RENAISSANCE STUDIES
In Honor of
HARDIN CRAIG

RENAISSANCE STUDIES

In Honor of

HARDIN CRAIG

Edited by

BALDWIN MAXWELL

W. D. BRIGGS

FRANCIS R. JOHNSON

E. N. S. THOMPSON

FOLCROFT LIBRARY EDITIONS / 1972

Limited to 150 Copies

RENAISSANCE STUDIES

In Honor of

HARDIN CRAIG

———

Edited by

BALDWIN MAXWELL

W. D. BRIGGS

FRANCIS R. JOHNSON

E. N. S. THOMPSON

———

STANFORD UNIVERSITY PRESS

Stanford University, California

LONDON: HUMPHREY MILFORD, OXFORD UNIVERSITY PRESS

Renaissance Studies in Honor of Hardin Craig is a joint publication of Stanford University and the University of Iowa. Both universities have contributed generously toward financing the volume and both are represented on the board of editors. Although Professor Craig left Iowa for Stanford more than a decade ago, he has in recent years returned frequently to teach in the Iowa summer session, and we at Iowa still regard him as a colleague.

The editors wish to thank two of Mr. Craig's publishers, Scott, Foresman and Company and the Macmillan Company, for their cooperation in helping to make this volume possible.

B. M.

CONTENTS

HARDIN CRAIG

By RUDOLF KIRK
Rutgers University

Hardin Craig came of pioneer stock. His father, Robert Craig, a native of Ayrshire, Scotland, migrated to Kentucky in 1852, settled near Owensboro, and became a tobacco exporter, and, after the War between the States, a farmer. His mother, Mary Jane McHenry Craig, was a great-granddaughter of Colonel John Hardin, a member of Washington's staff, who participated with General George Rogers Clark in the capture of Vincennes and who later was treacherously slain while on a peace mission to the Miami Indians. Her grandfather was Barnabas McHenry, a Methodist preacher of the South in the early days, and her father, John H. McHenry, was a fine scholar and a lawyer who served in Congress for a term or two.

Hardin Craig was born on his father's farm six miles from Owensboro, on June 29, 1875, and here he learned to hunt, fish, shoot and ride. He was particularly skilled in handling horses and liked to break colts. Anyone who has served his teaching apprenticeship under Craig can readily imagine that the colts were subjected to the same firm kindliness that has trained many a young man and woman to wear the academic harness. Craig was also a baseball player in the days when the catchers "took 'um off the bat" and to this day one of his front teeth bears the mark of a misjudged ball.

His education began in a one-room rural school which ran for five months of the year, where Mr. J. D. Burton instilled into his pupils an insatiable desire to learn for the sake of learning. Later he came under the influence of Mr. Malcolm McIntyre, a graduate of Bowdoin College, who had studied English composition and literature under Henry W. Longfellow, and who taught Greek, Latin, and mathematics in the local school. In 1893 and 1894, before he was ready for college, Craig was teaching in the district schools to earn money to put himself through college.

At Centre College, in the Blue Grass Country of Kentucky, Craig continued his study of mathematics, Greek, and Latin, and at the same time he entered into the athletic and literary life of his fellows. Here he studied under Professor Charles Henry Adams Wager—later of Oberlin College—to whom he refers as "one of the greatest teachers of English." On graduation he was Ormond Beatty Senior prizeman. Forty years later he delivered the commencement address at his alma mater and was honored by the degree of Doctor of Letters.

After receiving his A.B. degree, Craig took a position as principal of an academy at Stanford, Kentucky, in order that he might earn money to assist him with his graduate work. He chose Princeton, and, still a green Kentucky boy, set out from home in 1898 to study for his doctor's degree. In 1899, after one year at Princeton, he became a master of arts and was immediately appointed Charles Scribner Fellow in English Literature. This award, and its renewal a year later, permitted him to complete his work for the Ph.D. degree in 1901. He had studied under Professor Thomas Marc Parrott, who forty years later wrote: "Craig was my first graduate student. He and I started together years ago the study of the text of *Hamlet* which finally resulted in the critical edition of Q_2 that we published two years ago." Professor Parrott continues: "Then as now he was an indefatigable worker, and he, Clemens of the U. of Va., and Kennedy, now of Princeton, made up a group of graduates such as I've never had since."

Not satisfied with pursuing graduate study at one university, Craig spent the summers of 1899 and 1900 at the University of Chicago, where he came under the inspiring influence of Professor John Matthews Manly, who became his life-long friend. In 1902 he went abroad for fifteen months. A few weeks at the University of Jena convinced him that he must seek another atmosphere; so he journeyed to Oxford, where he matriculated at Exeter College. Here he found himself in congenial intellectual surroundings, and continued his study at Exeter for a year, and in the summer of 1904 returned for another term of residence. Immediately after completing the doctorate in 1901, Craig began his university teaching career as an instructor of English at Princeton. In 1905 he was appointed Edgerstoune preceptor, and in 1906 he married Miss

Gertrude Carr of Ashby, Massachusetts. Their son, Hardin, Jr., was born in 1907.

Craig was early a creative scholar. While working on the medieval drama, as a graduate student, the thought occurred to him that certain manuscripts of the old miracle plays might still be in existence at Coventry. When he had his opportunity to visit England, he went to the office of an ancient guild at Coventry and found two manuscripts of miracle plays which had lain hidden away for centuries, and these were published by the Early English Text Society in 1902. A few years later Craig joined with Dr. Henry van Dyke in arranging a large anthology of English poems which was published under the title *Little Masterpieces of English Poetry by British and American Authors* (1906). He also wrote during these years various articles and reviews.

Craig left Princeton in 1910 to accept a professorship at the University of Minnesota. His period of nine years at Minnesota was marked by successful teaching and by great scholarly productivity. In addition to a number of articles, he edited three books: *Richard II*, selections from Byron's poetry, and the *Works* of John Metham. When the World War began Craig entered the army and received his commission as a second lieutenant from the first R. O. T. C. camp at Fort Snelling, Minnesota. When he was discharged, December 30, 1918, he was a captain, and from 1919 to 1928 he served as a major in the Reserve Corps. His particular task during the War was that of teacher and organizer of educational activity. He served as senior instructor in the Quartermaster Training Camp at Camp Joseph E. Johnston, Black Point, Florida. Later he became director of the training division there and had under his charge a school of some fifty departments for enlisted men and an officers' training school with a total of from three to five thousand men. Craig remarked later, in speaking of his duties in the army, "So far as I was concerned, I worked almost day and night and hardly knew what was going on except in the command I held."

A few months after his return to academic work Craig received the offer of the headship of the Department of English at the State University of Iowa. Here from 1919 to 1928 he worked and here he showed his unusual administrative powers. Those who knew him in Iowa City will not forget the driving energy and the kindly attention to the problems of all members of the department. Never one to interfere capriciously with the teaching of his staff, Craig observed the work of every person and guided the young men and women so as to bring out their best qualities.

During these years at Iowa, Craig taught classes in American literature, Shakespeare, and nineteenth-century poetry. The undergraduates swarmed to hear his lectures, and the graduate students frequently sat in his courses a second time without credit. On the side of productive scholarship Craig was continually pushing ahead, though he seemed to be spending all of his immense vitality on his teaching. He founded *The Philological Quarterly,* and edited it from its beginning in 1922 to 1928. He began in these years to compile the annual bibliography of ''Recent Literature of the English Renaissance,'' which has appeared in *Studies in Philology* every year since 1926. He published in 1924 *Selections* from the works of Swift and in 1929 (with J. M. Thomas) *Great English Prose Writers.*

In 1922, on one of Craig's many periods abroad, he represented the State University of Iowa at the celebration of the six hundredth anniversary of the founding of the University of Padua. On this occasion he was granted the degree of Doctor of the University.

At the age of fifty-three, Craig accepted an invitation to go to Stanford University. At once he and Mrs. Craig moved to California and built a house on the Stanford University campus. Craig's productivity never lessened even amid the many calls on his energies made by a new position among new surroundings. Perhaps, however, a geographical and institutional change was not a radical one for Craig. So wrapt up has he always been in his work and so out-going in his human sympathies that he probably felt that he was not making any real change, rather that he was merely shifting from one classroom to another.

At Stanford he has taken a leading part in guiding the policies of the Department of English. From 1930 to 1933 he was Research Associate at the Huntington Library. He has also served on the governing bodies of many of the professional societies of the nation, including the Executive Council of the Modern Language Association (Vice President, 1931), the Executive Committee of the Philological Association of the Pacific Coast (President, 1938), the Council of the American Association of University Professors (Vice President, 1930), the board of Advisers of the National Council of Teachers of English, and the Supervising Committee of the English Institute. Again and again, sometimes more than once in a year, he has travelled across the continent to attend the meetings of these organizations. In the winter of 1935 he stayed in the East to serve as Visiting Professor at the University of North Carolina.

Meantime, Craig has never allowed even illness itself to interfere with his pursuit of scholarship. Since going to Stanford he has edited or written half a dozen volumes. Probably the most important of these are *The Enchanted Glass: The Elizabethan Mind in Literature* (1936) and the critical edition of the second quarto of *Hamlet* (1938), which he prepared in collaboration with Professor Thomas M. Parrott. Nor should we forget to mention his editing of the *Parrott Presentation Volume,* a collection of scholarly essays in honor of Professor Parrott, the dozen articles and reviews which have appeared in the professional journals, and the annual bibliography of "Recent Literature of the English Renaissance," in *Studies in Philology.* Only within the past half year a four volume series of Types of English Literature has appeared, under Craig's general editorship.

Like Tennyson's Ulysses, Craig still faces the future,

strong in will
To strive, to seek, to find, and not to yield.

In 1940, when the time came for his retirement from the service of Stanford University, he could not be spared. He was the third man in the history of the university to be asked to continue to teach beyond the age of sixty-five. Many of his friends and colleagues who have come to rely upon Craig's judgment, imagination, and unstinting generosity agree that he is one of the few men who indeed can not be spared.

THE YORK PLAY OF *CHRIST LED UP TO CALVARY*
(Play XXXIV)

By Mendal G. Frampton
Pomona College

Professor Charles Mills Gayley, at the close of his discussion of the group of York mystery plays which he felt showed the stylistic qualities of the great late York realist, concluded: "If we assume, and not without reason, that he also retouched the *Christ Led up to Calvary*, (XXXIV), and the *Crucifixion*, (XXXV), we may regard him as the Passion Playwright of York."[1] It is, perhaps, too much to go further and assert that York XXXIV actually was retouched by the great York master dramatist, but it is capable of demonstration that the play as we have it shows a rewriting of an extensive nature subsequent to 1415 when Roger Burton, town clerk, set down his famous list of the York plays, and was, therefore, at least rewritten at the time when the realist was doing his work. It is in Burton's list that we first find reference to the play. Of it the town clerk wrote:

To (undours). Jesus, sanguine cruentatus, portans crucem uersus Caluariam. Simon Sereneus, Judei angariantes eum vt tolleret crucem, Maria mater Jesu, Johannes apostolus intimans tunc proxime dampnacionem et transitum filii sui ad caluariam. Veronica tergens sanguinem et sudorem de facie Jesu cum flammeolo in quo imprimitur facies Jesu; et alie mulieres lamentantes Jesum.[2]

We next come upon mention of the play in Burton's "second list" where we find: "Shermen. Ductio Christi et ostensio Veronice."[3] The date of this "second list" is not given in the York Memorandum Book but the entries must have been made some time before January 31, 1422, (9 Henry V), because of extant records. In the first of these we find the Painters, Stainers, Pinners and Latoners petitioning the Mayor and Council of York that their two plays, the *Nailing to the Cross* and the *Raising of the Cross*, be combined into one play.[4] Their petition was granted and the new play appears in the Register as Play XXXV, the *Crucifixio Christi*. That the two

---

[1]Gayley, Charles Mills, *Plays of our Forefathers*, p. 157.
[2]Transcribed from Lucy Toulmin Smith, *York Mystery Plays*, p. xxv.
[3]Quoted from M. G. Frampton, *PMLA*, LIII (1938), 101, n. 79.
[4]*Surtees Society*, cxxv, 102-104. Entry dated January 31, 1422.

plays named in the petition were actually under production is verified by the following entries in the "second list":

(43)	Payntors.	Expansio et clavacio Christi.
(44)	Latoners.	Levacio Christi super montem.[5]

Obviously, if the second list had been set down after January 31,
1422, it would have contained but the one play of the Register, not
the two it contains.

In this same year we also find the following entry:

cum nuper in tempore Henrici Preston maioris (1422), de avisamento consilii
camere, pagina de lez Salsemakers ubi Judas se suspendebat et crepuit medius
in ludo Corporis Christi, et pagina de lez Tilemakers ubi Pilatus condempnavit
Jesum morti, et pagina de lez Turnors, Hayresters et Bollers ubi Jesus ligatus
erat ad columpnam et flagellatus, et pagina Molendinariorum ubi Pilatus et alii
milites ludebant ad talos pro vestimentis Jesu et pro eis sortes mittebant et
ea parciebantur inter se, fuerunt combinate simul in vnam paginam, ceteris
predictis paginis pro perpetuo exclusis, que quidem pagina decetero vocabitur
pagina condempnationis Jesu Christi.[6]

In accordance with this entry the Register contains but the one new
play entered as Play XXXIII. This union of four plays into one is
also verified by the "second list" where we find:

(38)	Sausmakers.	Suspencio Jude.
(39)	Tylemakers.	Condemnacio Christi per Pilatum.
(40)	Turnors and	
	Bollers.	Flagellacio et coronacio cum spinis.
(42)	Milners.	Particio vestimentorum Christi.[7]

These plays are, obviously, the four plays of the record we have just
quoted and just as obviously the one play of the Register and not
the four of the "second list" would have been entered in that list
had it been written after 1422. January 21, 1422 must be looked
upon, then, as the ultimate date for the "second list." As this list
contains seven more plays in the Passion Group than the 1415 list

---

[5] Same as note 3 above.

[6] *Surtees Society,* cxxv, 171. Miss Lyle thinks the new play thus authorized
went into a second form before being registered as Play XXXIII because that
play omits the Hanging of Judas and the Throwing of Dice (Marie C. Lyle,
"The Original Identity of the York and Towneley Cycles," p. 105). She
overlooked the words of the record when the play was authorized in 1422,
"ceteris predictis paginis pro perpetuo exclusis." (See full quotation above).
Miss Toulmin Smith, in turn, dates the earlier complaint of the Salsemakers
regarding the expense of producing their Burton play as "probably before
1410" (*York Mystery Plays,* p. xxiv, n.1). The actual date was 1417 (*Surtees
Society,* cxx, 155). Miss Lyle first made this correction (*Op. cit.,* p. 104).

[7] As note 3 above.

the entry probably dates from a time not far from the ultimate date. I suggest, elsewhere, c.1420.[8]

The only text of the play which has come down to us is that of the Register. Here again the date is uncertain, although the plays were probably entered between 1431 when the Masons were relieved of giving their play of *Fergus*,[9] "all trace of which is wanting in the Register,"[10] and 1476, when that play was resumed at York by the Lynenweavers, its sponsors in Burton's 1415 list.[11] Thus we have knowledge of our play, the York *Christ Led up to Calvary*, in 1415, again c.1420, and again sometime between 1431 and 1476.

Important in our study of this play, finally, is the fact that nine of the stanzas and two of the caudas of the York play are found in Towneley Play XXIIb.[12] These stanzas are iambic in movement and are organized into the stanza form $aa^4b^3aa^4b^3cdcd^3$.

These facts about the play may seem meager yet they offer adequate evidence of revision and even enable us to follow much of that revision in detail. To begin with, Burton, in his description of the play in 1415 quoted above, uses the words: "Veronica tergens sanguinem et sudorem de facie Jesu cum flammeolo in quo imprimitur facies Jesu," whereas in his "second list" he merely says: "ostensio Veronice." Clearly a change has been made in the play, a change which carries over into the registered play where Mary performs the function of the Veronica. Thus, between 1415 and c.1420 the play went through sufficient revision to at least bring about a changed treatment of the Veronica.

In the second place, the evidence shows clearly that the last five stanzas of the play as registered are new after 1415. Burton closes

---

[8]In 1419 the Ironmongers appealed to the Council for aid in giving their play of *Mary Magdalene*. If we knew the outcome of this petition we might date the list before 1419. Miss Sellers dates this record as 1490, an error corrected by Miss Lyle (*Op. cit.*, p. 105, n.32). Miss Lyle errs herself, however, when she thinks the Ironmongers continued to produce the play "as late as 1433 or 1434 because the play is included in the second Burton list" (*Op. cit.*, p. 105). I have shown that the list must date before January 31, 1422.

[9]*Surtees Society*, CXXV, 123-4.

[10]*York Mystery Plays*, p. xxvii, n.1.

[11]*Ibid.* In 1485 they, in turn, were relieved of the play although as late as 1517 there was still a possibility that the guild would resume its production (*Ibid.*). The play must have been entered in the Register, or at least a place left for it, as with Burton's play 22 and the Ironmonger's play (*York Mystery Plays*, p. xv), had the Register been undertaken close to the year 1431. The date of the Register must probably, therefore, be advanced some from the dates set by Miss Toulmin Smith, 1430-1440 (*Op. cit.*, p. xxviii).

[12]York stanzas 10, 12, 19, 23, 24, 26, 27, 28 and 29, with the caudas of stanzas 21 and 22.

his description of the previous play as known to him, **Play XXXIII**
as registered, with the words: "tres milites mittentes sortem super
vestem Jesu."[13]   This action, however, is entirely lacking in the
play as registered, a fact which led Miss Toulmin Smith to write:
"This last subject is contracted in the Register to a few lines at the
end of plays XXXIV and XXXV."[14]   Whatever the truth may be
about her statement as it applies to Play XXXV she was certainly
in error as regards Play XXXIV, our play.   For the discussion of
the lots at its close is no condensation of discarded material but a
definite preparation for a fuller treatment to follow.   The passage
reads:

32.	i Miles.	Take of his clothis be-liffe, latte se,	321
		A ha! þis garment will falle wele for mee,	
		And so I hope it schall.	
	ii Miles.	Nay, sir, so may it noght be,	
		þame muste be parte amonge vs thre,	
		Take euen as will fall.	
	iii Miles.	Ʒaa, and sir Pilate medill hym,	
		Youre parte woll be but small.	
	i Miles.	Sir, and ʒe liste, go telle hym,	
		Ʒitt schall he noght haue all,	
33.		Butte even his awne parte and nomore.	331
	ii Miles.	Ʒaa, late þame ligge still here in stoore,	
		Vntill þis dede be done.	333

Clearly this passage is anticipatory.   Some further treatment of the
theme, involving Pilate, is being prepared for.   What that treatment was is clear from the "second list" where, as we have shown
above, we find the entry: "(42) Milners.   Particio vestimentorum
Christi."   As the Millers had shared with the Tilemakers and others
in the giving of Burton's play 36, the play before ours,[15] it is perfectly clear that they left that relationship after 1415 and, taking
the lots material with which that play closed as their part of the
joint play, had developed it into the sole play of the "second list."[16]
As the lines just quoted could not have been written so long as the
lots material occurred in the earlier play, Burton's 36, the conclusion seems unescapable that they were written after the Millers

---

[13]Quoted from *York Mystery Plays*, p. xxv.

[14]*Idem*, p. xxv, n.2.

[15]*Idem*, p. xxv.

[16]These facts verify Burton's accuracy in placing the lots action at the end
of his play 36, the registered play XXXIII.   In the Towneley *Processus
Talentorum*, Play XXIV, Pilate squabbles with the soldiers over the casting of
the lots.

had seceded and written their sole play, particularly as our play is followed immediately in the "second list" by the Millers' new play.

The lines quoted, however, occupy a middle position in the last five stanzas of the York play, those not known to Towneley. The two plays have been proceeding as "identical" plays for six stanzas when, after York stanza 29, the identity ceases and Towneley is brought to an immediate close with a stanza in an entirely different stanza form, a stanza obviously preparing for the next Towneley play, Towneley XXIII, the *Processus Crucis*. Clearly the York play, as known to Towneley, ended here. The final five stanzas of York as registered must, then, have shared in the writing of the Lots passage and the whole must, therefore, have been written after Burton wrote his description of the play in 1415 and before the Miller's gave up their Lots play—as we know from another record that they did—in 1422.[17] The stanzas were certainly written new for the registered play.

Still other changes were made in Burton's form of the play before it was entered in the Register for, as Miss Frances Foster pointed out, Towneley picks up the York play with its second scene.[18] The present first scene of the registered play is in the manner of the late York realistic school even though the metrical form is that of the play as a whole. In it the soldiers gather ropes and nails for the crucifixion and call upon "Sir Wymond" to hurry with the cross for "wayt e(s) skathe."[19] The scene is so very fine and so much in the late manner that it must have been largely responsible for Gayley's remark with which we began this study. As the scene has exerted no slightest influence upon Towneley and as it is so distinctly more advanced than the rest of the play in its realism, I am confident that the scene represents creative writing on the part of

---

[17] *York Mystery Plays*, p. xxiv, n.1: *Surtees Society*, CXXV, 171. The placing of the casting of lots at the close of the last trial before Pilate in Burton's day and play was, of course, without authority. In all of the Gospels the action comes after the crucifixion. In the *Northern Passion*, however, it comes after the journey to the cross but before the crucifixion itself (*EETS*, CXLV, 187), and this placing in the "second list" is but one piece of evidence among many of the continued influence of the *Northern Passion* at York in Burton's day. The independence of Towneley in placing its Lots play after the crucifixion as in the Bible should not be overlooked.

[18] Frances Foster, *PMLA*, XLIII (1938), 133, n.48. The statement made first by Gayley (*op. cit.*, p. 164), and repeated by Miss Lyle (*PMLA*, XLIV (1929), 325), that the Towneley stanza 25 reflects stanza 2 of the first scene of the York play is in error (See M. G. Frampton, *PMLA*, LIII [1938], 98).

[19] York Play XXXIV, line 59.

the poet who was revising the play for the Shearmen, its new sponsors in the "second list."[20]   Thus Burton enables us to be assured that the opening and the closing scenes of the play as registered are new and that some revision of the middle of the play also took place.

It is clear, however, from internal evidence, that the opening fifteen lines of the play are also new.   Whether these lines were written at the time of the revision which we have been following or later I see no way to determine.   A poet is not confined to one meter or verse form and the lines differ from the rest of the play, in all probability, because of the fact that they fall into the Herod tradition of opening speeches in highly alliterative verse.   That they are late, however, will appear from the quoting of the opening five lines.

> i Miles.   Pees, barnes and bachillers þat beldis here aboute,   1
> Stirre noȝt ones in þis stede but stonde stone stille,
> Or be ȝe lorde þat I leue on, I schall gar you lowte,
> But ȝe spare when I speke youre speche schall I spille
> Smertly and sone.   5

These lines have all the earmarks of what Davidson considers very late writing.[21]   They are highly alliterative and are so burdened with extra syllables as to suggest scansion in five feet instead of four.   The stanza form, too, is very late.   The lines fall readily into two stanzas once we become aware that the second *b* line of the second stanza is lost.[22]   The form is abab⁴c²dd⁴c², a form unique in the York cycle but very like that of Play XLI, registered in 1558. The stanza of this play runs abab⁴c²ddd⁴c² throughout scenes 2, 3 and 4, although the stanza is obscured by the format Miss Smith uses in her transcription of the text.   The passage is certainly very late.

Thus far we have proceeded with confidence.   It is clear that the registered play differs from Burton's 37 in its opening fifteen lines, its first and last scenes, and in a revision involving the treatment of the Veronica.   In other words, just half of the extant play is new and part of the rest must be the result of revision.   It is just possible that we can determine the extent of this revision by comparing

[20]The fact that the play changed sponsorship from the Tunners to the Shearmen between the writing of the 1415 list and the entry in the "second list" is additional evidence favoring a rewriting at this time.

[21]Charles Davidson, *Studies in the English Mystery Plays*, p. 127.

[22]Miss Smith gives the lines consecutively with the remark: "These first lines appear so irregular (purposely so, perhaps) that I count the stanzas from line 16" (*York Mystery Plays*, 337, n.1).

the play with the Towneley Play XXIIb. Any conclusions will be rendered to a degree conjectural by the loss of a leaf from York after the pedes of stanza 13,[23] and by an interpolation in Towneley after its stanza 34, but these facts do not entirely blur the picture.

The ''identical'' stanzas in York and Towneley occur both before and after the York loss, and Towneley continues for five stanzas after the loss begins before its interpolation is thrust in. As the York leaves contain for this play an average of about six stanzas, the temptation is great to look upon the five Towneley stanzas as restoring most of the lost York text. Such seems not to be the case, however, for Towneley is innocent of the York stanza 13 after the pedes of which, as I have said, the York lacuna begins, knows nothing of the present York stanza 11 before the lacuna and stanzas 20 and 25 after the ''identity'' resumes,[24] and resumes that ''identity'' with York, not at the end of the lacuna but seven stanzas later. The conclusion seems to be reasonable that Towneley is not reflecting the registered version of the York play but the Burton version. Unfortunately, Towneley, whose treatment of the Veronica would be definitive, inserts its interpolation at this point, resuming identity with York immediately after, but only after, the York treatment of the subject. The point at issue, then, must be left in some degree of uncertainty. This uncertainty is so slight, however, that I am of the opinion that Towneley, in its ''identical'' stanzas and the five not in the registered York play, does reflect the earlier or Burton version of the play.

If this conclusion be accepted, fully two thirds of the registered play represents new or revised writing. On either count the York play as registered is at least half new and revised, as we have seen, and thus shares definitely in that great upsurge of play writing at York between 1415 and c.1420, an upsurge which increased the twelve passion plays of Burton's 1415 list to seventeen in his later list. If York XXIV is not the work of the great York realist, then, it at least shared in the great elaboration of the Passion Group which took place under his influence.

---

[23] The leaf & vij is lost.

[24] Towneley also recovers the caudas of York stanzas 21 and 22, caudas which the Towneley editor includes in his stanza 42. This difficulty in resuming York suggests that Towneley got hold of the York play after the Tunners had ceased to give it and after the new play for the Sledmen had been written. If this were true the borrowing would date well after 1415.

THE MIRACLE PLAY: NOTES AND QUERIES

By GEORGE R. COFFMAN
University of North Carolina

The essential unity of this brief paper resides in its concern with problems of origin, heritage, and nomenclature in a form of drama that appeared first in the eleventh or early twelfth century and continued into the early English Renaissance. Limitations of space permit me to sketch in critical review only the main outline of the materials involved and to suggest some further problems raised. The guiding considerations here are that circumstances and conditions of the period of a literary genre explain its origin; that with the development and passing of the fashion for this genre, it loses its original functional purpose and the accumulated literary product becomes a cultural heritage, possibly contributing to new forms; and that nomenclature in the meantime is the identifying mark for the immediate fashion and the cultural heritage.

Nomenclature for drama in the middle ages and in early Renaissance England emerges rather from the time and occasion of production, the temper and the mood of the product, than from an author's conscious artifice for a structural pattern, causal relationships in the situations involved, and consequent integrity of character. Official records show a regard for the former procedure and the preserved literary documents show a prevailing absence of the latter except as previously shaped by the narrative source.

The origin of the miracle play was the subject of a study by me, published in 1914.[1] Nine years later Professor Young followed this with an essential correction, related to the thesis of this study.[2] His article, distinguished by his usual clarity and definitiveness,[3] centered around *historia*, which he showed as a liturgical term, referred to the whole *cursus* of the services of a saint's day and not to his life and legends (*vita*), as I had assumed. Since his cor-

---

[1] *A New Theory Concerning the Origin of the Miracle Play* (Menasha, 1914).

[2] Karl Young, ''Concerning the Origin of the Miracle Play,'' *The Manly Anniversary Studies* (Chicago, 1923), pp. 254-268.

[3] I may add, also, presented with a graciousness and courtesy which those of us who have profited from his acumen and learning have come to associate with him in scholarly as well as personal relationships.

rection necessarily subordinated the outlines of my study as a whole and might well raise question in the mind of the reader as to the validity of my thesis, I make that study and his correction the basis for the first of my notes and queries.

In a word, the thesis of this study as paraphrased from Joseph Bédier's *Les Légendes Épiques*, to which I acknowledged my indebtedness, was "that circumstance and conditions of the eleventh century explain the origin of the miracle play, not only as to its type, but also as to its form and spirit." In support of this I surveyed briefly and selectively the renaissance of the eleventh century, the wide diffusion of the cult of St. Nicholas in Western Europe, especially during this period, and the activities of secular clerics as they brought humanistic influences from the outside world into monastic and cathedral centers. Then against an all too thinly sketched background, I posed the theory that the miracle plays of St. Nicholas in form and lyric quality suggest the mediaeval Latin hymn and that in spirit they are characterized by secular rather than churchly elements. Finally, I maintained that in two versions of a legend of St. Nicholas, of approximately 1050-1100, based on an incident centering around a prior and the monks of a monastic cell, there was to be found the clue to the origin of the miracle play. Specifically, the monks on St. Nicholas's day requested permission to sing a new and popular *historia* concerning him. The prior refused this request because he maintained, according to one version, that the music was not the ecclesiastical chant (*cantate*) and, according to the other, that the composition was a *nova saecularium cantica clericorum, immo jocularia quaedam.* In both versions, on the following night St. Nicholas appeared to the prior, flogged him severely, and forced him to learn and sing an antiphon in his honor. As a result the prior granted the monks their request. This *historia* I interpreted as a *vita*; and connecting the objections of the prior with the dramatized legends of St. Nicholas preserved and with the form and the spirit of the verse and the preserved music, as judged by authorities in those fields, I presented all this as a theory for the origin of the miracle play.

Professor Young through adequate illustration, exposition, and analysis showed, as I indicated above, that in mediaeval liturgiology "*historia* is the name given to the whole series of antiphons and responsories for the Canonical Office, or *cursus*, of a single day, especially when any or all of these musical pieces are given metrical form or are adorned with rhyme." Then he cogently pointed out that we have no evidence to prove that the miracle play originated as the result of a combination in a creative mind of the elements I have summarized above. I hope this summary gives an adequate epitome of my method and procedure; and I hope especially that I have not done injustice to Young's excellent article. To him we are indebted for exposition of an important liturgical term.[4] Further, his statement that we have no evidence to attach any of St. Nicholas's plays to such a *historia* is cogent. In fact, viewing my study objectively, I affirm, further, that even if my conception of *historia* had been correct, I had no more evidence supporting my theory as to the final process of creation than I had found in the farced epistle—a theory which I had already analyzed and rejected.[5]

Professor Young's latest word concerning the origin of the miracle play follows:

In so far, then, as we can judge from the extant miracle plays, they rest not upon short and summary references to the *vita* such as are found in liturgical embellishments, but directly upon the complete forms of the legends themselves. The plays represent the incidents of the traditional narratives with substantial fidelity, and they appear to have arisen through the application of the dramatic treatment to these stories.[6]

All of this accords with a view which was set forth by Dr. Manly over thirty-five years ago and which has influenced profoundly my thinking about creative processes in the field of literature. Stating that literature is not an organism and "that principles true of development of plants and animals have no necessary validity for works of art," he does, nevertheless, find what he regards as a pertinent biological analogy in De Vries's theory of mutation. Specifically, using mediaeval drama for illustration, he points to the fact that despite dramatic possibilities in the services of the Mass and in the narratives of saints' lives, through a long period of time, the first Easter play and the saints' play "came into existence by a

---

[4]This is to be added to his able exposition of other liturgical meanings of *historia*: "Chaucer and the Liturgy," *MLN*, xxx (1915), 97-99.

[5]*A New Theory*, Chapter II.

[6]*The Drama of the Medieval Church* (Oxford, 1933), ii, 310. Space does not permit quoting the entire passage (pp. 310-311), in which Young, without commitment, presents some conjectures and in which he summarizes logical reasons, through activities within the monasteries, for the plays, in verse, and set to music.

single bound and not by insensible gradations.''[7]   This emphasis
upon the creative genius of the individual author appears to me,
with the strictures I mention below, as thoroughly sound.   It is,
also, a necessary and effective antidote to the evolutionary theory as
it was then being applied to literature.

This apparent digression is very important in relation to the
thesis of my study: i.e., that circumstances and conditions of the
age explain the origin of a literary form. Manly's theory, properly,
emphasizes the immediate and individual act of a creative mind.
But that very emphasis tends to subordinate a fact to which space
is devoted in his article and which in informal lectures and conversations he recognized as of first importance: that the genius enriching old forms or creating new did not do so in a vacuum.   In
a similar manner, it seems to me, Professor Young's limiting all the
influences or immediately inspiring elements to the medieval church[8]
unduly subordinates, or ignores, the complex factors of the eleventh
century that surely kindled the creative processes of the author of
the first miracle play.[9] Now the entire burden of my thesis is that
the phrase ''secular intrusions'' epitomizes the forces and influences
which led finally to immediate creation of a St. Nicholas play by the
first author. *Mutatis mutandis*, we may affirm of the Dowry play

---

[7]John M. Manly, ''Literary Forms and the New Theory of the Origin of
Species,'' *MP*, IV (1907), 577-595. For his insistence on the proper interpretation of this article, see his presidential address before the Modern Human-
ities Research Association (1922-1923), p. 10.

[8]See also Young, ''Concerning the Origin,'' etc., pp. 265-268.

[9]See my fairly extended statement of this stricture, as applied to Professor
Young's exclusion in his entire monumental work, *The Drama of the Medieval
Church*, of all influences except that of the Church: review, *Speculum*, IX
(1934), 110-111: ''To this admirably concise and cogent introduction, differentiating the Church drama from the three other dramatic traditions of the
Middle Ages, the reviewer is inclined to add a word of caution. Though this
drama is remarkably independent of existing dramatic traditions, elements
alien to Christian worship exerted a constant influence upon it in every stage
of its development. From its inception in the tropes, up to the highest point
of its artistic development, it represents an essential intrusion into the liturgy
of the Church. In last analysis it is the product of monks and clerics who
recognized the claim and appeal of the senses and who were consciously or unconsciously groping toward something artistic—whatever their didactic *apologia*.
They were among the leaders who shaped the renaissances of the ninth and
eleventh centuries. In the broadest sense of the word they were humanists.
Considered from the point of view of these leaders, not members of the
hierarchy, the mediaeval Church was essentially inclusive rather than exclusive
in its interests. Young's rigid exclusion of all materials directly unnecessary
to his immediate exposition has, perhaps, at times unduly subordinated this
fact, important in any comprehensive and final interpretation of the plays included in his *corpus* and survey.''

of the three daughters saved from a life of shame, as the writer of
our St. Nicholas legend did concerning the author of the new
historia: "scripta quidem per hominem sed homini divinitus in-
spirata."

This leads us back to the legend in its two versions. Clearly the
prior and his monks of Holy Cross (Crux) had two different levels
of meaning for *historia*. The prior, evidently a conservative, disturbed by the new wine in his old bottles, objected to a *historia* that
was not set to liturgical music of his time (*in vestra ecclesia cantatur
cantate, et nil amplius*), that was composed by secular clerics and
that was, indeed, characterized by what appealed to him as a spirit
of irreverence (*nova saecularium cantica clericorum, immo jocularia
quaedam*).[10] Are we to accept the implications of the *liturgical
historia* and reject entirely the explicit and repeated objections of
the prior as misrepresentation or ignorance on his part? On the
basis of all the preserved St. Nicholas plays are they not in theme
and spirit what we might expect from secular clerics and their influences? If so, do we have proof here of the origin of the miracle
play? Decidedly not. But what we do have is indirect and direct
evidence that St. Nicholas is being treated in the secular spirit that
the testimony collected by such scholars as Gautier, Faral, and
Waddell would lead us to expect.[11] We do not have such immediate
evidence surrounding the creation of the miracle play as we find,
for instance, in the case of *Fulgens and Lucres*, the first interlude.
This will probably never be available. Consequently proof cannot
be established. Nevertheless, all the evidence I have presented at
different times and all that I know about the mediaeval drama and
the eleventh and twelfth centuries convince me that the most logical
explanation for the origin of the miracle play is to be found through
the intrusion of outside humanistic forces within the fold and their
absorption in monastic and cathedral centers. Also may we not find
essential acceptance of Manly's view if we suggest that mutation as
applied to literature is the result of definite external forces or elements stirring an original and creative individual to artistic activity? With all of this in mind, possibly a more acceptable title for

---

[10]For evidence concerning *historia*, in vernacular, as applied to saints' lives.
chanted or recited, also by jongleurs, see E. Faral, *Les Jongleurs en France au
Moyen Âge* (Paris, 1910), pp. 47-55.

[11]L. Gautier, *Histoire de la Poesie Liturgique au Moyen Âge. Les Tropes*
(Paris, 1886), esp. pp. 187-190; E. Faral, *op. cit.*; Helen Waddell, *The Wandering Scholars* (Boston, 1929), esp. pp. 64-103.

my monograph of almost thirty years ago would be: A Study of
the Seminal Environment for the Miracle Play in its Origins.

When the miracle play as an established fashion appears in the
vernacular literature of mediaeval England, it has the accompanying heritage of the bizarre, the spectacular, the romantic, that characterizes the dramatized legends with which its early auditors were
already familiar. The view that this heritage passed as dramatized
narrative into the romantic spectacles and dramas of the Tudors is
too well known to require more than passing comment. Dr. Manly
has made the best brief apologia for this.[12] Here is a thesis which
I have presented and defended with conviction for many years.
But how far the romance aspects and the romantic spirit and technique in Renaissance drama are the heritage of those elements and
of this fashion in miracle plays, and how far the inspiration to the
first Renaissance dramatists of this adapted type came from the
whole body of native mediaeval romances and how far from foreign
Renaissance importations—these are considerations that raise nice
questions. One of the most fruitful studies as a starting point for
this problem is Dr. Waldo McNeir's unpublished dissertation, *Elements of English Medieval Romance in the Plays of Robert Greene*
(Univ. of North Carolina, 1940).

Again, the issues of the question as to how far the term miracle
play was restricted in mediaeval England to the type represented by
its original content and spirit, and to what extent it included cyclic
plays comprehending the range of Biblical history, from the fall of
the angels to Judgment day, are too well known to require discussion or review.[13] Since, as Manly states, official records show no
confusion in the use of this term, would it not clarify the situation
to recognize in critical terms the actual distinction in content and
spirit between miracle plays and those treating of Biblical history?
As a word of caution, however, with reference to fugitive preserved
plays, it is well to remember that *The Pride of Life* is a *miracle de*

---

[12]"The Miracle Play in Mediaeval England." Transactions of the Royal
Society of Literature of the United Kingdom (London, 1927), pp. 133-153.

[13]See for latter view, e.g., E. K. Chambers, *The Medieval Stage* (Oxford,
1903), Vol. II, passim. Hardin Craig makes the best case for the Corpus Christi
plays officially recognized as a separate and distinct type: "The Corpus
Christi Procession and the Corpus Christi Play," *JEGP*, XIII (1914), 589-602.
See also Manly, "Miracle Play," *op. cit.*; and Coffman, "The Miracle Play in
England—Nomenclature." *PMLA*, XXXI (1916), 448-465; "The Miracle Play
in England—Some Records of Presentation, and Notes on Preserved Plays,"
SP, XVI (1919), 56-66.

Notre Dame as well as a morality; that though *Mary Magdalene* is certainly a miracle play, the author adapts to his purpose disparate elements from the morality, and through its microcosm of the little world of man it takes on cyclic pattern; and that *The Play of the Sacrament* is a miracle play, not because it has to do with a saint, but because it has the spirit and technique of a saint's play—in fact, interest centers around the relic which gave the impulse for Corpus Christi plays.

To close as I began, with a generalization, the longer I study problems of genres and types, of the progress of an idea through different periods of civilization, and of the cultural contribution which we call heritage, the more difficult adequate evaluation and conclusions appear to be. The elements that need to be considered are so varied, and rigid selection for any conclusion is so necessary, that oversimplification creates almost unavoidable pitfalls for the literary historian.[14]

---

[14]See, in this connection, my review article, ''Some Recent Trends in English Literary Scholarship, with Special Reference to Mediaeval Backgrounds,'' *SP*, xxxv (July, 1938), 500-513.

SOME ASPECTS OF THE ORIGIN OF ITALIAN HUMANISM

By B. L. ULLMAN
University of Chicago

Improved techniques of lighting have affected not only our homes and offices, but the Middle Ages as well. The darkness of the medieval blackout has all but disappeared. Certain medieval centuries indeed are said by some to be nearly as bright as day, for we now speak of a Renaissance in the ninth century and another in the twelfth. Consequently the dazzling brightness of what used to be *the* Renaissance to those who came to it from the medieval blackout now seems to have less candle power. Then too we have discovered medieval shadows lurking in the Renaissance. As a result of both of these developments some persons even maintain that they can see little or no difference in the brightness of the two periods. Furthermore the importance of the revival of letters and learning which used to bulk large in the minds of many has been diminished by the historians and other social scientists who have asserted that this movement was subsequent and subsidiary to the real Renaissance—to the development of trade, of a bourgeois society, of cities, and so on. Then too we have discovered a spiritual kinship with the Middle Ages, a discovery which has led to some rather remarkable results in the last twenty years. Among them is a depreciation of the Renaissance.

This paper will be regarded as reactionary by some because it assumes the fundamental importance of the revival of literature and the classics in the formation of the Renaissance.[1] It is not my ambition to present a new unified interpretation of the origin of the Renaissance, a movement so complex that no single interpretation or even many interpretations suffice to explain it. Scholars often tend to oversimplify the phenomena they study. I must confess to a distrust of any single, simple explanation, the kind that is easily conveyed to a notebook, for so many-sided a movement. It is my

---

[1]Protests against some of the current views are rare. A welcome emphasis on the classical revival is to be found in Douglas Bush, *The Renaissance and English Humanism*, 1939.

intention merely to trace out a few threads of the complicated pattern. I shall confine myself almost entirely to the beginnings of the movement in Italy in the fourteenth century.

But before considering Italy let us turn to neighboring France. As a result of the ninth-century awakening many manuscripts of classical Latin authors had been copied and were lying about in the libraries of France. In the twelfth century came another Renaissance. Continuing into the thirteenth century, it brought with it or was accompanied by the founding of the universities and of the Dominican and Franciscan orders. The interest turned to philosophy. The translation of works of Aristotle previously unknown was in keeping with the current interest, and all these factors led to scholasticism. It is clear that scholasticism had its roots in a revival of the classics, but it petrified into a form which was eventually regarded as the very antithesis of classical study. The scholastic movement spread everywhere, to England and to Italy. It is against this movement, in its later more quibbling form, that the early Italian humanists reacted most strongly—one classical revival against the ossified remains of another. This is not so strange as it seems, for some recent scholars have criticized the Italian Renaissance as well as certain tendencies of present-day classical study in much the same manner.

It is not without interest to note that the particular phase of scholasticism that the Italians attacked most fiercely was that of the British, whose leader was Ockham. In one of his letters, Petrarch belabors a Sicilian dialectician. i.e., a devotee of scholasticism. Scylla and Charybdis were bad enough without this new pestilence invading Sicily. says Petrarch; the pest seems to be one peculiar to islands, for in addition to the legions of British dialecticians we now have this new horde of Sicilians. Sicily first had Cyclopes, he continues, then tyrants, now it has a third pack of monsters, armed with syllogisms, and so on at some length.[2] Benvenuto da Imola, the commentator of Dante. calls "those modern English logicians" "spiders."[3] Coluccio Salutati bewails the fact that philosophy, so-called. has fled to Britain and urges his correspondent to rid the world of sophistry and equivocation.[4] Again in a defense of poetry against certain contemporary philosophers

---

[2]*Fam.*, I. 6.

[3]Novati, *Epistolario di Coluccio Salutati,* III (1896), 320n.

[4]*Ibid.*, pp. 319-320.

who are always ready to talk at length on any subject, he charges
that they do not understand Aristotle but instead quote certain
English treatises.[5]   Though the early humanists were not particularly fond of Aristotle. their attitude was one rather of indifference
than of hostility.

But to return to France with its many manuscripts of classical
authors which had been copied from the ninth century to the fourteenth.   Here then there was a continued interest in the classics,
one that waned from time to time to be sure, but the like of which
did not exist in Italy before the fourteenth century.   Cross-fertiliza-
tion between Italy and France. it seems to me, played an important
part in the revival of the classics in Italy.   What was it that brought
Italians. especially north Italians, into contact with French classical
culture?   For one thing it was the establishment of the papal court
at Avignon in 1309.   Hundreds of Italians came to Avignon and
France during the succeeding seventy years.   The papal court
played somewhat the same rôle in spreading classical culture to
Italy that the church council of Constance played a century later
(1415) in spreading the new Italian humanism to other parts of
Europe.

Among those who came to Avignon and spent many years in or
near it was Petrarch, the most remarkable figure among the early
humanists. a man far ahead of his time and one who, in spite of all
reservations, may still fittingly be called the first modern man.   In
France he found many of the manuscripts which gave him such an
enthusiasm for the classics.   It is this enthusiasm that is one of the
most striking and significant characteristics of Petrarchan and Italian humanism.   The world has seen nothing like it since.

Petrarch was in Paris (which he calls the foster-mother of learning) in 1333 and might, as Nolhac suggests.[6] have been in the Sor-
bonne library.   A catalogue of this library made in 1338 survives;
in it are several of the classical treasures listed by the thirteenth-
century humanist Richard de Fournival.   We would thus have a
direct connection between Petrarch and the French humanism of
the thirteenth century.[7]   From a Greek whom he met at Avignon

---

[5] *De laboribus Herculis* I. 1.   (Publication of my *editio princeps* of this work
has been delayed by the war).

[6] P. de Nolhac, *Pétrarque et l'humanisme*, ed. 2 (1907), I, 39.

[7] The fathers of both Petrarch and Boccaccio had been in Paris (Nolhac,
op. cit., p. 35).   Petrarch's father bought a manuscript of Isidore there which
passed to his son.   He was also an admirer of Cicero and his son no doubt

in 1353, Petrarch obtained the copy of Homer in the original Greek which he treasured but never learned to read. The ferment caused by this manuscript may have been partly responsible for the rise of interest in Greek among the humanists. It seems to me then that Petrarch's stay in Avignon and his travels through France were highly significant for the development of his interests and therefore for the humanistic movement in general, in which he was the dominant figure.

There are other indications that point the same way, that show that the curious, but intellectually somewhat narrow Italians of the fourteenth century, found in France just the right milieu for their development. Here is just one detail, dealing with a single Latin author, Seneca. In the Middle Ages Seneca's philosophical works were well known everywhere, but the plays first attracted attention in Italy in the early fourteenth century.[8] A Dominican cardinal from Prato, near Florence, became interested in the tragedies, how or why we do not know, and about 1314 wrote from Valence, not far from Avignon, to an English Dominican, Nicholas Trevet, or Trivet, to prepare a commentary on Seneca's plays, which the cardinal, with his scholastic background, found obscure.[9] He turned to Trevet, not because the latter was a humanist in any sense or had a special competence in Seneca, but because the cardinal had read and liked Trevet's commentary on Boethius and because he knew that Trevet had written a commentary on the *Declamations* of the Elder Seneca. Trevet produced the desired commentary, which is of no great consequence. The really significant point for us is that an interest in the tragedies should be awakened in the very Dominican circles which were the heart of scholasticism and that the clearing-house, so to speak, of this activity should be at Avignon. The significance of the cardinal's action is heightened when we consider, as we shall in a moment, the part that Seneca's tragedies played in the Renaissance. Incidentally the papal library

acquired some of his own love of Cicero from his father. The father's copy of Cicero's rhetorical works (where he obtained it is unknown) was cherished by the son.

[8]Medieval manuscripts of the tragedies are scarce, but some three hundred dating from the fourteenth and fifteenth centuries, written for the most part in Italy, are in existence. I have not space to go into details or to substantiate my belief that their archetype came from France.

[9]E. Franceschini, *Studi e note di filologia latina medievale,* 1938, p. 29.

at Avignon had a copy of them, with Trevet's commentary, as early
as 1317.[10]

Another example of Avignon's strategic position. This time the
example is Greek and of a somewhat later period. A Florentine
cardinal, Pietro de' Corsini, had been imbued with the humanistic
spirit, probably catching it from Petrarch. In Aulus Gellius, that
gossipy ancient who gives us all sorts of curious lore, the cardinal
found a quotation from Plutarch's essay on anger. This seems to
have impressed him so much (again we do not know why) that he
seems to have kept it in mind for years and to have looked for a
chance to get the entire essay. We can imagine the good cardinal
asking every new acquaintance if he had seen a copy of the essay.
In 1372 at the papal court of Avignon he met a Greek archbishop
named Simon and asked him the usual question. The quest was
ended, for Simon had a copy and translated it for his new acquaintance.[11]

Avignon played a part in establishing contacts between French
and Italian scholars.[12] It may be significant that the first phases
of humanism in France, represented by Jean de Montreuil, Nicolas
de Clamanges, the Col brothers, Gontier and Pierre, and others,
died out at just about the time that Avignon abandoned its papal
claims entirely and the schism came to an end. To be sure, political
conditions in France, as well as the departure of the papacy, played
their part too in bringing this period to a close.

Though Coluccio himself never went to Avignon he was in touch
with many Italians who did, and through them he became acquainted
with Frenchmen and other foreigners. So he writes to the Arag-
onese Juan Fernandez de Heredia, who spent much time in Avignon,
and asks for copies of the less well-known Roman historians.[13]

In spite of all the indebtedness to France which is merely hinted
at in my few examples, early Italian humanism retained its inde-

[10]We know, to be sure, only that the library had a manuscript of the tragedies
with a commentary, but I agree with Franceschini (*loc. cit.*) that Trevet's
commentary must be the one.

[11]Dean P. Lockwood in an unpublished paper (cf. *Proc. Amer. Phil. Assoc.*,
LXIV (1933), lxvi. Coluccio, in a letter which Novati (*Epist.*, II, 480) probably
dates too late, criticizes the style of this translation.

[12]A. Coville, *Gontier et Pierre Col et l'Humanisme en France au Temps de
Charles VI* (1934), has a chapter entitled *Les Relations avec l'Italie et l'Inter-
médiaire d'Avignon* (pp. 140ff.). The hint that I have given of the rôle of
Avignon should be thoroughly investigated.

[13]Novati, *Epist.*, II, 289 and note 1. Benedict XIII may have been the inter-
mediary (cf. Novati, *Epist.*, IV, 264).

pendence. Otherwise it would not have developed. The mysterious
urge was already there; Avignon and France furnished the opportunity. Notwithstanding his love for Vaucluse, Petrarch has some
sharp things to say about French barbarism. He admits that the
French are the most civilized of the barbarians, but insists that
after all only Italians are real Latins. It has already been pointed
out that humanism reacted strongly against scholasticism, nurtured
in France. Humanism did more than that, it cancelled all medieval
literature and started where the ancients left off. The French saw
their medieval literature as part of their continuous tradition. The
earlier French revivals could not be lightly cast aside by Frenchmen, but the Italians traveled without such useless baggage.

I do not want to give the impression that Italy had no classical
treasures and that the humanists found the classics only in France.
Such an impression would be far from the truth. Perhaps there
was something more exciting and enchanting in the books found
far from home. Nor do I mean to imply that the Italians found all
their inspiration in France. The ghost of Dante rises to challenge
any such implication. Scholars have placed him now at the end of
the Middle Ages, now at the beginning of the Renaissance. The
dispute is a good proof that the Renaissance did not come into being
full-grown, like Minerva from the head of Jove. Dante has some
humanistic qualities, though if I am forced to classify him I should
prefer to put him in the Middle Ages. Except for Petrarch, the
early humanists were enthusiastic admirers of Dante. Boccaccio
lectured on *The Divine Comedy* in the University of Florence.
Benvenuto da Imola, Dante's first commentator (in Latin at that)
was a friend of Petrarch and Coluccio. Dante's patriotic utterances, the prominence he gives to Virgil, and other aspects of his
work had their influence in shaping humanism.

I am ready then to take into account the twelfth (and thirteenth)
century French Renaissance. At the same time I vehemently reject
the view that the Italian Renaissance is a mere continuation of the
French. To my mind it is still to be regarded as something quite
new, quite as dazzling as it appeared to those who years ago saw no
glimmer of light in the medieval darkness.

In the thirteenth century much of the classical material was
taken by speakers and writers at second and third hand from hand-
books and anthologies, such as the works of John of Salisbury and
the enormously popular *specula*, or encyclopaedias, of Vincent of

Beauvais.[14] One striking result of the new humanistic curiosity which led to the acquisition of better libraries was that the originals were now read and quoted.   Petrarch acutely characterizes the French Renaissance of the thirteenth century when he accuses a certain Frenchman of having only a handful of extracts, a truly French work, and of regarding them, in accordance with Gallic lack of seriousness, as substitutes for a complete library.[15] An unusually interesting example of the difference between the two attitudes may be seen in the defense of literature by Coluccio Salutati and the attack on it by Giovanni Dominici in the early 1400's.[16] Dominici gets much of his material from secondary sources such as Vincent. Much of it he quotes from a faulty memory. Coluccio, on the other hand, regularly quotes scrupulously at first hand from the classical books in his library. In this way he is able to clear up many an obscurity and many a misunderstanding and to refute his opponent. "Quote correctly," he says on one occasion, "as the best manuscripts have it and as other evidence shows. If you cannot do that, do not quote at all rather than offer the reader something that is open to criticism."[17]

The work which Coluccio considered his most important, as it was his longest, the *De laboribus Herculis,* was an allegorical treatment after the manner of the "moralized Ovids" and similar works which gave the Middle Ages one of its chief characteristics. But Coluccio's work reveals a broad and first-hand knowledge of the Latin classics and an interest in neglected authors which no medieval writer can match.

Great weight must be attached to the influence of particular Latin authors in determining the direction that the Renaissance took. Though all authors were eagerly sought, the various humanists had their favorites. For Petrarch, who did more than any one else to chart the course of humanism, it was Cicero. As a child Petrarch was fascinated by the musical sound of Cicero's words even before

---

[14]B. L. Ullman, "Classical Authors in Certain Mediaeval Florilegia," *Classical Philology,* XXVII (1932), 40; "A Project for a New Edition of Vincent of Beauvais," *Speculum,* VIII (1933), 312.

[15]"Unum manipulum florum, opus vere Gallicum, et, quod Gallica levitas, pro omnibus libris habet" (*Contra Galli calumnias,* in *Opera,* ed. Bas., 1554, p. 1178).

[16]A new edition of Dominici has just been published by a student of mine: Edmund Hunt, *Iohannis Dominici Lucula Noctis* (Publications in Mediaeval Studies, The University of Notre Dame, IV), 1940.

[17]*Epist.,* IV, 83-84.

he could understand them.[18]   When the other boys were reading Prosper and Aesop, the regular pabulum of the medieval school, he was racing through Cicero.   He attributes such ability as he has in writing Latin to "the father of eloquence," as he calls Cicero.   But he was absorbed in Cicero's *Weltanschauung* as well as his style. Through Petrarch Cicero had far-reaching effects on the development of prose style in Latin and in the vernaculars and on the tendencies of political theory.   If Petrarch was the father of humanism, Cicero was its grandfather.

We are extremely fortunate in having a short list of favorite books which Petrarch put together before 1333, when he was still in his twenties.   The exact nature and therefore the importance of this list has not always been realized on account of the difficulty of deciphering its faded heading.   It can now be stated positively that it reads: *Libri mei peculiares.   Ad reliquos non transfuga sed explorator transire soleo,* "My specially prized books.   To the others I usually resort not as a deserter but as a scout.''[19]   The last part of the sentence is a quotation from one of Seneca's letters.   The difference between humanism and medievalism is well illustrated by this quotation.   Petrarch employs it to head a list of favorite books in which Cicero has first place.   The same sentence is quoted by a twelfth-century prior in answer to a request by an abbot of Corvey for a manuscript of Cicero.   The prior writes: "Although you want to have the books of Cicero, I know that you are a Christian, not a Ciceronian.   For you go into the enemy's camp not as a deserter but as a scout."   To the prior, Cicero is in the enemy's camp; the Christian writers are in his own.   To Petrarch, Cicero is a most precious friend, while the Christian writers, with the one exception of Augustine, are in the enemy's camp.

But to return to Petrarch's list.   Cicero's philosophical, or moral works, as Petrarch calls them, come first, headed by the sixth book of the *Republic* and the *Tusculan Disputations.*   Then follow the rhetorical essays and the orations.   After Cicero comes Seneca, leading off with the letters to Lucilius, the essay *De clementia* and the *De remediis fortuitorum,* followed by the tragedies.   The titles of three other essays were added later.   Petrarch's enthusiasm for

---

[18]The appreciation of the artistry of Latin literature was a fundamental characteristic of the early humanists. The Paduan group, to be mentioned below, interested themselves in the meters of Seneca.

[19]B. L. Ullman, "Petrarch's Favorite Books," *Trans. Amer. Phil. Assoc.,* LIV (1923), 21.

Seneca's philosophical works was more of an inheritance from the Middle Ages than a humanistic innovation. Aristotle's *Ethics* is squeezed in among the moral works and is the only Aristotelian work included. This too is a medieval inheritance; but of all the works of Aristotle the *Ethics* would naturally be among the few of greatest interest to the early humanists. Boethius' *Consolation of Philosophy* is also listed. After the moralists come the historians: Valerius Maximus, Livy, Justinus, Florus, Sallust, Suetonius, Rufus Festus, Eutropius. History was a favorite subject with Petrarch, and Livy his favorite historian. From Cicero and Livy in particular he got his ideas about the growth of Rome, ideas which he applied to the Italy of his day. Next come the two excerptors, Macrobius and Aulus Gellius. The poets listed are Virgil, Lucan, Statius, Horace, "especially in the *Odes*," Ovid, "especially in the *Metamorphoses*," and Juvenal. Virgil always had been a favorite of Petrarch's and along with Cicero's rhetorical works had been rescued from the fire into which Petrarch's father had thrown the son's books because he spent too much time in dalliance with them when he was supposed to be studying the practical subject of law at Montpellier. We really owe a great debt to the law for the many eminent persons who turned from it in distaste to pursue humanistic studies. Virgil of course was no discovery of the humanists but was now being read with greater insight and appreciation. The entry "Horace, especially in the *Odes*" attracts our attention. The Middle Ages were fonder of the *Satires* and *Epistles*. The personal, lyric character of the *Odes* would naturally appeal to the author of the *Canzoniere*.

The only Christian writer in the list is Augustine, of whom the *City of God* and the *Confessions* head the list of four works given. Petrarch and Augustine had some qualities of temperament in common, and it is not surprising that Petrarch should be drawn to these two books.

A slightly later list on the same page is somewhat briefer. The poets are the same; Cicero and Seneca are still favorites but the tragedies are expressly excepted. Aristotle and dialectic are omitted. Livy too is absent but this must be due to accident or to a temporary estrangement. Cicero and Livy, Virgil and Horace are Petrarchan favorites who continued to mold the thought of the Renaissance.

Petrarch's coolness toward Seneca's tragedies, a coolness that is only relative, however, by contrast with his other enthusiasms, and in another person and in a different age might be called warmth, is for once out of line with the Renaissance movement. About the same time that Trevet wrote his commentary for the Italian cardinal, several persons in Padua became deeply interested in Seneca's plays—just why is one of the many unanswered questions about the origin of the Renaissance. Franceschini has pointed out that, although Trevet really understood Seneca scarcely more than the cardinal for whom he wrote, the Paduans certainly did.[20] Marsiglio, the famous author of the *Defensor pacis*,[21] precursor of Machiavelli, was one of the Paduans who took an interest in Seneca. But most noteworthy among the Paduan contributions was the play called the *Ecerinis,* by Mussato. This was the first and best play to imitate Seneca; it was so successful that Mussato has been called the father of Renaissance tragedy. It is perhaps true that he was chiefly responsible for making Seneca the tragic poet of the Italian and European Renaissance down to the time of Shakespeare. Perhaps we should rather say, in the absence of other Roman tragedies than Seneca's, that Mussato raised Senecan tragedy to a high place among Renaissance literary genres.

The continued influence of Seneca's tragedies is worth tracing a bit farther. Coluccio Salutati, who with Petrarch and Boccaccio formed a triumvirate of Florentine humanism in the fourteenth century and who was largely responsible for making Florence the center of the movement in the next century, had a large library. I have located over one hundred manuscripts of this library, and of all these only one was transcribed by Coluccio himself. It is a beautiful copy, carefully made, of Seneca's tragedies, followed by Mussato's *Ecerinis,* at the end of which Coluccio proudly wrote: "I Coluccio copied this book myself." Coluccio's chief book, on the labors of Hercules, was inspired by Seneca's play on the mad Hercules.

While we are on the subject of Seneca's plays let us skip a bit in time and out of our particular field to get a glimpse of how the Italian Renaissance spread. In the British Museum there is a manuscript of Seneca's tragedies copied by an Englishman, John Gun-

---

[20]*Op. cit.,* p. 12.

[21]My theory that Franco-Italian relations contributed to the Renaissance gets some support from the fact that this budding humanist spent a number of years in France (C. W. Previté-Orton, *The Defensor Pacis of Marsilius of Padua,* 1928, p. x).

thorp, in 1460 while he was studying the art of poetry in Ferrara under the famous humanist Guarino of Verona.   The margins are filled with notes, presumably reproducing in part at least the observations of Professor Guarino.   Once again an Englishman writes a commentary on the tragedies, but how different a commentary and how different an Englishman from the commentary of Nicholas Trevet, written less than 150 years before.   A new world had come into being.   John Gunthorp is one of the figures in that early fifteenth-century Renaissance in England which prepared for but was so completely overshadowed by the great sixteenth century that it has received less attention than it deserves.

Let us turn to another Roman poet, Ovid.   Coluccio Salutati says of him: "I owe him much, for I had him as a sort of door and teacher when my passion for this sort of study first flared up as if by divine inspiration at the end of my adolescence.   Although I had no one to advise me and heard no one discuss the matter, after Ovid came into my hands, I of my own accord read all the poets and by divine gift, as it were, understood them."[22]   Ovid a door! A door to the great treasures of Roman poetry, a door into the future through the past, a door opening vistas of the coming Renaissance. To Dante Virgil had been a guide: "Tu duca, tu signore, e tu maestro,"[23] a guide into the Inferno of the life after death.   To Coluccio Ovid is a door into a paradise on this earth.

Coluccio himself could not understand how he took to Ovid so easily and so violently; to him it seemed a miracle.   Of unusual importance is his statement that he started his own Renaissance, so to speak, without outside suggestion.   Was humanism a seed spread by the winds?   Or had he at least heard or read some chance remark that germinated in his soul?   Here at the beginning of the Renaissance we are confronted by the usual mystery.   Significant too is the inspiration which Ovid gave him to read more widely. He was by no means the first to read Ovid; in fact Ovid was very popular in the Middle Ages, and the twelfth century has been called the *aetas Ovidiana,* the age of Ovid.   But the Italian of the fourteenth century had a mysterious something, a germ or an excess of some secretion or an imbalance of salts that caused him to behave in a different way from his predecessors.   Others would call it economic independence or something similar.   Be that as it may, Ovid

---

[22]*De lab. Herc.,* III.11.

[23]*Inf.,* 2.140.

remained a favorite of the humanists, again down to the time of Shakespeare.

In this paper I have merely hinted at the possible rôle of France in feeding the culture-hungry Italians of the fourteenth century and thus contributing to the origin of humanism. The sketch should be filled in with scores of minutiae. In the same way the influence of certain classical authors which I have outlined should be traced in detail. By following the procedure of Voigt, Sabbadini, and others like them we may achieve a point of view and a method which will help correct some current views about the Renaissance.

FORTUNE IN THE TRAGEDIES OF GIRALDI CINTIO

By ALLAN H. GILBERT
Duke University

Professor Craig, in his paper on *The Shackling of Accidents,* has indicated that Renaissance tragedy presented the idea "that those in high station were the most subject to the onslaughts of evil fate."[1] Then, inquiring whether the dramatists presented any ideal which can "subordinate change and accident to fortitude and self-command," he decides that man can master himself and thus control outer ills so far as they affect his own spirit. Concluding, he quotes from Cleopatra:

> 'Tis paltry to be Caesar;
> Not being Fortune, he's but Fortune's knave,
> A minister of her will; and it is great
> To do that thing that ends all other deeds,
> Which shackles accidents, and bolts up change   (V, ii, 2-6).

As Professor Craig suggests, accident and change were commonly expressed by the Renaissance under the figure of Fortune. Conventional many references to Fortune in the sixteenth century are, but that does not mean that they lack reality. On the contrary, the Renaissance may be said to have seized on Fortune as the explanation of its view of the world as unstable, shifting, irrational, and unpredictable. In recent times man has been inclined to talk of Progress and to emphasize the stability of life. This tendency, however, was more marked before 1914 than since; conquest, war, and depression have had some effect on current philosophy, leading man to think more of the uncertainties of his existence than of its stability. We can better appreciate the attitude of Machiavelli when he declared that in his time Fortune was the more fully believed in because of the great variations in human affairs that had been seen and that still were to be seen every day.[2] Fortune, then, is the metaphorical statement of a fact. This is often apparent in the structure of narrative. When Giraldi wishes to make the transition to another part of a *novella,* he has only to say: "Volle la sorte,"[3]

---

[1] *Philological Quarterly,* XIX (1940), 1-19.
[2] *The Prince,* chap. 25.
[3] *Ecatommiti,* II, 6.

just as Spenser introduces a new incident with "It fortuned." This is not Aristotle's plot built according to necessity; it is rather his probability that many things will happen contrary to probability. But it was realism to the sixteenth century.

Consequently when references to Fortune were observed in the *Poetics* of Aristotle as it became the rule book for writers of tragedy,[4] the age was quite prepared to take at its fullest value what the Philosopher had said. Giraldi renders Aristotle's Τύχη by Fortune,[5] as does Pazzi.[6] Trissino, who perhaps knew Greek literature and criticism better than any other critic of the century, also uses the word *fortuna* in translating Aristotle.[7] In general the age was willing to echo Theophrastus, who called tragedy a "reversal of heroic chance."[8]

Giraldi is familiar with the usual metaphors for Fortune. Her wheel is ever-turning.[9] As the sea is ever in motion, so is man's life swayed by Fortune, often pictorially represented as standing among the waves.[10] Fortune also is indicated by the figure of the ship tossed by the billows,[11] and by the less frequent figure of the glass of the window:

> Sò che di vetro è la Fortuna, e tanto
> Ella più fragil è, quanto più splende.[12]

The figure of Opportunity indicates that man is not wholly at the mercy of Fortune:

> *Agn.* Anzi già messa
> La man le hò ne capegli. *Pag.* Più non temo,
> Ch'ella ci possa rivoltar le spalle (*Arren.* 3.1, p. 63).

---

[4]The first Latin translation circulated in the Renaissance is that of 1498, by Giorgio Valla. For mediaeval Latin translations that apparently did not circulate widely, see Alfred Gudeman, *Aristotle's Poetik* (Berlin, 1934), pp. 29, 458.

[5]Giovambattista Giraldi Cintio, *Delle Comedie e delle Tragedie*, (Milano, 1864), pp. 33, 62, 67—(pp. 220, 241 of the ed. of 1554; the second reference was added later). He speaks also merely of moving "dalla infelicità a stato felice" (pp. 7, 13). Aristotle uses various derivatives, such as εὐτυχία.

[6]Vincentii Madii Brixiani et Bartholomaei Lombardi Veronensis *in Aristotelis Librum de Poetica Communes Explanationes* (Venetiis, 1550), pp. 124, 137, 152.

[7]Giovan Giorgio Trissino, *Opere* (Verona, 1729), II, 99ff. (*Poetica*, div 5).

[8]Reported by Diomedes (Keil, *Grammatici Latini*, I, 487).

[9]*Cleopatra* 1.1, p. 10; *Arrenopia* 3.11, p. 88; etc.

[10]*Orbecche* 2.2, p. 35.

[11]*Orbecche* 3.5, pp. 83-6; 5.4, p. 126.

[12]*Antivalomeni* 1.2, p. 16. For illustrations see Jean Cousin, *The Book of Fortune (Liber Fortunae)*, Paris and London, plate LV.

Generally Fortune exercises her power for the ill of men; the Chorus of *Altile* complains of

> la Sorte, da cui rette
> Sono le cose humane, ò per dir meglio,
> Da cui il Mondo è sotto sopra volto (4,3, p. 90).

The desolate Semne bewails the fate of women exposed "a strali suoi."[13] Even though unfavorable Fortune may be expected to change to the opposite,[14] yet generally she opposes man's happiness. The adjective most commonly applied to her is *rea*. The tragic character hopes nothing good from her hand. Learning of the horrible deception that ruins the happiness of Epitia, her chamberlain declares that Fortune is the worse the more favorable she seems.[15] Liscone, the noble captain of the *Altile,* laments the promotion that has raised him only to make him an instrument of cruelty.[16] The tragic character is forced to conclude:

> Se la Sorte
> Esser ci vuol nemica, trova tale
> Via di darci martir, e 'human pensiero
> Non vi puote arrivare (*Selene* 4.1, p. 84).

He who is prosperous, deservedly or not, may expect the inconstant goddess to overthrow him.[17] On the other hand, he who is down may expect equally unaccountable restoration.[18] Yet it is still true that Fortune prefers to favor the wicked:

> Ugali
> N'habbia prodotti qui l'alma natura,
> Se la cieca fallace, & ria fortuna,
> Ch'a ogni spirto gentil sempre è nemica,
> Riguardo havesse havuto à la virtute (*Orbecche* 3.2, pp. 61-2).

Above all in war, Fortune shows herself irrational; an experienced soldier contemplates the military skill of the opposing army, yet knows that it may be in vain.[19] Against such irrationality man can find partial remedies. One is "accomodarsi al tempo, a la Fortuna,"[20] according to the advice of the wise adviser of the king in

---

13*Arrenopia* 1.4, p. 27. Cf. Hamlet's "slings and arrows of outrageous Fortune."

14*Arrenopia* 2.8, p. 60.

15*Epitia* 3.1, pp. 48-9.

16*Altile* 4.4, p. 91.

17*Cleopàtra* 1.1, p. 10.

18*Altile* 5.2, p. 118.

19*Arrenopia* 3.11, pp. 85-6.

20*Orbecche* 3.2, p. 55.

the *Orbecche*. Had King Sulmone heeded this exhortation to adapt himself to the time, he would have changed tragedy to comedy. Courage is another defence, for "Fortune friends the bold,"[21] as Spenser wrote.

So Gripo exhorts his follower:

> La Fortuna, in cui man son l'human'opre,
> Gli animosi, i gagliardi aita sempre,
> Et à chi teme, vien del tutto meno (*Selene* 4.2, p. 91).

Yet courage fails to prevent the ruin of this villain. When all the qualities that the Renaissance put under Virtue are united against Fortune, even they do not always avail; looking on the fate of her mistress, a servant of the *Arrenopia* declares:

> I'veggio manifestamente,
> Che non giova virtù punto, ò bontade
> Quando Fortuna ci vuol dare assalto   (4.2, p. 92).

The typical passages thus far cited suggest how often the characters of Giraldi attribute their sufferings to the malice of Fortune, and how the tragic atmosphere of the play depends on reminders to the auditor that the persons before him are in the hands of a malignant force against which man has but slight protection. Even the strong and the good find that Fortune's dominion means tears and misery. In addition to such lines as have been quoted, there are also many, often not dissimilar, that bear on the central theme of the play, and seem to represent the author himself saying that his concept of tragedy is that of a noble character suffering from the ills of a world mastered by a force that is irrational or even inclined to evil rather than good. Such passages may be thought to show the tragedian explaining the power of Fortune in his plot, so far as the characters of a drama may be allowed to speak for their creator. In *Euphimia* there are two soliloquies by Thuamastio, a minister of the king who does not elsewhere speak; obviously he is a sort of extra chorus, not to carry on the action but to give the "notable morality" Sir Philip Sidney wished in tragedy. His name, derived from the Greek for wonder and astonishment, suggests Giraldi's belief that one of the functions of tragedy was to rouse the feeling of wonder; the wailing and lamentation of tragedy should, he says, cause in the spectators "maraviglia, misericordia, e orrore."[22] And he writes further:

---

[21]*Faerie Queene* 4.2.7.6.

[22]*Discorso sulle Comedie e sulle Tragedie*, p. 117 (p. 283 of the ed. of 1554).

Gente . . . volentieri vengono a quella terribile e lagrimevole azione, se acconciamente ella è condotta nella scena. E cercando io tra me la cagione di ciò, mi son risoluto che la tragedia ha anco il suo diletto, e in quel pianto si scopre un nascosto piacere che il fa dilettevole a chi l'ascolta e tragge gli animi alla attenzione e gli empie di maraviglia.[23]

At any rate Thaumastio emphasizes the *maraviglia* we should feel in the diversities of human fate caused by Fortune:

> Chi non sapesse quanto la Fortuna
> Aggiri, e turbi le mortali cose,
> Miri quel, ch'è avenuto in questa corte.
> Che n'havrà essempio tal, che vedrà chiaro,
> Che fermezza non hà cosa mortale,
> Qual'hor questa inconstante, a vaga Dea
> Vi pon la mano à rivoltarle tutte (*Euphim.* 4.3, p. 83).

He then summarizes the action of the play as illustrating the power of Fortune. In *Orbecche*, the hero Orontes soliloquizes:

> Chi con san' occhio ben le cose humane
> Mira, vedrà, che non è tanto polve
> Minuta, e lieve da' soffianti venti
> Menata in giro, quanto la Fortuna
> Queste cose mortai volve, e rivole (3.5, pp. 83-4).

Then he tells the story of his life as connected with the tragedy. In the same play the heroine shows her knowledge of Fortune:

> Non sai, Nodrice mia, che quanto lieta
> Si mostra a noi piu la Fortuna, tanto
> Piu devemo temerlo, e men fidarsi,
> De le lusinghe sue sempre fallaci? (5.2, p. 109).

After this she gives her immediate suspicions, confirmed by a terrifying dream portending the fate of her husband and children. The reader, moreover, knows what the princess does not, namely, that her tyrannical father has already murdered his son-in-law and grandchildren, after luring them to his presence with signs of favor that promised a happy conclusion to a time of anxiety. In other plays comparable passages are little less striking; the reader hardly can escape the feeling that the author intends the plot he is presenting to exemplify the work of Fortune. In some such passages appear also general reflections on Fortune, as though to darken the atmosphere of the tragedy. Such speeches frequently are assigned either to characters speaking in soliloquy or to the Chorus. Usually they are set off by quotation marks, according to the common prac-

---

[23] *Discorso sulle Comedie e sulle Tragedie*, p. 120 (p. 285 of the ed. of 1554).

tice of the age for indicating sententious passages.[24] Cleopatra's
servant meditates on the fall of her mistress:

> Quanto bene
> Sarebbe, che quando da sommo grado
> Cade un Signor ad imo, cosi anchora
> La Fortuna gli dessé un cor humile,
> Convenevole al grado, in ch'elle il pone (*Cleop.* 4.4, p. 117).

In *Didone* the messenger who comes with the tidings of the death
of the Queen soliloquizes:

> Ahi che il di non sappiam quel, che ci apporti
> La sera tarda: e nulla si puote hoggi
> Prometter di dimane huomo mortale;
> Tanto lo stato human Fortuna aggira,
> Con varii modi: sol gli Dei felici
> Si posson dire, & i mortali tutti,
> Per legge natural, tristi, e infelici (5.4, p. 119).

In such passages the tragic character is representative of mankind,
showing the fate to which all are subject as they are men. Any of
us may suffer in the same fashion, as the critics understood. Trissino, for example, said that "generally those will be compassionate
who remember that to themselves or some of their relatives similar
accidents can come, or who fear that they will come to themselves
or some of theirs."[25] Giraldi himself did not say as much, though
it seems likely he would have accepted the idea, for he did write:

La conformità che ha l'essere umano col lagrimevole, gli induce a mirar
volentieri quello spettacolo, che ci dà indizio della natura nostra e fa che
l'umanità che è in noi ci dà ampia materia di aver compassione alle miserie
degli afflitti.[26]

Since men universally are subject to the malice of Fortune, all can
feel compassion for any character whose ills can be charged to the
fickle goddess.

Yet in most of the plays there is a character who denies Fortune's
ultimate control over man. Still more, the majority of Giraldi's
tragedies end happily, as did the *Iphigenia among the Taurians*
admired by Aristotle. It is true that a blind and irrational goddess
might at times bring the deserving to happiness, but such accident
is not enough. There is after all an ultimate power that rises up

---

[24]Quotes are not used for this purpose in the *Euphimia* and the *Arrenopia*,
and only in the first act of the *Epitia*. They are not printed in the *Orbecche*,
but some reader long ago supplied them in my copy of the edition of 1583.

[25]*Poetica*, div. 5, p. 108; translated in Gilbert, *Literary Criticism: Plato to
Dryden* (New York, 1940), p. 221. From Aristotle's *Rhetoric*, II. 8.

[26]*Discorso sulle Comedie e sulle Tragedie*, p. 120 (p. 285 of the ed. of 1554).

against Fortune with absolute certainty: the power of God. In some
of the plays there is a final assurance by the Chorus that Heaven
rules, as in the *Didone*:

> Lassa à noi non tien fede,
> Nè ria Fortuna, nè fallace Amore,
> E chi si fida in lor misero more,
> Però huom non fia, che la sua speme fermi
> Ne l'instabilita de la Fortuna, . . .
> Dunque chi questo vede,
> Per ischifare, e l'uno, e l'altro errore,
> Volga al verace ben subito il core.

Similarly at the end of *Epitia* the Chorus asserts:

> Puo Fortuna aggirar le cose humane,
> Con la natia inconstanza,
> Ma una viva speranza
> C'habbia l'huom nel Signore,
> Che del tutto è fattore,
> Le forze sue fà vane.

In *Selene* a like affirmation is made by the Chorus at the end of
the fourth act; the play closes with the assertion that men get
justice, implying the conquest of Fortune. *Arrenopia* and *Altile*
declare that *rea Sorte* is ultimately powerless over the righteous.

The conclusion of *Cleopatra* seems to make the opposite assertion:

> Quanto miseri, oime, sono coloro,
> Che, perche hanno felice
> La fallace Fortuna a' desir loro,
> Mai provarla non temono infelice. . . .
>   À lei sola lice
> Le gioie altrui far vane,
> Et abbassar tutte le altezze humane.

But the meaning is probably not far from that of the last Chorus
of *Orbecche*, namely that mortal things are fleeting and only the
Lord of Heaven is firm. Both the chief characters of *Cleopatra* are
far from good, and both are wholly overthrown; there is no reason
why in this instance True Divinity should intervene against Fortune.

Evidently there is a logical difficulty in the theory of Giraldi:
the world cannot be ruled by both Fortune and the Lord of Heaven.
In most of the tragedies our author makes no attempt to reconcile
the contradiction; once, however, there is something of the sort. In
the *Euphimia* one of the characters is Eudocimo (by derivation,
Judicious), the good adviser of the almost incredibly egotistic king.
His function is merely to give good counsel and soliloquize on it,
for he appears only in the early scenes of Act 2, and has no active

function in the plot. He asserts the subjection of the mobile goddess:

> Quanto più può, più dee penser chi regge,
> Di far sol quel, che si conviene al giusto.
> E se Fortuna auttorità gli dona,
> Di far, di dir, pensar deve egli sempre,
> Che in quanto occhio si gira ella si muta,
> E dietro lascia poi la penitenza,
> Che de' misfatti altrui prende la pena;
> Disponendo cosi l'alto Motore (2.1, p. 32).

The Judicious Man is apparently brought in to utter the truth, that is, the beliefs of the author himself. Even he, however, addresses the villain of the play, not the morally blameless heroine, who until the end is left to censure Fortune without comfort from the suggestion of a higher control.[27] Even after this play, then, it is possible to say that the main actions of the tragedies run on as though Fortune ruled the world. In other words, their course is generally Senecan.

This condition Giraldi allowed as possible in a tragedy. In one of the additions to his *Discourse on Comedies and Tragedies,* apparently representing his mature thought, he writes that spectators may get from tragedy its proper effect, that of comfort in tribulation, because they see that afflictions are normal to human nature, "which naturally is exposed to all the blows of Fortune."[28] Though allowing this as an acceptable theory, he does, however, prefer the tragic effect derived from seeing afflictions come to those who deserve them through their errors, but not through extreme wickedness. Apparently it was his desire for moral effect that led him to prefer tragedies showing the overthrow of the wicked, though he well knew this was not acceptable to Aristotle.[29] This method, as he says, he used in the *Altile* and the *Selene,* in which he displayed the defeat of the strong, the unjust, the wicked. Still further, he felt a preference, at least on the stage, for tragedies ending happily; but three of his nine tragedies end unhappily: the *Orbecche,* the *Didone,* and the *Cleopatra.* One of his reasons is that of Aristotle, who says that a play having an unhappy issue for the wicked and a happy issue for the good pleases the spectators, because of their weakness, or, as Giraldi puts it, their ignorance.

---

[27]She blames Fortune in Act 3, sc. 3, p. 60, in Act 4, sc. 2, p. 82, and in Act 5, sc. 4, p. 115.

[28]P. 29.

[29]*Discorso sulle Comedie e sulle Tragedie,* p. 23 (p. 215 of the ed. of 1554).

Admitting Aristotle's censure,[30] he still asserts that it is better with some lesser excellence to satisfy the audience than with a little more greatness to displease those for whose pleasure the play is put on the stage. Moreover, the happy ending enables him to adapt himself better to "l'uso dei nostri tempi."[31] This has been interpreted to mean that, like Guarini later, he thought the older form of tragedy antiquated and looked on tragicomedy, or a similar form, as better adapted to modern times.[32] Such an opinion is in harmony with Giraldi's championship of contemporary literature. Though his chief success was with the *Orbecche,* he still indicates that the tragedy ending in ruin is proper rather for the closet than the stage.

It might be supposed, however, that a firmer basis in theory would have been given for his choice of the prosperous issue. He might have said that the dramatist fulfills his moral function by showing the reward of the good. Such a theory was held by Benedetto Varchi, who writes: "For the sake of example the poet introduces now a vicious man, who receives the proper punishment for his evil deeds; now a virtuous man, to whom come from either God or men proper rewards for his virtues."[33] This concept was known to Giraldi, but he mentions it only in dealing with the romances. saying that the poet presents his illustrious actions not as they are but as they should be, and accompanies the vicious with the terrible and miserable, thus purging our minds from such passions and rousing them to virtue.[34] If he seems to apply no such standard to tragedy, perhaps it was because he considered that form more strictly bound by truth to nature than was the epic. Tragedy

---

[30]*Poetics,* chap. 13, 53 a 30.

[31]*Discorso sulle Comedie e sulle Tragedie,* p. 34.

[32]Giambattista Guarini, *Il Compendio della Poesia Tragicomica* (Venice, 1602), p. 13. Translated selections in Gilbert, *Literary Criticism: Plato to Dryden,* pp. 505-33. See also Camillo Guerrieri Crocetti, *G. B. Giraldi ed il Pensiero Critico del Sec. XVI* (Milan, 1932), pp. 648-51.

[33]*Della Poetica in Generale,* parte 1, particella 3. First published in 1553. Cf. Sir Philip Sidney: "Poetry ever sets virtue so out in her best colors, making Fortune her well-waiting handmaid, that one must needs be enamored of her. . . . And of the contrary part, if evil men come to the stage, they ever go out (as the tragedy writer answered to one that misliked the show of such persons) so manacled as they little animate folks to follow them" (*The Defense of Poesie,* in Gilbert, *Literary Criticism,* p. 425).

Bacon writes: "True history propoundeth the successes and issues of actions not so agreeable to the merits of virtue and vice; therefore poesy feigns them more just in retribution. and more according to revealed providence (*Advancement of Learning,* bk. 2).

[34]*Discorso dei Romanzi* (Milan, 1864), p. 66 (p. 59 in the ed. of 1554).

must have a plot "in conformity with natural habits and not remote from what can happen and often does happen."[35] As a tragedian he was not willing to abandon the probable, though as the author of the *Ercole* he might give it up in the romance.

But if the conflict between Fortune and Divine Providence and the necessary victory of the latter was not formally introduced into Giraldi's theory of tragedy, it yet seems that a desire to assure his audience of God's power must have affected him. Fortune rules his plays until almost the end, and the interposition of Heaven is hardly more appropriate than in Euripides, whom he cites in justification. Yet he doubtless believed that in his own dramas, as in the *Ion*[36] of Euripides, the force mastering *rea Fortuna* appeared only when warranted by a proper regard for the construction of the plot, and that such "shackling of accidents" was in harmony with the genius of tragedy.

In his employment of Fortune our tragedian is not very different from Rucellai or Alamanni, or from Tasso, or even Ben Jonson and Beaumont and Fletcher. Indeed in his likeness to them lies his value in assisting toward a characterization of Renaissance tragedy. Though the dramatists inherited Fortune from Roman Seneca, they adopted it not so much because it enjoyed the approval of the moralist, as because it expressed the truth of existence in its unpredictable uncertainty, and satisfied a desire for an image of life. Suffering, the fate of man who is born to evil as the sparks fly upward, is usually inflicted by Fortune. Existence is a struggle against the fickle goddess, usually adverse, though quite as dangerous when she turns her smiling face on a hero. In this conflict, the best of man's qualities appear; victory can be his only when his virtue bars Fortune from any control of his spirit; even in outward things prudence and courage are necessary to the power that "bolts up change." If man won in this struggle he was, as Sidney thought, worthy of imitation, and the tragedy that presented him had done its duty by the morals of the spectators. If on the other hand he was overthrown, he still conformed with the purpose of tragedy, in stirring up pity and fear. Indeed the pity and fear of Renaissance tragedy is almost wholly for the victims of adverse Fortune. The type of poetic Aristotelianism then popular is hardly possible without it; the Renaissance, though conscious of Aristotle's theory of

[35] *Discorso sulle Comedie e sulle Tragedie*, p. 15 (p. 209. ed. of 1554).
[36] *Apology for Dido*, p. 138; *Discorso sulle Comedie e sulle Tragedie*, p. 19.

the tragic flaw, seems to have done little with it. It preferred to let the afflictions of relatively good characters come from Fortune rather than from within their own hearts. The evil man overthrown is not an Aristotelian hero.

Fortune, too, exempted the sixteenth-century dramatist from insisting too much on the Aristotelian sequence of probability and necessity, and on the nexus of character and plot. He acted in the spirit of Aristotle's saying that it is probable that many things will happen contrary to probability,[37] and did not feel moved to ask whether Aristotle would have wished the solution of the plot to depend on character.[38] Such emancipation from logical sequence enabled the poet to satisfy one of the prime demands of Renaissance critics, that for variety. Variety indeed appears to be one of the defining characteristics of the non-classical epic and drama of the age.[39] Could any power contribute more to variety than irrational Fortune, unceasing in her motions and making no discrimination between the just and the unjust, the wise man and the fool?

The ethics of a tragedy based on Fortune are primarily pagan. Even good Christian characters can rail against Fortune without offending piety. But nothing in the theory of Fortune can provide a Christian solution. The utmost in virtue, that is, goodness, capacity, energy, and prudence, may be unable to stop the course of the wheel that raises and lowers men without regard to their qualities. If God will keep the wicked from rejoicing and raise merit from the dust, he must adopt Fortune for his own minister. But if the goddess becomes intelligent and discriminating she ceases to be Fortune. If she keeps her power, God can but overrule her. When Providence does not exert its power, tragedy is pagan. A Christian tragedy such as Sidney desired, and Giraldi provided, means the rejection of Aristotle as a proponent of character working out its own fate. It also means that such realism as the century saw in the presentation of Fortune at work in the world is abandoned. Moreover, when Providence overrules Fortune to determine the outcome of a play as disastrous for the wicked and happy for

---

[37] *Poetics*, chaps. 18, 25.

[38] This statement is to be found only in the most recent text of the *Poetics*, chap. 15 (Gilbert, *Literary Criticism*, p. 90). The Renaissance probably would have not been much interested in it if it had had it.

[39] Not that classicists did not admire variety; see, e.g., Scaliger, *Poetice*, IV, 48.

the good, the coming of the tragi-comic type of play, as distinguished from pure tragedy, is hastened.

The whole process is so complex and the interrelations and exceptions so numerous that a simple formula has its dangers. Yet it seems hardly too much to call the tragedy of the sixteenth century the tragedy of Fortune. At least that tragedy can hardly be interpreted except by one who realizes how largely it is determined by *rea Fortuna.*

FRACASTORO AND THE IMAGINATION

By Murray W. Bundy
State College of Washington

Girolamo Fracastoro's *Turrius sive De Intellectione*,[1] a psychological treatise complementary to his dialogue on poetry,[2] contains an account of imagination and related powers not only at variance with other Renaissance views but in some important respects anticipating the utterances of Wordsworth, Coleridge, Leigh Hunt, and their contemporaries. If this account had been better known in its time, or if Fracastoro had made the obvious applications of his psychology to poetry, literary criticism might have undertaken much sooner the necessary redefinition of powers which in his day were generally described as concerned with the apprehension, reproduction, and recombination of images from sensory experience. From such an empirical tradition there could hardly evolve a theory of the imagination adequately describing the processes of poetic insight and creation, a view of the imagination as "the living power and prime agent of all human perception."[3] Fracastoro, departing from this rigid empiricism, discovered some of the materials which were to become basic in Romantic theory. He pointed the way to a new psychology, but he failed to see the implications of his view for the theory of poetry. The reasons for this failure are for the student of criticism quite as important as the discoveries themselves.

Fracastoro's age inherited a medieval tradition, chiefly Aristotelian, colored at times and distorted by Neoplatonism and Stoicism, and modified by Christian and Arabian thinkers.[4] In this tradition

---

[1] In *Hieronymi Fracastorii Veronensis Opera Omnia, Secunda editio* (Venice, 1574), pp. 121-148. The first edition is dated 1555, two years after his death. The dialogue is undated.

[2] *Naugerius, sive De Poetica Dialogus*, in *ibid.*, pp. 112-120; for a translation see Girolamo Fracastoro *Naugerius, sive De Poetica Dialogus*, with a translation by Ruth Kelso, . . . in *University of Illinois Studies in Language and Literature* (August, 1924), IX, 3.

[3] S. T. Coleridge, *Biographia Literaria*, Chapter XIII.

[4] See my *Theory of Imagination in Classical and Mediaeval Thought*, in *University of Illinois Studies in Language and Literature* (May-August, 1927), XII, 2-3. For typical Renaissance views see Gianfrancesco Pico della Mirandola *On the Imagination*: the Latin text with an introduction, an English translation, and notes by Harry Caplan, in *Cornell Studies in English*, (1930), XVI; Iacopo Mazzoni, *Difesa di Dante* (Cesena, 1587), pp. 145ff.; and Thomas Fyens, *De Viribus Imaginationis Tractatus, Editio postrema*, (Lyons, 1635).

the words "phantasy" and "imagination," usually synonymous, were used to describe a series of processes of the passive intellect beginning with simple apprehension, in which the image was called a phantasm or appearance, and culminating in the use of images or phantasies as the schemata of thought, and in the recombination of sensory materials in the idealizations of painter and poet, such as a Madonna or a Venus, a composite of separately beautiful features derived from many sources. The power by which images were recalled when the stimulus was no longer present was also called phantasy or imagination; and, in spite of efforts throughout the Renaissance to distinguish between phantasy and memory, the confusion persisted. There was also uncertainty regarding the capacity of the imagination or phantasy to determine the correspondence of the image to the external object. The prevailing tradition, especially in popular literature, questioned the trustworthiness of our phantasies, and a profound distrust was based upon their dangerous alliance with the appetites and passions. Occasionally, however, there was recognition of a judicial capacity, resident in the lower soul, and therefore not to be identified with reason. This was sometimes called phantasy, but more frequently a *vis cogitativa*, a term popularized by the Averroist controversy.[5]

There was also uncertainty regarding the phantasy which was responsible for the Venus of the painter and the feigned Cyrus and the ideal commonwealth of the poet. These were the creations of the same phantasy which was responsible for chimaeras, castles in Spain, centaurs, and the delusions of the lunatic and the lover.

All of these processes and all of the controversies concerning their trustworthiness both in knowledge and conduct involved either "phantasy" or "imagination" or both words. The terms were also used to describe, in addition to the faculty and the processes, the part of the brain where these operations took place, usually the foremost of three cells or ventricles.[6] When, however, the highest of these processes, usually phantasy, was described as approximating the life of reason, then it was placed in the foremost part of the central cell, assigned to reason, and it was sometimes called

[5] See A. H. Douglas, *The Philosophy and Psychology of Pietro Pomponazzi* (Cambridge, 1910), pp. 207 and 210.

[6] See, for examples in English, Thomas Vicary, *Anatomie of Man's Body* (1548), in *Early English Text Society, Extra Series*, No. 53, v. 30, p. 31; and Sir John Davies, *Nosce Teipsum*, ed. Grosart, (London, 1876), I, 71-72; and *Faerie Queene*, 2.9.49-58.

phantasy and sometimes *vis cogitativa*.[7] To the extent that phantasy found its way into the central cell, close to reason, imagination as a lower power was the more securely confined by contrast to the lower cell. In spite of the continued confusion of imagination and memory, the latter was assigned to the third ventricle at the rear of the head.

In the light of this summary of Renaissance views one can easily understand the difficulties involved in dissociating a lofty role of the imagination from functions essentially related to the life of the senses, and associated with reason only in the capacity of a hand-maid admitted to the presence of a mistress.

This psychology of the imagination, which underlies many aspects of Renaissance thought, such as ethics, epistemology, demonology, and medicine, was also the foundation of much of its critical theory. It is conveniently summarized in Mazzoni's *Difesa di Dante*[8] as essential to his reply to the charges of Bulgarini and others that Dante's poem is only a dream and thus the untrustworthy product of the phantasy or imagination. It is also explicit in varying degree in the critical utterances of Varchi,[9] Tasso,[10] Ronsard, Puttenham, Sidney,[11] Huarte,[12] and Bacon.[13] In the views of these men its limitations as a basis for an adequate conception of the poetic imagination are apparent. They may seem to glorify the imagination as the poet's faculty; but they all struggle against obstacles inherent in the name and its associations. "Imagination" as the power of poetic insight and creation was in bad company. This term, used to describe the capacity of poetry "to give some shadow of satisfaction to the mind of Man in those points wherein the Nature of things doth deny it,"[14] was the same power which, allied to the appetites, passions, temperaments, and humors, was prone to false reports concerning the external world, responsible for bad behavior,

---

[7]Cf. Mazzoni, *op. cit.*, p. 145, and Davies, *Nosce Teipsum*.

[8]Mazzoni, *op. cit.*

[9]Benedetto Varchi, *Sopra la Pittura et Scultura*, in *Lezzioni* (Florence, 1590), pp. 162ff.

[10]*Discorsi*, tr. in *Literary Criticism: Plato to Dryden*, ed. by A. H. Gilbert (New York, 1940), pp. 474-475.

[11]See my " 'Invention' and 'Imagination' in the Renaissance," in *Journal of English and Germanic Philology* (October, 1930), XXIX, 4.

[12]Juan Huarte[s], *Examen de Ingenios*, tr. by Mr. Bellamy (London, 1698), pp. 190-193.

[13]See my "Bacon's True Opinion of Poetry," in *Studies in Philology* (April, 1930), XXVII, 2.

[14]See *op. cit.*, p. 244.

and as likely to fabricate monsters and delusions as perfect heroes and ideal commonwealths.

Shakespeare made his Theseus express this prevalent view when, asked by his bride to accept as reliable the account by the lovers of the events of the night, he replied by asserting that the lunatic, the lover, and the poet were "of imagination all compact."[15] For him there was no essential difference in terms of imagination between the lunatic's hallucination of "more devils than vast hell can hold," the lover's idealization of his gypsy love into Helen's beauty, and the poet's transformation of "airy nothing" into something having "a local habitation and a name," an excellent characterization, one observes, of the "poetry" of this play, "antique fables" and "fairy toys." Shakespeare also made Theseus typical of Renaissance thought about imagination in poetry when he asserted:

> Lovers and madmen have such seething brains,
> Such shaping fantasies, that apprehend
> More than cool reason ever comprehends.

"Cool reason" is his criterion of credibility; and, in comparison, lovers, madmen, and, by implication, poets are untrustworthy as having imaginations which were hot and moist. Conditions were hardly ripe for describing the imagination as "Reason in her most exalted mood."[16]

The Renaissance thus reached a kind of impasse in its thought about the poetic imagination or phantasy. Ronsard, Puttenham, and Sidney had tried to find one way out by their identification of "imagination" and "phantasy" with rhetorical "invention"[17]; but in doing so they were constantly aware of the dangers of imagination: poets as men of good phantasy (*euphantasioti*) must be distinguished from mere *phantastici*.[18] Mazzoni, making use of Plato's distinction between "icastic" and "phantastic" imitation, faithful reproduction of reality and poetic freedom to recombine the images of experience, and boldly identifying poetry with the second type,[19] found himself in conflict with many contemporaries, including Tasso,[20] and also failed to describe the process by which he asserted

---

[15]*Midsummer Night's Dream*, V, i, 2-8.

[16]Wordsworth, *Prelude*, 14. 192.

[17]" 'Invention' and 'Imagination'," *op. cit.*

[18]George Puttenham, "Of Poets and Poesy," in *Elizabethan Critical Essays*, ed. Gregory Smith (Oxford, 1904), II, 20.

[19]Translated in *Literary Criticism*, ed. Gilbert, *op. cit.*, pp. 361ff.

[20]*Op. cit.*, p. 474.

that Dante achieved his freedom. Bacon, after giving lip-service
to the commonplace that the imagination enables the poet to make
"unlawful matches and divorces of things" resulting in new creations, concluded that this is only a play of the imagination.[21]

Fracastoro pointed the way to a redefinition of imagination which
might have precluded this inevitable apology for the poetic power
as concerned with unideal functions. Although he failed to apply
this new psychology of the imagination to poetry, he provided the
most promising psychological basis to be found in the Renaissance
for the description of the poetic imagination.

He saw that there must be a process of differentiation to free
"phantasy" and "imagination" from common associations. He
also saw that, if one faculty was to be described as higher than another, it must be analyzed as a state of mind more conscious of its
own processes. In the traditional psychology, there had been little
place for the recognition by any one of these faculties of the significance of its own functions. The processes were usually described
as mechanical in a passive intellect each of the parts of which was
necessarily passive. It is true that, at the outset, Fracastoro insisted that he adhered to the Aristotelian tradition of a passive intellect;[22] but we shall discover that, in comparison with contemporary Aristotelian accounts, his explanation made the imagination
an essentially active agent.

After a description of *species* presented by external *sensibilia*,
he gave the name "subnotion" to what was ordinarily called the
simple imagination or phantasy: "the simple and separate presentation of one sensible object after another."[23] This, he added, was
not memory; and this distinction he reiterated as vital. Aware that
the subnotion was usually included under the general term "phantasy," he accepted the comprehensive term as a concession to Aristotelian usage. He described the subnotion as the first and simplest
function in which the mind, a passive agent, wanders from image
to image, attracted by desire to the species of the good, repelled
by aversion from the species of evil.[24] This is the human equivalent
of animal appetite, a kind of instinctive life regulated by pleasure
and pain, involving the spirits, nerves, and membranes. This power

---

[21]"Bacon's True Opinion," *op. cit.*, p. 260.
[22]Fracastoro, *op. cit.*, p. 122.
[23]*Ibid.*, p. 125.
[24]*Loc. cit.*

of subnotion has no capacity for distinguishing the true and the false.[25] In this description Fracastoro makes no contribution, save that he refused to call the power either phantasy or imagination, and he refused to connect it with memory.

He was also familiar, of course, with the notion of a common sense, wherein impressions derived from separate senses coalesce in a single image. This power he regarded as the first aspect of phantasy proper,[26] although at some points he wrote about a "common sense" as a separate power.[27] Then, in his description of an orderly process, in which the mind is always impelled by the desire to learn, this phantasy undertakes to distinguish the similarities and differences in simple sensory images in respect to form, figure, location, and function.[28] This habit of comparison enables phantasy to determine that an image is like its object, and the function of observing the differences enables phantasy to detect the lack of correspondence. Phantasy, in Fracastoro's system, asserting "It is" and "It is not," is fixed as the mind's first power of judgment: it is fundamentally the mind's consciousness that there is a problem of appearance and reality.

Fracastoro is no innovator here. This had been recognized, almost from the beginning, as a function of phantasy. Having refused, however, to employ the term "phantasy" for the unreflective capacity of dealing with images, he divorced "phantasy" from "opinion," two words persistently confused in the Renaissance in spite of qualifying adjectives supplied by both Aristotelian and Stoic traditions in an attempt to avoid the confusion. "Phantasy" denoted an altogether trustworthy process. There was no necessity for finding another name, such as *vis aestimativa* or *vis cogitativa* for this judicial operation, since the unfavorable associations of "phantasy" had been broken. Nor was there necessity for regarding this check upon the reliability of sense-experience as specifically rational and therefore to be contrasted with the uncontrolled and irrational phantasy. Milton's Adam reflects the traditional Renaissance contrast which Fracastoro sought to avoid:

> But know that in the Soul
> Are many lesser faculties that serve
> Reason as chief; among these Fancy next

[25] *Loc. cit.*

[26] *Loc. cit.*

[27] *Op. cit.*, p. 147.

[28] *Op. cit.*, p. 125 et verso.

Her office holds; of all external things,
Which the five watchful Senses represent,
She forms Imaginations, Aery shapes,
Which Reason joining or disjoining, frames
All what we affirm or what deny, and call
Our knowledge or opinion.[29]

Here Milton explicitly assigned to Fancy a function which Fracastoro described as a subnotion, and, in turn, he assigned to Reason the function of Fracastoro's phantasy. In spite of Fracastoro, the tradition which Milton embodied was to prevail, hardening into the contrast, a commonplace of seventeenth and eighteenth century criticism, of Fancy and Judgment, Imagination and Reason. If Fracastoro's view had obtained, "phantasy" would have achieved the dignity of a faculty intent upon determining the veracity of images. One must remember, however, that phantasy is a power primarily concerned with the reality of external objects and that it is no longer concerned with the recombination of sensory images into ideal pictures.

Imagination describes an altogether higher kind of mental process: the mind proceeds to transform the materials supplied by subnotions and evaluated by phantasy. "Then it learns, moreover, to enumerate, to imagine, and to remember, and, after that, to achieve many other greater ends."[30] Although at the outset enumeration is regarded as a kind of intermediate function between phantasy and imagination, it is evident that it is a first aspect of imagination, just as common sense was a first aspect of phantasy. By this first basic aspect of the power one recognizes individual items as belonging to the same series. To enumerate is to accept the many in so far as they may be gathered into a unity.[31] One grasps the notion of many separate phantasies having similar qualities as belonging to the same genus. Here is the primary function of that power which was later to be described as the discovery of unity in variety. Enumeration is the simple mathematical aspect of the imagination.

In the lower processes involving subnotions and phantasies the mind knows the many only as many and disparate; but

if we consider these many in every respect in which they are comparable, then we say that we imagine. For to imagine is nothing but to receive the many as many, to compare them in respects in which they are related, and to see how each individual is related to the whole. This can be done in every instance in which the many can be compared, whether in place, station, form, figure,

---

[29] *Paradise Lost*, 5, 100-108.

[30] Fracastoro, *op. cit.*, p. 125 verso.

[31] "Nihil enim aliud est numerus, quam acceptio plurium, quatenus in unitate conveniunt, et ab illa pluries mensurant."

action, or similarity, or in any other way in which they happen to be associated.[32]

In the Renaissance Fracastoro seems to be alone in claiming this capacity exclusively for the imagination; and he took pains to set it off as essentially a higher function than the highest power ordinarily attributed to phantasy, the comprehensive term. "These greater functions that faculty performs which others call phantasy. Now we are reluctant to use 'imagination' as the inclusive term; but, the better we know our subject, we call 'imagination,' not all of these operations, but only one."[33] Fracastoro, like the Romantic critics more than two centuries later, having described the imagination as essentially a higher power, guarded against its identification with the phantasy, a power primarily concerned with the relation of the mental image to its object. This elevation of imagination over phantasy is unique in the Renaissance. It points, not only in its preference, but in the reasons for that preference, to Coleridge and Wordsworth; but one cannot add that it is a source of their views.

We shall shortly discuss Fracastoro's illustrations of his new theory of imagination; but, before we do, we shall glance at his conception of memory. Fracastoro had insisted, one recalls, that subnotions are not memories. After analyzing phantasy (in his restricted meaning) and imagination, he was ready to describe memory as dependent upon them. Memory is the recollection, not of sensory images as such, but of the associations which the mind in virtue of phantasy and imagination had previously established. Thus the memory of Dion, a servant, is the recollection of a servant in his relation to his master, and of those situations in which the mind had previously contemplated him. One remembers, not an isolated visual image or subnotion, but a complex of associations.

If Fracastoro's view had been generally accepted, critics such as Wordsworth and Ruskin might have been led to recognize memory as an essential part of the poetic process. For them, however, memory was a capacity essentially related to imagery. Wordsworth, for example, in his censure of Taylor's definitions of imagination and fancy, wrote: "It is not easy to find out how imagination thus explained, differs from distinct remembrance of images: or fancy from quick and vivid recollection of them: each is nothing

---

[32] "Nihil enim aliud est imaginari, quam plura ut plura recipere, et comparare ad id, in quo coniuncta sunt, et videre, qualiter unumquodque sese in illo habeat."

[33] *Op. cit.*, p. 126.

more than a mode of memory."[34] Fracastoro established a place for a higher kind of memory to accompany his higher imagination. One could wish that Wordsworth had had access to such a view, since his own poetry required such an explanation in terms of memory as well as imagination. Again, however, one must add that Fracastoro's psychology did not prevail.

We have now described the psychology which might have become the foundation for a new and illuminating theory of poetry. Why did Fracastoro fail to relate this penetrating analysis of the imagination to his conception of the poet in *Naugerius*? The answer is to be found, first of all, in the professions to which he went for examples of men of imagination. Having defined the imagination as a power receiving "the many as many, comparing them in respects in which they are associated, and seeing how each individual is related to the whole," he added:

This [faculty of imagination] mathematicians, architects, and painters especially demonstrate, and those who are concerned with the arts. For mathematicians consider with precision angles, lines, and figures simultaneously as they are related. And painters study man, the parts of man, and the parts of those parts, each in minutest detail, in what order and in what relation they stand, and how the other parts function in relation to one member. In similar fashion architects are busied with buildings, and others with their arts.[35]

In a later passage discussing the psychological aptitudes of men for various professions, he included musicians with men of imagination: "Musicians are men who are strong in that kind of imagination which is concerned with sounds in the same way in which mathematicians are with quantities."[36]

His conclusion shows clearly that in bringing together mathematicians, painters, architects, and musicians as examples of men of imagination he had in mind the contemporary distrust of the power: "In all fields we should consider carefully the orders and parts of objects as they are related. On this account we say that some are *bene imaginativos*, others *male*."[37] The prevalent tradition, founding its claims for a creative imagination in the arts on the freedom to recombine images derived from sensory experience, had found

[34]*Preface to Poems* (1815), in *Wordsworth's Literary Criticism*, ed. Nowell C. Smith (London, 1905), p. 156.

[35]Fracastoro, *op. cit.*, p. 125 verso, 126. For the relation of mathematics and anatomy to painting, sculpture, and architecture see Gilbert and Kuhn, *A Hitory of Aesthetics* (New York, 1939), pp. 177-179.

[36]Fracastoro, *op. cit.*, p. 148.

[37]*Ibid.*, p. 126.

it necessary, as has been pointed out, to distinguish between *euphan-tasioti* and *phantastici*, between men who made a right use of the power, and those who exhibited a wrong use in delirium, ecstasy, and the "phantastical" creations of painting and poetry. For Fracastoro this distinction was to be based, not upon the freedom or restraint involved in the combination of simple images, but upon the architectonic capacity of the artist or the absence of it—upon the quality of the imaginative mind. Fracastoro shifted the criterion from the acceptable nature of the product, a feigned invention which a rational man would accept as probable, to the structural capacity of the mind as it approximated that of the mathematician. One hardly needs to add that in having accomplished this he provided an aesthetic standard much closer to great Renaissance practice in the fine arts than that which he was attempting to supplant. This is an aesthetic of the imagination which in directing the attention to the relation of the arts to anatomy, mathematics, physical laws, and kindred studies, offers a much more adequate explanation of the processes of creation. Fracastoro enables one to understand, for example, the imagination of a Leonardo and a Michelangelo, the mental processes which resulted in "The Last Supper" and the frescoes of the Sistine Chapel. It is the only Renaissance theory of imagination which does so.

Like many a later thinker, however, such as Wordsworth, he was capable of slipping back, almost unconsciously, into contemporary attitudes.[38] Thus he could write, as though making a concession to the popular view: "But, indeed, in those matters which are feigned [i.e., invented by the free combinatory phantasy] there is also imagination, both in future [visions] and things made now."[39] This is obviously connected with another passage: "For, from this similarity, moved by a certain desire, it [the mind] imagines what it received as separate as connected, either in place, in subject, or in some other respect. Whence it feigns to itself chimaeras, centaurs, gardens, and palaces; *and the poet does precisely this*."[40] This is

---

[38]Fracastoro, after having described a system which has little place for a separate faculty, common sense (see p. 125), later not only recognized common sense as separate, but definitely placed it in the first ventricle (p. 146 verso), and then debated whether phantasy was also in the first ventricle or in the front of the second (p. 147). He also offered a typical Renaissance account of the relation of phantasy to the passions in dreams, fevers, frenzies, and religious ecstasy (pp. 141-143). See also *De Symp. et Antipath.*, in *op. cit.*, 70ff.

[39]*Ibid.*, p. 126.

[40]*Ibid.*, p. 128 verso. The italics are mine.

the only passage in which Fracastoro connected the imagination and poetry: the poetic imagination for him was specifically of this type. It is important to observe that, although he had been discussing the truly synthetic imagination, this reference to the "lower" manifestation of the comprehensive power led him to inquire whether animals can also imagine. He concluded that they can, since they are apparently frightened in their sleep by images which do not correspond to external reality.[41] The psychology of poetry was related for him to this lower realm of subnotions and phantasies, a realm which he had left when he entered the higher region of imagination of the architect, the painter, and the musician.

Why did Fracastoro fail to include poetry with the plastic arts and with music as a striking illustration of his psychology of the synthetic imagination? The answer lies in part, of course, in the failure of his time to achieve a comprehensive aesthetic. It lies more essentially in the nature of the Renaissance apologetic for poetry. This goes back ultimately to Plato's charge that poetry was not good philosophy. The Renaissance, answering that charge, instead of finding a true criterion for poetry, frequently attempted to show that it was good philosophy, or good history, or the loftiest kind of rhetoric. In his dialogue on poetry Fracastoro chose the third kind of defence: the poet was the star pupil of the master of rhetoric, an expert in *elocutio*, the technique of expression.[42] In the opening sentences of his *Turrius* he stated that he was turning from *locutio*, the concern of the poet, to *scientia*, the proper subject of a psychological treatise.[43] In other words, poetry as a function, as a creative act, is concerned, not with knowledge, with mental processes as such, and their products, but with their adequate expression in terms of beauty (an aesthetic concept which he failed to define). The poet *as poet* is a consummate stylist seeking every appropriate means of adorning subjects which he has drawn from sources outside of his own nature and his own field as a poet.

Although Fracastoro found for the moment an interesting avenue of escape from the charge brought against poetry, and, incidentally, found a true explanation of much of the poetic impulse of his own day, he knew that in *Naugerius* he had justified Renaissance poetic practice on the grounds of technique alone and that he had done

[41]*Loc. cit.*
[42]See my introduction to *Naugerius*, tr. Kelso, *op. cit.*, pp. 16ff.
[43]Fracastoro, *op. cit.*, p. 121.

nothing to establish the poets in society, along with the learned professions, as having a congenial field or subject. He had, in fact, gone so far as to say that poets may choose any theme.[44]

At the end of *Turrius* he returned to this question in his analysis of fitness for professions in terms of the relative vigor of faculties and spirits. Here one finds the poets classified with the philosophers as concerned with universals: "The latter love to inquire into the nature of hidden matters; and on this account they are by nature thoughtful and taciturn. . . . In them that seat in the central fold [of the brain] in which intellect reigns supreme is especially well disposed, and is both ample and vigorous."[45] The reasoning by which Fracastoro attempted to establish the kinship psychologically of the philosopher and the poet is both ingenious and unconvincing. The poet is like the philosopher in virtue of a capacity for wonder, a quality stressed in the treatise on poetry,[46] which he now attempts to identify with philosophic curiosity. He is interested in preserving the magnitude and beauty of things, and this involves wonder. Like the philosopher, therefore, he also finds delight in discovering the causes of things, "Whence it follows that many poets are great philosophers, just as many philosophers are poets."[47] This, of course, as a reply to the Platonic attack upon poetry as unphilosophical, is only the assertion that the poet is a kind of philosopher. It is hardly a valid argument, since it is based wholly upon the assumption that wonder is the poetic equivalent of the impulse which leads to the philosophic quest for hidden causes. It has little relation to any quality of intellect noteworthy for the comprehension of universals. At best, it claims for the poet a keen interest in subjects of philosophical speculation.

The superficial character of the poet's "philosophy" becomes more apparent in the subsequent comparison:

They differ, however, in this: that those who are by nature more philosophers than poets stress the investigation of causes and rejoice more therein; but those who are more poets than philosophers, captivated more by the beauties of objects, love to imitate and explain them, and they are not able to endure it if any beauty or appropriateness be lacking in the objects. Therefore, if perchance these are lacking, they add them: they feign, and in some way they create more perfect objects. For this reason poets rejoice in bringing to birth, philosophers in holding within the womb.[48]

[44]*Naugerius, op. cit.*, p. 58.

[45]Fracastoro, *op. cit.*, p. 148.

[46]*Naugerius, op. cit.*, p. 66.

[47]Fracastoro, *loc. cit.*

[48]*Loc. cit.*

Fracastoro had undertaken to give standing to the poet as a kind of philosopher interested in virtue of his "wonder" in the life of the intellect or reason. In terms of *locutio* he was an expert in style; in terms of *scientia* he was a younger brother of the philosopher searching into "the hidden causes of things." The contemporary tradition, however, was too strong; and Fracastoro, differentiating his poet from the philosopher, accepted the current notion that the poet's chief attribute as a thinker was that he could improve upon his originals. He had apparently joined the ranks of the Renaissance critics who stressed the poet's power of "feigning" or "inventing," usually in virtue of the combinatory capacity of the phantasy.

His view, however, is strikingly different from that of Ronsard, Sidney, Puttenham, and Bacon, and the difference saves Fracastoro from the charge of inconsistency. Bacon, who is typical of a long tradition, in his conception of poetry as "feigned history," was to assert that the process of "feigning" or "inventing" lies in the capacity of the poetic imagination to improve upon the imagery derived from experience.[49] The poet is imaginative only in reference to external reality, summarized for Bacon in history. Fracastoro was not thinking primarily of history but of a larger body of intellectual materials comprehended by the terms *philosophia* and *scientia*. Thus the poet, impelled to feign because he does not find in the materials at hand the beauty which satisfies him, embroiders both the "history" of *Joseph* and the *scientia* of *Syphilis*, Fracastoro's two important poems illustrative of his own theory. As we have said, he never defined the "beauty" which impelled him; and one may add that he never described the process by which poets "create more perfect objects." He was apparently unwilling to find his way out by accepting the theory of imaginary composites, which included in the same category ideal gardens and castles in Spain, heroes and satyrs and sirens.

Fracastoro had discovered psychological materials which his age, deterred both by its prevailing empiricism and by its poetic practice, was not ready to apply to literary criticism. He indicated the direction of a new aesthetic of the imagination and memory, and he made tantalizingly brief applications to painting, architecture, and music. He pointed the way to a more adequate explanation than his contemporaries could provide of "The Last Supper," St.

---

[49]See "Bacon's True Opinion," *op. cit.*, p. 253.

Peter's, and a composition of Palestrina. The application to poetics was to come only after the pictorial quality of Renaissance poetry had lost its emphasis and men sought to explain insight and vision as qualities of mind essentially more active and introspective than those then denoted by "imagination" and "phantasy." Fracastoro, with his new theory of imagination, was a kind of prophet born out of due season.

CURRENT ENGLISH TRANSLATIONS OF *THE PRAISE OF FOLLY*

By HOYT H. HUDSON
Princeton University

So far as available records indicate, four different English versions of Erasmus's *Encomium Moriae* have been published:

(1) Sir Thomas Chaloner, *The Praise of Folie*, 1549, reissued 1560?, 1577; also reprinted in a limited and expensive edition, London, 1901.

(2) John Wilson, *The Praise of Folly*, 1668; reprinted 1906, as one of a series of sixpenny texts for schools, the whole under the editorship of W. H. D. Rouse; again reprinted, with expurgations and amendments and an Introduction, by Mrs. P. S. Allen, Oxford University Press, 1913, and kept in print.

(3) White Kennett, or Kennet, *Witt against Wisdom*, 1683; second edition entitled *Moriae Encomium, or a Panegyrick upon Folly*, 1709, several more editions in the eighteenth century (sixth ed., 1740); many editions published both in England and the United States in the nineteenth and twentieth centuries (though the earliest seen is 1870), several undated, some entitled *In Praise of Folly*. Few editions bear the translator's name, but Kennett's version may be recognized by this opening:

> How slightly soever I am esteemed in the common vogue of the world, (for I well know how disingenuously Folly is decried, even by those who are themselves the greatest fools,) yet it is from my influence alone that the whole universe receives her ferment of mirth and jollity.

(4) James Copner, *The Praise of Folly*, 1878; this translation, apparently never reprinted, is so rare that a copy cannot be located except in the British Museum and Bodleian Library.

In addition, F. M. Nichols made his own translation of the prefatory letter to More and of a short section concerning cardinals and popes, in *The Epistles of Erasmus*, Vol. II, 1904.

The purpose of this essay is to examine the adequacy of these translations from the point of view of a modern reader who wishes to become acquainted with *The Praise of Folly*. This point of view virtually excludes the first and fourth on our list. Chaloner's rendering is an excellent one on many counts, but its language forms a great barrier to a reader unaccustomed to any English older than Shakespeare's; furthermore, the work is not generally available. This last objection holds also against Copner's translation, which is so difficult to find in this country as to be practically non-existent. There can be no doubt that Wilson's translation of 1668 and Kennett's of 1683 have had the widest reading, although a wide reading of Wilson has prevailed only since the modern reprints were made early in the present century. For the eighteenth and nineteenth centuries Kennett's version for all practical purposes was *The Praise of Folly* for English readers. And to judge from copies in the Princeton University Library and in other libraries visited, this is still the translation most likely to be hit upon by anyone who does not make a point of avoiding it. This fact is unfortunate, because Kennett's is the worst rendering of the three examined; as will be shown, it does not fairly represent Erasmus's meaning, it fails to transmit a true impression of his style, and it even obscures the essential tone and temper of the book.

White Kennett (1660-1728), who made this version, became Bishop of Peterborough, renowned for his scholarship in the field of English history. When he translated Erasmus, however, he was twenty-two years of age and had just been graduated from Oxford University. His principles of translation and the spirit in which he undertook the work may be learned from his own address "To the Reader." A large quotation is made (from the second edition, 1709), because Kennett comments on Chaloner and Wilson and is very explicit upon matters pertinent to our subject:

[sig. b] . . . I must divert the Apology for the *Author*, to one more requisite for the *Translator*. Against whom (beside all other Piques and Exceptions) there will no question be pointed this thrusting Objection, namely, That this same Piece of Wits Pageantry has been Twice already cloath'd in our Mother [b^v] Tongue, so that the *Republishing* at least of one of these Translations might have superceeded the Trouble of a new one. It may, I hope, be no Scandal to confess, that till after my first Onset I had neither by Sight nor Report gathered any Intimation of the Forestalment herein; of which I were yet the less inquisitive, because the Person who imposed on me the Undertaking, took the Negative for granted, though he stood in better Circumstances of being informed, and was more concerned in the Consequence. But allowing the worst, *Retranslations* of late have been so successively performed, so much to the *Service* of the *present* Times, and *Justice* to the first Authors, that Attempts of like nature can be no longer invidious, if they are grounded on the same Inducements, and do answer the same End and Design. How far I can square my Apology by this [b 2] Rule will in part appear by this following Observation: *Originals* of one Language are differently to be rendred into another, according to their respective Matter and Subject; in an Argument of *History*, but more especially of *Physicks*, and *Mathematicks*, so much depends on the Critical Genuine Sense of the Author, that there can be no Latitude or Deviation allowed, but a *harsh Cadence* is far more preferrable, than a *bold*, though *tunable Variation*: Whereas on the contrary, in *Poesie, Oratory, Panegyrick, Satyr*, or such like loser Subjects, the Excellency resulting rather from the Stile and Fancy in general than from the strictness of particular Periods, there may, nay, there must, be some such Judgment or Discretion Tolerated, as shall within due Bounds new Marshal the Words, and in some Measure Plaister over the Abruptness and Incoherence of Sense. Accordingly the Design of [b 2ᵛ] Translations seems then best answered, when the respective Renderers square their Attempts by the foregoing Rule; the same Liberty being an unpardonable *Extravagance* in the one, which is no worse than a becoming *Freedom* in the other: as the Painter, who is employed to draw a Face to the Life, must confine his Pencil to an exact Transcript of the Natural Strokes, without any room to Fancy or Flattery, Limning even *Venus* herself with a *Blemishing Mole*; whereas in the copying after a *Landskip*, or other flourishing Draught, both Colours and other Features for the Lustre of Prospect may be so far altered, as the Judgment of the Artist shall with Liberty recommend. The Result of this it is my interest to have thus understood. Our Language hath been so much Polish'd and Refin'd since the first Appearance of this Declamation in English,* [Marginal Note: **Done by Sir* Thomas Chaloner, *and Printed at London,* 1549, *in* 4to] that had it [b 3] fallen into my Hands e'er I entred on this Work, the Perusal of it would have scarcely discourag'd me from pursuing the Undertaking: For to have adventured abroad a Second Edition of this antiquated Version, would doubtless have been Interpreted as Design rather of Exercising the Reader in the unpleasant Task of laboriously picking out the meaning of obsolete Words and Expressions, than of fairly leading him into the True and Genuine Sense of the Original; although what is here asserted might be easily made out beyond all Possibility of Exception; yet the Learned Author acquitted himself so very well herein, that he comes fully up, even to the most commendable Way of Writing, which obtain'd in his Time. The Modern Translator (to whom I intended the Rule, but now laid down, to be chiefly applied) tied himself so strictly to a Literal [b 3ᵛ] Observance of the *Latin*, that to a reader, unacquainted with Allusions to the Eloquence of the *Latin* Tongue, his Version is sometimes puzzling and obscure, at least never so smooth and voluble, as the Gaiety of the Argument would better have dispens'd with; whereas in this *Rehearsal* of mine, I have (more I confess to my own Ease, and more gratefully, I question not, to the Palate of others) allowed my self such Elbow-room of Expression, as the Humoursomeness of the Subject, and the Idiom of each Language, did *invite*, if not *command*. Yet I would not have it hereby suspected that I have taken a straying Frisk or Jaunt, beyond the Limits of a just *Decorum*; no, I have been so *free*, I hope, as not to be *licencious*, so *bold*, as not to be *immodest*: I considered, that Rambling Variations, as well as *Verbatim* Constructions, are both the Scandalous Tasks of *School-boys*; [b 4] therefore I so far consulted the avoiding of each Extreme, that I have this *Disjunctive Plea* to gag the Men of *Teeth* with, where-ever the *Latin* appears to have been seemingly injured, and receded from, there I doubted a too close Adherence would have been rough and jarring: Again, where the *English* wants anything of Cadence or Coherence, there I check'd my Range, and was afraid of treading too wide from the Footsteps of the Original. For that the same Harangue, compleatly Eloquent in one Tongue, would be less winning and perswasive when close Interpreted in another, is as obvious, as that *Travellers*, if they adapt not their Garb to the Mode of the Country they reside in, are rather an Object to *Stare* and *Gaze* at, than to *Bow* to, *Reverence*, or be in any way *Respected*. The Reason on which this is grounded being a *Propriety* in each Language to peculiar Tropes, Figures, Phrases, [b 4ᵛ] &c. is so known a Topick, that to them who understand the original *Latin* it is wholly *superfluous*, and to those that do not it is altogether as *needless*.

Sentiments expressed by Kennett which are most relevant to our criticism are these : he is more interested in coherence and a "tunable" and "voluble" cadence than in fidelity to the original; he believes that freedom should be the rule when one is translating poetry or oratory; and yet, with a necessary allowance made for the difference in idiom between Latin and English, he believes that he has not permitted himself too much license. He considers that in translating *The Praise of Folly* he was not under as much obligation to fidelity as would be the painter of a portrait; and, what is more disconcerting, he strongly implies that if there is any roughness or incoherence in his translation, it results from following the Latin too closely. Elsewhere he says that the translator's duty is to "Plaister over the Abruptness and Incoherence of Sense." From his own remarks, then, we can say that Kennett worked on the assumption that the style of the original was something to be disguised and altered. This assumption is hardly a fair one, and manifests a lack of any proper piety on the part of the translator toward his original.

The only criticism of Kennett's translation appearing in books consulted is that of Mrs. Allen, who wrote in the Introduction of her reprint of Wilson: "Kennet . . . is long-winded and prosy, and his 'elbow-room' has resulted in a coarseness of expression surprising in a future Church dignitary." That Kennett is "long-winded" can be shown by figures: his version runs to about 44,000 words, whereas that of Wilson is about 38,500 words.[1] The difference would be still greater if Kennett had not skipped many sentences or phrases of his original. Mrs. Allen speaks of Wilson's "truer though faint echo of Erasmus's terse vivacity." If *The Praise of Folly* is characterized by "terse vivacity," then certainly Kennett misrepresents the style. He is vivacious, perhaps—or at least sprightly; but he is not terse.

We may get a view of the nature of Kennett's translation by analyzing a specimen chosen to illustrate a number of its characteristics. This is fairly typical, and its faults could be matched in a score of other passages. What is quoted follows upon Erasmus's description of foolish old women who use cosmetics, dress as young girls, go to dances, and have love affairs. Folly is speaking :[2]

---

[1] Both figures include the prefatory letter to Thomas More.

[2] References to Erasmus are by column to Vol. IV (1703) of the Le Clerc (Leyden) edition of his *Opera Omnia*. References to Wilson are to Mrs. Allen's edition, Oxford, 1913. References to Kennett are to the undated edition, with Holbein's sketches, issued by Brentano's, New York; and corresponding page references to the undated edition of Peter Eckler, New York, have been placed

Erasmus, col. 433: Porro quibus haec deridicula videntur, illud secum expendant velim, utrum satius ducant hujusmodi stultitia vitam plane mellitam exigere, an trabem, ut ajunt, suspendio quaerere. Porro quod haec vulgo putantur infamiae obnoxia, istud nihil ad stultos meos, qui malum hoc aut non sentiunt, aut si quid sentiunt, facile negligunt. Si saxum in caput incidat, id vere malum sit. Caeterum pudor, infamia, probrum, maledicta, tantum adferunt noxae, quantum sentiuntur. Si sensus absit, ne mala quidem sunt. Quid laedit, si totus populus in te sibilet, modo tute tibi plaudas? /Atque ut id liceat, sola Stultitia praestat Sed mihi videor audire reclamantes Philosophos. Atqui hoc ipsum est, inquiunt, miserum, Stultitia teneri, errare, falli, ignorare. Imo hoc est homini esse./ Porro miserum cur vocent, non video, quandoquidem sic nati estis, sic instituti, sic conditi, ea est communis omnium sors. Nihil autem miserum, quod in suo genere constat, nisi forte quis hominem deplorandum existimet, qui neque volare possit cum avibus, &c.

Wilson, pp. 61-62: But I would have them to whom these things seem ridiculous. to consider with themselves whether it be not better to live so pleasant a life, in such kind of follies, than, as the Proverb goes, "To take a Halter and hang themselves." Besides though these things may be subject to censure, it concerns not my fools in the least, in as much as they take no notice of it, or if they do, they easily neglect it. If a stone falls on a man's head, that's evil indeed; but dishonesty, infamy, villany, ill reports, carrie no more hurt in them than a man is sensible of; and if a man has no sense of them, they are no longer evils. What art thou the worse if the people hisse at thee, so thou applaud thy self? /And that a man be able to do so, he must ow it to Folly.

But methinks I hear the Philosophers opposing it, and saying 'tis a miserable thing for a man to be foolish, to erre, mistake, and know nothing truly. Nay, rather, this is to be a man./ And why should they call it miserable, I see no reason; forasmuch as we are so born, so bred, so instructed, nay, such is the common condition of us all. And nothing can be called miserable that suits with its kind, unless perhaps you'l think a man such because he can neither flie with Birds, &c.

Kennett, pp. 62-63 [111-12]: As for those that think them herein so ridiculous, I would have them give an ingenuous answer to this one query, whether if folly or hanging were left to their choice, they had not much rather live like fools, than like dogs? But what matter is it if these things are resented by the vulgar? Their ill word is no injury to fools, who are either altogether insensible of any affront, or at least lay it not much to heart. If they were knocked on the head, or had their brains dashed out, they would have some cause to complain; but alas, slander, calumny, and disgrace, are no other way injurious than as they are interpreted; nor otherwise evil, than as they are thought to be so: what harm is it then if all persons deride and scoff you, if you bear but up in your own thoughts, and be yourself thoroughly conceited of your deserts?//And prithee, why should it be thought any scandal to be a fool, since the being so is one part of our nature and essence; and as so, our not being wise can no more reasonably be imputed as a fault, than it would be proper to laugh at a man because he cannot fly in the air like birds and fowls; &c.

The sentences between virgules are left untranslated by Kennett. Counting words, we find that 96 words of Latin (down to the first

in square brackets. These have been added because Eckler's reprint seems to have enjoyed the widest circulation in the United States of any edition, although it is expurgated, suffers from a number of misprints, and gives absurdly mistaken titles to several of the Holbein illustrations.

virgule) become 137 words in Wilson's rendering and 156 in Kennett's. After that, Kennett's apparent advantage in brevity is gained only by his complete omission of three sentences and his compression of the next into a clause which misrepresents its meaning. The worst offense is that by his omission he fails to indicate that Folly is here continuing her running battle with Stoics and philosophers, who appear in a manner similar to this at various points in the eulogy. The argument to be refuted, in Kennett's wording, is that it is a "scandal" to be a fool, but that has already been refuted; and the larger context, both before and after, relates to happiness and unhappiness. Kennett has been forced to change the subject in the last part of this passage in order to connect with the few sentences preceding and to cover up his failure to reproduce the transition which Erasmus made. By so changing the subject, however, he is then forced to mistranslate *deplorandum* absurdly as "proper to laugh at." Going back to the first part of the passage, we notice that Kennett has been very free with Erasmus's choice between living as a fool and committing suicide, having rendered it by the antithesis, "rather live like fools, than die like dogs." Such a liberty, in view of the balance and compression of the phrase, may be allowable; it exemplifies what he means by "a *bold*, though *tunable Variation*." Yet why does he then translate the four words, *modo tute tibi plaudas*, by such a weak expansion as "if you bear but up in your own thoughts, and be yourself thoroughly conceited of your deserts"? This variation is neither bold nor tunable, and Wilson's literal "so thou applaud thy self" is better. Kennett's expansion of *Si saxum in caput incidat* into "If they were knocked on the head, or had their brains dashed out," is typical of his usual manner; but with this particular clause a certain "abruptness" might be preferable. Certainly Wilson's "that's evil indeed" for the ending of this sentence is better than Kennett's "they would have some cause to complain." By inserting "alas" in the next, Kennett misrepresents the attitude of Folly, who is not lamenting the shamelessness of her fools but pointing to it with pride. Finally, he omitted the terse sentences, *Atque ut id liceat, sola Stultitia praestat* and *Imo hoc est homini esse*. A translator should not be blamed for combining some short units separated by periods in Latin into longer sentences of English. But to suggest to any degree the style of the original, some of these pithy bits must be allowed to stand alone. They do not so stand often enough in Kennett.

We may turn to other and briefer specimens. The following will show that again Kennett overlooked a definite transition, and will find him up to his trick of omitting at will. These sentences come after the fine comparison of human life to a play on the stage, wherein Erasmus says that if an intruder should strip the clothes from the actors and let the audience see them as they really are, the play would be spoiled. He goes on to say that in the human comedy the same actor may be called upon to play a king and then a beggar. The comparison ends with the sentence, *Adumbrata quidem omnia, sed haec fabula non aliter agitur* ("Thus all things are but shadowed forth, but this comedy is played in no other way"). Then the analogy is applied in this fashion:

Erasmus, cols. 428-29: Hic si mihi sapiens aliquis coelo delapsus subito exoriatur, clamitetque hunc quem omnes ut Deum ac dominum suspiciunt, nec hominum esse, quod pecudum ritu ducatur affectibus, servum esse infimum, quod tam multis, quamque foedis dominis sponte serviat. Rursum alium, qui parentem extinctum luget, ridere jubeat, quod jam demum ille vivere coeperit, cum alioque vita haec nihil aliud sit quam mors quaedam. Porro alium stemmatis gloriantem, ignobilem ac nothum appellet, quod a virtute longe absit, quae sola nobilitatis sit fons, adque eumdem modum de caeteris omnibus loquatur, quaeso, quid is aliud egerit, nisi ut demens ac furiosus omnibus esse videatur？

[Literally]: Suppose, at this point, some wise man that has dropped down from heaven should get up before me and cry out that a certain man whom everyone looks upon as a god and lord is not even to be classed as a man, because he is led sheepwise by his passions; that he is the basest slave, because he willingly serves so many and such foul masters. Again, let him bid another man, who mourns for his deceased father, to laugh, because now his father has at last begun to live— since this life is no other than a kind of death.[3] Another man who glories in his ancestry let him call ignoble and base-born, because he is so far from virtue, which is the only true fount of nobility. And in the same manner let him speak about all other people. What would he have accomplished, I ask, except to make himself appear to everybody as raving and insane？

Kennett, pp. 54-55 [100]: Now if there should arise any starched, formal don, that would point at the several actors, and tell how this, that seems a petty god, is in truth worse than a brute, being made captive to the tyranny of passion; that the other, who bears the character of a king, is indeed the most

---

[3] Wilson went wrong as to the intention of the author in this sentence, and made one of his rare insertions. He translates it (p. 54, insertion italicized): "Again if he should bid a man that were bewailing the death of his Father to laugh, for that now he began to live *by having got an Estate, without which* Life is but a kind of Death." His primary error was making the son, and not the deceased father, the subject of the verb *coeperit*. Erasmus assumes the premise that life after death is more truly to be called life than is life on earth.

slavish of serving-men, in being subject to the mastership of lust and sensuality; that a third, who vaunts so much of his pedigree, is no better than a bastard for degenerating from virtue, which ought to be of the greatest consideration in heraldry, and so shall go on exposing all the rest; would not any one think such a person quite frantic, and ripe for bedlam?

Here it is unfortunate that Kennett carries over the figure of the actors from the preceding passage, without marking the transition which Erasmus makes; for Folly is now talking about the real world, with real kings and nobles. Kennett may possibly know this, but his phrase "point at the several actors" seems to confine the whole to the stage and to make what follows a diatribe against the private lives of actors! To clear up his own intention he might have said "point at the several actors on the stage of the world." His most serious fault, however, is missing the point about the man dropped down from heaven. Folly uses a device, often appearing in modern literature, of introducing a character from outside the world— usually "a man from Mars"—in order to have an observer who is himself untouched by the customs and follies he comes upon. But this observer has become "any starched, formal don"—hardly the person to speak the blunt truth about things. Folly gives three examples of this heavenly visitant's plain speaking. Kennett divides the first one into two and completely omits the second.[4] To turn to a lesser question, is "virtue, which ought to be of greatest consideration in heraldry" an improvement upon the literal "virtue, which is the only true fount of nobility"?

At times Kennett omits translating some of the original because of the difficulty in making it understandable to his readers. The following passage comes from the attack upon theologians; it begins with the closing units of a long sentence which has said that no authority of the Church can any longer make a man a Christian—

Erasmus, col. 469: nisi Baccalauriorum calculus accesserit, tanta est in judicando subtilitas. Quis enim sensurus erat eum Christianum non esse, qui diceret has duas orationes, *matula putes, & matula putet,* Item *ollae fervere, & ollam fervere,* pariter esse congruas, nisi sapientes illi docuissent? Quis tantis errorum tenebris	[Literally]: except as the vote of these academic bachelors is added, so great is their subtlety in passing judgment. For who would have thought that a man is not a Christian if he says that the two expressions, *matula putes* and *matula putet,* or these two, *ollae fervere* and *ollam fervere,* are equally grammatical, if these wise

[4]Kennett probably could not be expected to have notice that the passage about the unworthy and slavish king merely echoes and compresses what Erasmus had written a very little before (col. 428): *Quis Regem non & opulentum & dominum fatetur? Atqui nullis animi bonis instructus est, atqui nihil illi satis est, jam videlicet pauperrimus est. Tum animum habet plurimis addictum vitiis, jam turpiter servus est.*

liberasset Ecclesiam, quos ne lecturus quidem unquam quisquam feurat, nisi magnis sigillis isti prodidissent? Verum, an non felicissimi dum haec agunt?

men had not instructed us? Who would have freed the Church from such shades of error—which no one would ever have read about if these theologians had not published them under their great seals? Are they not most happy, forsooth, while they do these things?

Kennett, p. 141 [225]: except he have the joint suffrage of these novices in learning, who have blessed the world no doubt with a great many discoveries, which had never come to light if they had not struck the fire of subtlety out of the flint of obscurity. These fooleries sure must be a happy employ.

Kennett's surgery is severe and not wholly necessary; for even in literal translation the passage yields most of its meaning. The added image of the fire and flint is quite un-Erasmian.

In the following passage, the allusion to Plato's myth of the cave proved to find no response from Kennett, and he substituted a vague reference to the doctrine of ideas:

Erasmus, col. 451: Num quid interesse censetis inter eos, qui in specu illo Platonico variarum rerum umbras ac simulacra demirantur, modo nihil desiderent, neque minus sibi placeant? & sapientem illum qui specum egressus, veras res adspicit?

Wilson, p. 94: Or what difference, think ye, between those in Plato's imaginary Cave, that stand gaping at the Shadows and Figures of things, so they please themselves and have no need to wish; and that Wise Man, who, being got loose from 'em, sees things truly as they are?

Kennett, p. 103 [172]: What difference is there between them that in the darkest dungeon, can with platonic brain survey the whole world in idea, and him that stands in the open air, and takes a less deluding prospect of the universe?

The next passage, which comes where Erasmus is suggesting that skilled scholastic disputants, trying to convert the pagans, might meet with disputants equally skilful, is similarly weakened and shortened:

Erasmus, col. 468: ut jam par sit pugna, perinde quasi Magum cum Mago committas, aut si gladio fortunato pugnet aliquis cum eo, cui gladius sit fortunatus: tum enim nihil aliud quam tela Penelopes retexeretur.

[Literally]: so that now the battle would be equal, just as if you should match a wizard against a wizard, or some one with a charmed sword should fight a person who also had a charmed sword; for then it would be nothing but reweaving the web of Penelope.

Kennett, p. 138 [219]: and this last way the victory would be altogether as hopeless, as if two persons were engaged of so equal strength, that it were impossible any one should overpower the other.

For a final bit of weak translation we might notice a clause from the passage wherein Folly argues that her turning of old men into children is a more benevolent metamorphosis than any fabled to have been performed by "the gods of the poets." They turn a man or woman into a tree, a bird, a cicada, or even a snake. Then comes this clause (col. 414): *quasi vero non istud ipsum sit perire, aliud fieri* ("as if, indeed, to be made into something else were not the same as to perish"). Wilson translates it well (p. 24): "As if there were any difference between perishing, and being another thing!" Kennett's version is this (p. 20 [60]): "but alas, their very change into somewhat else argues the destruction of what they were before." Yet this is the man who thought Wilson's translation too much like a work of history or physics.

Some of Kennett's expansions result from his desire to explain allusions, leading him to put into the text much material which an editor would put into notes. Perhaps this is the least of his sins, and yet it brings it about that there are several long sentences and many clauses which are purely of his composition; and whether he is to be trusted to maintain the tone and vitality of the original is a great question. In the passage (cols. 424-26) wherein Folly shows how people are persuaded by trivial fables and analogies rather than by sober argument, she cites a number of classical instances such as the fable of the belly and its members, that of the fox and the hedge-hog, the white hind of Sertorius; the whole passage consists of about 115 words of Latin. Wilson translates it (pp. 48-49) in about 140 words. Kennett adds synopses of all the stories alluded to, with the result that his corresponding English (pp. 46-48 [95-96]) runs to more than five hundred words. In the same context Folly asks a question which is fairly well (but verbosely) translated by Kennett thus (p. 49 [96]): "For farther, what city would ever submit to the rigorous laws of Plato, to the severe injunctions of Aristotle? or the more unpracticable tenets of Socrates?" But then Kennett answers the question, with no Latin whatever to authorize him: "No, these would have been too straight and galling, there not being allowance enough made for the infirmities of the people." It seems possible that a translator who answers the rhetorical questions of his original thereby may alter the style and falsify the tone of the composition.

We have suggested that some of this translator's insertions are out of key. Speaking of the wretched life of the scholar, Erasmus says, according to Kennett (p. 77 [133]) that he "is always stingy, poor, dejected, melancholy, burthensome to himself, and unwelcome to others, pale, lean, thin-jawed, sickly, contracting by his sedentari-

ness such hurtful distempers as bring him to an untimely death,
like roses plucked before they shatter."[5]   The simile at the end,
however, is Kennett's addition.   Perhaps it is intentionally incon-
gruous, for the sake of humor; if so, the humor is not that of Erasmus, and in order to insert it Kennett omitted the point which
Erasmus did make.   A fairly close rendering of the passage (col.
439) gives this: "always frugal, impecunious, sad, austere, unfair
and strict toward himself, morose and unamiable to others; afflicted
by pallor, leanness, invalidism, sore eyes, premature age and white
hair; dying before his appointed day.   By the way, what difference
does it make when a man of that sort dies?   He has never lived."
Nothing in Kennett corresponds to the last two sentences here; instead we have his roses.

Many people have read Kennett's translation with delight, and
for that reason perhaps one is graceless in bringing an indictment
against it.   The book is sprightly, as we have said.   Some of the
sentences and paragraphs roll and romp along in a merry way which
is admirable.   It seems likely that Kennett had read Urquhart's
version of Rabelais (1653) and that he tried to carry over some of
the spirit of that work, which is not entirely an alien one, into this.
The following passage will illustrate these remarks (pp. 30-32 [74-
79]):

> But now some blood-chilled old men, that are more for wine than wenching,
> will pretend, that in their opinion, the greatest happiness consists in feasting
> and drinking.   Grant it be so; yet certainly in the most luxurious entertain-
> ments it is Folly must give the sauce and relish to the daintiest cates and
> delicacies; so that if there be no one of the guests naturally fool enough to be
> played upon by the rest, they must procure some comical buffoon, that by his
> jokes, and flouts, and blunders shall make the whole company split themselves
> with laughing: for what purpose were it to be stuffed and crammed with
> so many dainty bits, savoury dishes, and toothsome rarities, if after all this
> epicurism of the belly, the eyes, the ears, and the whole mind of man, were
> not as well foistred and relieved with laughing, jesting, and such like diver-
> tisements, which like second courses serve for the promoting of digestion?   And
> as to all those shooing horns of drunkenness, the keeping every one his man,
> the throwing of hey-jinks, the filling of bumpers, the drinking two in a hand,
> the beginning of mistress' healths; and then the roaring out of drunken
> catches, the calling in a fiddler, the leading out every one his lady to dance,
> and such like riotous pastimes, these were not taught or dictated by any of the
> wise men of Greece, but of Gotham rather, being my invention, and by me
> prescribed as the best preservative of health; each of which, the more ridiculous
> it is, the more welcome it finds.

In view of these excellences, a defender might argue that since
Kennett gives the spirit of *The Praise of Folly* and the general

---

[5]In the Eckler edition, the last phrase reads: "like rose-buds plucked before they bloom."

drift of its argument he has made a good enough translation. But the fact is that he entirely misses much of the spirit of the piece. He misses, or badly blurs, the mock-scholarly tone of much of it. This eulogy in its whole conception is an academic burlesque, a carefully worked out rhetorical structure that follows precisely all the best traditional rules for pronouncing a eulogy. Its argument is perfectly concatenated, its transitions skilful, and its logic exemplary in outer form. The whole is almost pedantic in its precision. This aspect does not appear in Kennett and does appear to some degree in Wilson. Kennett, as we have seen, does not even follow the track of an extended argument and omits the necessary transitions which introduce new arguments or new divisions of an argument. And yet within this large framework Erasmus shows a great variety of feeling and attitude, the changes running from sheer horse-play to tenderness, from satiric derision to poetic contemplation, earnest piety, and even mysticism. This range Kennett fails to reflect. He is competent for the humorous and satiric parts; he is not so good with the salty wit of the original, for he frequently substitutes something of his own which is quite different. And in the poetic or deeply religious parts he is likely to be either flat or unbecomingly vivacious. Thus half, or perhaps more, of the book is right in tone—except for the mock-academic details of which we have spoken—while the rest of it is either toneless or out of key. With this expansive feeling of freedom, moreover, he overlooks many touches and turns of thought, each of little importance in itself but all together constituting an important manifestation of the author's mind. Readers have rightly enjoyed Kennett, and may well go on doing so; but they should know that they do not read Erasmus, who has vitality as well as vivacity, and who, while giving us some fireworks, also burns steadily with a dry light.

John Wilson (1627-1696) is best known as a playwright of the Restoration, author of *The Cheats* (1664). Our discussion of his version of Erasmus can well be brief, for he shows fewer faults than Kennett, and almost none which affects more than a sentence or a clause. On the whole Wilson made a sound, honest translation, and his mistakes are honest mistakes. So far as the style of the piece goes, he is worlds nearer to Erasmus than is Kennett. He falls too often into over-simplification, to be sure, being less subtle than Erasmus and less complex. These characteristics will appear *in petto* from an analysis of the following brief passage:

Erasmus, col. 409: Nomen igitur habetis: Viri, Quid addam epitheti? Quid nisi stultissimi? Nam quo alio honestiore cognomine Mystas suos compellet Dea Stultitia?

Wilson, p. 13: I have giv'n ye my name; but what Epithet shall I adde? What but that of the most Foolish? For by what properer name can so great a goddess as Folly be known to her Disciples?

Wilson's chief blunder here was his decision that Folly was seeking for an epithet to be applied to herself. Having made this decision, he omitted to translate the vocative *Viri*. But the intention was rather to apply the epithet to Folly's hearers, as the form *stultissimi* and the next question indicate. Kennett is better (p. 8 [34]):

Of my name I have informed you, Sirs; what additional epithet to give you I know not, except you will be content with that of most foolish; for under what more proper appellation can the goddess Folly greet her devotees?

Kennett chose, or picked up from Wilson, the rendering of *honestiore* as "more proper"; but the better meaning would seem to be "more honorable," for Folly is trying to effect a transvaluation of values and to insist upon folly as an honorable state. For the disclosure of the dramatic nature of this passage, in which Erasmus means to represent Folly as pausing and groping for an epithet, some such device as the following might be used:

You have my name, gentlemen . . . gentlemen . . . what shall I add by way of an epithet? What but "most foolish"? For with what more honorable style could the goddess Folly address her devotees?

The fact that in Latin the epithet might come after the noun, whereas in English it must come before it, makes the repetition of the word helpful; but even with the repetition the exact effect is hard to give.

Except for the insertion already discussed,[6] Wilson's worst misconstruction of the sense of a passage will be found in the comparison of life to a play. Immediately after imagining the intruder who pulls off the costumes and disguises from the actors, Erasmus writes (col. 428):

Exorietur autem repente nova rerum species, ut qui modo mulier, nunc vir: qui modo juvenis, mox senex: qui paulo ante Rex, subito Dama: qui modo Deus, repente homunculus apparent. Verum eum errorem tollere, est fabulam omnem perturbare.

Wilson, p. 54:

But nothing is more common with them than such changes; the same person one while personating a Woman, and another while a Man; now a Youngster, and by and by a grim Seigniour; now a King, and presently a Peasant; now

---

[6]In footnote 3, above.

a God, and in a trice agen an ordinary Fellow. But to discover this were to spoil all.

Wilson missed the point and substituted for it one made by Erasmus a little farther on. The contrast Erasmus makes here is not between an actor now playing a woman and presently a man; it is between an actor playing a woman and the same actor as seen the moment his theatrical trappings are removed. The passage means something more like this:

Immediately there will come about a new order of things: the actor who played the lady will now be seen to be a man; he who a moment ago appeared young is old; he who only now was the king is suddenly shown to be an ostler; and he who played a god is a manikin. Indeed, to destroy the illusion is to ruin the whole play.

An unfortunate mistranslation of a single word appears on p. 128 in the passage representing the monks as appearing before Christ to be judged and pleading their merits. Says Wilson: "One shall shew ye a large Trough full of all kinds of Fish"; but the word he translates as "a large Trough," *aqualiculum* (col. 473), has a secondary meaning of paunch, or belly, and the clause means rather: "One will display a paunch fattened upon all kinds of fish."[7] Again, Wilson missed a negative when he wrote (p. 30), "that which Momus onely has the priviledge of speaking at length." The Latin reads (col. 417): *quae ne Momus quidem impune proloquutus est.* On p. 65, "most men laugh at [the profession of law] as the Ass of Philosophy" should be rather "philosophers usually laugh at [the profession of law] as an ass." A slightly more serious error appears on p. 131 in the clause, "And first they [the preaching friars] invoke what ever they have scrapt from the Poets," which represents this Latin (col. 475): *Primo loco invocant, id quod a Poëtis mutuo sumserunt.* The meaning is rather: "The first thing they do is utter an invocation, a trick they have borrowed from the poets." The expurgations made for Mrs. Allen's edition account for as great alterations as do Wilson's errors. After the sentence on p. 18, "In fine, that Wiseman who ever he be, if he intends to have Children must have recourse to me," four sentences of Latin (col. 412) are left unrepresented; the translation of these in Kennett (p. 14) runs to 84 words. Other expurgations have been made in at least five places,[8] all of them quite unnecessarily.

---

[7]Kennett changes the point, as he does so often (p. 148 [231]): "one will brag how he mortified his carnal appetite by feeding only upon fish."

[8]Six words of the original (col. 421) are left untranslated after "A man is laughed at," p. 39, and *moechae* is rendered as "weeping wife"; thirteen

To sum up, it appears that those of us who have to do with introducing students or others to Erasmus should favor Wilson's translation of *The Praise of Folly*, and be on our guard against that of
Kennett. We should understand that even Wilson does not wholly
compass the variety, subtlety, and richness of the original, and to
some degree actually mistranslates or misrepresents what Erasmus
wrote. But of course this brings us back to what we have always
known, that no translation can do full justice to an author. Perhaps our real duty is to become good enough Latinists to work with
Erasmus in the tongue he used. A better version of *The Praise of
Folly* might be made, however, better for every purpose, if a translator could follow his author with complete piety and at the same
time naturalize the idiom in crisp phrasing which should reflect
neither the merely contemporary nor the antique in language. That
such a translator would have an opportunity to bring into English
more of Erasmus than either Kennett or Wilson brought must be
concluded from our findings here. As a final enforcement of this
conclusion, we may consider two brief passages which were badly
rendered by both translators, each erring in his own typical
fashion.[9] The first comes early in the eulogy, after Folly has announced her name (col. 408):

Quamquam quid vel hoc opus erat dicere, quasi non ipso ex vultu fronteque,
Quod ajunt, satis quae sim prae me feram, aut quasi si quis me Minervam,
aut Sophiam esse contendat, non statim solo possit obtutu coargui, etiam si
nulla accedat oratio, minime mendax animi speculum.

Kennett, p. 6 [30]: But why need I have been so impertinent as to have told
you this, as if my very looks did not sufficiently betray what I am; or sup-
posing any be so credulous as to take me for some sage matron or goddess of
wisdom, as if a single glance from me would not immediately correct their
mistake, while my visage, the exact reflex of my soul, would supply and
supercede the trouble of any other confessions.

Wilson, p. 11: Or what need was there to have said so much, as if my very
looks were not sufficient to inform ye who I am? Or as if any man, mistaking me for Wisedome, could not at first sight convince himself by my face,
the true index of my mind.

Both Englishmen overlook the fact that the last five words of the

---

words of the original (col. 432) are unrepresented after "still catterwawling,"
p. 61; fifty-four words (cols. 440-41) not translated after "some tang or other
of madness," p. 77; a sentence of five words (cols. 445-46) not translated
after "fall of a house," p. 84; eleven words (col. 483) untranslated after "so
many Bankers," p. 146.

[9]Questions of another nature are raised by the fact that both translators
render the important sentence near the end (col. 504), *Atque, haec est Moriae
pars . . . perficitur*, as if the text read *Mariae* and not *Moriae* (Kennett, pp.
218-19 [325]; Wilson, p. 186).

Latin constitute a *sententia*, "Speech [is] the most faithful mirror of the mind," or something like that. Both not only miss the universality of the statement, applying it personally to Folly alone, but also actually negate it by putting the last phrase into apposition with *vultu fronteque*, far back in the sentence, instead of with *oratio*. Wilson simply omits the entire reference to *oratio*; Kennett typically covers it up with verbiage. Both also omit the definite allusion to Minerva, although it seems that here this should be kept definite, for Folly is identifying herself as one of the goddesses and saying that anyone can tell by looking at her that she is not the goddess Minerva or one who might be called Sophia. Both translators compress *ipso ex vultu fronteque, quod ajunt* into "my very looks." Kennett's "a single glance from me" is wrong; the person to be corrected is the one to give the glance, and the phrase should be "a single glance at me"—except that *obtutu* is not a glance, but rather a stare or intent look. With these corrections made, we get a translation something like this:

Still, what need was there to tell this, as if in my very face and front, so to speak, I do not sufficiently announce who I am? As if anybody who might assert that I am Minerva or the Spirit of Wisdom could not immediately be set right by one good look, even if I were not speaking—though speech is the least deceptive mirror of the mind.

Finally, there is an interesting sentence near the close of Folly's argument that half-wits or natural fools are the happiest of all people. A most original suggestion comes at the end, namely, that these fools will serve as jesters and entertainers in the other world. Kennett smothers the point in a vague general statement; Wilson falsifies it by inserting "their"; again the faults are typical.

Erasmus, col. 438: Igitur ut ad fatuorum felicitatem redeam, multa cum jucunditate peracta vita, nullo mortis vel metu, vel sensu, recta in campos Elysios demigrant, & illic pias atque otiosas animas lusibus suis delectaturi.

[Literally]: Let me return to the topic of the happiness of fools. After a life lived out in much jollity, with no fear of death, or sense of it, they go straight to the Elysian fields, there to entertain the pious and idle shades with their jests and gambols.

Kennett, p. 76 [130]: But to return. An additional happiness of these fools appears farther in this, that when they have run merrily on to their last stage of life, they neither find any fear nor feel any pain to die, but march contentedly to the other world, where their company sure must be as acceptable as it was here upon earth.

Wilson, p. 73: But to return to the happiness of Fools, who when they have past over this life with a great deal of Pleasantness, and without so much as the least fear or sense of Death, they go straight forth into the Elysian Field, to recreate their Pious and Careless Souls with such Sports as they us'd here.

THE PROVERB "THE BLACK OX HAS NOT TROD ON HIS FOOT" IN RENAISSANCE LITERATURE

By ARCHER TAYLOR
University of California

The proverb "The black ox has not trod on his (or: her) foot" was familiarly used by English writers of the Renaissance and was, we may be sure, readily understood in its general tenor, but it has almost completely disappeared from use,[1] and the Renaissance examples do not indicate its origin. The proverb has the following closely related meanings,[2] which I arrange in the order of their appearance:

1. He has not known trouble in the married state.

1546. It was yet but honeymoone: The black oxe had not trode on his or her foote. J. Heywood, *A Dialogue conteinyng ... proverbs*, I, ch. vi.

1557. I think he passeth not xxiii, the blacke oxe neur trode on hys fote. Erasmus, *A mery dialogue*, ll. 749-51, fol. 16ᵛ-17ʳ (see facsimile ed. in H. de Vocht, *The Earliest English Translations of*

---

[1]My friend Bartlett Whiting gives me two examples from modern English fiction, viz., "She was ready to settle down and let the Black Oxen do their will with her" (Theda Kenyon, *Witches Still Live* [New York, 1929], p. 343) and "The black ox hath trodden on her toe" (Wyndham Lewis, *The Apes of God* [New York, 1932], p. 593). The plural "oxen" appears again in the title of Gertrude Atherton's *Black Oxen* (1923). These uses of the proverb appear to have been suggested by acquaintance with a literary rather than an oral tradition and are intended to suggest "atmosphere." Sir Walter Scott's use of the proverb (*The Antiquary*, Ch. XL; *Fortunes of Nigel*, Ch. II middle) may, on the contrary, have an origin in oral tradition, for the proverb is said to be current in Scotland; see J. Jamieson, *Etymological Dictionary of the Scottish Language* (1825), new ed., Paisley, 1879, s.v. "black ox"; G. V. Irving, *Notes and Queries*, 3d Series, XII, 488; T. F. Dyer, *Domestic Folk-Lore* (London, 1881), as cited in *Notes and Queries*, CLXVII, 376.

[2]For many of these examples I am indebted to Professor M. P. Tilley, who has generously given them to me.

Some instances which are found in proverb collections give no indication of their meaning and serve therefore only to prove that the proverb was known at the time of printing. See, e.g., a manuscript note written about A.D. 1598 in Fergusson, *Scottish Proverbs* (ed. Beveridge), p. 102; William Camden, *Remaines concerning Britain* (3d ed., London, 1623), p. 279 (not found in ed. 1614). There are no proverbs in ed. 1 (1605); J. Howell, *Paroemiographia* (1659), "British Proverbs," p. 23; N. R., Gent., *Proverbs* (1659), p. 21; Thomas Fuller, *Gnomologia* (1732), p. 189, No. 4427.

Erasmus' Colloquia, Oxford U. Press, 1928).   The original is: nondum novit, quid sit esse patremfamilias.

1573.   See the quotation from Tusser, below § 4.

1575.   They never prove stayed until the blacke oxe hath trodden on their toes. G. Gascoigne, *Glasse of Government* in *The Complete Works of George Gascoigne*, ed. J. W. Cunliffe (Cambridge, 1910), II, i, p. 81, v. 6.

1587.   The blacke Oxe neuer troade on their feete.   Greene, *Penelope's Web*, in *Works* (ed. Grosart), v, 5, p. 152.

1616.   The blacke Oxe neuer trode on his foot.   Th. Draxe, *Treasurie of Ancient Adages*, s.v. "Unexperienced," No. 2271 = *Anglia*, XLII (1918), 417.

Before 1720.   Alas! my son, you little know, /The sorrows that from wedlock flow./ . . . The black cow on your foot ne'er trod.   D. Herd, *Ancient and Modern Scottish Songs²* (Edinburgh, 1726), II, 120, "Wayward wife," ll. 1-2, 9.

1721.   The black Ox never trod on your Foot. (You never had the Care of a Family upon you, nor was press'd with severe Business or Necessities).   J. Kelly, *A Complete Collection of Scottish Proverbs*, p. 327, No. 198.

  2.   He is inexperienced, has not known sorrow or care.

1580.   The blacke Oxe neuer trode on your foote yet, you neuer came where it grewe.   Anthony Munday, *Zelanto, the fountain of fame*, p. 126b.

1581.   Till the blacke oxe tread upon his toes, and neede make him trie what mettle he is made of.   Mulcaster, *Positions*, XXXVI (1887), 139.

1589.   I hope his Canterburinesse will looke to this geare, and suffer them to haue liberty neither to write, nor to dispute, the blacke Oxe hath troden on his foote, he hath had some trial by woful experience, what smal credite . . . there is to be had, either in writing or disputing with these fellows.   *Marprel. Tr., Epitome*, B ii b.

1590.   They travelled by the space of two or three days without seeing any creatures, being often in danger of wild beasts, and pained with many passionate sorrows.   Now the black oxe began to tread on their feet. T. Lodge, *Rosalynde* (ed. W. W. Greg, London, 1931), pp. 34-35.

1590.   Sonne, as yet thou hast not eaten bread with one tooth, nor hath the blacke Oxe trodden upon thy foote. Robert Greene, *Mourning Garment* (ed. 1616), p. 6.

1605.   At last the black ox trod o' my foot, /And I saw then what long'd unto't. J. Marston, *Eastward Ho*, V, v, 80 (ed. Bullen, III, 119).

1610.   . . . when men feele the Reines of liberty on their necke and may take a course without controlement, . . . then when the black Oxe hath trod vpon their feete, . . . in the end they come home by weeping crosse. Samuel Rowlands, *Martin Marke-all his Apologie, Works,* II (Glasgow: Hunterian Club, 1880), separately paged, p. 29, ll. 5ff.

1611.   Tis true as your father said, the black ox hath not trode upon that foot of yours. Robert Tailer, *The Hog Hath Lost His Pearl* (Dodsley's *Old Plays,* 1744), II, i, p. 198.

1616.   The blacke Oxe neuer trode on his foot.   Th. Draxe, *Treasurie of Ancient Adages,* No. 2271, s.v. "Unexperienced," *Anglia,* XLII (1918), 417.

1633.   Well young squire, the black ox never trod on your foot. B. Jonson, *Tale of a Tub,* IV, 6, 16.

1639.   The black ox has trod on's foot.   J. Clarke, *Paroemiographia,* p. 165, s.v. "Infortunii sive exitii."

1652.   I chose . . . not to write to them on whose foot the black Oxe had not already trod, as the Proverbe is, but to those only, that are weather-beaten in the Sea of this World. Fulke Grevill, *Life of Sir P. Sidney,* Ch. XVIII, p. 245.

1670.   The black ox never trode on his foot. (That is, he never knew what sorrow or adversity meaned). J. Ray, *A Collection of English Proverbs,* p. 188.

1850.   The 'black ox' trod on the fairy foot of my light-hearted cousin Fan. Leigh Hunt, *Autobiography,* I, iv, 171.

1883.   "The black ox has not trodden on you"—i.e., care has not come near you—is an old Shropshire saying.   C. S. Burne, *Shrop-shire Folk-Lore,* p. 209.

3.   She has not suffered the ravages of old age.

1578.   When the black crow's foot shall appear in their eye or the black ox tread on their foot . . ., who will like of them in their age who love none in their youth?   Lyly, *Euphues,* p. 37.

1584.   Now crowes foote is on her eye, and the black oxe hath trod on her foote.   Lyly, *Sapho and Phao,* IV, ii, 20-21.

1601.   The crow shall set his foot in their eye, and the black ox tread on their foot.   Lyly, *Love's Metamorphosis,* IV, i, 135-36.

1611.   The black ox hath not trode on Phrinaes fine foote.   John Davies, *Scourge of Folly, Complete Works* (ed. Grosart, [Edinburgh], 1878), II, separately paged, 50, Vpon English Prouerbes, No. 391.

1621.   Time, care rivels (wrinkles) her . . .; after the blacke oxe hath trodden on her toe, she will . . . waxe out of favor.   R. Burton, *Anatomy of Melancholy,* III, ii, v, iii.

1654.   Alas! the neatest foot that ever came / In the most super-cillious royal shoe,/ By the blacke oxe is often trodden lame.   [G. Tooke], *Annæ-dicata* (London), p. 108.   Quoted from *N. and Q.,* CLXVII (1934), 376.

1738.   The black ox has set his foot upon her already.   Swift, *Polite Conversations,* IX, 418.

19th Cent.   J. Wright, English Dialect Dictionary (London, 1898-1905), s.v. "black," 5 (11).

4.   He has not known want.[3]

1564.   And of late I traueiled into Terra Florida, whereas I felt both wealth and woe; the blacke oxe neuer trode upon my foote before, a dogge hath but a daie.   William Bullen, *A Dialogue Against the Fever Pestilence,* E. E. T. S., Ex. Ser., LI, p. 96, ll. 15-17.

1573.   Why then do folke this prouerbe put, The blacke oxe near trod on thy fut, If that way were to thriue?   Hereout a man may

---

[3]The editor of Tusser's *Husbandrie* quotes the following from Bernard's *Terence:*   "Prosperitie hangs on his sleeue; the black oxe cannot tread on his foot."

soone picke forth, Few feeleth what a pennie is worth, Till such time as they wine. T. Tusser, *Five Hundred Points of Good Husbandrie* (Engl. Dialect Soc., ed. 1875, § 67, ch. 56, stanza 6, p. 153).

1590. Sonne, as yet thou hast not eaten bread with one tooth, nor hath the blacke Oxe trodden vpon thy foote. R. Greene, *Mourning Garment* (ed. 1616), p. 6.

1630. The blacke oxe has trod upon their feet. *Wine, Beere and Ale* (1915), p. 34, l. 387.

1634. The blacke oxe hath not yet trod on their toes. J. Harington, *The Orlando Furioso of Ariosto,* in *English Heroical Verse,* p. 46, Canto VI, Stanza 72.

1639. The black Ox treads sore on's toes. J. Clarke, *Paroemiologia Anglo-Latina,* p. 245, s.v. "Paupertas."

1659. The black Oxe never trod on thy foot, viz. thou wast never in want. J. Howell, *Paroemiographia, English Proverbs,* p. 5.

1670. The black ox never trode on his foot. (That is, he never knew what sorrow or adversity meaned). J. Ray, *A Collection of English Proverbs,* p. 188.

1690. The black Ox has not trod upon his Foot, of one that has not been Pinch'd with Want, or been Hard put to it. B. E., *Dictionary of the Canting Crew,* reprinted in *New Cant. Dict.,* (1725), s.v. "Ox."

1721. The black Ox never trod on your Foot. (You never had the Care of a Family upon you, nor was press'd with severe Business or Necessities). J. Kelly, *A Complete Collection of Scottish Proverbs,* p. 327.

There remain a few instances of the proverb which are not readily interpreted. John Heywood's epigram

> The blacke Oxe neuer trode on thy foote:
> But the dun Asse hath trode on both thy feete.
> Which Asse and thou, may seeme sproong of one roote;
> For the asses pace, and thy pace are meete[4]

involves an obscure allusion to the dun ass, which seems to be a symbol of sloth. The precise significance of these references is obscure. Equally obscure is the dialectal "Th' black bull's trodden

---

[4] *Epigrams* (ed. J. S. Farmer, 1908), p. 139, No. 79, "The blacke oxe."

on him; that is, he is in a very bad temper."[5] When W. B. Yeats writes "The years like great black oxen tread the world, / And God the herdsman goads them on, / And I am broken by their passing feet,"[6] we probably need not see a reference to the proverb.

These examples of the proverb permit us to draw several inferences. Although the proverb serves to describe the feminine fear of old age, no particular importance should be attached to the pronouns "he" and "she." In other words, the origin of the proverb is not suggested by a reference peculiarly applicable to males or to females. The early and long-continued use of the proverb to describe unhappiness in the married state might suggest some special connection between an unhappy marriage and a black ox, but this clue does not lead us to anything definite. The allusions to unhappiness in marriage are concerned rather with poverty and distress than with marital difficulties. As we shall see, the continental parallels do not apply the proverb to marriage. Consequently, it seems probable that the original implication of serious misfortune has been replaced by such vague generalizations as "He has not known sorrow," or such special applications of the idea as "He has not known trouble in the married state" and "She has not suffered from old age."

The continental European parallels to "The black ox has not trod on his foot" offer much the same picture as do the English examples. In Germany, the proverb names either a black ox or a black cow, but as in the case of the pronouns "he" and "she," we cannot find anything significant in the variation.[7] An important and curious early German example of our proverb occurs in Nicolaus Herman's verses on the Prodigal Son which were published in 1562. A similar context is seen in Samuel Richardson's allusion: "The common phrase of wild-oats, and black oxen, and such-like qualifiers."[8] After the Prodigal Son has squandered his substance in riotous living, he suffers distress:

> Do jn so tratt die schwartze Kuh,
> Kam der alt Reul vnd bisz mit zu.[9]

---

[5]E. Peacock, *A Glossary of Words Used in the Wapentakes of Manley and Corringham, Lincolnshire*[2] (English Dialect Soc., LVIII; London, 1889), p. 51.

[6]*Countess Cathleen*, as quoted in *Notes and Queries*, CXLIX (1935), 67.

[7]Wander, *Deutsches Sprichwörter-Lexikon*, II, col. 1687, "Kuh," 521 and III, col. 1108, "Ochs," *350, *360, *361. The form varies slightly: "Die schwarze Kuh hat ihn gedrückt" or "Die schwarze Kuh hat ihm auf den Fuss getreten."

[8]Quoted from the *New English Dictionary*, s.v. "ox."

[9]P. Wackernagel, *Das deutsche Kirchenlied*, III (Leipzig, 1870), 1210, No. 1413, Stanza 8. For comment see *Deutsches Wörterbuch*, s.v. "Kuh," 6.

This obscure passage has been satisfactorily explained as a reference to Reuel (penitence) as a dog.[10] A confusing variant:

> In des so trat jn auch die schwartze Kuh,
> Kam der alte keil auch darzu.[11]

is probably a misreading of "der alt Reul." There is an occasional example of the proverb of the black ox in later literary use, e.g., "Wissens auch nicht, weil ihre augen gut und gesund sein, und keine augenbrechen gehabt noch versucht haben, oder wie man zu sagen pfleget, welche die schwarze kue noch nicht getreten hat,"[12] "auf die letzt trat mich zwar die schwarze kuh, aber zu spät,"[13] "er hat sich viel Unglücks genietet, die schwarze Kuh hat ihn oft getreten," and "jedes rauschend Blatt ist ihm ein geharnischter Mann, die schwarze Kuhe hat ihn zu oft getreten,"[14]—which have the meanings familiar in English.

The proverb is found in German collections of traditional materials, especially in provincial collections, and we can safely assume that it is—or was—familiarly used. To these German instances we may add the Lithuanian "Vom schwarzen Ochsen getreten sein," a phrase signifying "having suffered poverty" (Elend erlebt haben),[15] which seems to be current in the neighboring Baltic states;[16] the Hungarian "Er ist noch nicht auf die ferse der schwarzen kuh getreten," a phrase signifying "He has had no particular misfortunes";[17] the Albanian "The black ox has not yet

---

[10]*Deutsches Wörterbuch*, VIII, col. 835-36. See also F. Koldewey (ed.), B. Wapdis, *Streitgedichte* (Halle, 1883), p. xvi.

[11]J. Bergmann, *Ambraser Liederbuch*, "Bibliothek des litterarischen Vereins," XII (Stuttgart, 1845), 147 (No. 128, Stanza 8). The variant reading also appears in the *Liederbüchlein* (Frankfurt a.M.: N.Basse, 1580), the *Liederbüchlein* of 1584, and the *Gross Liederbuch* (Frankfurt a.M., 1599). For description of these texts see C. A. Williams, *JEGP*, VIII (1909), 489-500. Professor Williams has given me counsel about these texts.

[12]G. Bartisch, Ὀφθαλμοδουλεία *Das ist, Augendienst* (Dresden, 1583), 3 as quoted in *Deutsches Wörterbuch*, s.v. "Kuh," 6.

[13]Christian Weise, *Die drei ergsten Erznarren*, Ch. 6 as quoted in *Deutsches Wörterbuch*, s.v. "Kuh," 6.

[14]V. Herzberger, *Herz-Postille*, I, 780 and *Trauerbinden* as quoted by G. Schoppe, *Mitteilungen der schlesischen Gesellschaft für Volkskunde*, XXIX (1928), 300.

[15]A. Schleicher, *Litauische Märchen, Sprichwörter, Rätsel und Lieder* (Weimar, 1857), p. 174 (the original is not given).

[16]A parallel (German) from Estonia in A. W. Hupel, *Idiotikon der deutschen Sprache in Lief- und Ehstland* (Riga, 1795), p. 131. Grimm's reference (*Deut. Myth.*, p. 631) to Etner is obscure.

[17]Ipolyi, *Zeitschrift für deutsche Mythologie*, I (1853), 271. The original is not given. The aberrant form of this Hungarian version suggests that the translation may not be accurate.

mounted on you," a phrase signifying that your parents have not yet died and that consequently you have not yet known suffering;[18] and the Modern Greek "The black ox has trod on him."[19] These do not bring us much farther. The proverb appears to be generally known in Germany and in countries east of Germany. The absence of parallels in the Romance languages is curious. As a possible parallel Riegler adduces the Neapolitan "passa (l)a vacca," meaning "to suffer want or hunger."[20] When the phrase is spoken, the speaker passes his outstretched thumb and forefinger back and forth across his chin. Riegler suggests that the gesture is a symbolic presentation of the cow's horns. It seems more plausible to adopt an interpretation given me by my friend Herbert H. Vaughan. The saying might refer to the primitive manner of delivering milk by driving a cow through the streets and milking her for each customer. When the cow has passed, the chance of obtaining milk has passed.

The variations in details are just what we would expect to find in oral tradition: the ox is occasionally replaced by a cow, and the act is described in slightly varying terms, e.g., the ox has pressed or squeezed him, the ox has walked on his foot or his toes. Especially interesting in this connection is the Renaissance Dutch "Die bonte os heeft hem niet betreden." (The pied ox has not trod on him).[21] This variation in the color calls our attention to the tenacity with which tradition has retained the adjective "black."

The Albanian parallel is definitely associated with death and suggests that we might look farther in this direction for the explanation of the symbolism. The collections have already noted for us the Turkish "Der Tod is ein schwarzes Kameel, das niederkniet vor jeder Tür.[22] There is no reason to think of an immediate connection between this phrase and ours; a similar symbolism comes to mind in the description of the death of Theodoric, who is borne

[18]J. G. von Hahn, *Albanesische Studien* (Jena, 1854), II, 154, No. 73.

[19]N. G. Polites, *Paroimiai*, III (Athens, 1903), 200-201, "Beta," No. 45. The extensive commentary represents the most thorough investigation of the proverb. I am indebted for the reference and other substantial assistance to my friend Richard Jente.

[20]R. Riegler, *Die neueren Sprachen*, XXXIII (1925), 369-70.

[21]*Gemeene Duytsche Spreckwoorden: Adagia oft Proverbia ghenoemt* (Campen, 1550), p. 11 = Harrebomée, II, 154 a.

[22]*Osmanische Sprichwörter* (Bernstein, 3522), pp. 32-33, No. 95.

away on a black horse.[23] We may infer that the phrase "The black ox has not trod on his foot," like the Turkish phrase referring to a camel and the story of Theodoric's riding off on a black horse, describes death symbolically by referring to an animal. We shall be supported in this inference if we can find the black ox used as a symbol of death. The explanation will be all the more plausible if it supplies a symbolism of the black ox which was once generally known in Christian Europe, was freely used in the late Middle Ages or the Renaissance, and is no longer readily recognized. For the symbolism which connects a black ox with death scholars have suggested various sources, viz., customs of sacrifice in classical antiquity, ideas found in Germanic mythology, ideas found in popular belief, traditions of the Devil, and a Welsh idiom. It is scarcely pertinent to think of treading on the foot as a symbol of marriage, for the implication of marriage is found only in English uses of the proverb and furthermore marriage to an ox conveys no particular meaning. We shall now examine these various suggested sources.

Long ago, an explanation of our proverb was sought in Greek sacrifices of black oxen.[24] Groschuff, who advanced this explanation, maintained that German knights brought the phrase to Prussia from the Levant. He cited no Levantine examples. Professor Clarence Paschall reminds me of such typical references to black sacrificial oxen as *Aen.* VI, 153-55, 243-47, but there does not appear to be an allusion to a black ox treading on a man's foot. Probably no one will care to defend this explanation.

A more serious effort was made to find an explanation in Germanic mythology. Jacob Grimm, who called for an explanation of the phrase, collected some materials suggesting its relation to

23 H. Massmann, *Kaiserchronik* (Quedlinburg, 1854), III, 951-54; F. Liebrecht, *Des Gervasius von Tilbury Otia Imperialia* (Hanover, 1856), p. 126; E. L. Rochholz, *Schweizersagen* (Aarau, 1856), II, 21-22; Brothers Grimm, *Kinder- und Hausmärchen*, III (Göttingen, 1856), 298; R. Köhler, "Eine Sage von Theodorichs Ende in dem 'Libro de los Enxemplos,'" *Germania*, XVIII (1873), 147-52 = *Kleinere Schriften*, II (Berlin, 1900), 266-72; Heiberg, "Theodorich som den vilde Jaeger," *Dania*, IX (1903), 239-40; J. Bolte and G. Polívka, *Anmerkungen*, IV (Leipzig, 1930), 140-41. Compare Herman Schneider's explanation of the story in *Germanische Heldensage*, I (Berlin, 1928), 278-82.

24 *Neuer Büchersaal der schönen Wissenschaften*, VI (1748), 449-58. Wander, *Deutsches Sprichwörter-Lexikon*, II, col. 687, "Kuh," * 521 cites J. G. Bock, *Idioticon prussicum* (Königsberg, 1759), pp. 38-39, but this contains nothing pertinent. A. M Hyamson, *A Dictionary of English Phrases* (London, 1922), p. 49, offers the same explanation and adds that the phrase means "He is henpecked."

mythological ideas, but he seems not to have been firmly convinced of a connection, for he left the matter in the form of a question.[25] Those who followed in his footsteps were less cautious and declared, e.g., "Doch wird diese Redensart aus der deutschen Mythologie erklärt."[26] We need only indicate the kind of evidence which Grimm collected, viz., the Slovene *mavra* (black cow) as name for the rainbow, the modern superstition that slaughtering a black ox and black cow brings misfortune,[27] and some miscellaneous allusions to cows with no apparent bearing on the phrase. Felix Liebrecht added a reference which Jacob Grimm would probably have considered very important: a pestilence in Vig was foretold to Óláfr Geirstaðaálfr by a dream of a black ox. The ox came from the East, went from farmstead to farmstead, and most of those on whom it breathed fell before it.[28] Since he would scarcely have defended these combinations after his views on German tradition and mythology changed, we need not go into the details. The case for an origin of our phrase in Germanic mythology rests on very tenuous inferences. In particular, the *Óláfsþáttr Geirstaðaálfs,* which might be considered to be its best support, is a late vision embellished with materials from Christian legends.[29] If we can find a better explanation, we shall not rely upon Germanic mythology to explain our phrase.

An ingenious explanation which is more in accord with modern ideas of popular tradition seeks an explanation of "The black ox has not trod on his foot" in the idea of the nightmare (Alpdämon).[30] Omens are often communicated by dreams, and the creatures which appear in nightmares often symbolize unhappiness and misfortune. Riegler, the author of this explanation, collects examples of oxen in

---

[25]*Deutsche Mythologie,* 1st ed., p. 631, n. 1 (4th ed., p. 554, n. 1).

[26]Wander, *Deutches Sprichwörter-Lexikon,* II, col. 1687, "Kuh," *521. This positive assertion is typical of ideas prevalent about the middle of the nineteenth century.

[27]*Deutsche Mythologie,* III, 467, No. 887.

[28]*Des Gervasius von Tilbury Otia Imperialia* (Hanover, 1856), p. 92. The Óláfsþáttr Geirstaðaálfs may be found in Fornmannasögur, x, 209-15. The pertinent passage is conveniently reprinted in G. D. Kelchner, *Dreams in Old Norse Literature and Their Affinities in Folklore* (Cambridge, 1935), p. 127.

[29]Eugen Mogk in Paul's *Grundriss der germanischen Philologie,*2 II, i (Strassburg, 1901-9), 824.

[30]R. Riegler, "Zur Redensart: Die schwarze Kuh hat ihn gedrückt (getreten)," *Die neueren Sprachen,* XXXIII (1925), 368-70. See also G. Schoppe, "Sprichwörtliche Redensarten," *Mitteilungen der schlesischen Gesellschaft für Volkskunde,* XXIX (1928), 300, who independently offers the same explanation.

nightmares. but concedes that they are very few. What a pity that he did not find the dream of Óláfr Geirstaðaálfr! In the absence of anything more satisfactory, we might be willing to accept this explanation.

Wander does not defend his suggestion that the black ox is a symbol of the Devil.[31] Since the proponent of the explanation makes no great matter of it, we may pass on.

In *A Glossary and Etymological Dictionary of Obsolete and Uncommon Words*, W. Toone sharply corrects the prevailing explanation of the phrase and offers another:

The proverbial expression, "the black ox has trod on your foot," has no reference to the explanation given of it by Archdeacon Nares; it is derived from an historical fact, and signifies that a misfortune has happened to the party to which it is applied. The saying is deduced from the Ancient Britons, who had a custom of plowing their land in partnership, and if either of the oxen died or became disabled during the operation, the owner of the land was compelled to find another animal, or give an acre of land to the aggrieved partner, which acre was usually styled *erw yr uch ddu*, "the acre of the black ox," and many single acres in Wales now bear this title, and hence the proverb arose.[32]

Whatever the significance and origin of the Welsh phrase may be, it can not be the origin of a phrase known from Scotland to Estonia, Hungary, and Greece. We can only admire the ingenuity of this attempt to explain the phrase.

There remains a last possibility, viz., that the proverb has connections with Christian ideas. This has not been suggested before, and we may therefore begin with a brief examination of the idea of Death riding on a black ox.[33] It appears at the beginning of the fourteenth century in contexts which suggest that it was already familiarly known. Konrad Burdach points out an example in an Amiens missal of 1323 which is now at The Hague.[34] Unknown to

---

[31]*Deutsches Sprichwörter-Lexikon*, III, col. 1108, "Ochs," *350.

[32]London, 1832. See p. 106. According to Archdeacon Nares, the proverb signifies the burdens of old age, but he offers no comment. See *A Glossary or Collection of Words* (New ed., London, 1901), II, 625.

[33]Comte A. de Laborde, "La Mort chevauchant un boeuf," *Comptes rendus des séances de l'Académie des inscriptions et belles-lettres*, 1923, pp. 100-13; Alois Bernt and Konrad Burdach (eds.), *Der Ackermann aus Böhmen* (Berlin, 1917), pp. 237-52, "Das römische Bild des Todes und die bildhaften Elemente der Todesvorstellung im 'Ackermann,'" especially pp. 248-49; Istvan Kozáky, *Anfänge der Darstellungen des Vergänglichkeitsproblems* ("Bibliotheca humanitatis historica, I; Budapest, 1936), passim. Kozaky's important study is the first of three volumes on the origin, development, and modern forms of the Dance of Death. The high merits of the first volume have not been adequately noticed in any review that has come to my attention.

[34]A. Bernt and K. Burdach, *Ackermann*, pp. 248-49; Kozáky, p. 184.

him is a somewhat later unpublished Latin dialogue between Death and a youth from which Kozáky extracts the following lines:

> Juvenis equitans cum accipitre ait:
> O lente, quid queris? Frustra me ledere queris!
> Velox sum, fortis sum, non horreo iacula mortis.
>   Mors dicit iuueni:
> Cursu quo (qui?) te gerit equus albus cum pede nigro,
> Cursus uanus erit: te sequar cum boue pigro.[35]

These instances which are a commentary on a famous passage in the *Ackermann aus Böhmen*, 16: 19-24: "Du (der Ackermann) fragest, wo wir (der Tod) sein: Vnbescheidenlich sein wir, do man vnser figure zu Rome in einem tempel an einer want gemalet fant als einen man auf einem ochsen sitzende, dem die augen verbunden waren; der selbe man furte ein hawen in seiner rechten hant vnd ein schaufel in der linken hant. Damite fachte er auf den ochsen" are earlier than the allusion in Pierre Michault's *Danse des Aveugles* (second half of fifteenth century). Consequently, Comte de Laborde should not attempt to derive certain contemporary miniatures representing Death and a black ox from Michault's poem to the exclusion of other possibilities. To be sure, neither the Latin verses nor the German passage specifically calls the ox "black," but since they mention no color, we need not suppose these passages imply a disagreement with the current usage. The idea of Death riding a black ox is perhaps not to be separated from descriptions and pictures of Death riding in a vehicle drawn by black oxen.[36] Pictures of this sort are conventional in paintings suggested by Petrarch's *Trionfi*. Kozáky alone has sought to pursue the symbolism of Death and the black ox to an ultimate origin.[37] He connects it with the game of Blindman's Buff, which the Germans call "Blinde Kuh," and maintains that the representation of Death as an animal can be

---

[35] Kozáky, p. 229.

[36] De Laborde, p. 106. These pictures supply a better explanation of the French and Breton traditions of death symbolized by vehicles drawn by black oxen than does Riegler's theory. A painting suggested by Petrarch's *Trionfi* and belonging to an artist of the school of Mantegna hangs in the Metropolitan Museum (New York). I am indebted to Mr. Harry B. Wehle of the Museum for confirming my recollection of the painting. For iconographic parallels see E. Panofsky, *Studies in Iconology* (New York, 1939), p. 11, n. 58.

[37] See Kozáky, p. 185. On Blindman's Buff see Groschuff, "Gedanken über das in Deutschland übliche Blindekuhspiel," *Neuer Büchersaal der schönen Wissenschaften*, VI (1748), 431-58; F. M. Böhme, *Deutsches Kinderlied und Kinderspiel* (Leipzig, 1897), p. 628; J. Lewalter and G. Schläger, *Deutsches Kinderlied und Kinderspiel* (Kassel, 1911), p. 406, No. 98. Kozáky would have found support in S. Singer's remarks in *Zeitschrift des Vereins für Volkskunde*, XIII (1903), 50.

traced to Oriental sources, and in particular to Tibetan masks.[38]
The relations would be difficult to establish to the satisfaction of all
readers and since they are not essential to the present discussion,
we need not pursue them farther here.

Let it suffice to say that a literary and iconographic tradition of
Death riding a black ox is well established in late medieval Christian
use. Since the evidence for this tradition begins not very long before the first appearance of the proverb ''The black ox has not trod
on his foot,'' a connection between the two seems altogether probable. The Albanian proverb ''The black ox has not yet mounted
on you,'' which is said to mean ''Death has not yet taken away
your parents and consequently you have not known suffering,''
suggests how readily an allusion to Death can pass into a more
general allusion to sorrow, care, and poverty.

---

[38]See Kozáky, pp. 185, 266, 337.

ASPECTS OF SPENSER'S VOCABULARY

By FREDERICK M. PADELFORD
University of Washington

"The pure flowing streame of Chrystallin Spenser" was fed by native springs, but not by them alone. Richard Mulcaster observed in his *Elementarie* that the English tongue would prove very pliable "if our learned cuntriemen will put to their labor." Spenser was one pupil who took the precepts of his master seriously and who did put to his labor, but he early recognized that while the full resources of the native language should be explored and employed, it should likewise be enriched with judicious importations from abroad. Spenser was second to none in his patriotism and his proud dreams for a greater England in both material and spiritual realms, but agreeing as he doubtless did with Daniel's condemnation of "displacing our words, or inventing new, only upon a singularity, when our own accustomed phrase set in the due place, would express us more familiarly and to better delight than all this idle affectation of antiquity or novelty can ever do," he nevertheless appreciated that through proper coinage the language was daily growing in strength and beauty. He did not hesitate to coin a word or to give a new meaning to an old word, if occasion required. This paper is concerned with his contribution to the language of words derived outright from the classical or Romanic languages, and words devised by adding classical or Romanic prefixes or suffixes to existing words, whether those words were of native or foreign descent. The paper is also concerned with a cognate problem, the relative range of the poet's vocabulary in his earlier and in his later work.

A comparison of the Spenser *Concordance* with the *New English Dictionary* reveals 103 words derived wholly or in part from the classical or Romanic languages for which the first citations are from Spenser.[1] This does not necessarily mean that Spenser was the first to use each of these words, but it creates a strong presumption

---

[1] One of my former students, Mrs. Dorothy Haggett Lister, made such a comparison several years ago. I have made a recheck, and our findings are substantially in accord.

to that effect. Indeed for many of the words the only citations are from Spenser and most of them are so poetical in quality that their authorship is not open to question. It is interesting to note the sources of these words, how often and at what period of his writing the poet employed them, and the extent to which they have survived.

In the first column of the following table the words are listed, with linguistic sources indicated, *L.* standing for Latin, *Fr.* for French, etc., and *H.* for hybrids—words with foreign prefixes or suffixes. In the second column all of the occurrences of the word are indicated; the abbreviations of the *Concordance* are employed, Roman numerals standing for the books of the *Faerie Queene*. If a word is used more than once in a particular poem or book, the number of times it occurs is shown in parentheses. The third column gives for each word the date of the latest citation in the *N.E.D.*; a dash means that the only citation is from Spenser.

accoil *Fr.*	II	——	captivance *Fr.*	III, V	——
accourage *Fr.*	II, III	——	capuccio *It.*	III	——
accourt *H.*	II	——	cerule *Lt.*	*Gn.*	1830
addeem *H.*	V, VI	——	chevisance *Fr.*		
addoom *H.*	VII	——	(？) (a flower)	*S.C.* (2)	1620
admirance *Fr.*	V	——	compacture *Lt.*	II	1641
adviceful *H.*	IV	1607	comportance *Fr.*	II	1644
affrap *It.*	II, III	——	comprovincial		
affret (n.) *It.*	III, IV (3)	——	*Lt.*	III	1652
affriended *H.*	IV	——	concent *It.*		
aggrace (n.) *It.*	II	——	("to make		
aggrace (v.) *It.*	I, II	1825	accord")	IV	——
aggrate *It.*	*TM.*, II (4),		concrew *Fr.*	IV	——
	III (2), IV,		counterfeisance		
	V, VI	1755	*Fr.*	*Hub.*, *T.M.*, I,	
aguise *H.*	*Hub.*, II (3),			III, IV	1656
	III, V	1598	creatress *H.*	III	1892
amenage *Fr.*	II	——	crumenal *Lt.*	*S.C.*	1647
amenance *Fr.*	*Hub.*, II (2),		daedal *Lt.*	III, IV	1872
	III, IV	1739	decrew *Fr.*	IV	——
avengeful *H.*	*T.M.*, IV (2),		disadventurous		
	H.L., *H.H.B.*	1841	*H.*	*Hub.*, I (2),	
battailant *Fr.*	*Van.*	——		IV (2), V	
beastlihead *H.*	*S.C.*	1616		(2)	1702
belgard *It.*	II, III, *H.B.*	1616	disentrail *Lt.*		
blatant [beast]			or *Fr.*	IV, V	1692
Lt. (？)[2]	V-VI freq.	1874	disleal *It.* or *Fr.*	II	——
bonnibel *Fr.* or			disloign *Fr.*	IV	——
It.	*S.C.*	1823	dispace[3]	*Gn.*, *Mui.*	1610
busket *Fr.*	*S.C.*	——	dispart (v.) *Lt.*	II, III (2),	
camis *Lt.*, *Fr.*,				IV (2), VI	1868
It., or *Sp.*	II, V	——			

[2]From *blatare？*
[3]di + spatiari (*Lt.*), di + spaziari (*It.*), or dis + pace (*H.*)

dispurveyance H.	III	—
dispread H.	Gn., Mui., Ded. Son. 14, II (7), III (3), IV (2), V (3), VI	1863
disshiver H.	IV	1638
distent (v.) Lt.	II	1880
drapet It.	II	1799
dreariment H.	S.C., Ti., I (3), II (4), III (2), IV, V, VI, Epith.	1867
dureful H.	IV, Am.	1614
effierce (v.) H.	III	—
embay H. ("to drench, plunge")	Mui., I (2), II (3), III (4)	1762
emboil H.	I, II	—
embrave H.	Ro., S.C., II	1874
emmarble H.	H.L.	1864
empurple H.	II, III (2), IV	1884
engore H. ("to gore, infuriate")	II, III (4), IV, VI	—
entrail Fr. ("a coil")	I	—
entrenchment H.	II	1876
equipage (n.) Fr.	S.C., Hub., I, IV	1867
equipage (v.) Fr.	II	1847
gallantry Fr. ("gallants collectively")	Col. [overlooked in N.E.D.]	1688
giust⁴ (equiv. of "joust")	III, V	1808
grapplement Fr.	II	—
habitance Fr.	II	—
hazardize H.	II	—
indignance Lt.	III	1845
indignant Lt.	III (2), V (2), VI	1880
indignify Lt.	Col.	1743
interdeal H.	Hub., V	1612
intuse Lt.	III	—
irrenowned H.	II	—
jolliment H.	II, IV, VI	—
joyance H.	T.M., Mui., As., I (2), III, IV (3), V, VI (2), VII (2), Epith., H.L.	1878
lucid Lt.	Hub.	1893
martel (v.) Fr.⁵	III	—
mercify H.	VI	1733
misdesert H.	VI	1865
obliquid Lt. or Fr.⁶	VII	—
pallid Lt.	Ro. (2), Gn. (2), II, III, V, VI, Proth.	1876
paravant Fr.	III, Col., VI	—
penurious Lt., Fr., or It.	V	1894
pictural (n.) H.	II	—
portance Fr.	II (3), III (2), VI	1881
protense Lt.	III	—
pupillage H.	Ded. Son. 7, II	1882
redisburse H.	IV	1655
renfierce H.⁷	II	—
renverse Fr.	I, IV	1681
riotise H.	Gn., Hub. (2), I (2), III (2)	1637
saliaunce H.	II	—
scerne It.	III	—
scorse It. ("to chase")	III, VI	—
sdeign (n.) It.	V, Am.	—
sdeign (v.) It.	Hub., Ded. Son. 2, III (2), IV, V	1667
sdeignful H.	T.M., Mui., D., III (2), V (2)	1748
sdeignfully H.	Hub.	—
singult Lt.	T.M., Col., III, V	1820
subverse Lt.	Hub., III	1870
thrillant H.	I, II	1594
unruliment H.	IV	—
wariment H.	IV	—

---

⁴"quasi-It. spelling of joust."

⁵Spenser derives this verb from the noun which had been in use for over a century.

⁶"Apparently for obliqued from oblique (v.)." No occurrence of oblique as a verb, however, is cited prior to 1775.

⁷fierce (v.) from adj.; analogy of renforce?

Twenty-two of these words are clearly taken from the French, sixteen from the Latin, thirteen from the Italian, plus one quasi-Italian word, two from one or the other of the Romanic languages, and four from Latin or a Romanic language. One—*dispase*—may be from the Latin or Italian, or may be a hybrid; two—*blatant* and *chevisance*—presumably are from the Latin and French respectively. The remaining forty result from adding prefixes or suffixes to words already extant.

For forty-five of these words the citations are confined to Spenser. Two words—*aguise* and *thrillant*—were employed by imitators of Spenser—Sylvester and Greene—in 1598 and 1594, but apparently did not survive the century. Nineteen enjoyed some vogue in the seventeenth century, the period of Spenser's strongest influence, but went out of use before 1700; eight others failed to outlive the eighteenth century. The remaining twenty-nine have survived, or at least were employed in the nineteenth century. With the exception of *blatant, creatress, daedal, equipage, lucid, pallid, penurious* and *pupillage*, these words strike us as somewhat archaic or at least poetical in connotation.

Especially significant, as throwing light upon Spenser's workmanship, is the fact that fifty-four of these words are confined in use to the first part of the *Faerie Queene* and the minor poems written prior to 1590,[8] whereas only twenty-three occur exclusively in Books IV-VII and the later poems.[9] Moreover, there are, all told, 131 occurrences of the words in the earlier books and only eighty-two in the later. It is thus clear that Spenser was more interested in coining words or giving currency to new words in his earlier period than in the later. That he used a larger vocabulary in the earlier period also seems to be implied.

In addition to the above, there are forty-nine words, likewise of foreign origin, to which, on the basis of the citations in the *N.E.D.*, Spenser gave new meanings. They are as follows: *abet, aret, assoil, attaint, banderol, bullion, canticle, chevisance, cloy, cognizance, court (v.), debatement, deify, discountenance, efforce, efforced, enchase, endue, feculent, fencible, gyre, imbrue, imitate, impicture, indignity, insolence, insupportable, intendiment, intimate (v.), invest, jouissance, jovial, lourd, macerate, malefice, moil, overture, platform,*

---

[8] The *Hymne of Love* and *Hymne of Beauty* are classed as early as poems, which of course is conjectural, but only four references are involved.

[9] *Blatant* is counted only once since it was used as a proper noun.

race (*n.*), *rencounter, renforce, reprise, respire, respondence, rowell, stour, stupefy, suborn, tyrannize.*

These words also are worthy of special study, for perhaps to an even greater degree than those borrowed or originated by the poet they reveal the workings of his mind. Sometimes a word is recalled to its etymological significance; at other times a word leaps boldly from one meaning to another. That there are sixty-seven instances of the novel uses of these words in the earlier books of the *Faerie Queene* to thirty-three in the later, supports the conclusions deduced from the words which Spenser added to the language.

That Spenser used a more varied vocabulary in his earlier than in his later work finds still further evidence in a numerical study of words used only in one or the other part of the *Faerie Queene*. Exclusive of articles, pronouns, prepositions, conjunctions, interjections and auxiliary verbs, there are 2090 such separate words—no word being counted more than once—in Books I-III, and 1428 separate words in Books IV-VI. Thus, of the total number of words confined to one part of the poem, 59.1 per cent, or approximately three-fifths, are in the earlier books, and 40.9 per cent, or approximately two-fifths, in the later. As 53.3 per cent of the stanzas are in the earlier books and 46.7 per cent in the later, it thus becomes evident that Spenser used an appreciably larger vocabulary in Books I-III than in Books IV-VI.

A classification of these words as parts of speech is also significant:

Books I-III			Books IV-VI		
Parts of Speech		Percentage	Parts of Speech		Percentage
Verbs	301	14.4	Verbs	248	17.4
Adverbs	130	6.2	Adverbs	131	9.1
Nouns	938	44.9	Nouns	596	41.7
Adjectives	318	15.2	Adjectives	183	12.8
Ppl. adjs.	332	15.9	Ppl. adjs.	176	12.3
Verbal nouns	71	3.4	Verbal nouns	93	6.5

It will be seen that the percentages of nouns, adjectives and participial adjectives are larger in the earlier books, and of verbs, adverbs and verbal nouns larger in the later books. Only one conclusion can be drawn from this: the first part of the poem is more given to description, and the second part, to action.

THE NEO-PLATONIC LADDER IN SPENSER'S *AMORETTI*

By Edwin Casady
Brown University

Although the relation of Spenser's *Fowre Hymnes* to Neo-Platonic writings has been studied in detail[1] and the influence of the Neo-Platonic interpretation of love on specific sonnets of the *Amoretti* has been pointed out,[2] the extent to which Spenser may have drawn upon Neo-Platonic thought in developing his sonnet sequence has not been fully realized. In fact, a detailed comparison of the *Amoretti* with Renaissance Italian expositions of Neo-Platonism suggests the possibility that in constructing his sequence Spenser may have had in mind the Neo-Platonic Ladder.

To weigh the evidence revealed by such a comparison we need first to review the conceptions of the Neo-Platonists. The basic conception of Neo-Platonism is that every soul derives from the One, of which all beauty (both physical and abstract) is a radiation, and every soul potentially desires and can attain reunion with the One. Such is the nature of the soul, however, that it frequently fails to realize its potentialities until aroused by external stimulation. Since beauty is a radiation of the One, the perception of beauty can act as such a stimulus. Therefore, in Neo-Platonic literature, where "love" aroused by the perception of beauty is interpreted as the desire of the soul for reunion with the One, the means by which the human soul becomes conscious of its potentialities and climbs back to reunion with the One is often represented as a "Ladder" having the following "rungs":[3]

---

[1] For example, in W. L. Renwick's edition of *Daphnaïda and Other Poems* (London, 1929), pp. 209-224; in Lilian Winstanley's edition of *The Fowre Hymnes* (Cambridge, 1930); and in Mohinimohan Bhattacherje's *Platonic Ideas in Spenser* (Calcutta, 1935).

[2] For example, by Lu Emily Pearson, *Elizabethan Love Conventions* (Berkeley, 1933), pp. 173-175; and by Mohinimohan Bhattacherje, *op. cit.*, pp. 177-195.

[3] In Messer Pietro Bambo's explanation as reported in Castiglione's *Il Cortegiano* the "rungs" are not numbered; nor are they always sharply differentiated; but I have based this exposition upon *Il Cortegiano* for two reasons: 1) in the sixteenth century this work was among the most widely known expositions of the Neo-Platonic conception of love; 2) Spenser was certainly familiar with it. As Bembo draws upon Pico della Mirandola's commentary on Benivieni's *Canzona delo amore celeste et divino*, I have also made particular use of Pico's commentary.

1. Sensual love forms the lowest rung. In Neo-Platonic phraseology, the sight of physical beauty in a human being can arouse in the soul a "flame" which first takes the form of desire for physical union with that beauty.

2. The lover so aroused, having a mind previously trained to distrust sense and appetite, must call upon reason[4] to extinguish his sensual desire. If reason is unable to extinguish the "flame," the lover can safeguard himself only by accepting the failure as evidence that the attraction derives from spirit, not body. He can then subordinate sensual desire by reminding himself that beauty, being of divine origin, "is most perfect when wholly separate"[5] from body and consequently can "in no wise be enjoyed, nor can the desire which it excites in our minds be satisfied, by means of touch."[6] By means of such reasoning, the lover can convince himself that he can best, or most nearly, satisfy the desire within him by means of the sense least dependent on bodily substance—the power of vision. Having resolved to shun "wholly every stain of vulgar love"[7] and to draw himself fully onto this rung of the Ladder, the lover seeks to be as constantly as possible in the physical presence of his beloved; for only when he is actually in her presence can he as yet, his eyes being turned outward, see clearly and enjoy the image of beauty which his beloved embodies.

3. Since the lover cannot be constantly in the physical presence of his beloved and is tormented when absent from her by desire to look upon her beauty, he learns to give his attention when with her to fixing in his mind that image of beauty which she embodies. With the aid of reason, which assures him "that the body is something very different from beauty, and not only does not enhance it, but diminishes its perfection,"[8] he turns his eyes inward and finds that he can gratify his desire by seeing in his mind the image

---

[4] "In our soul there are three modes of perceiving; that is by sense, by reason, and by intellect: from sense springs appetite, which we have in common with the brutes; from reason springs choice, which is peculiar to man; from the intellect, by which man is able to commune with the angels, springs will." (*The Book of the Courtier*, trans. by L. E. Opdycke [Immortal Classics, 1929], p. 285. Hereafter cited as *The Courtier*.) Throughout this article I quote *Il Cartegiano* in Opdycke's translation because his phrasing is more easily followed by the modern reader than is that of Hoby; for example, in the quotation given in this note Opdycke uses the word *intellect* to translate Castiglione's *intelletto*; Hoby (Everyman Edition, p. 303) uses *understanding*.

[5] *The Courtier*, p. 295.

[6] *Ibid.*

[7] *Ibid.*

[8] *Ibid.*, p. 299.

of beauty which he at first could see only when in his beloved's presence. While he contemplates the image in his mind, his imagination[9] begins to fashion it into an image more beautiful than the one he sees when he turns his eyes outward to look upon his beloved. Consequently, the image in his mind becomes more beautiful than the physical beauty from which he derived it, and the lover soon learns to prefer contemplating the image he has constantly within him to looking upon his beloved. By so doing he turns his desire wholly from that body to the image of its beauty and pulls himself fully onto the third rung of the Ladder.

4. Standing on the third rung, the lover keeps his eyes turned inward to enjoy the idealized image of one body's beauty. While he contemplates this image, he gradually adds together the beauties of all bodies to form the universal concept ("Idea") of all bodily beauty. Once the lover has, with eyes turned inward, seen the beauty of this Idea, he finds it so much more attractive than even the idealized image of one body that "he will esteem lightly that which at first he so greatly prized"[10] and give his mind solely to contemplating his Idea of all bodily beauty. By so doing he pulls himself fully onto the fourth rung of the Ladder.

5. Although the lover who has reached the fourth rung is far happier than one who makes any concession to sensual desire, he has not yet attained the greatest felicity that he can attain. Contemplating this universal Idea of the beauty of all bodies, the lover discovers that beauty is more fully realized in the beauty within his soul than it is in any physical beauty.[11] This discovery, because it brings the lover to contemplate his own nature,[12] enables him to

---

[9]"The same order is in the lesser World, our Soul: the inferiour faculties are directed by the superiour, whom following they erre not. The imaginative corrects the mistakes of outward sense: Reason is illuminated by the Intellect, nor do we at any time miscarry, but when the Imaginative will not give credit to Reason, or Reason confident of it self, resists the Intellect." (*A Platonick Discourse upon Love by Pico della Mirandola*, trans. by Thomas Stanley [1651] and edited by E. G. Gardner [Boston, 1914], p. 65. Hereafter cited as Pico.)

[10]*The Courtier*, p. 300.

[11]Pico, pp. 73-74: "Reflecting upon her own Operation, the knowledge of universal Beauty, and considering that every thing found in Matter is particular, she [the soul] concludes this universality proceeds not from the outward Object, but her Intrinsecal Power: and reasons thus: If in the dimme Glasse of Material Phantasmes this Beauty is represented by vertue of my Light, it follows that, beholding it in the clear Mirrour of my substance devested of those Clouds, it will appear more perspicuous: thus turning into her self, she findes the Image of Ideal Beauty communicated to her by the Intellect, the object of Celestiall Love."

[12]Because it awakens "the soul . . . [and] opens those eyes which all possess but few use" (*The Courtier*, p. 300).

comprehend that the beauty he has discovered by looking inward is the reflection of heavenly beauty as manifested in his particular intellect.[13] Having recognized the heavenly origin of this "Image of Ideal Beauty," the lover is moved by spiritual desire far more overpowering than any love he has previously felt and finds within himself the ability to pull himself fully onto the fifth rung of the Ladder.

6. Once the lover has attained the fifth rung and escaped completely the distraction of things earthly, he can contemplate without interruption this reflection of heavenly beauty. As love formerly guided the lover from the contemplation of the image of one particular bodily beauty to the Idea of the universal beauty of all bodies, now spiritual love guides the lover who contemplates the reflection of heavenly beauty that he has found within himself[14] to the Idea of the universal beauty of all intellect.[15] When the lover has thus pulled himself fully onto the sixth rung of the Ladder, his "soul, kindled by the most sacred fire of true divine love, flies to unite herself with the angelic nature ['universal intellect'], and not only quite forsakes sense, but has no longer need of reason's discourse; for, changed into an angel ['intellect'], she [his soul] understands all things intelligible, and without veil or cloud views the wide sea of pure divine beauty, and receives it[16] into herself, and enjoys that supreme felicity of which the senses are incapable."[17]

7. Although Bembo in *The Courtier*[18] protests that he thinks "love is not willing that its secrets should be further disclosed, or that the Courtier should pass beyond that stage [the sixth rung] which it has been pleased to have me show him," other Neo-Platonists differentiate a seventh rung, or more properly, a "landing

---

[13] "The Image of Ideal Beauty communicated to her [the soul] by the Intellect, the Object of Celestiall Love" (Pico, p. 74). For the meaning of *intellect* see above, note 4.

[14] "In her [his soul's] own particular intellect" (*The Courtier*, p. 301).

[15] "Guides her [his soul] from the particular to the universal intellect" (*Ibid.*); cf. Pico, p. 74: "She [the soul] ascends from this Idea in her self, to the place where Celestial Venus is, in her proper form: Who in fullness of her Beauty not being comprehensible, by any particular Intellect, she, as much as in her lies, endeavours to be united to the first Minde, the chiefest of Creatures, and general Habitation of Ideal Beauty."

[16] "The wide sea of pure divine beauty."

[17] *The Courtier*, p. 301.

[18] P. 304; cf. Pico, p. 74.

stage''[19] on the top of the Ladder. At this "landing stage" the soul passes through union with universal intellect[20] into ecstatic mystic union ("reunion") with the One. To quote Plotinus:

> If then a man sees himself become one with the One, he has in himself a likeness of the One, and if he passes out of himself, as an image to its archetype, he has reached the end of his journey. And when he comes down from his vision, he can again awaken the virtue that is in him, and seeing himself fitly adorned in every part he can again mount upward through virtue to Spirit, and through wisdom to God. Such is the life of gods and of godlike and blessed men; a liberation from all earthly bonds, a life that takes no pleasure in earthly things, a flight of the alone to the Alone.[21]

In reading the *Amoretti,* no one familiar with Neo-Platonic writings can overlook the prevalence of Neo-Platonic phraseology or fail to recognize the rungs of the Ladder in such individual sonnets as No. 22,[22] of which lines 5-8 are:

> Her temple fayre is built within my mind,
> in which her glorious ymage placed is,
> on which my thoughts doo day and night attend
> lyke sacred priests that neuer thinke amisse.[23]

Such obvious reflections in individual sonnets, added to our knowledge of the Neo-Platonic Ladder's influence on *The Fowre Hymnes,* suggest the possibility that the Ladder may also have had some influence on the construction of the whole sequence. If we test this possibility by making a detailed comparison of the *Amoretti* with Bembo's exposition of the Ladder in *The Courtier,* we can find evidence of relationship which cannot be lightly dismissed.

Such evidence, although it can be found throughout the sequence, is most easily recognized in Sonnet 60 and those immediately following. Therefore, without meaning to imply that Spenser, abandoning his usual practice, intended only one meaning in each sonnet and drew that meaning from a single source, let us begin our comparison with these sonnets.

In Sonnet 60 Spenser writes that the year he has been in love has seemed longer than the previous forty he has lived. Nevertheless, in the last two lines he expresses the hope that his beloved will let him come closer during the ensuing year. This hope be-

---

[19]Cf. J. B. Fletcher, *Literature of the Italian Renaissance* (New York, 1934), p. 113.

[20]"Celestial Venus"; Pico, p. 74.

[21]W. R. Inge, *The Philosophy of Plotinus* (London, 1918), II, 142.

[22]Other good examples are Nos. 27, 35, 45, 72, 78, 79, 88.

[23]Throughout, quotations from Spenser's sonnets are from W. L. Renwick's edition of *Daphnaïda and Other Poems* (London, 1929).

comes much more meaningful if we recall that the purpose of Bembo's exposition in *The Courtier* of the Neo-Platonic interpretation of love is "to prove that old[24] men can love not only without blame but sometimes more happily than young men."[25] He who has attained that age when "knowledge is at its true prime"[26] and aspires to "love in a way that would bring him not only no blame, but much praise and highest happiness unaccompanied by any pain—which rarely and almost never happens with young men"—[27] is better able, Bembo asserts, to keep constantly in mind the Neo-Platonic doctrine that "the beauty . . . which is seen in the bodies and especially in the faces of men, and which excites this ardent desire that we call love . . . is an effluence of divine goodness."[28]

Having in Sonnet 60 acknowledged his more than two score years, Spenser in Sonnet 61 reminds himself of the divine origin of the beauty he loves; and by asserting that *Such heauenly formes ought rather worshipt be, then dare be lou'd by men of meane degree,*[29] he defines, as does Bembo, "in what way old men ought to desire beauty, and what they ought to seek from women, and with what they ought to be content,"[30] and thus implies a resolve to "enter on the path of divine love, with reason for guide."[31]

In Sonnet 62 the lover who has suffered a *weary yeare* in the toils of false love repeats, with the coming of the new year, his resolve to eschew *the old yeares sinnes forepast.* This decision to *chaunge eeke our mynde and former liues amend* by (as he has implied in the foregoing sonnet) climbing the Neo-Platonic Ladder enables the lover to look forward to changing *old yeares annoy to new delight.*

In Sonnet 63, as soon as he makes this resolve, the poet, who has previously been *tossed sore* by *long stormes and tempests sad assay,* finds his eyes able to *descry the happy shore in which I hope ere*

---

[24] "Taking this word *old*, however, not in the sense of decrepit, nor when the bodily organs have already become so weak that the soul cannot perform its functions through them, but when our knowledge is at its true prime" (*The Courtier*, p. 288).

[25] *Ibid.*, p. 285.

[26] *Ibid.*, p. 288.

[27] *Ibid.*, p. 284.

[28] *Ibid.*, p. 286.

[29] To maintain a distinction, here and following all quotations from Spenser's sonnets are italicized, and all quotations from *The Courtier* are enclosed in quotation marks.

[30] *The Courtier*, p. 289.

[31] *Ibid.*, p. 295.

long for to arryue; and he forgets all former pains in confident anticipation of gaining there *eternall blisse*.

In Sonnet 64 the poet celebrates the joys of the lover who has reached the second rung of the Neo-Platonic Ladder. Having "arouse[d] his reason, and therewith arm[ed] the fortress of his heart, and so shut the way to sense and appetite that they cannot enter there by force or trickery,"[32] the poet finds his proud faire, who has previously scorned his importunings as *base things that to her loue too bold aspire*,[33] willing to permit him *to kisse her lyps*. An explanation of her willingness to grant him *such grace* can be found in *The Courtier*:

> And to the end that you may still better understand that rational love is happier than sensual, I say that the same things ought sometimes to be refused in sensual love and granted in rational love, because they are unseemly in the one and seemly in the other. Thus, to please her worthy lover [who has climbed up to the second rung of the Ladder], besides granting him pleasant smiles, familiar and secret discourse, and leave to joke and jest with her and to touch her hand, the lady may in reason even go so far as kissing without blame, which is not permitted in sensual love. . . . For since the kiss is the union of body and soul, there is danger lest the sensual lover incline more in the direction of the body than in that of the soul; while the rational lover perceives that although the mouth is part of the body, yet it gives issue to words, which are interpreters of the soul, and to that inward breath which is itself even called soul. Hence a man delights to join his mouth to that of his beloved in a kiss . . . because he feels that bond to be the opening of a passage between their souls.[34]

That his love is rational love, the poet demonstrates by proclaiming in Sonnet 64 that his appreciation of her beauty is as chaste as his appreciation of the beauty of flowers,[35] whose particular physical beauty Neo-Platonic doctrine would teach him to find in the higher manifestation of beauty embodied in the human form.

Sonnet 65 is often interpreted as the expectant bridegroom's reassurances to his fiancée, but the argument that *when loosing one, two liberties ye gayne, and make him bond that bondage earst dyd fly* takes on quite another significance when we note that the poet not only offers it immediately after he has been granted a kiss; he

---

[32]*Ibid.*, p. 295.

[33]Sonnet 61.

[34]P. 297.

[35]The Neo-Platonists recognized that beauty could be chastely enjoyed by means of senses other than sight, and the hierarchy of the senses was a subject of considerable interest to them. (Cf. R. V. Merrill, "Platonism in Pontus de Tyard's *Erreurs amoureuse* (1549); *MP*, xxxv, 2 (Nov., 1937), p. 144, n. 8, and the references cited there.) As hearing and smell can operate at a distance from their objects, they were differentiated from taste and touch, which were commonly admitted to be means of chaste enjoyment only under such specified conditions as those quoted above in the text.

also plays upon the word *bond* and the relationship of *one* and *two* precisely as does Bembo in asserting that the lover climbing the Ladder

delights to join his mouth to that of his beloved in a kiss, not in order to arouse any unseemly desire in him, but because he feels that bond to be the opening of a passage between their souls, which, being each drawn by desire for the other, pour themselves each into the other's body by turn, and so commingle that each has two souls, and a single soul (thus composed of these two) rules as it were over two bodies.36

Moreover, such a lover, as Bembo assures us, "will do no injury to the *husband*,37 father, brothers, or kinsfolk of his beloved lady,"38 for his desire is neither for illicit favors nor for a wife. He loves in his lady "not less the beauty of mind than that of body,"39 and while on the second rung of the Ladder he seeks

by admonition and good advice . . . to lead her on to modesty, to temperance, to true chastity, and [to] see to it that no thoughts find place in her except those that are pure and free from every stain of vice; and by thus sowing virtue in the garden of her fair mind, he will gather fruits of fairest behaviour too, and will taste them with wonderful delight. And this will be the true engendering and manifesting of beauty in beauty, which . . . is said to be the end of love.40

In Sonnet 65, therefore, the rational lover can assure his doubtful *fayre loue* that in *the league twixt them . . . fayth doth fearlesse dwell in brasen towre, And spotlesse pleasure builds her sacred bowre.*

In Sonnet 66 the poet—having become conscious that his beloved's beauty is a "heavenly beam"—41 protests his own unworthiness in a manner which demonstrates that in his progression up the Ladder he has reached that state in which "the soul [in the presence of the beloved's beauty] delights, and trembles with awe and yet rejoices, and as in a stupor feels not only pleasure, but that fear and reverence which we are wont to have for sacred things, and speaks of being in paradise."42 The conclusion of the sonnet—

> For now your light doth more it selfe dilate,
> and in my darknesse greater doth appeare.
> Yet since your light hath once enlumind me,
> with my reflex yours shall encreased be.

36*The Courtier*, p. 297.
37Italics mine.
38*The Courtier*, p. 299.
39*Ibid.*, p. 295.
40*Ibid.*, pp. 295-296.
41 *Ibid.*, p. 295.
42 *Ibid.*, p. 298.

—continues the Neo-Platonic interpretation, for as Bembo explains,

The influence of her beauty gives the lover wonderful delight when she is present, and by warming his heart weakens and melts certain dormant and frozen forces in his soul, which (being nourished by the warmth of love) spread and blossom about his heart, and send forth through the eyes those spirits that are very subtle vapours made of the purest and brightest part of the blood, which receive the image of her beauty and fashion it with a thousand various ornaments.[43]

When he has fashioned the image of her beauty with a thousand various ornaments and succeeded in fixing that idealized image in his mind, he will have attained the third rung of the Ladder.

In Sonnet 67 the poet compares his experience to that of the weary huntsman in order to reiterate that "rational love is happier than sensual."[44] He develops the comparison to assert that not until he had spent the violence of his sensual love in long, unsuccessful pursuit of the *gentle deare* could he get close to the object of his desire. But once he had put on the *mylder looke*[45] of rational love, the *gentle deare* immediately permitted him to approach *and with her owne goodwill hir fyrmely tyde*.

In Sonnet 68 ("the Easter Sonnet") the poet proclaims his appreciation of the divine origin of love, as exemplified by Christ's sacrifice for man, and prays that he and his *deare* shall be able to heed the lesson Christ taught and love *lyke as we ought*—spiritually.

In Sonnet 69 the lover proclaims that his verse shall be the *immortall moniment* of his *loues conquest, peerelesse beauties prise, adorn'd with honour, loue, and chastity*. If we appreciate that his verse constitutes an immaterial "image" of his beloved's beauty, we are able to comprehend how consistent is this ancient conceit of immortality in verse with Neo-Platonic thought and to understand why it was used so frequently by Neo-Platonic poets.

Sonnet 70, on the surface a conventional Valentine's Day or May Day sonnet, can also be interpreted as an expression of the lover who would progress upward from the second to the third rung of the Ladder. In discussing Sonnet 66 we noticed a part of Bembo's warning,

It is very dangerous to stop . . . [on the second rung]. . . . Even if no other evil flowed therefrom, absence from the beloved object brings much suffering . . ., because the influence of her beauty . . . when she is present . . . by warming his heart weakens and melts certain dormant and frozen forces in

---

[43] *Ibid.*

[44] *Ibid.*, p. 297.

[45] "With mylder looke" in the phrase "There she, beholding me with mylder looke" almost certainly modifies *me*.

his soul, which (being nourished by the warmth of love) spread and blossom about his heart.[46]

He who would love wisely, therefore, and

escape the torment of this absence and . . . enjoy beauty without suffering . . . need[s] . . . with the aid of reason, wholly [to] turn his desire from the body to the beauty alone, and contemplate it in itself simple and pure, as far as he can, and fashion it in his imagination apart from all matter; and thus make it lovely and dear to his soul, and enjoy it there, and have it with him day and night, in every time and place.[47]

The sonnet, therefore, can be interpreted thus: Only he who so arouses his love from *where she is carelesse layd, yet in her winters bowre, not well awake* in order *to wait* with her *on loue amongst his louely crew* in the manner prescribed by reason shall escape the *penance dew* which sensual love exacts—penance, in Bembo's words, "such as jealousies, suspicions, disdainings, angers, despairings, and certain furies full of madness whereby they are often led into such error that some of them not only beat the women whom they love, but deprive themselves of life."[48]

In Sonnet 71 the poet repeats the assurances he offered to his beloved in Sonnet 65. He uses the conceit of the Spyder and the Bee to explain again that *as your worke is wouen all aboue,* so the origin is heavenly of the love *in whose streight bands ye now captiue are so firmely, that ye neuer may remoue.*

In Sonnet 72 the rungs of the Ladder are unmistakable. The poet, having from Sonnet 60 raised himself steadily from rung to rung, in the first quatrain confesses:

> *Oft when my spirit doth spred her bolder winges,*
> *In mind to mount vp to the purest sky:*
> *it down is weighd with thoght of earthly things,*
> *and clogd with burden of mortality.*

In other words, at such times as reason enables him to rise from the third to the fourth rung and, while he rests on this elevation, urges him to reach mentally[49] up towards the fifth rung, he feels his spirit *weighd with thoght of earthly things,* for as Bembo warns,

This stage of love, although it be very noble and such as few attain, still cannot be called perfect; for since the imagination is merely a corporeal faculty and has no perception except through those means that are furnished it by the senses, it is not wholly purged of material darkness; and hence, although

---

[46]*The Courtier,* p. 298.

[47]*Ibid.,* p. 299.

[48]*Ibid.*

[49]Notice that the phrase *In mind* (line 2) has the double meaning of *intending* and *mentally.*

it considers this universal beauty in the abstract and intrinsically, yet it does not discern that beauty very clearly or without some ambiguity, because of the likeness which phantoms bear to substance. Thus those who attain this love are like tender birds beginning to put on feathers, which, although with their frail wings they lift themselves a little in flight, yet dare not go far from their nest or trust themselves to the winds and open sky.[50]

Too closely to be mere coincidence does the sonnet reproduce the meaning and the imagery of Bembo's warning as the poet confesses his inability to purge his *fraile fancy* wholly of material darkness.[51]

In Sonnet 73, moreover, the poet continues to make use of the figure of the "tender birds." He explains that his *hart, whom none with seruile bands can tye*, is as yet like a tender bird which, although with frail wings it lifts itself a little in flight, yet dares not go far from its nest or trust itself to the winds and open sky. He asks, therefore, that the beloved permit him to return to lodge again where he can feed his heart on the direct sight of her beauty; for by so doing *perhaps he there may learne . . . to sing your name and prayses ouer all*, and by implication, thus gain strength to sustain a flight in the open sky.

Having in Sonnets 72 and 73 slipped back down to the second rung of the Ladder to contemplate again the particular physical beauty of his beloved, the poet in Sonnet 74 fixes his mind on the image of beauty represented by the letters spelling Elizabeth—an image which embodies the beauty of two other kinds as well as the beauty of her *by whom my spirit out of dust was raysed*. In other words, he pulls himself up onto the third rung again.

In Sonnet 75 the poet further develops the conceit of alphabetical letters by combining it with the conceit of immortality in verse. The particular physical letters, he admits, are always washed away, but his act of embodying the abstract image of his beloved's beauty in verse *shall eternize* that beauty as well as the beauty of their spiritual love.

In Sonnet 76 the poet demonstrates that "always contemplating beauty in the body often perverts sound judgment,"[52] even if the contemplator's eyes have been instructed by reason to look upon a *Fayre bosome* as *the sacred harbour of that heuenly spright*. He acknowledges that *whiles diuing deepe through amorous insight,*

---

[50] *The Courtier*, p. 300.

[51] The often cited similarity of this sonnet to Tasso's *L'alma vaga di luce,* which Tasso himself annotated to point out its Neo-Platonic significance (*Le rime di T. Tasso*, Angelo Solerti, ed. [Bologna, 1898], II, 98), argues for, rather than against, the present interpretation.

[52] *The Courtier*, p. 298.

he feels himself so *rauisht* by the physical attractiveness of her breasts that his sound judgment becomes perverted, and his *frayle thoughts, too rashly led astray,* sprout *wanton winges.* In other words, he slips back down the Ladder to the first rung again.

The evidence of relationship produced by the foregoing comparison of these seventeen sonnets with Bembo's exposition of the Ladder in *The Courtier* is not, of course, conclusive. Nor does a similar comparison of the entire sequence, which space does not permit including here, do more than increase the quantity of the evidence. Nevertheless, if we remember that even the Neo-Platonist who attained the seventh rung of the Ladder, being human, could remain there only briefly before returning to earth again,[53] we shall find in the *Amoretti* no obstacle to prevent interpreting the sequence as a study of a lover's attempt to climb the Neo-Platonic Ladder— as a study of the lover who in his struggle to attain spiritual love succeeds now and again in raising himself up to rung three or four, only to be drawn back each time to a lower rung by physical love.

That the *Amoretti* can be so interpreted supports the other evidence we have found to demonstrate that the reflections of the Neo-Platonic interpretation of love are more frequent and clearer in Spenser's sonnets than has been generally realized. Moreover, as great differences of opinion continue to exist among scholars concerning the *Amoretti*, the consistency of this evidence has encouraged me to suggest the possibility that Spenser may have had the Ladder in mind as he organized his sequence.

To formulate an hypothesis for use as a basis for further investigation, let us assume, as do many scholars, that when Spenser undertook to publish a sonnet sequence he had already written a number of sonnets for other purposes. Our hypothesis can then become: to produce the *Amoretti* Spenser selected from the sonnets he had previously written those which he found could be used for his present purpose, ordered them as best he could, and then wrote such additional ones as were necessary to make the sequence a consistent study of the lover climbing the Neo-Platonic Ladder.[54]

---

[53] See the quotation from Plotinus above, p. 96.

[54] To test this hypothesis thoroughly, as well as to find evidence of whether or not Spenser was being original if he so organized a sonnet sequence, it is necessary to reëxamine the relationship of Neo-Platonism and Petrarchism and to investigate the extent to which Neo-Platonic thought influenced other Renaissance sonnet sequences. Such a study Professor A. T. MacAllister of the Department of Romance Languages, Princeton University, and I are undertaking.

GREENE'S PANTHER

By John Leon Lievsay
Stanford University

A recent article by Don Cameron Allen[1] adduces a staggering
amount of evidence to indicate that the details of Robert Greene's
euphuistic "science," except when he dealt with astrology, derived
largely from his own fertile imagination rather than from the
traditional or assigned sources. In thus demonstrating that
Greene's acquaintance with classical and contemporary authorities
was considerably slighter than the pretensions of one who styled
himself *utriusque Academiae in Artibus Magister* might lead the
unsuspecting to believe, Mr. Allen has performed a service which
merits our thanks. Many another Elizabethan reputation is in
need of just such deflation. Mr. Allen's article, however, is slightly
marred by one lacuna which I find difficult to justify: namely,
the omission of any reference to the panther. Since this remarkable beast is mentioned at least twenty-three times in Greene's
prose[2]—a greater number of references than Mr. Allen lists for
any other single stone, bird, fish, animal, reptile, insect, tree, or
herb in his long catalogue[3]—there would seem to be some warrant
for here examining Greene's treatment of so obvious a favorite.
What characteristics, in brief, does Greene attribute to the panther
and to what degree are they conventional, to what degree invented?

The panther, we read, has a sweet breath[4] and a "beautifull hide"

---

[1] "Science and Invention in Greene's Prose," *PMLA*, LIII (December, 1938),
1007-1018.

[2] *Works*, ed. A. B. Grosart (London, 1881-86), II, 20, 44, 51, 60, 232, 255,
279; III, 239; IV, 82, 115; VI, 174; VIII, 67, 138, 142; IX, 74, 129, 138, 190,
207; XI, 23, 41-42, 203, 206.

[3] *Op. cit.*, pp. 1011-1013.

[4] *Works*, II, 44, 51, 279; VI, 174. How he "got that way" is explained by
John Swan in his *Speculum Mundi, or a Glasse representing the Face of the
World* (1635): "Now the reason why these beasts have such a sweet breath
is in regard that they are so much delighted with the kinde of spices and
daintie aromaticall trees; insomuch that (as some affirm) they will go many
hundred miles in time of the yeare when these things are in season, and all
for the love they bear to them. But above all, their chief delight is in the
gumme of camphire, watching that tree very carefully, to the end that they
may preserve it for their owne use." Quoted from E. F. Hulme, *Natural
History Lore and Legend* (London, 1895), p. 152.

or "painted skinne";[5] is "rauenous" and a "murtherer," a creature with a "tyrannous heart" and a "beastly paunch";[6] is the very type of a deceiving flatterer, covering an iniquitous inside with a fair outward show.[7] Not only does he symbolize, through the unchangeable nature of his spots, a brutish perseverance in evil,[8] but "the longer he liues the more spots hee hath in his skinne."[9] He is an enemy to the ounce,[10] whose company he "escheweth" and "cannot abide," but he exerts a special charm upon the ermly[11] and the leopard.[12] Moreover, "the Panther hauing the fairest skinne hath the most infectious [i.e., alluring, and therefore destructive] breath."[13] And, as with the enchantress of old Nile, age cannot wither, nor custom stale, for "the aged Panther [hath] the purest breath."[14] Most remarkable of all, perhaps, is the fatal attraction of the panther's pleasant breath (or handsome skin: Greene says both) for other creatures, his means of luring them to their destruction.[15]

Such is the panther as he appears in the prose of Robert Greene—a mixture, one sees, of tradition and invention. Examination of the apparently invented elements,[16] not in themselves particularly astonishing, reveals that in frequency of occurrence they are four or five times outnumbered by the traditional elements. The only invented element to be repeated, and that but once, is the enmity between the panther and the ounce. Here, then, is at least one important, though scarcely invalidating, exception to the hypothesis advanced by Mr. Allen. Since nothing seems likely to be gained

[5] *Works*, II, 44, 51, 255; IX, 129; XI, 203.

[6] *Ibid.*, II, 20, 51, 232, 255; IX, 207; XI, 203.

[7] *Ibid.*, II, 20, 232; VIII, 138.

[8] *Ibid.*, VIII, 142. Cf. Emma Phipson, *The Animal-Lore of Shakspeare's Time* (London, 1883), p. 22; Thomas Nashe, *Works*, ed. R. B. McKerrow (London, 1904-8), II, 52 and McKerrow's note, *ibid.*, IV, 219.

[9] *Works*, XI, 206.

[10] *Ibid.*, IV, 115; XI, 41-42.

[11] *Ibid.*, VIII, 67.

[12] *Ibid.*, IV, 82; XI, 23. Allen, *op. cit.*, p. 1012n, under the invented attributes of the leopard, erroneously assigns this last reference to XII, 23. Greene, it should be noted, was not always either consistent or clear in his distinctions between the leopard and the panther; but then neither were other early writers. Cf. Phipson, *op. cit.*, p. 22.

[13] *Works*, VI, 174.

[14] *Ibid.*, II, 279.

[15] *Ibid.*, II, 60; III, 239; IV, 82; IX, 74, 190; XI, 23.

[16] Enmity to the ounce; attraction of the ermly; the fairer skin, the sweeter breath; purifying of breath with age.

from any attempt to assign Greene's traditional material to individual sources,[17] we may now consider certain interesting special
circumstances in his treatment of panther-lore. Before doing so,
however, I should like to pose an objection to one suggested source.

This is Lauchert's suggestion that Greene, along with other
euphuists, drew upon the *Physiologus* for his information regarding the panther.[18] For several reasons this seems to me improbable.
First, among the various references to the panther in euphuistic
works, Lauchert cites six from Greene.[19] Yet of the six or seven
attributes of the panther mentioned in the *Physiologus*,[20] Greene
employs but two: the sweetness of his breath and the attractiveness of his skin, neither of which, surely, could be called distinctive.
Second, whereas Greene apparently invents an antipathy between
the panther and the ounce, he remains silent about the much more
striking enmity already specified by the *Physiologus*, namely, that
between the panther and the dragon.[21] Third, the *Physiologus*
depicts the panther as quiet and gentle; Greene characteristically
treats him as rapacious, tyrannous, murderous. Fourth, Greene
entirely disregards the Christian symbolism of the panther as a
type of Christ, the basis of the treatment accorded the animal in
the *Physiologus*. To see the "influence" of the *Physiologus* in such
a faint reflection seems to me as ridiculous as this other explanation
of Lauchert's in reference to Lyly's phrase "a sweet panther":[22]
"Dieses epitheton 'sweet' kann *nur aus dem Physiologus* verstanden

---

[17]The facts that the two parts of *Mamillia*, Greene's earliest prose work,
contain more references to the panther than does any other of his works and
that virtually identical phrasings of the same common-places occur in Lyly's
Euphues may be taken to indicate that work as a *likely* source. *Mamillia*
shows other borrowings from Lyly; cf. Allen, *op. cit.*, p. 1008, note 10. Much
of the most striking panther-lore (largely, though not entirely, from Pliny)
is drawn together in *A Greene Forest* (1567), by John Maplet, who signed himself, like Greene, "M. of Arte and student in Cambridge"; see the reprint,
ed. W. H. Davies (London, Hesperides Press, 1930), p. 162. No doubt Greene
was also familiar with the vast body of emblem literature afloat in his day.
In such a book as Geoffrey Whitney's *A Choice of Emblemes and Other Devises*
(Leyden, 1586) he could have found much of his traditional lore.

[18]Friedrich Lauchert, "Der einfluss des Physiologus auf den euphuismus,"
Englische Studien, XIV (1890), 188-210.

[19]*Ibid.*, p. 197.

[20]*Physiologus*, tr. James Carlill (London, n.d.: Broadway Translations),
p. 190.

[21]Cf. Bartholomaeus Anglicus on the enmity between the panther and the
dragon; *Medieval Lore* (selections from Trevisa's tr. of the *De Proprietatibus
Rerum*, ed. Berthelet, London, 1535), ed. Robert Steele (London, 1893), p. 135.

[22]*Euphues*, ed. Croll and Clemons (London, 1916), p. 36.

werden, wo wir lesen, dass der panther durch die süssigkeit seines athems alle anderen thiere an sich ziehe. . . .''[23]

To resume. The peculiarities of Greene's panther-lore—they can hardly be called innovations—lie not so much in what he says or implies as in the manner of application and in his choice of details for repetition. He is particularly fond, for example, of comparing the lure of the panther's "painted skinne" with the wiles of meretricious "syrens": "Oh *Gwydonius*, hast thou not heard . . . that the Leopard looking at the Panthers painted skinne, is taken as a praie, and that hee which taketh too much delight to gaze vpon beautie, is oftentimes galled with grief and miserie";[24] "our curtizans of *Troynouant* . . . haue in their eyes adamants that wil drawe youth as the Iet the strawe, or as the sight of the Panther the Ermly";[25] "Oh *Francesco* she hides her clawes, but lookes for her pray with the Tyger, she weepes with the Crocodile, and smiles with the Hiena, and flatters with the Panther, and vnder the couert of a sugred baite, shrowdes the intent of thy bane";[26] "For women, my sonne, oh for them take heede: they bee Adamants that drawe, Panthers that allure, and Syrens that intice.''[27] Similarly, varying the application slightly, he likes to use the panther to point a contrast (frequently the result of hypocritical feigning) between appearance and reality.[28] Again, not without propriety in one who alternated between extremes of prodigal revelry and queasy-conscienced repentance, he shows a partiality for figures juxtaposing the panther and the mouse: "But perhaps you wil cay, *Mamillia*, that the beasts which gase at ye Panther, are guilty of their own death; that the Mouse taken in the trap, deserueth her chaunce";[29]

---

[23]*Op. cit.*, pp. 196-7. Italics mine.

[24]*Greenes Carde of Fancie* (1587), *Works*, IV, 82. That Greene was more than commonly pleased with this figure appears from the fact that he repeats it word for word in *Orpharion* (1589 ?; ed. 1599), *Works*, XI, 23: "But as the fish Ramerà listning to the sound of the trumpet, is caught of the Fishers: as the Porcupine standeth staring at the glimmering of the Starres, and is ouertaken with dogges: *as the Leopard looking at the Panthers painted skinne, is caught as a pray: so he which taketh too much delight to gase vppon beautie, is oft times galled with greefe and misery.*" My italics.

[25]*Greenes Neuer too late* (1590), *Works*, VIII, 67.

[26]*Greenes Neuer too late*, Pt. II (1590), *Works*, VIII, 138.

[27]*Greenes Mourning Garment* (1590; ed. 1616), *Works*, IX, 138; again in virtually identical wording at p. 190, and with minor variations at p. 207.

[28]*Works*, II, 20, 51, 232, 255; VI, 174; IX, 203.

[29]*Ibid.*, II, 60; and, identically, IX, 74.

"But I perceiue as no time wil alter the Panther from his spots, the Mouse from hir feare, nor the Tyger frō his fiercenes; so,'' etc.[30]

There is nothing in Greene to suggest, as some earlier authors and some of his contemporaries insist, that the attractions of the panther's appearance and odor are exercised only upon quadrupeds and not at all upon man. Nashe, for instance, is clear as to this limitation: "But as the Panther smelleth sweetlie but onely to brute beastes, which shee draweth vnto her to theyr destruction, not to men, in like maner, so these men seeme learned to none but to Idiots. . . .''[31] One passage in Greene's *Arbasto, the Anatomie of Fortune* (1584), though doubtfully worded, seems in fact to indicate that he considers man no exception in the matter: "Ah cruell and accursed *Arbasto,* I see now that it fareth with thee as with the Panther, which hauing made one astonished with his faire sight, seeketh to deuoure him with bloudy pursute.''[32] With regard to the method of attraction, although he clearly recognizes the drawing power of both the panther's fair skin and his sweet breath, Greene most definitely and frequently attributes the panther's charm to his appearance.[33] Inasmuch as others of his contemporaries[34] make the same observation, this should probably be regarded not so much a departure from the traditional matter as a slightly unorthodox emphasis upon it.

The most curious circumstance in Greene's treatment of the panther, however, is that, being as patently obsessed with the lore of the beast as he was, he should have been content to repeat such relatively colorless items of the traditional repertory and to frame such tame inventions. Truly, as Mr. Allen remarks,[35] "Greene's innovations are by no means superior to the material that he could have found in the conventional encyclopediae.'' Consider, for example, how much more striking is the following passage written by his

---

[30] *Ibid.*, VIII, 142.

[31] *Works,* I, 21. McKerrow's note (*ibid.,* IV, 21) cites Erasmus' *Parabolae*: "Panthera bene olet, sed non nisi bestiis . . . hominibus non item.''

[32] *Works,* III, 239.

[33] *Ibid.,* II, 20, 60, 232, 255; III, 239; IV, 82; VIII, 67; IX, 74, 129, 190, 207; XI, 23, 203.

[34] Cf. Spenser, *Amoretti,* Sonnet LIII; Sir William Seger (quoted by Phipson, *op. cit.,* pp. 23-24, from Harleian MS 6085): "The panther is admired of all other beasts for the beauty of his skyn, being spotted with variable colours, and beloved and followed of them for the sweetness of his breath, that streameth forth of his nostrils and ears like smoke, which our paynters mistaking, corruptly doe make fire.''

[35] *Op. cit.,* p. 1012.

fellow Nashe in the prefatory epistle "To the Gentlemen Students of both Vniuersities" of Greene's own *Menaphon* (1589): "Wherein I can but resemble them to the Panther, who is so greedie of mens excrements; that if they be hangd vp in a vesseil higher than his reach, he sooner killeth himselfe with the ouer-stretching of his windlesse bodie, than he will cease from his intended enterprise."[36] Yet this is perfectly obvious material, at hand in the Aristotle[37] and Pliny[38] whom Greene allegedly follows, and repeated in other popular works derived from them.[39] It seems a shame, too, that Greene should have passed by without comment (if he knew it: Mr. Allen suspects that his familiarity lay more with the index than with the text of Pliny) the belief recorded by Pliny "that the panther has, on the shoulder, a spot which bears the form of the moon; and that, like it, it regularly increases to full, and then diminishes to a crescent."[40] With that as a clapper, how he might have rung the changes on the fickleness of women, of fortune, of what not! And your panther, Greene might have found without much expenditure of effort, is none of Falstaff's breed to entertain qualms at being disemboweled; for, says Pliny, "it will continue to fight long after its intestines have been dragged out of its body."[41] Aristotle also would have supplied him with the information—which could only have proved most edifying and useful—that the female of the species is more deadly than the male.[42]

I have already indicated that Greene passed over unheeded the Christian symbolism of the panther as represented in the *Physiologus*. The reason for this neglect is, I think, that he had no time for more than surface comparisons; that he was never deep in anything save wine—and debt. Nevertheless his tendency, convention-

---

[36]Greene, *Works*, VI, 14.

[37]*Historia Animalium* (*Works*, Oxford tr., IV, 1910), 612ᵃ.

[38]*The Natural History of Pliny*, tr. John Bostock and H. T. Riley (London, 1855-7), II (bk. viii, ch. 41), 293; V (bk. xxvii, ch. 2), 219.

[39]McKerrow's note on the passage (Nashe, *Works*, IV, 447) quoted above says that it was "probably taken by Nashe from the *Parabolae* of Erasmus (in Lycosthenes' *Apophthegmata*, 1574, p. 1229), 'Panthera sic auida est excrementorum hominis, ut si in vase suspendatur altius quam possit attingere, enecat sese defatigati porrectu corporis: ita nonnullis quod est foedissimum, id dulcissimum est.'" As a sort of *advocatus diaboli* I should perhaps point out here that neither Aristotle nor Pliny attributes this debased taste to the innate perversity of the panther; the animal resorts to such a diet only as an antidote for poisoning from panther's-bane (παρδαλιαγχές).

[40]*Op. cit.*, II (bk. viii, ch. 23), 274.

[41]*Nat. Hist.*, II (bk. viii, ch. 41), 293-4.

[42]*Op. cit.*, pp. 608ᵃ-608ᵇ.

al as it is, to treat the panther as a type of flatterer does show the beginnings of symbolism. It is therefore hard to see how, had he been familiar with it, he could have failed to turn to his own uses the following illustration at once of tender maternal solicitude and the quasi-mythical virtue of gratitude:

Demetrius, the natural philosopher, relates an equally remarkable instance, in relation to a panther. The animal was lying in the middle of the road, waiting for some one to pass that way, when he [!] was suddenly perceived by the father of one Philinus, an ardent lover of wisdom. Seized with fear, he immediately began to retreat; while the beast rolled itself before him, evidently with the desire of caressing him, at the same time manifesting signs of grief, which could not be misunderstood in a panther even. The animal had young ones, which had happened to fall into a pit at some distance from the place. The first dictates of compassion banished all fear, and the next prompted him to assist the animal. He accordingly followed her, as she gently drew him on by fixing her claws in his garment; and as soon as he discovered what was the cause of her grief and the price of his own safety, he took the whelps out of the pit, and they followed her to the end of the desert, frisking with joy and gladness, in order that she might more appropriately testify how grateful she was, and how little she had given him in return; a mode of acting which is but rarely found, among men even.[43]

But it is the omission of still another traditional trait which bears most telling witness to Greene's inattentive and lackadaisical handling of even the best-known conventional details. To the old authorities and to Greene's contemporaries alike[44] it was a commonplace observation that the panther, for all the attractions of his fair skin and pleasing odor, possesses a frightening countenance capable of striking terror into the heart of the beholder. To capture his prey, therefore, he resorts to the stratagem either of hiding himself completely and letting the scent of his body serve as a lure, or of hiding his head and trusting to the charm of his appearance to provide for his larder. Nashe makes a punning allusion to the second practice in his *Christs Teares ouer Ierusalem* (1593): "The inwarde Atheist is he that deuoures widowes houses vnder the pretence of long prayers, that (like the Panther) hideth his face in a hood of Religion, when he goeth about his pray."[45] In *The Vnfortunate Traveller* (1594) he phrases the idea more directly: "There were no sweete-breathing Panthers that would hyde their terrifying heads to betray. . . ."[46] Spenser, too, observes that

---

[43]Pliny, *op. cit.*, II (bk. viii, ch 21), 272-3; repeated in Primaudaye, *op. cit.*, p. 831.

[44]Aristotle, *Hist. Anim.*, p. 612ᵃ; Pliny, *Nat. Hist.*, II (bk. viii, ch. 23), 274; Bartholomaeus Anglicus, *De Prop. Rerum*, p. 135. Maplet, *op. cit.*, p. 162, follows Pliny.

[45]*Works*, II, 117.

[46]*Ibid.*, p. 284.

> The panther, knowing that his spotted hyde
> Doth please all beast, but that his looks them fray,
> Within a bush his dreadful head doth hide,
> To let them gaze while he on them may prey.[47]

One further expression of the same idea may be cited for its quaint language and moralizing application, the latter being in the very key of Greene:

It is reported that all beasts are wonderfully delighted with the sent of the breath of the panther, a beast fierce and cruell by nature, but that they are else affrighted with the sternesse of his lookes: for which cause the panther, when he hunts his prey, hiding his grimme visage, with the sweetness of his breath allures the other beastes vnto him, who, being come within his reach, hee rends and cruelly doth dilaniate them. Even so, those patrons and *minions of false pleasures, the flatterers,* that they may prey vpon the credulitie of the abused GREAT ONES, imitate the panthers, extenuating, and, as much as in them lyes, hiding the grossnesse, the vglinesse, the deformitie of those follyes they perswade vnto; and with a false glosse varnishing and setting out the paradise of vncontrolled pleasures, to the ruine, oftimes, of the informed, and glorie of their owne pietie.[48]

No one less haphazard than Robert Greene would have overlooked a feature so essential to the lore of the panther and at the same time so pat to his purpose. In his faulty presentation of even so congenial a matter as panther-lore, Greene is merely paying once again the inevitable price of his hack work.

---

[47] *Amoretti,* Sonnet LIII.

[48] John Ford, *Linea Vitae: A Line of Life,* Shakespeare Soc. xix (London, 1843), pp. 58-9.

BACKGROUNDS FOR MARLOWE'S ATHEIST LECTURE

By Paul H. Kocher
Folger Shakespeare Library

The day has passed when it was necessary to doubt that Marlowe made the anti-Christian declarations ascribed to him by Richard Baines in a memorandum submitted to the Privy Council shortly before the dramatist's death. Agreement is now widespread that Marlowe did make them substantially as charged. It is time, therefore, to become very inquisitive about the meaning of his statements, especially in their connection with the religious controversies of his own and earlier periods. In spite of the impossibility of exhausting so huge a subject, I hope to make it clear that the Marlowe of the Baines note, far from being a mere jester at religion, was a serious thinker who had for his views both ancient precedent and contemporary parallel; furthermore, that his utterances represent a carefully designed attack on Christian dogma, often with very dexterous use of the language of Scripture itself. Greatly daring, brilliantly sardonic, and fortified with Scriptural learning, he was an heir of all the ages of protest against Christianity and a voice for the inarticulate and nameless of his own day.

As I have argued elsewhere,[1] the statements set down by Baines fall readily into some four groups so naturally consecutive in thought that they seem to have been spoken during a single conversation. Moreover, there is reason to believe that they reflect the substance and method of one of Marlowe's tracts against Christianity, which he was never able to publish. The discussion begins with an attack on the date given by the Old Testament for the creation of Adam, obviously intended to discredit the whole Mosaic cosmogony and everything dependent on it. Then comes a denunciation of Moses himself as an impostor attaining selfish power by means of juggling tricks. If that were true, the Law transmitted by Moses would also be false, and deep foundations of Christianity would be swept away. The logical next step is to abolish Christ.

---

[1] "Marlowe's Atheist Lecture," *JEGP*, xxxix (Jan. 1940), 98-106. With some slight modifications, the present paper takes up the items of the Baines note in the order there suggested, and carries farther towards proof the theories of its predecessor.

Accordingly, Jesus is interpreted as a trickster and criminal who deserved crucifixion. For apostles he was able to enlist, Marlowe says, only men base, cowardly, and subject to his vilest desires, men whose ignorance of all culture is evident in their abominable writing in the New Testament. Neither he nor they knew anything about the technique of establishing a religion.

From this rough paraphrase of the Baines note it seems evident that Marlowe's argument against Scripture was quite the opposite of random. It was drawn up chronologically and directed against the central elements of faith. A closer analysis of the individual parts of it will likewise reveal much learning and care, as well as incidental mockery.

The first charge is, "That the Indians and many Authors of antiquity haue assuredly writen of aboue 16 thousand yeares agone whereas Adam is proued to haue lived within 6 thowsand yeares."[2] It is usual to say that Marlowe got this idea from Harriot, who has left notes on the chronology of Genesis.[3] Perhaps he did. We should be a little wary of this conclusion, however, because calculation of Old Testament chronology was a favorite occupation of the sixteenth century. Placing creation of the world variously between 5505 B.C. and 3759 B.C., all orthodox computations were based solely on Biblical texts.[4] Nevertheless, many of them found it hard to ignore and even harder to reconcile the very different accounts given by Greek, Egyptian, Babylonian and other ancient historians. Philip de Mornay's way of disposing of the Chaldee records is characteristic:

> . . . they make their vaunt that they haue the natiuities of Childred noted & set downe in writing . . . for aboue the space of three and fortie thousand yeres afore the reigne of the great Alexander. And that is true. But . . . when they speake after their Schoolemaner, they meane alwaies (as witnesseth Diodorus) the moneth yeere, that is to say, euery moneth to be a yeere.[5]

---

[2] All references to the Baines note are to the text reprinted by C. F. Tucker Brooke, *The Life of Marlowe* (London: Methuen & Co., 1930), pp. 98-100.

[3] Harriot's notes have never been published, and no descriptions of them have been available to indicate whether or not his calculations were unorthodox, and, if so, to what extent. One notices that Marlowe bases his objection on the authority of the ancients, not on science or mathematics.

[4] See M. Hanmer, *A Chronographie*, London, 1585 p. 554; Iohn More, *A Table From the Beginning of the world to this day*, Cambridge, 1593; and many others.

[5] *The Trewnesse of the Christian Religion*, translated by Sidney and Golding, London, 1587, chap. viii, p. 115. This work, over six hundred pages long, contained one of the finest compilations of anti-Christian arguments ever assembled during the Renaissance, each accompanied by Mornay's reply. See

This is a very convenient method. Raleigh, therein markedly differing from Marlowe, likewise applied it in his *History of the World* to Egyptian traditions said to be 13,000 years old.[6] Clearly, the possibility that the world might be older than Scripture permitted was something to be reckoned with. In one form, the idea was even imputed to the Family of Love by John Rogers, who said, "They holde, that there was a worlde before Adams time, as there is now."[7] In fact, the issue had a long history and was probably as old as the Church itself. It was debated for the Christians as early as c.170 A.D. by Theophilus of Antioch.[8] And the amount of pagan authority which had to be denied or explained away was very great. For example, Egyptian history was said by Herodotus to go back more than 17,000 years, by Diodorus Siculus 23,000 years, by Pomponius Mela above 13,000, by Plato 8,000, by Diogenes Laertius 48,000.[9] Babylonian claims of an antiquity of over 400,000 years were reported by Alexander Polyhistor and Abydenus, but ridiculed by Cicero.[10] A Persian civilization 6,000 years before the fall of Troy is mentioned by Diogenes Laertius.[11] Finally, Aristotle and many other philosophers held that the world had always existed. Marlowe, therefore, had good reason to say that "many Authors of antiquity" opposed the Christian chronology. He chose a limit of 16,000 years apparently because sixteen contrasted to six made a good rhetorical jingle, and because the figure was con-

---

similarly, Calvin, *The Institution of Christian Religion*, trans. T. Norton, London, 1578 (hereafter cited simply as Calvin), Lib. I, chap. 8, fol. 20r; N. Gibbens, *Questions and Disputations Concerning the Holy Scripture*, London, 1601, chap. 2, p. 56.

[6] (Oxford University Press, 1829) Bk. I, chap. viii, sec. xi, p. 298. Lodowick Lloyd's *Consent of Time*, London, 1590, p. 142, also refers to the 13,000 years of Egyptian antiquity and explains them in the same way.

[7] *Displaying of . . . the Familie of Loue*, London, 1578, sig. K2r.

[8] *Theophilus to Autolycus* in Ante-Nicene Christian Library, Vol. III, Bk. III, chap. xvi, p. 120. Here Apollonius the Egyptian is quoted as declaring the world to be 153,075 years old. Our question was usually merged into the question whether the books of Moses were the oldest writings of mankind. On this point the Church fathers were vehement. Each nation contended that its own records were oldest and therefore most reliable.

[9] Herodotus (Loeb Library) Bk. II, 43, p. 329; Diodorus Siculus (Loeb) Bk. I, 44, p. 157, also pp. 73, 77, 83; Pomponius Mela, *The Situation of the World*, trans. A. Golding, London, 1590, p. 19; Plato *Timaeus* (Loeb) p. 37; Diogenes Laertius (Loeb) Bk. I, Prologue.

[10] Extracts from Alexander Polyhistor and Abydenus are given by I. P. Cory, *Ancient Fragments* (London: Wm. Pickering, 1832) pp. 21, 26, 32, 33. Cicero *De Divinatione* (Loeb) Bk. I, xix, 37.

[11] Bk. I, Prologue.

servative. But why he specified Indian writers is not so easy to discover. Most of the accessible references to Indian antiquities were vague. Strabo and Diodorus Siculus, for instance, wrote descriptions implying great age for the Indian nation but risked no particular dates whatever. The most definite figures I have seen appear in Arrian's *Indica*[12] and in the *Polyhistor* of Julius Solinus,[13] where events in India considerably more than 6,000 years before the conquest by Alexander the Great were narrated.

In the succeeding portion of the Baines note, Marlowe shifts his attack from the Mosaic cosmogony to Moses himself, saying "that Moyses was but a Jugler & that one Heriots being Sir W Raleighs man Can do more then he." This type of argument was giving some concern to Renaissance divines, as can be seen in Calvin's *The Institution of Christian Religion*:

> But because the matter was plainlier knowen, than that the prophane coulde deny that miracles were done by Moses: the father of lyeng hath ministred them an other cauillation, saying that they were done by Magicall artes and sorcerie . . . Truely no such deceiuer useth his iugglinge castes, but that he studieth to amase the mindes of the people to get himselfe a fame. But what doth Moses? . . . he crieth out, that himselfe and his brother Aaron are nothing, but doth onely execute those things that God hath appointed . . . how oft did sometime the people prowdely and impudently make insurrections . . . how could he haue begyled their furor with illusions?[14]

The questions troubling Calvin had been raised long ago in various quarters hostile to Jew and Christian. Of those classical writers who were aware of the existence of Moses, a few, like Strabo, gave him a favorable character, as a man of superior intelligence and leadership, but the majority considered him an evil worker in magic.[15] Flavius Josephus, the first-century Jewish historian so often cited by the Elizabethans, thus rebukes certain of the Greeks: "Apolonius Molon, and Lysimachus, and certaine others, partly for ignorance, partly for madnesse, haue most iniuriously belied our lawmaker Moses, and the lawes he made, detracting him as a deceit-

---

[12](Loeb) Bk. VIII, 9, p. 333. Marlowe can scarcely be thinking of the Indians of America, whose sparse records were generally acknowledged to be of recent date.

[13]Trans. A. Golding, London, 1587, sig. Dd2v. L. Thorndike, *A History of Magic and Experimental Science* (N. Y., 1923) II, 898, says that Petrus de Abano's *Conciliator* lists "various estimates of the number of years since creation . . . up to the enormous figure of 1,474,346,290 years given by the Indians and Persians".

[14]Lib. I, chap. 8, fol. 21r.

[15]Strabo, *Geography* (Loeb) 16.2.35-6; and *contra*, Apuleius, *Apologia* (London: Bell & Sons, 1888) p. 336, and Justin, *Philippine History*, cited in Cory, *Ancient Fragments*, edition of 1876, p. 80.

full Magician, and then as the author of all malice and impietie amongst us.''[16]   A century later, Celsus struck at Christianity through Judaism with the same charge: ''Those herdsmen and shepherds who followed Moses as their leader, had their minds deluded by vulgar deceits'' and ''they worship angels and are addicted to sorcery, in which Moses was their instructor. . . .''[17] There can be no doubt that others in the sixteenth century besides Calvin knew of these pagan blasphemies, for we find Henry Smith, in *Gods Arrow Against Atheists*, denying at some length the views of Porphyry and Apion that the miracles of Moses ''were done by Art Magicke, and not by the power of God,''[18] and Mornay admitting that ''some Authors haue attributed those myracles to Magicke, and othersome to naturall reasons.''[19]

Nevertheless, one distinction must be made. Some of these opponents of Moses seem to ascribe to him real magical powers. Marlowe's rationalism forbids him to do so. His idea is, rather, that Moses, although an ignoramus by comparison with Harriot, knew enough science to produce optical illusions and other phenomena useful to his ambitions. Quite similarly, Marlowe once said in the hearing of Kyd that ''things esteemed to be donn by devine power might haue aswell been don by observation of men.''[20] The latter phrase seems to mean the observation, by men, of the laws of nature

[16]*Against Apion*, in *Works*, Trans. T. Lodge, London, 1602, Bk. II, p. 790.

[17]*A True Discourse* (c. 180 A.D.) by Celsus the Greek Platonist was one of the most profound, eloquent, and uncompromising attacks delivered against Christianity by the paganism of the ancient world. Although the original work was destroyed by Church censorship, large fragments of it were preserved in Origen's refutation, *Against Celsus* (c. 250), which was known to the Renaissance in both Greek and Latin versions. The quotations given in the text above are from Origen's refutation as translated into English in the Ante-Nicene Christian Library, ed. A. Roberts, Edinburgh, 1869 (hereafter cited simply as Origen), Bk. I, chaps. xxiii and xxvi. Origen likewise notes that a heavy assault upon Moses came from Egyptian writers, who alleged that his miracles ''were wrought by sorcery, and not by divine power,'' Bk. III, chap. v, p. 89. The underlying design of Celsus in derogating Moses is thus analyzed by Origen: Celsus ''thinks that he will be able the more easily to establish the falsity of Christianity, if, by assailing its origin in Judaism, he can show that the latter also is untrue'' (Bk. I, chap. xxii, p. 419). It is interesting to see Marlowe pursuing the same scheme. Marlowe may or may not have read Origen directly, but it is safe to say that Origen, as an influential forefather of controversy, helped to determine the nature of both the attack and the defence in Elizabethan theological dispute and in that way inevitably had some indirect effect on Marlowe.

[18]London, 1604, p. 42; first published in 1593.

[19]*Op. cit.*, chap. xxvi, p. 467.

[20]Tucker Brooke, *op. cit.*, p. 107.

and application of such knowledge to effect consequences hitherto unknown.

But to return to the Baines paper. Marlowe supports his assertion that Moses was a juggler by two quotations from Scripture and a generalization of his own, as follows:

> That it was an easy matter for Moyses being brought up in all the artes of the Egiptians to abuse the Jewes being a rude & grosse people.
>
> That Moyses made the Jewes to travell xl yeares in the wildernes, (which Jorney might haue bin done in less then one yeare) ere they Came to the promised land to thintent that those who were privy to most of his subtilties might perish and so an everlasting superstition Remain in the hartes of the people.
>
> That the first beginning of Religioun was only to keep men in awe.

The first of these is based on *Acts* 7:21 and 22. I give the Geneva version: "And whē he was cast out, Pharos daughter took him up, & nourished him for her owne sonne. And Moses was learned in all the wisedome of the Egiptians, and was mightie in wordes and in deedes." Now the change from the Bible's "all the wisedome of the Egiptians"[21] to Marlowe's "all the artes of the Egiptians" may be only an accident, a slip in the reporting by Baines, but to the Renaissance mind it would embody all the difference between legitimate learning and the magical arts for which Egypt had long been notorious.[22] The substitution fits in with Marlowe's whole argument so neatly and is so typical of his deft irony that I cannot think it came from anyone but the dramatist. He says, in effect, "Of course Moses was a juggler. Your own Bible says that he learned everything the Egyptians could teach him, and you know what arts of illusion they were famous for. The Jews, poor devils of slaves and herdsmen, had no chance with him." This emphasis on the lack of education among the Jews was frequent enough in

---

[21]The Bishops Bible has "al manner of wysedome of the Egyptians"; the Vulgate, "omni sapientia Aegyptiorum"; and the King James, "all the wise-dome of the Egyptians."

[22]Elizabethans would be likely to think immediately of Pharaoh's magicians in *Exodus*. Celsus several times likens the miracles of Jesus to "the feats performed by those who have been taught by Egyptians" (Bk. I, chap. lxviii, p. 475); and Origen says that this very text in *Acts* 7: 22 does not mean that Moses acquired black lore in Egypt: "And in the Acts of the Apostles Stephen bears witness to the great learning of Moses ... For he says: 'And Moses was learned in all the wisdom of the Egyptians.' And therefore with respect to his miracles, it was suspected that he wrought them perhaps, not in virtue of his professing to come from God, but by means of his Egyptian knowledge, in which he was well versed. For the king, entertaining such a suspicion, summoned the Egyptian magicians, and wise men, and enchanters, who were found to be of no avail against the wisdom of Moses ..." (Bk. III, chap. xlvi, p. 128).

the Renaissance, as is exemplified in Gibbens' *Questions and Disputations*: "It is manifest hereby that the Scripture applieth it selfe in a sort unto the rudenesse of the Iewes, to whom it was first directed."[23]

Marlowe's second argument from Scripture is clumsier. According to the Pentateuch, the Jews first reached the borders of Canaan within a relatively short time, but the Lord in His wrath sent them back into the wilderness for forty years in order that all the adults (save two) might perish there for disobedience.[24] Marlowe brushes aside the supernatural and calls on Machiavelism for the true explanation. Moses kept the Israelites in the desert because he wished, by killing those who knew his secrets, to perpetuate his power and the religion which sustained it.

The generalization follows naturally: ". . . the first beginning of Religioun was only to keep men in awe." In other words, religions have always been invented by the ambitious who have understood that the arm of a man is a far less terrifying instrument of power than the voice of a god. No doubt this idea first glimmered in the mind of some primeval savage annoyed by the dealings of the witch-doctor and the tribal chief. In Roman times, it received moving expression in Lucretius' *De Rerum Natura*. And in the sixteenth century it worried Hooker, Sidney, Mornay, Calvin, Henry Smith, the writers of plays like *Selimus* and *Life and Repentance of Mary Magdalene,* and countless others.[25] Calvin, for example, declares that all men have an instinctive knowledge of God: "Wherefore it is most vayne which some doe say, that religion was deuised by the suttletie and craft of a few, by this policie to keepe the simple people in awe, whereas they them selues that procured other to worship God, beleeued nothing lesse than that there was any God at

---

[23]Chap. 3, p. 120.

[24]Raleigh, *op. cit.*, Bk. II, chap. v, secs. iii & iv, estimates, on the basis of pertinent Scriptural passages, that the first journey to Canaan took slightly less than two years.

[25]*Selimus* (ll. 335ff.) is quoted by Danchin and Tucker Brooke, p. 62. See *Life and Repentance of Mary Magdalene* (ed. F. J. Carpenter), ll. 500-11; Henry Smith, *op. cit.*, p. 6. G. T. Buckley, *Atheism in the English Renaissance* (University of Chicago Press, 1932), pp. 75 and 89, cites Hooker, *Ecclesiastical Polity* Bk. V, sec. 2 and Sidney's *Arcadia*, Bk. III, chap. x. In the latter, the temptress Cecropia derides ". . . zeale of Deuotion, indeede the best bonde, which the most politicke wittes have found to holde mans witte in well doing. . . So are these bugbeares of opinions brought by great Clearkes into the world. . . Feare, and indeede, foolish feare, and fearfull ignorance, was the first inuenter of those conceates. . ."

all.''[26] Mornay states that Numa Pompilius originated the Roman
religion ''and under pretence, he bewitched the ignorant people
with a thousand superstitions,'' and then continues: ''Sceuola the
Highpriest of the Romans . . . made three sortes of Gods: Poetical,
worse than the worst men, Philosophical, whom they taught to haue
bin men, howbeit ⸔ it was not good for the people to know it; and
Ciuill, made by the Princes to hold their people in awe with. . .''[27]
There is nothing unique, then, about Marlowe's assertion. One may
even find Tacitus applying it explicitly to Moses: ''To establish
his influence over this people for all time, Moses introduced new
religious practises, quite opposed to those of other religions.''[28]

If Marlowe's onslaught on Moses is severe, that on Christ is
savage. Besides the underlying accusation of quackery, there are
express charges of bastardy, fornication, and homosexuality. Some
admirers of Marlowe, unwilling to believe that the poet could have
said such things, hold that his real words are here misrepresented.
Others consider him guilty of something between gross violation of
good taste and deep and final depravity. Both attitudes, I think,
are unnecessary. In the course of the next few pages I hope to
show that there is a high probability that Baines was reporting
Marlowe quite accurately. For the moment, however, I am primarily concerned to show why the dramatist chose to make so scur-
rilous an attack.

It is true that his impiety might well have taken a more generous
form. Christ and Moses could have been explained as self-deceiv-
ers, at worst, or as superlatively gifted men whose accomplishments
had been magnified and teachings distorted by popular hallucination
and the long working of rumor. But such moderation was not for
the Elizabethans. The analogy of their defamation of Mohammed,
for instance, is very revealing. A respectable divine like Henry
Smith could write,

Mahomet himselfe was such a fleshly fellow, as though modest eares are loth
to heare, yet because the filthinesse of this Prophet may not be concealed, I
must utter it: He committed buggerie with an Asse, Bonfinius writeth it.
Againe, he committed adulterie with another mans wife. . . [p. 56] As
Mahomets religion is defended by force of sword and fraude . . . so likewise
did it begin . . . and was established through wiles, deceit, subtiltie, and lies.
For first hee hauing the falling sicknes, perswaded his wife and others, that it
was the power of God, and the presence of the Angel Gabriel that caused him
to fall downe. Sergius the hereticall Monk was at hand, and bare false wit-

26Lib. I, chap. iii, fol. 4v.
27Op. cit., chap. xxii, pp. 380-81.
28Histories (Loeb), Bk. V, iii-iv.

nesse to the same (saith Zonaras). . . He had three companions all of a con-
federacie, to deuise and face out his lies with him.   When hee perceiued that
men gaue eare to him, hee fained that the Angell Gabriel had carried him to
Jerusalem, and thence to haue lifted him up to heauen, and there to haue
learned his law. . .[29]

How strangely parallel to what Marlowe says about the deserved
crucifixion of Jesus is this comment on Mohammed by Mornay, surely one of the most temperate of men: "Whether he were a good
man or no, let the people of Mecha (who woorshippe him at this
day) iudge, which condemned him to death for his Robberies and
murthers.   And he himself in his Alcoran confesseth himself to bee
a sinner, an Idolater, an adulterer, giuen to Lecherie, and subiect
to women. . ."[30]   And of course the arraignment for sorcery often
turns up: "The enuious Monke Sergius . . . picked foorth Mahomet, the most proud, arrogant, and insolent person of Arabia to
take upō him to be a prophet, & by magick wrought such counter-
feit miracles, as to this day a great part of the world are led $_w^t$ his
error."[31]

All Elizabethan comment on Mohammed is in the same general
vein.   At the root of it lies the doctrine that every rival Messiah is
of the devil, and therefore a seat of congregated vices.   This intolerance had been one of the strengths of Judaism, and, wrought
into the fabric of the New Testament, it became a strength of
Christianity in the days when the new faith had to conquer or die.
The apostles denounced Simon and Elymas as deceivers and magicians because they tried to found religions of their own (*Acts* 8.9;
13:8).   How badly fared the reputations of heresiarchs and
apostates in the first centuries of the Christian era can be read in
the pages of Eusebius' *Ecclesiastical History,* Irenaeus' *Against
Heresies,* or Hippolytus' *Philosophumena.*   Manes, Callistus, Mar-
cus, Emperor Julian, and an infinity of others all seem to have been
wizards, hypocrites and degenerates, and to have met very unhappy
deaths.[32]   Coming down to more recent times, everyone remembers

---

[29]*Op. cit.,* pp. 55-56.

[30]*Op. cit.,* chap. xxxiii, p. 624.

[31]Geo. Whetstone, *The Censure of a loyall Subiect,* London, 1587, sig. D3r.
For similar Elizabethan opinions of Mohammed, read M. Hanmer, *The Baptiz-
ing of a Turke,* London, n.d. [1586?], sigs. B3r, C7r, D2v, and *The Mahumetane
or Turkish Historie,* trans. R. Carr, London, 1600, fol. 1ff.

[32]Socrates Scholasticus, *Ecclesiasticall Historie,* trans. M. Hanmer, London,
1585, Lib. I, cap. xvii, pp. 242-43; Eusebius (in same volume), Lib. III, cap.
xxiii, p. 50; Irenaeus, *Against Heresies* (Ante-Nicene Library), Bk. I, chap.
xiii.

what the Catholics thought of Luther, what stories the Protestants circulated about the witchcraft and abominations of the Popes, and what filth a bishop like John Bale could write about the Catholic saints.[33] Later on, the leaders of some of the more bizarre Puritan sects became victims of the same tradition. One must emphasize again that the men who wrote such abuse were reputable, excellent authors, most of them churchmen. It seems a little hard on Marlowe to require him to have more charity in his soul than did the ministers of God in his own century. The amenities of theological debate being what they were, Marlowe would see no reason for not adopting against Jesus the same tactics used by the Christians against their adversaries.

Let us go back to the details of the Baines memorandum. Marlowe makes three alternative assertions respecting the birth of Christ, all three calculated to impugn his divine origin. One is an obscene jest aimed at the Immaculate Conception: ''. . . the Angell Gabriell was baud to the holy ghost, because he brought the salutation to Mary.'' As might be suspected, similar ribaldries were not unknown in Elizabethan London. Thomas Lodge, in his *Wits Miserie, and the Worlds Madnesse,* is probably drawing a picture from life when he writes of the devil Derision who ''neuer sitteth but in the chaire of Pestilence, his meerest profession is Atheisme: . . . Christ his Sauior is a Carpenters sonne: Christians, Galileans in contempt: Nay such blasphemie uttereth he betwixt the Holy ghost and the blessed and Immaculate Virgine Marie, as my heart trembleth to thinke them.''[34] But the humor of Marlowe's remark should not disguise for us the thoroughly serious place it has in the program of his argument.

Now, assuming the idea of a virgin birth to be fabulous and untenable and Jesus to have been born in the natural course of human kind, Marlowe's next contention is, ''That Christ was a bastard and his mother dishonest.'' This slander had been spread by Jews, Mornay declares: ''The Prophets haue told us that he [Christ] should be borne of a Virgin. The Gospell affirmeth Mary his mother to haue bin such a one; and yet the Iewes which haue come

---

[33]*The actes of English votaryes,* London, 1546, *passim.*

[34]Cited by Buckley, *op. cit.,* p. 87. Origen, Bk. VI, chap. lxxiii, p. 415, mentions some ridicule of the virgin birth by Celsus, but nothing exactly like Marlowe's.

afterward, haue written that she was taken in adulterie.''[35] Celsus introduces it in his *True Discourse* through a dialogue between Jesus and a Jew, in which the Jew

accuses Him of having 'invented his birth from a virgin', and upbraids Him with being 'born in a certain Jewish village, of a poor woman of the country, who . . . was turned out of doors by her husband, a carpenter by trade, because she was convicted of adultery; that after being driven away by her husband, and wandering about for a time, she disgracefully gave birth to Jesus, an illegitimate child, who naving hired himself out as a servant in Egypt on account of his poverty, and having there acquired some miraculous powers, on which the Egyptians greatly pride themselves, returned to his own country, highly elated on account of them, and by means of these proclaimed himself a god.[36]

Celsus later even designates the supposed father of Jesus, "a certain soldier named Panthera." It seems valid to conclude that Marlowe is drawing on this Jewish tradition.

His third alternative argument is that if Jesus was not illegitimate, at least he was merely the child of ordinary wedlock between Joseph and Mary: ". . . he was the sonne of a Carpenter and . . . if the Jewes among whome he was borne did Crucify him theie best knew him and whence he Came." As previously Marlowe cited Scripture against Moses, so here he cites it against Christ. Two texts are appealed to. The first is the cry of the doubting Jews of Nazareth upon hearing Jesus preach: "Whence cōmeth this wisedome and great workes unto this man? Is not this the carpenters sonne? Is not his mother called Marie, and his brethren Iames & Ioses, and Simon and Iudas?" (*Matthew* 13:54-5). Later scoffers made the phrase a standard term of reproach. So at the time of the early Christian persecutions "Libanius a singular Sophist, but an enimie to the truth, and a follower of Iulian [Apostata], looking and longing after his maisters victory in regard of his threates, came to a godly Schoolemaister . . . in Antiocha, & scoffing at his religion scornfully asked him, Fabri filius quid nunc putas agit? What thinkest thou nowe doeth the Carpenters

---

[35]*Op. cit.*, chap. xxx, p. 543. Cf. Smith, *op. cit.*, p. 48. *The Malleus Maleficarum*, famous witchcraft treatise by Institor and Sprenger (trans. M. Summers, Rodker, 1928), Pt. II, Ques. 1, chap. 12, describes the practise of witches to "utter the filthiest words against the Purity of the Most Glorious Virgin MARY, casting the foulest aspersions on the Nativity of Our Saviour from Her inviolate womb."

[36]Origen, Bk. I, chap. xxviii, p. 426, and chap. xxxii, p. 431.

sonne?'"[37]   The other text used by Marlowe is, similarly, the denial
by the Jews of Jerusalem that Jesus is the Christ:

> Howbeit we know this man whence he is but when the Christ commeth, no
> man shal know whence he is.
> Then cried Iesus in the Temple as he taught, saying, Ye both know me &
> knowe whêce I am: yet am I not come of my self, but he that sent me, is
> true, whom ye know not. (*John* 7:27-8.)[38]

Since both texts relate the incredulity of the Jews among whom
Jesus lived, their combination is highly appropriate and can only
be the result of conscious planning.   Also striking is the fidelity
with which the Baines note preserves the Biblical language.   The
inference is unmistakable that Baines is really transmitting the
words of Marlowe, if not with absolute accuracy, then at least with
substantial accuracy.   The only other alternative is that Baines, or
someone else-unnamed, was clever enough to piece together the two
texts into a damaging Scriptural argument and then diabolical
enough to father it on Marlowe.   In addition, the fabricator would
have to achieve a mocking irony very like that displayed in Marlowe's works, and as a last stroke he would have to throw in some
convincing references to the dramatist's acquaintances, Harriot,
Cholmley, and Poole.[39]   A theory like that cannot be taken seriously.

No, the argument is Marlowe's clearly enough, and if further
proof be needed the next allegation of the Baines note will help to
provide it: ''That Crist deserved better to dy then Barrabas and
that the Jewes made a good Choise, though Barrabas were both a
thief and a murtherer.''   Here is continued the line of reasoning
begun in the statement preceding.   The Jews among whom Christ
spent his life were the best judges not only of his real parentage but
also of his crimes and deceptions.   If they decided to crucify him
instead of Barabbas, they knew what they were doing, ''though
Barrabas were both a thief and a murtherer.''   The exact words of
this last clause are worth careful notice.   They disclose knowledge
of a ticklish point in the harmonizing of the gospels.   Barabbas is
described by Matthew (27:16) only as ''a notable prisoner called
Barabbas''; by Mark (15:7) as ''one named Barabbas, which was

---

[37]W. Averell, *A merxailous combat of contrarieties*, London, 1588, sig. E4v.
Notice especially the quotation from Lodge's *Wits Miserie* in the text, *supra*.
And cf. Mornay's *Treatise of the Church*, London, 1581, p. 52.

[38]The Bishops and King James Bibles have almost exactly the same words.

[39]Tucker Brooke, *op. cit.*, pp. 98, 99.

bound with his fellowes, that had made insurrection, who in the insurrection had committed murder''; by Luke (23:19) as Barabbas ''Which for a certeine insurrection made in the citie, and murder was cast into prison'';[40] but in John (18:40) according to the Vulgate, Bishops Bible, and King James Bible, the words simply are ''This Barabbas was a robber'' (''erat latro''). Now the Geneva translation renders John ''. . . this Barabbas was a murtherer,'' evidently in order to avoid conflict with the other three gospels. It seems very much as if Marlowe knew and relished the differences. To him they would be one of those ''Contrarieties oute of the Scripture'' which he had drawn up to show to certain great men. At the risk of seeming superfine, I suggest that in the clause ''. . . though Barrabas were both a thief and a murtherer'' Marlowe puts the verb ''were'' into the subjunctive for a condition contrary to fact, and uses the word ''both'' to stress the contrasts between the gospels versions. The necessary presupposition for this view is that Baines is here transcribing Marlowe with minutest accuracy.

One further word as to Marlowe's argument that the Jews were in the best position to know the truth about Jesus. I have not seen these particular texts used elsewhere as Marlowe uses them. But, of course, the argument in its general tenor had long been employed by the Jews: ''If Jesus (say they [Jews]) were the Christ; who should haue knowen and receiued him, rather than the great Sinagogue which was at that time? The obiection is very old. . . . it is expressly sayd by the Prophetes, that when the Messias came unto them, they should be so blynde as not too knowe him, and so unthankeful as to despise him.''[41]

Shameful in birth, shameful in death, and most shameful in life— such was Jesus according to Marlowe's indictment: ''the woman of Samaria & her sister were whores & . . . Christ knew them dishonestly. . . . St. John the Evangelist was bedfellow to Christ and leaned alwaies in his bosome . . . he used him as the sinners of Sodoma.''

The most that can be said for such charges is that they would not have been made but for certain Biblical passages:

The woman of Samaria answered, and said, I haue no husband. Iesus said unto her, Thou hast wel said, I haue no husband.

---

[40]All three of the foregoing quotations are given in the language of the Geneva Bible, but the Bishops, Vulgate, and King James versions are substantially the same.

[41]Mornay, *The Trewnesse of the Christian Religion*, chap. xxxi, pp. 572-73.

For thou hast had fiue husbands, and he whom thou now hast, is not thine husbād: that saidest thou truely (*John* 4:17-18; Geneva).

Nowe there was one of his disciples, which leaned on Iesus bosome, whom Iesus loued (*John* 13:23; Geneva).[42]

In his libel on St. John, Marlowe's retention of the Scriptural phrase is again noteworthy. If his conclusions seem fantastic, it is well not to waste too much twentieth-century disgust on what is, after all, only too typical of sixteenth-century theological malice and ingenuity.

As in previous instances, Marlowe seems entitled to whatever credit for originality there may be in the elaboration of these particular points and the use of these particular texts, but the volume of similar abuse of Jesus among the pagan classics and the Jews is immense. It is so much like what was suffered by Moses and Mohammed that only a few representative examples need be offered. Celsus, for one, said that Christ lived "a most infamous life" and "was punished by the Jews for his crimes."[43] To Porphyry he was a "dead god, who was condemned by right-minded judges, and perished ignominiously by a violent death."[44] Lucian classified him among the impostors as "that Syrian adept from Palestine."[45] And the attitude of the Jews was thus described by Justin Martyr:

. . . you have sent chosen and ordained men throughout all the world to proclaim that a godless and lawless heresy had sprung from one Jesus, a Galilean deceiver, whom we crucified, but his disciples stole him by night from the tomb, where he was laid when unfastened from the cross, and now deceive men by asserting that he has risen from the dead and ascended to heaven.[46]

Marlowe is not reported as mentioning Christ's miracles or the resurrection, but what he would think of them is obvious.

---

[42]Bishops Bible: "There was one of Iesus disciples leaning on Iesus bosome (euen he) whom Iesus loued." Vulgate: ". . . unus qui recumbebat in sinu ipsius, is quem-diligebat Ieschua." From earliest times, no one doubted that the allusion was to John the Evangelist himself. Marlowe has no Biblical authority for giving the woman of Samaria a sister.

[43]Origen, Bk. VII, chap. lvi, p. 478, and Bk. II, chap. v, p. 7.

[44]From Porphyry's early work, "On the Philosophy Derived from Oracles," cited in A. B. Hulen, *Porphyry's Work Against the Christians*, Yale Studies in Religion, No. 1, 1933, p. 16.

[45]*The Liar*, cited by Buckley, *op. cit.*, p. 7.

[46]*Dialogue With Trypho* (Ante-Nicene Library), chap. cviii, p. 235. Also, Tertullian's *Against Marcion* in the same set. Bk. III, chap. vi, p. 130. In the Gospels the Pharisees accuse Christ of magic, and the same charge is refuted, for example, by Justin Martyr, *First Apology*, chap. xxx, the pseudo-Clementine *Recognitions*, Bk. I, chap. lviii, and Mornay, *op. cit.*, chap. xxx. Within Christianity itself many sorts of heretics expressed views upon Christ's divinity, from the Ebionites who believed him to be an ordinary man, to the Arians who thought him a subordinate part of God; but none of these was disrespectful of him. All were very widely known and discussed during the Renaissance.

The order of statements in the latter part of the Baines note becomes harder to determine, but the next shafts seem directed not so much against Christ personally as against the ceremonies established by him and his Church:

That if there be any god or good Religion, then it is in the papistes because the service of god is performed with more Cerimonies, as Elevation of the mass, organs, singing men, Shaven Crownes & cta. That all protestantes are Hypocriticall asses.
That if Christ would haue instituted the sacrament with more Ceremoniall Reverence it would haue bin had in more admiration, that it would haue bin much better administred in a Tobacco pipe.[47]

Paraphrased, the argument amounts to this: the only good religious ceremonies are those which keep the people most wonderstruck and submissive. Christ bungled the job by not surrounding his sacrament of the eucharist with more impressive decorations. Herein the Catholics have improved upon their master, and are far ahead of the Protestants, who hypocritically envy and condemn them on that account.

In other words, this is a new phase of the argument Marlowe had made before in connection with Moses, ". . . the first beginning of Religioun was only to keep men in awe." There is a passage in Agrippa which helps to suggest this interpretation:

Of the members of Religion, the pompes of rites, and Ceremonies be not the least, in apparrell, in vessels, in lightes, in belles, in organs, in singing, in encensinge, in sacrifices. . . Numa Pompilius was the firste that commaunded ceremonies to the Romans, that under theire pretence or colour he might allure men to deuotion, faithe, iustice, and religion, and more easily gouerne the rude and fierce people, which had usurped the rule of the Realme with force and iniurie.[48]

Apparently, then, Marlowe shifted naturally from disparagement of Jesus as a pretender into the scornful charge that he was not even good enough at his business to know the psychology of religious deception. Thence flowed a discussion of the relative merits of Catholic and Protestant ritual. Marlowe's compliment to the "papistes," although a poisonously back-handed one, must have been particularly enraging to his Protestant auditors. Some of the

---

[47]Marlowe's phrase "instituted the sacrament" is a technical term customarily used by theologians, as by Adamo [pseud. for A. Mainardi] *An Anatomi . . . of the Mass*, Strasburg[?], 1556, fol. 112r: "As though Christ had instituted the sacramēt, to thentent that it should be bileued that he were in that host. . ." Four more instances of its use occur in Mainardi, fols. 109v, 119r, 120r, 153v. Similarly, Smith, *op. cit.*, p. 71; Mornay, *Treatise of the Church*, pp. 37, 109, 174. By "Elevation of the mass" Marlowe means the lifting up of the host by the priest during the mass.

[48]*Of the Vanitie . . . of Artes and Sciences*, London, 1569, cap. 60, fol. 85r.

bitterest English invective was expended on the idolatry and superstition of the Catholic mass. The whole episode serves well to show Marlowe's living concern in contemporary religious questions. Nowhere is his satire so double and triple edged.

Even more remarkable, but for a different reason, is his statement that holy communion "would have bin much better administred in a Tobacco pipe." Why should Marlowe have chosen that particular comparison? Probably because of a general association of ideas between the Christian sacrament and the Indian use of tobacco for religious ceremonies. A vivid description of such ceremonies was given by Harriot in his book, *A briefe and true report of the newfoundland of Virginia*, published in 1588:

> The Spaniards generally call it Tobacco. The leaues thereof being dried and brought into powder: they use to take the fume or smoke thereof by sucking it through pipes made of claie. . .
> This Uppówoc is of so precious estimation amongst thē, that they thinke their gods are maruelously delighted therwith: Wherupon sometime they make hallowed fires & cast some of the pouder therein for a sacrifice: being in a storme uppon the waters, to pacifie their gods, they cast some up into the aire and into the water . . . but all done with strange gestures, stamping, sometime daunsing, clapping of hands, holding up of hands, & staring up into the heaues, uttering therewithal and chattering strange words & noises.[49]

Of course, this passage does not declare that tobacco pipes were used during the rites, but it shows how the idea of the Christian sacrament might bring into Marlowe's mind the thought of tobacco, which in turn would draw in the image of a pipe. If this theory is correct, we have here a uniquely intimate view of the swift workings of his consciousness. To be sure, since other books on America also had accounts of tobacco ceremonies,[50] we cannot say definitely that Marlowe was remembering either Harriot's conversation or his book. But Harriot's narrative on this subject seems to have been one of the best of its kind, and certainly it is the closest, most likely source of suggestion for the dramatist. In view of Marlowe's naming of Harriot earlier in the Baines note, it would be surprising if Harriot's book were not also in his thought here. At any rate, it seems difficult any longer to dismiss the tobacco pipe as a merely random irreverence. Marlowe used that comparison because he had in mind the religion of the Indians. And he was much

---

[49]London, sig. C3.

[50]Monardes, *Ioyfull Newes Out of the newe founde worlde*, trans. J. Frampton, London, 1577, Pt. 2, fol. 38; J. Acosta, *The Naturall and Morall Historie of the East and West Indies*, trans. E. G., London, 1604, Lib. 5, chap. 26, p. 404.

too fine a satirist not to intend all the sardonic implications of a parallel between the rites of the dancing, chattering savages of Virginia and those of the Christian Elizabethans.

The discussion of ceremonies then shades into two strictures on the Apostles:

> That if he were put to write a new Religion, he would undertake both a more Exellent and Admirable methode and that all the new testament is filthily written.[51]
> That all the apostles were fishermen and base fellowes neyther of wit nor worth, that Paull only had wit but he was a timerous fellow in bidding men to be subiect to magistrates against his Conscience.

Beside these statements may be put Kyd's averment that Marlowe esteemed "paul a Jugler."[52] The objectives here seem to be to damage both Jesus and the New Testament by discrediting those who published his teachings. The New Testament made no secret of the fact that most of the apostles were men of the humblest origin, and that some of them on occasion had denied or betrayed Jesus. This had therefore seemed a vulnerable point to antagonists like Celsus: "Jesus having gathered around him ten or eleven persons of notorious character, the very wickedest of tax-gatherers and sailors, fled in company with them from place to place, and obtained his living in a shameful and importunate manner."[53] Celsus also dwells on the treachery of the apostles, and reasons that if Jesus could not win more faithful, better educated followers than these he could not have been much of a Messiah. As far as Paul was concerned, Celsus was silent; Paul would make against his case. But Julian the Apostate had singled Paul out as the one "who surpassed all the magicians and charlatans of every place and every time."[54] Paul's "wit" (intelligence) there could be no denial of by anyone who remembered the Bible stories of the many disputations he won, and Marlowe is careful to admit it expressly. In the opinion that Paul "was a timerous fellow in bidding men

---

[51]With "more . . . Admirable methode" connect ". . . would haue bin had in more admiration . . ." in the comment on the sacrament, just analyzed.

[52]Tucker Brooke, op. cit., p. 107.

[53]Origen, Bk. I, chap. lxii, p. 466; also Bk. II, chap. xlv, p. 46. Highly interesting evidence of Renaissance study of Celsus comes in Mornay's reference to this opinion: "For whereas Celsus the Epicure obiecteth, that Jesus chose Publicanes and men of wicked conuersation to be his Disciples: euen therein peculiarly hath he shewed the effectualnes of his doctrine in the curing of mens soules." Trewnesse of the Christian Religion, chap. xxx, p. 557.

[54]In his famous polemic against Christianity, Against the Galileans (c. 363 A.D.), translated by W. C. Wright for the Loeb Library, 1923, I, 341.

to be subject to magistrates against his Conscience'' he is certainly relying on what Paul wrote in *Romans* 13 :1 and 5 :

Let euerie soule be subiect unto the higher powers: for there is no power but of God: and the powers that be, are ordeined of God.

Wherefore ye must be subiect, not because of wrath onely, but also for conscience sake.[55]

I confess to some difficulty in seeing how Marlowe knows that Paul is here acting against his conscience. A suggestion may be ventured, however: Marlowe means that Paul gave this bidding to his followers in order to ingratiate himself with the Roman authorities, although his conscience told him that if Christians always obeyed it they would sometimes have to violate the law of God. All Renaissance exegesis stipulated an exception to the command in such cases, but Paul makes no exception.[56] It is noteworthy to see Marlowe bringing in this text because it had great contemporary importance as a storm center in the struggles between civil and ecclesiastical power. It was always being cited by the dominant Catholics against the Huguenots in France, by the Protestants against the Catholic minority in England, and within the English church by the Anglicans against the Puritans, to justify maximum control of those bodies.

In speaking of the apostles Marlowe had also criticized the New Testament as ''filthily written'' and had offered to write a new religion according to a ''more Exellent and Admirable methode'' upon request. This is a cavil rather against literary style and organization than against subject matter,[57] the argument apparently being that from ''fishermen and base fellowes''; one could expect nothing better. It is an opinion which was shared by a considerable number of humanists, as Agrippa complains,

---

[55]The Geneva Bible has an important marginal note to this verse: ''. . . here he speaketh of ciuill Magistrates: so that antichrist and his cannot wrast this place to establish their tyrannie ouer the conscience.'' This Puritan interpretation explains why Marlowe used the phrase ''subiect to magistrates.''

[56]*E.g.* Bishop Hooper ''Annotations on Romans xiii'' in *Later Writings of Bishop Hooper* (Parker Society, 1852) p. 102; and Henry Bullinger, *Decades* (Parker Society, 1849) Decade 2, Sermon 9, pp. 390-91.

[57]The French translation of Origen's *Against Celsus* published at Amsterdam in 1700 expresses Origen as saying that the apostles spread the gospel by divine aid only, ''. . . ni par la force de leur éloquence, ni par la netteté de leur Méthode, ni par les autres artifices de la Rhétorique & de la Dialectique, qu'on apprend dans les Ecoles des Grecs. . .'' (Bk. I, p. 38). The English translation has, in place of ''Méthode,'' ''any orderly arrangement of their message. . .'' (Bk. I, chap. lxii). J. Anwick, *Meditations*, London, 1587, Epistle Dedicatory, contrasts ''Method and ornamentes of arte'' with ''goodness in substaunce'' of a book.

I see many waxe prowde in Humane learning and knowledge, that therefore they do despise and lothe, the Sacred and Canonicall Scriptures of the Holie Ghoste, as rude and rusticall, because they haue no ornamentes of woords, force of sillogismes, and affectate perswasions, nor the strange doctrine of the Philosophers.[58]

And in so official a place as the authorized *Sermons* it is said that "... the phrase of the Scripture is sometime so homely, grosse, and playne, that it offendeth the fyne and delicate wittes of some courtiers."[59]   One need scarcely go back into antiquity except to mention that Celsus and his contemporaries had no respect for the style of the Greek originals either.[60]

Omitting two items which do not deal with religion, we come to Baines' final allegation, that Marlowe "saieth likewise that he hath quoted a number of Contrarieties oute of the Scripture."   The prevalence of this sort of analysis in Elizabethan times may be judged by the fact that Arthur Broke in 1563 wrote a whole book, *The Agreemente of Sondry Places of Scripture*, to prove that 107 cases of seeming contradiction in texts were only apparent and not real.   His Epistle to the Reader runs:

There are also diuerse whiche (not caring for any religiō but rather wishing $\frac{t}{y}$ al thing wer disordered, & $\frac{t}{y}$ euery one shold do what semeth hĩ best) wickedly take certain scrapings of $\frac{e}{y}$ holy scriptures, and assone as they haue foũd in thē some litle shew of discord, they lay hand on $\frac{t}{y}$ as if they had ouer come al, tending to no other end but to brĩg $\frac{e}{y}$ word of god to be despised & hated. . .

In like fashion, Nicholas Gibbens clarifies some two dozen places where "perhaps a Manichee or some blasphemous Atheist, will argue a contradiction in the Scripture."[61]   And a great many other citations could be brought to show that the Elizabethans realized the acuteness of the danger.   But it was a danger which had confronted the Church ever since its earliest days, and the defense against it had engaged some of the ablest champions of Christendom.[62]   Probably most troublesome were discrepancies in the

---

[58]*Op. cit.*, sig. A4r.   For other excellent statements see Mornay, *op. cit.*, chap. xxvi, pp. 452, 455; P. Viret, *The Worlde possessed with Deuils*, London, 1583, Dial. 4, sig. D5; E. Bulkeley, *Answere to Ten friuolous . . . reasons*, London, 1588, p. 13.

[59]*Certaine Sermons appointed by the Queenes Maiestie. . .* London, 1587, II, sig. T5r.

[60]Origen, Bk. VI, chap. ii, p. 337.

[61]*Op. cit.*, p. 38.

[62]Origen, Bk. VII, chap. xviii, p. 440; Tertullian, *Against Marcion*, Bk. IV, chap. i, p. 175; St. Augustine, *Reply to Faustus the Manichaean* (*Works*, ed. M.

genealogies of Christ given by Matthew and Luke, and the varying accounts of the passion and resurrection. A long history might be written on this subject alone.

On leaving the Baines note, one has the sense that tantalizing secrets yet lie hidden there. But some things about it are now plain. Baines has given us a more faithful transcript of Marlowe's words than we have ever realized. No doubt it suffers from some omissions, some dislocations in the sequence of the statements reported, and possibly a few minor verbal misquotations. But through these obscurities appears the shape of an ordered argument. And as individual units the statements seem to be recorded with a high degree of accuracy. Almost every one refers to a definite Scriptural text; several unmistakably repeat the phraseology of the Bible. Such things do not happen by chance or by the malevolence of Richard Baines.

I should not like to say that there are no light or careless touches in Marlowe's argument. Probably Marlowe himself would smile ironically to hear that said. But the predominant seriousness of his purpose is not to be mistaken Marlowe has not only searched the Scriptures; he has also read many books and plucked from many orchards of the ancient and modern worlds. If specific books must be mentioned as influencing him, Mornay's *Trewnesse of the Christian Religion* and Origen's *Against Celsus* are likeliest to have done so,[63] but indebtedness to them cannot be absolutely proved. It is better to conclude generally that the thoughts of the ethnics, of the Jews, and of his own Elizabethan contemporaries all left their mark on him. Into these ideas he breathed the living reality of his convictions, and dared to utter them abroad at the risk of his career and his life that other men might share the truth. He became one of the spokesmen of a tendency. For free-thought was stirring in England in a vague, unorganized way during the last fifty years of the century. Underneath the intonations of the orthodox writers, one can hear it rising, this mutter of revolutionary dissidence. For the most part it was scattered and anonymous. But in Marlowe we can see the quintessence of it drawn together and revealed. This

---

Dods, Edinburgh. 1872) Bk. III, p. 152; Macarius Magnes, *Apocriticus* (ed. T. W. Crafer, N. Y., Macmillan, 1919) Bk. II, chaps. xii and xvii.

[63]Buckley, *op. cit.*, chap. x, has suggested that Marlowe knew the anonymous work *De Tribus Impostoribus*, which assailed Moses, Christ, and Mohammed. Scholars are still debating whether the book we now have under that title is not a late seventeenth-century production. I incline to think it is.

is the unique historical importance of the Baines note, to which we have never sufficiently awakened. Of whom among the Elizabethans have we such another record? Not Raleigh, not the scientists, nor any of Marlowe's fellow dramatists, nor any other literary Englishman whose work we know. For revolutionary impact and scope it stands alone, an extraordinary document in the history of English free-thought.

THE TAMING OF A SHREW

By Henry David Gray
Stanford University

The belief that *The Taming of a Shrew* was not the source of Shakespeare's *Taming of the Shrew* but another of the "bad" quartos did not gain currency until Mr. Peter Alexander's statement of the case in 1926,[1] and many scholars have not accepted it for reasons which I wish to examine. As far back as 1850 Hickson had called attention to some passages in which *A Shrew* apparently depended upon the reading which appeared first in the Folio; Creizenach added the point that the Bianca story in *The Shrew* is closer to the source and consequently earlier than the corresponding story in *A Shrew*; Ten Brink threw out the casual suggestion that both went back to a common source and that this source was a "Jungendarbeit Shakespeares."[2] After Pollard had made us all "bad quarto conscious"—if I may so say—it was easy to see that this early work of Shakespeare was merely *The Shrew* as it was when *A Shrew* was stolen from it. Alexander's predecessor at the University of Glasgow, John Semple Smart, realized that we had before us all the evidences of a bad quarto.

Alexander's more elaborate statement of the case was accepted by Wilson in the New Cambridge edition of *The Shrew,* but with a concluding comment which is my point of departure in this paper:

> If the reader be prepared to accept this conclusion, let him not shut his eyes to the consequences. One of them is that Shakespeare at this early date was already capable of the verse we find, for instance, in Petruchio's speech at the end of 4.1. or Katharina's at the end of 5.2. . . [a feat] that orthodox Shakespearian criticism will, unless we are mistaken, find it very difficult to credit.

That Wilson was not mistaken was promptly proved by an anonymous reviewer,[3] who announced that the passages cited by Hickson and Alexander were inconclusive "because they are just as naturally explained on the old assumption that Shakespeare was re-working the quarto play, in which it is possible he had previously had

---

[1] *TLS*, Sept. 16, 1926.
[2] "Über den Sommernachtstraum," *Jahrbuch*, XIII, (1878), 92.
[3] *TLS*, 1928, p. 374.

a hand." Alexander at once demanded to be told *how* the old assumption explains certain peculiarities which the bad quarto hypothesis accounts for perfectly.[4] This challenge received in reply only a profound silence.

Yet anybody can see that the speeches Wilson refers to, and others throughout the taming scenes, as well as the masterly ease with which the Induction is handled, are characteristic of Shakespeare about 1597, and are wholly unlike the work he did before 1593 when the Pembroke company, which had acted *A Shrew,* went to pieces. The answer is both easy and inevitable: *The Shrew* was an early work; *A Shrew* was derived from it; and when the play was revised Shakespeare rewrote those portions which clearly are not early. Of course if we recognize the undoubted fact that Elizabethan plays often underwent revision, and remember at the same time that Shakespeare was an Elizabethan, Sir. E. K. Chambers will call us "disintegrators," but we must bear that as best we may.

It was unfortunate, I think, that Alexander rejected the idea of an earlier version. He proved that an earlier version would be identical with the Folio text at certain points, but it is quite possible to show that they were not identical at other points. I give, for example, the speech of Katharina in *A Shrew* when she yields at last to Ferando (Petruchio) and greets an old man as if she mistook him for a young girl, and then the corresponding speech from *The Shrew:*

> Fair lovely lady, bright and crystalline,
> Beauteous and stately as the eye-trained bird,
> As glorious as the morning washed with dew,
> Within whose eyes she takes her dawning beams,
> And golden summer sleeps upon thy cheeks,
> Wrap up thy radiations in some cloud,
> Lest that thy beauty make this stately town
> Inhabitable like the burning zone
> With sweet reflections of thy lovely face. (*A Shrew*, xv, 36ff.)

> Young budding virgin, fair and fresh and sweet,
> Whither away, or where is thy abode?
> Happy the parents of so fair a child!
> Happier the man whom favorable stars
> Allot thee for his lovely bed-fellow! (*The Shrew*, iv, v, 37ff.)

The first line of the hack poet's version contains three of his favorite words: lovely, bright and crystalline, and would be naturally explained as derived from Shakespeare's vaguely remembered line; but "As glorious as the morning washed with dew" is taken from

---

[4] *Ibid.*, p. 430.

Petruchio's "As morning roses newly washed with dew" (II, i, 173), and such a transference from one part of the play to another is recognized as one of the characteristics of a bad quarto. The hand of the revising poet can be recognized also by the omission of the word *roses*. That morning roses can be washed with dew makes good sense; but how the *morning* can be washed with dew the imitating poet does not stop to consider. The rest of the passage shows a dependence upon Shakespeare, for surely no other poet wrote the line,

> Wrap up thy radiations in some cloud.

Shakespeare uses "inhabitable" for "uninhabitable" in *Richard II* (I, i, 65), but this was an allowed usage at the time, and he repeats "the burning zone" in *Hamlet* (V, i, 165), but any other poet might do that. It is the Shakespearean ring in the passage, and especially the highly poetic and imaginative figure in the line just quoted, that show an imperfectly preserved passage from the original play, which must have been revised at this point. Why Shakespeare threw away so good a speech for the one he substituted is perhaps to be explained by his increased interest in the characterization. The first speech, so far as we can judge by the hack poet's report of it, contained amusing and pretty lines; but in the revised speech we can feel the personality of the newly-tamed shrew as she enters upon her rôle with abandon and a relish of the humor in it. Therefore we are not compelled to believe that Katharine's final speech, to which Wilson calls attention, was written by Shakespeare at a time when he was not writing in this manner; for *A Shrew* gives us at this point a different speech, one that is obviously based on a Shakespearean original quite assignable to him in his first period.

The present theory, that *A Shrew* is a bad quarto based upon *The Shrew*[5] before it underwent revision, avoids a difficulty which puzzled the older critics. Regarding *A Shrew* as the source of *The Shrew*, they found two plays in each of which the Induction and

---

[5] For convenience I use Shakespeare's title for his play even in its earlier form, though I agree with those who believe that his original title was *The Taming of a Shrew*. The makers of the bad quartos of the *Contention* and *True Tragedy* obviously would not have invented these titles in trying to reproduce Shakespeare's dramas. Shakespeare's title for *Henry VIII* was *All Is True*. It must, I believe, have been Heminges and Condell who grouped all the English plays after the Norman conquest, arranged them in chronological order and named them for the kings. This has been misleading to young students who suppose that a history play is a sort of chronicle play; whereas obviously *Richard III* is a tragedy and *Anthony and Cleopatra* and *Troilus and Cressida* are chronicle plays.

taming scenes were written in one style and the younger sister story in another; so they were forced to suppose that two men collaborated on *A Shrew,* and then Shakespeare and a collaborator revised it, Shakespeare almost slavishly copying his source while his collaborator for some strange reason wrote a very different story, scarcely touching his source. This was so incredible that every possible variation of it was suggested. Kuhl stoutly maintained[6] that *The Shrew* was wholly Shakespeare's, a view which it is much easier to accept on the bad quarto-revision theory, since the fainter characterization and less fluent verse of the Bianca story would be due to the contrast between Shakespeare's earlier and later work. That Shakespeare did something with the Bianca story in revising the play Mrs. Ashton makes abundantly clear,[7] but that he was chiefly concerned with the Induction and the taming scenes nobody who accepts the revision theory will deny. And the contrast between the two styles in *A Shrew* also finds a possible solution when we accept the bad quarto idea.

For just such a difference would be the inevitable result if the play was stolen by an actor whose rôles brought him into the Induction and the taming scenes, and left him so completely out of the Bianca scenes that he was not even called when those scenes were rehearsed. The difference in style would be the difference in the work of a second-rate poet when he is remembering more or less of what Shakespeare had written and his work when he remembers nothing but the general idea of a milder younger sister, and so has to fall back on his own ability to write blank verse and to put into it some high-sounding quotations from Marlowe.

Some scholars seem to have an antipathy to the actor-thief explanation of a bad quarto, though it is so in keeping with what the conditions of the time would make likely, and prefer to believe that a shorthand writer using Bright's *Characterie* system could take down the rapid interchange of dialogue confused by the stage business of the various actors as readily as he could take a sermon. Because Heywood said, in the always-quoted lines,

> Some by stenography drew
> The plot, put it in print, scarce one word true,

these scholars feel that they have first-hand evidence in the matter.

---

[6] "The Authorship of *The Taming of the Shrew,*" by Ernest P. Kuhl, *PMLA,* XL (1925), 551ff.

[7] "The Revision of the Folio text of *The Taming of the Shrew,*" by Florence H. Ashton, *PQ,* VI (1927), 151ff.

But we ourselves are not always correctly informed about what goes on in our own time. Stenography was in use, and his play was stolen: and that is apparently all that Heywood knew about it. *The Taming of a Shrew* is perhaps the farthest of all the bad quartos from a possible explanation on the shorthand hypothesis, yet even in this case Van Dam made the attempt.[8] He was driven to suppose that actors' substitutions and interpolations could account for an entirely different set of scenes in the younger sister story, which scarcely touch the scenes of Shakespeare which these actors were supposed to have learned.

It seems to me perfectly clear that the fairly close—at some points extremely close—approximation to Shakespeare's Induction and taming scenes, and very remote suggestion of his Bianca story in the story of the two younger sisters in *A Shrew*, can be reasonably explained only on the hypothesis I have suggested. It is true that the greater vividness and interest of the Induction and taming scenes would make them better remembered than the Bianca story. Anyone who attempted to reproduce the play from memory would undoubtedly do much better with the former than the latter. But the difference in *A Shrew* is too great to be accounted for in this way. In the Bankside edition, edited by Albert R. Frey, the lines in the quarto which correspond closely to those in the Folio are marked, and this gives us an easy method of testing. The taming story has 164 lines so marked, while the younger sister's story has only 23, of which 7 have reference to the taming story. The scene where the correspondence is closest is that which introduces the Haberdasher and Tailor, though all of the scenes in Petruchio's house are well reported. I think it almost certain that the pirate took the rôle of the Tailor, and that he was also one of Petruchio's servants. If anyone in the audience recognized the servant in the Tailor, it would seem all a part of Petruchio's hoaxing; and for a cloak to serve as disguise enough to keep Katharine from recognizing him, that would go all the better with an Elizabethan audience. Half a dozen rehearsals would make any actor able to reproduce the greater part of those hilarious scenes. There was apparently no reason for altering these scenes in the revision; but where the lines were rewritten, as appears so clearly in the Induction, it is impossible to test the accuracy of the pirate or even to tell which

---

[8]*The Taming of a Shrew*, by B. A. P. van Dam, *English Studies*, x (1928), 97.

part he took. The followers of the nameless lord would naturally
be used as Petruchio's servants, and it would be strange indeed if
our pirate had not been employed in just about the capacity in
which he apparently was employed.

But like so many dramatic poets of this time, from the greatest
to the least—and the two extremes meet in the play before us—our
pirate worked under the dominating influence of Marlowe. He not
only stole brazenly from him but he was able to imitate him with
considerable skill. He was naturally impressed by the majesty of
the lines spoken by Faustus when he ventures out into the grove
at night to begin his incantations, and to the four lines he purloins
he adds a fifth of his own,

And darksome night o'ershades the crystal heavens,

and Smart includes it as part of the theft from Marlowe! With a
few stolen phrases like *crystal heavens, orient pearl, sable night*,
etc., a pseudo-poet can decorate his own verse until it appears like
poetry. But with ridiculous inappropriateness this pirate-poet gives
those thrilling somber lines of Faustus to the humorous lord as he
returns from the chase, gives orders to have the dogs well fed, and
then begins to play his practical joke on the drunken Sly.

The thefts from Marlowe in *A Shrew* are listed by Bond.[9] They
come from the two parts of *Tamburlaine* and *Dr. Faustus*, which
presumably means that the pirate had acted in these three plays
of Marlowe and not in his other dramas. All the borrowings from
both parts of *Tamburlaine* come from scenes where Usumcasane is
on the stage, or, in one instance, waiting to come on, and in all but
one instance Techelles is also present. (The latter part would probably be taken by one of the leading members of the company.) The
lines quoted are not the pirate's own; poor Usumcasane had only
filling-in lines to speak; but it seems to me probable that the pirate
had acted this small part with the Admiral's men. No assignment
to him of a particular rôle, however, would account for the pilfer-
ings from *Faustus*.

The problem as to the identity of the revising poet is interesting
for its own sake, but of course has no bearing on the conclusions
reached up to this point. The claim of Samuel Rowley was put forward by Sykes.[10] The recurrence of such exclamations as *souns*

---

[9] *The Taming of the Shrew*, Arden edition, 1904, p. xxxviii.

[10] The Authorship of "The Taming of a Shrew," "The Famous Victories
of Henry V," and the Additions to Marlowe's "Faustus," in *Sidelights on
Elizabethan Drama*, 1924.

(*swounds, zounds*), *O brave*, and of such expressions as *I warrant you, as't passes, let me* (or *him*) *alone to* do something, together with some parallels both of diction and ideas, led Sykes to claim identity of authorship for *A Shrew* and *The Famous Victories of Henry V*; then, noting that some of the expressions appeared in *Faustus B* (the 1616 quarto) in what seemed to be the additions for which Henslowe paid William Birde and Samuel Rowley, and also that some of them occurred in Rowley's *When You See Me You Know Me,* he concluded that Rowley was the man he was seeking. He added also *Wily Beguiled* and, at Wilson's suggestion, the clown scenes in Greene's *Orlando Furioso.* Wilson thought that Sykes had made his point. Chambers was seriously impressed. Greg considered the test of real significance and value, but thought that perhaps a group of men rather than one man might be involved, that, for example, some of the Queen's men might have picked up these tricks of speech from Tarlton. In general, the scholars who had given most attention to subjects of this sort seemed to be those who were most inclined to accept Sykes's test. I emphasize this because the reader is entitled to know that my more skeptical attitude is out of line with the opinion of those who are most entitled to be heard.

Sykes proved beyond reasonable doubt that almost all of the verse in *Faustus B* is built on the same pattern as the verse in *When You See Me*; but the latter play has a very slim showing of the colloquialisms which abound in the other plays considered.[11] As there is a fairly even division of verse scenes and clown scenes in the *Faustus* additions, and the verse scenes were undoubtedly by Rowley, the natural conclusion is that the clown scenes were by

---

[11]As Sykes realized, for one character to use *souns* or its variants a great deal would mean that this character swore profusely, whereas if most of the characters were involved it would be the author who was addicted to profanity. In *A Shrew souns* is used by various characters nineteen times, and *Gogs wounds, sownes* or *sownds* occur in *The Famous Victories* thirty-five times, with no distinction as to the user; but *souns* occurs in *When You See Me* only four times and all four times it is said by Black Will, who is distinctly characterized as a most profane scoundrel. Except for a single *O brave*, the few remaining test words occur in a single scene, sig. C, 3 and 4, and can be matched in Dekker's *Shoemakers' Holiday*, V, ii, and more than matched in *Look About You* and in Porter's *Two Angry Women of Abington*. Rowley makes his clown Will Summers as different from the clowns of the other plays as he could possibly be: Will gives his ironic opinions regarding matters of state and is amazingly clever at capping rhymes. The second clown, Patch, is remotely descended from Shakespeare's clowns and does not speak the language of the other clowns either.

Birde.[12] In *A Shrew*, as Sykes realized, the verse is obviously not by Rowley, and Sykes therefore gave him the prose scenes only; but the verse and prose are too closely interwoven to make this possible. The test words and phrases are not confined to a separate set of scenes. Rowley is therefore definitely out as a possible claimant to the authorship of *A Shrew*, and the question becomes whether there is enough evidence in the Sykes test to warrant a claim for William Birde.

Birde was a member of the Pembroke company when it was reorganized in 1597, and may have been a member in 1592-3. This connection with the company that produced *A Shrew*, taken in connection with the fact that he uses the Sykes expressions in *Faustus*, brings him definitely under suspicion. And there is one parallel which is so striking that it deserves special consideration. Sander's speech in *A Shrew*, "Boy[1] O disgrace of my person! souns, boy of your face! you have seen many boys with such pickadevants, I am sure," is repeated word for word in *Faustus B* except for the mere change of *of* to *in* and the substitution of *beards* for *such pickadevants*, which the author probably thought no longer sufficiently familiar. *Faustus A* gives the speech differently: "How, boy? swouns, boy! I hope you have seen many boys with such pickadevants as I have! Boy, quotha!" This was a natural way of speaking under the circumstances. In *Eastward Ho* (II, i, 82) it is, "Pickle? Pickle in thy throat! zouns, pickle!" And "disgrace of my person" comes in *Two Angry Women* as well as in *Wily Beguiled*. But the correspondence in the case of *A Shrew* and *Faustus B* is too extended and too exact to be explained by anything but identity of authorship or direct quotation. Direct quotation does not seem possible; for in making his additions to *Faustus* Birde would have a manuscript of the play in front of him, and in revising this scene he would not depart from the speech under his eye to look up a variant of it that came in a play of a dozen years ago, nor would he remember the speech in *A Shrew* so exactly unless he had written it himself, unless it was his way of putting it.

But *Faustus A* does not represent the drama as it was when the *Shrew* pirate made use of it. It is possible that the speech may have stood in the manuscript Birde used very much as he left it in *Faustus B*, and that *Faustus A* is a debased version of it. It has been not-

---

[12] Mr. Sykes in a personal conversation was by no means hostile to this suggestion, and we left the matter open in our discussion of it.

cd that the reference to Dr. Lopez must have been written in later, and that there are lines of genuine Marlowe in the 1616 quarto which are not in that of 1604, showing that this quarto represents the play as it was cut down in some places and added to in others. *The Merry Wives of Windsor* (IV, v, 68) refers to an episode which, as others have pointed out, is preserved in *Faustus B* but not in *Faustus A*. It is in the speech which introduces this episode that the parallel occurs: "Or hew'd this flesh and bones as small as sand" (*Faustus B*); "And hew'd thee smaller than the Libian sands" (*A Shrew*. Noted by Dyce in his ed. of Marlowe, p. xxi). This may be only another of the *Shrew* pirate's borrowings.

Sykes realized that Rowley's verse ends and Birde's begins at Act IV, scene ii.[13] From this point the verse is characterized by the frequent use of antithesis, and, as Sykes remarks, no similar bent is traceable in Rowley's drama.[14] This verse (including the last appearance of the Good and Evil Angels, but not counting a few lines mixed in with the prose of the clown scenes) contains 44.4 per cent of rhyme. The *Shrew* pirate avoids rhyme altogether; his verse is full of borrowed beauties and inappropriate classical allusions, of which there is no trace in the *Faustus* additions. Sykes realized that the verse in *A Shrew* could not have been written by Rowley, and so gave him only the prose; but this is impossible because the prose and verse are closely intertwined. But the non-Rowley verse of the additions is also not that of the pirate poet, and this fact, it seems, is stronger evidence against Birde's authorship of *A Shrew* than the presence of a few colloquialisms is evidence for it. I had hoped that by substituting Birde for Rowley I would arrive at the true solution of the problem; but I found that in clearing the way I had destroyed the goal, and that I had only, so far as the authorship of *A Shrew* is concerned, a negative answer to offer. I believe, however, that a negative conclusion is better than a false one.

---

[13]It was therefore he who gave the name Benvolio to the Knight of *Faustus A* and introduced in the same scene a character named Martino. This suggests the possibility—one might even say the probability—that Rowley took the part of the Clown in *Romeo and Juliet*. To the Clown and Benvolio Romeo reads the list of guests beginning, "Signior Martino and his wife and daughters." It seems unlikely that anyone but the man who played the Clown in 1602 associate the names of Benvolio and Martino. We know nothing of Rowley before he joined the Admiral's company in 1597.

[14]There is a characteristic couplet in the prose scene of Robin and Dick with the Vintner: First, be thou turnèd to this ugly shape, For apish deeds transformèd to an ape. This is an added proof, if one were needed, that it was not Rowley who wrote the scenes containing the Sykes test words.

THE TWO ANGRY WOMEN OF ABINGTON AND WILY BEGUILED

By BALDWIN MAXWELL
University of Iowa

The only surviving play known to have been written by Henry Porter, *The Pleasant History*—or according to the running head of the first quarto, *A pleasant Comedie—of the two angry women of Abington,* was printed in 1599, "As it was lately playde" by the Lord Admiral's servants. Seven years later, in 1606, there was printed anonymously *A Pleasant Comedie, Called Wily Begvilde.* Beyond the not uncommon similarity in the wording of the titles, there are several striking similarities between these two plays— similarities in style, in situation, in phraseology, and especially in technique.

Let me first note briefly some of the more general similarities. The style of both plays and the spirit of their comedy, as has frequently been observed, are reminiscent of earlier comedy than that at the end of the sixteenth century.[1] A case can indeed be made— although not here—for both plays, being revisions of much earlier plays.[2] Both plays reveal a particular fondness for popular sayings and proverbs, although, thanks to the appearance of Nicholas Proverbs, *T.A.W.* has many more than *Wily*. Both plays are homely comedies of village life, but both at times deviate into conscious poetic effort and bombast. In *Wily* this artificiality is to be found in nearly all of the speeches of the lovers; in *T.A.W.* it appears more seldom, but is evident in such speeches as that closing scene xiii, which I shall quote later (p. 143). There is in Porter's play much less use made of the comedy of abuse, so prominent in *Wily*, but how similar that which does appear is to that in *Wily* may be seen in the passages quoted on p. 145. Finally, both plays have been

---

[1] C. R. Baskervill, reviewing Boas, *University Drama*, in *JEGP*, XIV (1915), 620; W. Creizenach, *English Drama in the Age of Shakespeare* (London, 1916), p. 323; A. W. Ward, *History of English Dramatic Literature*, 3 vols. (London, 1899), II, 605; C. F. Tucker Brooke, *Tudor Drama* (Boston, 1911), p. 404.

[2] I have argued elsewhere (*SP*, XIX [1922], 220-37) that *Wily* is indebted to the lost *Wylie Beguylie* of 1567, and Mr. Oliphant has shown that the character of Nicholas Proverbs of *T.A.W.* was well known as early as 1589 (*Shakespeare and his Fellow Dramatists*, 2 vols. [New York, 1929], II, 38).

shown to draw upon the early plays of Shakespeare. Reflections in *Wily* of passages from *The Merchant of Venice* and *Romeo and Juliet* have frequently been cited;[3] and Gayley has called attention to the debt of *T.A.W.* to *Romeo and Juliet* and *A Midsummer Night's Dream.*[4]

To turn to more specific resemblances—

The central situation is much the same in the two plays. In *Wily* the main plot concerns the love of Lelia and the scholar, Sophos, a match which Lelia's father, Gripe, bitterly opposes but which is finally effected through the assistance of her brother, Sophos's sworn friend, Fortunatus. In the *T.A.W.* it is Mall's mother who opposes her daughter's match with Franke Goursey, but it too is finally accomplished with the aid of Franke's friend, Mall's brother. In both plays the brother plans an elopement by having the lovers go separately to a prearranged meeting place.[5] In both plays the heroine escapes from her watchful parent during the darkness of night. In *Wily* before the following scene, which takes place the next morning, a song is introduced to advise the audience that

> *The Larke doth chante her chearefull lay*:
> Aurora *smiles with merry cheere*
> *To welcome in a happy day* (ll. 2186-88).

Similarly in *T.A.W.*, after the confusions of the night, Sir Raph Smith closes scene xiii with the lines,

> Twill not be long ere that Aurora will,
> Deckt in the glory of a goldon sunne,
> Open the christall windowes of the east,
> To make the earth enamourde of her face,
> When we shall have cleare light to see our way:
> Come; night being done, expect a happy day.

In addition to the slight verbal similarity in these lines—and a

---

[3] J. W. Hales, ''Wily Beguiled and the Merchant of Venice,'' *Notes and Essays on Shakespeare* (London, 1884), pp. 212-13; F. G. Fleay, *Biographical Chronicle of the English Drama*, 2 vols. (London, 1891), II, 159; A. W. Ward, *op. cit.*, II, 612; etc.

[4] C. M. Gayley, *Representative English Comedies, from the Beginnings to Shakespeare* (New York, 1907), p. 533. All quotations from *T.A.W.* are from Gayley's text; those from *Wily Beguiled* are from the Malone Society reprint, except that like Gayley I modernize *u* and *v*.
It is, of course, quite possible—but perhaps hardly probable—that Shakespeare borrowed from Porter in these plays and in *The Merry Wives of Windsor*. (Cf. J. M. Nosworthy, ''Notes on Henry Porter,'' *MLR*, xxxv [1940], 517-21).

[5] *T.A.W.*, viii, 272ff; *W.B.*, ll. 1430ff.

poetic effort similar to that in many passages in *Wily*—there is an obvious similarity in technique.

A like similarity in expository technique, combined with similarity in content and in phraseology, is to be found in the lines in which the two fathers tell of their plans for their daughters. In *T.A.W.* Master Barnes soliloquizes:

> I have a daughter . . . .
> Well, well, I would my daughter had a husband,
> For I would see how she could demeane her selfe
> In that estate; it may be, ill enough,—
> And, so God shall help me, well remembred now!
> Franke Goursey is his fathers sonne and heyre,
> A youth that in my heart I have good hope on;
> My sences say a match, my soule applaudes
> The motion: O, but his lands are great,
> Hee will looke high; why, I will straine my selfe
> To make her dowry equall with his land (*T.A.W.*, iii, 85-99).

And so Barnes, having decided to propose such a marriage, makes his exit with ''I will goe write about it presentle'' (*T.A.W.*, iii, 174). In the opening soliloquy of *Wily*, the usurer Gripe says:

Let me see, I have but two children in al the world to bestow my goods upon, *Fortunatus* my son & *Lelia* my daughter . . . . now for my daughter she is my only ioy, & the staff of my age, and I have bestowed good bringing up upon hir (barlady) . . . Now if I can harken out some wealthy mariage for hir, I have my only desire. Mas, and well remembred, heer's my neighbour *Ploddall* hard by, has but one only sonne, and (let me see) I take it, his Lands are better than five thousand pounds; now if I can make a match betweene his sonne and my daughter, and so ioine his Land and my mony together, O twil be a blessed union. Well, Ile in, and get a Scrivener, Ile write, to him about it presently. . . (*W.B.* ll. 10-31).

After receiving and reading Barnes's letter, Master Goursey remarks ''I like this motion'' (*T.A.W.*, vi, 5); and when he meets Gripe, Ploddall says ''Marrie I like wel of the motion'' (*W.B.* l. 337).

The quoted soliloquies resemble each other not only in situation, in technique, and in phraseology, but also in the order in which the thoughts are presented. Either or both may be summarized as follows, the identical words italicized: *I have a daughter,* whom I wish to see married. *Well remembered!* My neighbor has an only *son* and heir. That would be a fine *match*. But his *lands* are great. Yet I have money to offer as dowry. *I'll go write about it presently.* And later, to both letters there is the reply, *I like* this *motion.*

Less striking in verbal similarity, but quite alike in technique are the outbursts of the two thwarted parents, when braved by

their children. When Mistress Barnes is told by her son that her
husband loves her "but too weli . . . unlesse ye knew much better
how to use him," she cries:

> Doth he so, sir? Thou unnaturall boy!
> 'Too well,' sayst thou? That word shall cost thee somwhat:
> O monstrous! have I brought thee up to this?
> 'Too well'! O unkinde, wicked, and degenerate,
> Hast thou the heart to say so of thy mother?
> Well, God will plague thee fort, I warrant thee:
> Out on thee, villaine, fie upon thee, wretch!
> Out of my sight, out of my sight, I say! (*T.A.W.*, iii, 256-263).

In *Wily* when Gripe offers Peter his daughter's hand, she plucks it
away.

> *Nurse.* Sheele none she thankes you Sir.
> *Gripe.* Will not she? Why how now I say?
> What? You pewling peevish thing, you untoward baggage:
> Will you not be rul'd by your Father?
> Have I tane care to bring you up to this?
> And will you do as you list?
> Away I say, hang, starve, begge; begone, packe I say;
> out of my sight (*W.B.*, ll. 1170-1177)

Exclusive of Churms, the conycatcher, who is not openly a suitor,
Lelia, the heroine of *Wily*, has two wooers, Sophos, the favored
lover, a scholar, and Peter Ploddall, the rich farmer's son. So
Mall in *T.A.W.* is wooed by Franke, who at first is afraid that wedlock may prove too curst to his "scholler thoughts" (vi, 30), and
by a farmer's son, of whom Phillip gives the following account:

> There came a farmers sonne awooing to her,
> A proper man, well landed too he was,
> A man that for his wit need not to aske
> What time a yeere twere good to sow his oates. . . .
> After a two monthes labour at the most,
> And yet twas well he held it out so long,
> He left his love, she had so laste his lips
> He could say nothing to her but 'God be with yee'! (*T.A.W.*, v, 25-34).

Just so the "well-landed" Peter Ploddall goes courting, talks of
the barnyard, and, mocked and laughed at by Lelia and the Nurse,
takes his departure with "Mistresse *Lelia*, God be with you" (*W.B.*,
l. 913).

There are, in addition, scattered through the two plays a number
of minor similarities. Several proverbs are in common, but as
proverbs are so frequent in both plays, some repetition is to be
expected. I refer, rather, to such similarities as the following.
Coomes like Churms has travelled for his experience (*T.A.W.*, viii,
319; *W.B.*, l. 66). Hodge "scorns" being called drunk as Will

Cricket "scorns" being called "good fellow" (*T.A.W.*, iv, 39;
W.B., l. 309). And in both comedies there is the play on the words
court and *cart* (*T.A.W.*, viii, 63; *W.B.*, l. 172).

With one exception there are no similar characters in the two
plays. I have called attention to the similar situations in which
Mall and Lelia are placed. But with the situation, all likeness between the two girls disappears; there is no resemblance whatever
in their characters. But Mall's prototype is found in *Wily* in
Pegge Pudding. Pegge pretends to a certain naïveté when with
Will Cricket, though she is at bottom as much of the animal as
Mall. She well deserves the scoldings she receives from her mother
and grandmother. Both girls have grown tired of the bonds of
maidenhood. Both, therefore, put on their "cork shoes" (*T.A.W.*,
iii, 167; *W.B.*, l. 1902) and begin search for a husband, determined
that they shall never lead apes in hell.

If it be recognized that there are resemblances between *Wily* and
T.A.W., how are they to be explained? The arguments of the two
plays, although strikingly similar, follow a formula too common in
Elizabethan comedy to suggest any necessary relationship. Except
in the soliloquies of the two fathers, the verbal similarities are certainly insufficient to warrant the belief that the author of one play
borrowed from the other. The most striking resemblances seem to
be in technique, and even in the case of the two soliloquies the similarities, although they can hardly be explained as coincidence, seem
unconscious rather than conscious. At first glance they suggest, perhaps, that the same author wrote both soliloquies and unconsciously
fell into the same progression of ideas and some of the same phrases
which he had used in a like situation in an earlier play. And that
view is to some extent supported by what little we know of Henry
Porter. He appears to have been, if not a writer of limited in-
ventiveness, yet one content to use the same or similar themes in
many of his plays,[6] and perhaps likely, therefore, to express himself in much the same way, although possibly in different language,
whenever he was in his writing faced by similar situations. Yet
T.A.W. so far surpasses *Wily* as a work of merit, its characters are
so much better drawn and its situations so much more amusingly

---

[6]Though all are lost, the titles recorded by Henslowe suggest similarity to
the extant [Part I of?] *T.A.W.*: *Love Prevented*, II *T.A.W.*, *Two Merry
Women of Abington* (possibly the same as II *T.A.W.*), and (with Jonson and
Chettle) *Hot Anger Soon Cold*. His only recorded participation in a play
clearly different was in *The Spencers* (with Chettle).

treated, that it is difficult to imagine *Wily* as written by the same man—especially if it were the later play.[7]

The similarities which I have pointed out, however, do have some value—even though it be negative. For the oft-repeated ascription of *Wily* to Peele, there was no evidence at all. But Mr. Sykes more recently, citing a great many verbal parallels between *Wily* and *Taming of a Shrew*, wrote confidently that "it can scarcely be necessary to give further evidence of Rowley's hand" in *Wily Beguiled*.[8] But an infinitely larger number of verbal parallels have been noted between *Wily* and the works of Kyd,[9] parallels which Mr. Sykes correctly dismisses as clearly implying plagiarism. The indebtedness to *A Shrew* appears to me to be of much the same sort, and this view is supported, I believe, by the similarities between *Wily* and *T.A.W.* The only thing of which we may be certain is that the author of *Wily* was widely acquainted with the drama of his time.

---

[7] There can, I believe, be no doubt that *Wily* in its present form should be dated 1601 or 1602. See *SP*, xix (1922), 207-12. If the resemblances I have noted are the result of indebtedness by the author of *Wily*, it could not have been written in 1596 as has frequently been assumed on the preposterous ground that it imitates no play of Shakespeare dated after that year!

[8] H. Dugdale Sykes, *Sidelights on Elizabethan Drama* (London, 1924) pp. 69-74.

[9] Gregor Sarrazin, *Thomas Kyd und sein Kreis* (Berlin, 1892), pp. 75-77; Frederick S. Boas, *The Works of Thomas Kyd* (Oxford, 1901), pp. xciv—xcv.

AIMS OF A POPULAR ELIZABETHAN DRAMATIST

By George F. Reynolds
University of Colorado

What Elizabethan pseudo-classic dramatists were aiming at is clear enough. To find out we have only to notice Ben Jonson's pronouncements. He specifies what he thought the most important considerations for Tragedy in his "To the Readers," prefixed to *Sejanus*: "truth of argument, dignity of persons, gravity and height of elocution, fulness and frequency of sentence." To these, which he carried out in the play, may be added "the strict laws of time" and "a proper chorus," which he excused himself for disregarding. Similarly for Comedy the prologue to *Every Man in His Humor* makes his aims in that form just as definite through his ridicule of what his contemporaries had done. This prologue is so familiar its points need only be summarized: reasonable observance of the unities of time and place, avoidance of ineffective stage effects, a sane presentation of the follies of men—these were his principal demands in comedy. Jonson, it need scarcely be said, was no slavish classicist. In the introduction to *Every Man out of his Humor*, Cordatus objects to Mitis' enumeration of "the laws of comedy" as "too nice observations": "the equal division of it into acts and scenes, according to the Terentian manner; his true number of actors; the furnishing of the scene with Grex or Chorus, and that the whole argument fall within compass of a day's business." In the Prologue to *Volpone*, however, "the laws of time, place, persons" are mentioned as observed in that comedy, and in its Dedication he says he has "labored for their instruction and amendment to reduce not only the ancient forms, but manners of the scene, the easiness, the propriety, the innocence, and last the doctrine, which is the principal end of poesy to inform men in the best reason of living."

Even these few citations from Jonson are enough to show his independent attitude toward the pseudo-classic critical dogmas, but his general acceptance of most of them, and make it unnecessary further to labor the point that his aims as a dramatist were quite clear to him and that he made them clear by precise statement to his audience and his readers.

Any even fairly comparable statement of what the popular romantic dramatists of the period were trying to do is less easy to find. They mostly wrote their plays without critical prefaces and prologues. We can, of course, deduce from their plays what they considered the main items of their job, but such deductions lack the vivid certainty of contemporary statement. The only such statement which I have noticed as even remotely approaching Jonson's in comprehensiveness and precision is the seldom quoted prologue to Thomas Dekker's *If It Be Not Good the Devil Is in It*, acted at the Red Bull between 1610 and 1612 and published in 1612. It is printed in Volume III of the Pearson Dekker; here it is copied from the 1612 quarto in the Huntington library:

Would t'were a Custome that at all New-playes
The Makers sat o'th, *Stage,* either with *Bayes*
To haue their *Workes Crownd,* or beatē in with *Hissing,*
Pied and bold *Ideotes,* durst not then sit *Kissing*
A *Muses* cheeke: *Shame* would base *Changelings* weane,
From *Sucking* the mellifluous *Hypocrene:*
Who write as blinde-men shoote, by (*Hap,* not *Ayme,*)
So, Fooles by lucky *Throwing,* oft win the Game.
Phoebus has many Bastards, *True Sonnes* fewe,
I meane of those, whose quicke cleare-eyes can viewe.
Poesies pure *Essence,* It being so diuine,
That the *Suns Fires,* (euen when they brightest shine)
Or *Lightning,* when most subtillie *Ioue* does spend it,
May as soone be approchd, weyed, touchd, or comprehēded.
    But tis with *Poëts* now, as tis with Nations,
    Thil-fauourdst *Vices,* are the brauest *Fashions.*
A Play whose *Rudenes, Indians* would abhorre,
Ift fill a house with Fishwiues, *Rare, They All Roare.*
It is not Praise is sought for (Now) but *Pence,*
Tho dropd, from Greasie-apron *Audience.*
Clapd may he bee with *Thunder,* that plucks *Bayes,*
With such *Foule Hands,* & with *Squint-Eyes* does gaze
On *Pallas Shield;* not caring (so hee *Gaines,*
A Cramd *Third Day,* what *Filth* drops frō his *Braines.*
Let *Those* that loue *Pans pipe,* daunce still to *Pan,*
They shall but get *long Eares* by it: Giue me *That Man,*
Who when the *Plague* of an Impostumd *Braynes*
(*Breaking* out) infects a *Theater,* and hotly raignes,
Killing the *Hearers* hearts, that the vast roomes
Stand empty, like so many Dead-mens toombes,
Can call the *Banishd* Auditor home, And tye
His Eare (with golden chaines) to his Melody:
Can draw with *Adamantine Pen* (euen) creatures
Forg'de out of the' *Hammer,* on tiptoe, to *Reach* vp,
And (from *Rare silence*) clap their *Brawny hands,*
T'*Applaud,* what their *charmd* soule scarce vnderstands.
That Man giue mee; whose Brest fill'd by the *Muses,*
With Raptures, Into a second, them infuses:

Can giue an Actor, Sorrow, Rage, Ioy, Passion,
Whilst hee againe (by selfe same Agitation)
    Commands the *Hearers*, sometimes drawing out *Teares*,
    Then smiles, and fills them both with *Hopes* & *Feares*.
That Man giue mee; And to bee such-a-*One*,
Our *Poet* (this day) striues, or to bee *None*:
Lend not (*Him*) hands for *Pittie*, but for *Merit*,
If he *Please*, hee's *Crownd*, if *Not*, his *Fate* must beare it.

The prologue's first demand is for Poetry, words that will "tye [the hearer's] Eare (with golden chaines) to his Melody." That this is put first is all the more significant when we remember our modern almost complete disregard of the appeal of words, except perhaps in wisecracks, slang and dialect. The Elizabethans were fascinated by words, even the understanding gentlemen of the yard, though, as the prologue bluntly says, they were not expected to understand them. Already the prologue itself illustrates this; Dekker must have expected to have so 'charmed their souls' by his involved phrasing and his classical allusions that they would not resent his references to their brawny hands, their greasy aprons, and their iron brains. Or were they so accustomed to such jibes that they took them lightly? At any rate there are in many Elizabethan plays which we have every reason to believe popular successes, innumerable stretches where a large part of the audience in the yard must have been pretty much at sea as to what was meant, and where neither business nor spectacle could have helped to hold their attention. It must have been the sheer incantation of words as delivered by the Elizabethan actors that 'tyed their Eares.' Much, no doubt, depended upon the actor, and many robustious, perriwiged-pated fellows, when they had to deliver such passages, probably helped them out by tearing passion to tatters and splitting the ears of the groundlings. But however abused, Poetry, or at least Rhetoric, certainly was one of the first considerations of the popular dramatists.

The next specified demand on the dramatist is the quick creation of vivid audience responses. There is no call for logically arrived at climaxes, but rather for speed—"into a second"; no emphasis on "truth of argument," "fulness and frequency of sentence," but on "raptures." The temperatures, so to speak, of the two ideals are completely different. This is, of course, almost the most obvious distinction between pseudo-classic and Elizabethan romantic drama; that Dekker puts the matter as clearly as he does is what we naturally expect.

Similarly with the third—the dramatist must give the actor a good opportunity to display strong emotions, ''Sorrow, Rage, Joy, Passion.'' Perhaps nothing about the Elizabethan drama needs more emphasis than this. Meeting most of these plays only in our libraries, we are likely to forget that they were, in their own day, especially vehicles for the actors—Marlowe's for Edward Alleyn, Shakespeare's and the other Chamberlain-King dramatists' for the leading members of that company. To say that this explains why Marlowe's plays, except *Edward II*, are built around one dominating part, while most of the plays of the King's company have many good parts would of course be absurd, but certainly these company arrangements were not without their influence on the dramatists in writing their plays. Most of them knew who their actors would be, what they could do best, and their desire for strong scenes. Thus this demand of the prologue's emphasizes an undeniably important consideration.

Moreover, these emotions must be arranged to provide striking contrasts—''sometimes drawing out Teares, then smiles.'' For Dekker and his audience the doctrine of Kinds had no potency. Their taste and that of their forebears was rather suggested in the illuminating title of *Cambises,* ''A Lamentable Tragedie, Mixed Full of Pleasant Mirth.'' Even in the scripture plays this desire for sharp contrasts is manifest: the chastisement of Noah's wife comes in the Chester play not many lines before his moving prayer of thanksgiving for their escape from the terrors of the flood; the tossing of Mak in a blanket is immediately followed in the Wakefield plays by the Gloria of the angels; and the carpenters in the York play of the Crucifixion make jokes while they nail Jesus to the cross. Dekker's prologue only records a long standing English taste which still continues, though perhaps in somewhat milder form.

Thus Dekker's demands, as expressed in this prologue, on a successful playwright—Poetry, Speed, strong Emotional Scenes to give the actors the greatest opportunities for stirring their audiences, Sharp Contrasts,—do pretty well sum up what the Elizabethan romantic plays actually do offer. The statement is as significant, too, as has already been indicated, for what it omits as for what it says. There is nothing about decorum, nothing about the unities, no regard for the different Kinds, no hint of trying to improve the audience, but only the main motive of stirring their emo-

tions. On only the one point, the importance of language, do Dekker and Jonson approach each other, and even then the "gravity
and height of elocution" call for more of state and dignity than
Dekker's "golden chaines" and "raptures." Thus it is, I think,
not claiming too much for his prologue to say that it may fairly
serve as a statement of what the Elizabethan romantic dramatist
was—'by Aime, not Hap'—consciously trying to do.

THE FALL OF ICARUS

By J. W. ASHTON
Kansas University

In the spread of enlightenment in England during the Renaissance two conflicting forces were at work. On the one hand were the exuberant and varied efforts to extend the powers of man by every possible device. Believers in progress, in the increasing perfectibility of mankind, patriots looking toward a glorious future for England, tried to make available to Englishmen the treasures of the "sciences" as they had been ordered and arranged and commented upon in the learned tongues, to spur Englishmen on to new wisdom, to a new understanding of the world in which they lived. It is this expansive spirit that we most often associate with this period of English life.

On the other hand, however, there were voices raised to decry this consuming ambition of man for knowledge. Some men insisted on the need for humility rather than far-reaching ambition, and they pointed out the practical dangers of too wide and free a spread of learning. Man was not, after all, on the same level as the angels; even if he was only a little below them, that little constituted a significant difference. To aspire too high in the realm of learning was to endanger one's soul just as surely as in the sphere of politics, for though man might know much, there were bounds beyond which he might not trespass with impunity. Long before the sixteenth century the story of Icarus had been taken as a symbol of that rash and headlong attempt to fly too high. The *Ovide moralisé* summarizes the penalty in its commentary on the story of Icarus:

> En enfer ert sa sepulture;
> Cil qui met s'entente et sa cure
> En vaine sapience aquerre.[1]

Later commentators, like Sandys, saw in the fable a symbol of the golden mean, only by inference perhaps concerned with learning.

This fable applaudes the golden Meane, and flight of virtue betweene the extreames. *Icarus* falls in aspiring. Yet more commendable then those, who

---

[1] *Ovide Moralisé Poeme du Commencement du Quartorzieme Siecle.* Edited by C. de Boer (Amsterdam, 1931), III, 153-4.

creepe on the earth like contemptible wormes, such the other extreame: where-as this hath somthing of magnanimity, and mounts like the bird of *Ioue* to his kindred Heauen. . . . *Lucian* will haue *Dedalu*, an excellent Astrologian; who instructed his sonne *Icarus* in that art: when hee, not content with com-petent knowledge, but searching too high into those heauenly mysteries, and so sweruing from the truth, was said to haue fallen from aloft into a sea of errors.[2]

This restraint on man's curiosity took many forms. It marked the last efforts of a truly or at least distinctively learned class to maintain its position in the face of new inventions and new ideas that threatened to destroy it. The most obvious example of this is to be found in the disputes over the translation of the Bible in the first half of the sixteenth century, and the consequent general dis-cussion of the popularizing of theological works. Here was a very special field of knowledge, long the exclusive or almost exclusive sphere of a limited group. And now all manner of men came vociferously demanding a new order, demanding not only the right to be taught but also, and far worse, the right to teach. The issue was not a simple one, but strong among its component parts was this question whether knowledge should be kept to the "well-quali-fied" few or whether it should be made available to the many. The point was presented vigorously by Erasmus in one of the great landmarks of the quarrel.

I totally dissent from those who are unwilling that the sacred scriptures should be read by the unlearned, translated into their tongue, as if Christ had taught such subtleties that they can scarcely be understood by a few theologians, or as if the strength of the Christian religion lay in men's ignorance of it! I wish they were translated into all languages, and I long that the husbandman should sing portions of them as he follows the plough, that the weaver should hum them to the tune of his shuttle, and the traveller beguile with their stories the tedium of his journey.[3]

Such a liberal point of view was rejected by many, however, as John Standish bore witness in 1554. In his *Discourse wherein is debated whether it be expedient that the scripture should be in English for all men to read that wyll* he takes exactly the opposite position to Erasmus and men like Gerrard.[4] Indeed, he goes so far

---

[2] *Ovid's Metamorphosis Englished, Mythologiz'd And Represented in Figures* by G[eorge] S[andys] (Oxford, 1632), p. 290.

[3] Prologue to the New Testament, quoted in Routh, *Sir Thomas More and his Friends* (Oxford University Press, 1934), pp. 55-56.

[4] Phillippe Gerrard, *A Godly Inuectiue in the defence of the Gospell, against such as murmure and woorke what thei can that the Bible shoulde not haue free passage* . . . London, 1547. The more philosophical aspects of the subject are treated in Peter Martyr's *Commentary on Romans* (London, 1568), where it is pointed out that human reason cannot hope to know and understand all that God does, and furthermore, that God is not to be brought to order by human laws (p. 124).

as to say that all the difficulties of the past few years have grown
from the fact that whoever wanted to could read the Bible.   Ob-
stinacy, disobedience, fleshly liberty, loss of devotion, swarms of
errors, heresies, with damnation of thousands of souls have resulted.
He gives interesting reasons: in addition to the basic problem of
inaccuracy in translation there is the fact that the scripture is very
hard to understand because God has so designed it that all men
may not understand.   The details of his argument need not be
presented here; it is sufficient to note his insistence on the dangers
from a spread of learning for which common men can not be qualified and which in many instances is the result of an iniquitous and
perverse curiosity.

This lengthy and vituperative quarrel was representative of the
problem.   At its worst it was sheer obscurantism such as Agrippa's insistence that all knowledge was vanity.[5]   "Vanity of vanities,
all is vanity; for in much wisdom is much grief, and he that increaseth knowledge increaseth sorrow."   Or it expressed itself in
that perennial denial of man's right to better his condition which
Ward attacks in his Dedicatory Epistle to the 1567 edition of *The
Secrets* of Alexis of Piemont.   Ward represents the "expansion-
ists."   He points out that the whole world was created for man and
his use and pleasure; so he ought to make the most of all that is
provided to give him comfort and health.   Then he pays his respects
to the obscurantists.   Some there are who refuse to have anything
to do with physic, saying that if God had appointed that a man
should die, it is impious to try to prevent that death.   But if his
initial premise is true, it is God who has prepared herbs and simples
for mankind's use.   Much, therefore, should be made of medicine.[6]

These are manifestations of a deep-seated suspicion of too great
intellectual curiosity which even in less obviously practical situations spread through English life in the sixteenth century.   As has
been indicated, the suspicion was associated with the concern for
the observance of the mean in all aspects of human life, but it went

[5]Henry Cornelius Agrippa, *Of the Vanitie and vncertaintie of Artes and
Sciences,* Englished by Ja[mes] San[ford] Gent. London, 1569.

[6]*The secrets of the reuerende Maister Alexis of Piemount: . . . Newely corrected and amended. . .* Translated out of French into English by William
Warde. London, 1568.   The title of this work suggests another phase of this
problem, the proprietary nature of medical knowledge and the reluctance of
physicians to divulge their most successful methods.   Through the sixth and
seventh decades of the century an active debate raged as to whether medical
lore should be made available in the vernacular.

beyond that.   It became a denial of the right of man even to attempt fields that were beyond his capacity to know and understand.
Even more perniciously, it set limitations on the right of man to
investigate the secrets of the universe.

That this was not merely a literary convention is shown by the
instances already noted and more particularly by the experience of
Dr. John Dee, at times (when in company with his malignant
familiar, Kelley) seemingly a little more than half quack, but at
other times quite clearly a man of real genius, one of the true scientists of the sixteenth century.   In spite of the Queen's interest
and the patronage of great nobles like Leicester, Dee was several
times in danger from the London mob, and when he went on his
travels in 1583 his excellent library, his furniture, and other posses-
sions were destroyed by a superstitious and vindictive mob.   The
reason was simple.   He knew too much, and the age could explain
such extraordinary knowledge only by believing him to be in league
with the devil.   The situation is summarized with clear understanding in a complaint he included in his Preface to Euclid's *Elements*
(1570) :

> And for these, and such like marueilous Actes and Feates, Naturally, Mathe-
> matically, and Mechanically, wrought and contriued: ought any honest Student,
> and Modest Christian Philosopher, be counted & called a Coniurer?   Shall the
> folly of Idiotes, and the Mallice of the Scornfull, so much preuaile, that He,
> who seeketh no worldly gaine or glory at their handes: but onely, of God,
> the threasor of heauenly wisedome, & knowledge of pure veritie: Shall he (I
> say) in the meane space, be robbed and spoiled of his honest name and fame?
> He that seketh (by St. Paules aduertisement) in the Creatures Properties, and
> wonderful vertues, to finde iuste cause, to glorifie the Aeternall, and Almightie
> Creator by: Shall that man be (in hugger mugger) condemned, as a compan-
> ion of the Helhoundes, and a Caller, and a Coniurer of wicked and damned
> Spirites?   He that bewaileth his great want of time, sufficient (to his con-
> tentation) for learning of Godly wisedome, and Godly Verities in: and onely
> therin setteth all his delight: Will that man leese and abuse his time, in
> dealing with the Chiefe enemie of Christ our Redeemer: the deadly foe of all
> mankinde: the subtile and impudent peruerter of Godly Veritie. . .?   Surely
> (for my part, somewhat to say herein) I haue not learned to make so brutish,
> and so wicked a Bargaine.[7]

He recognized clearly, as he had reason to, that the spirit of
scientific inquiry was at war with the forces of ignorance and prejudice, and he insisted on both the validity and the necessity of the

---

[7] *The Elements of Geometry of the most auncient Philosopher EVCLIDE of
Megara.* Faithfully (now first) translated into the Englishe toung, by H.
Billingsley Citizen of London. . . . With a very fruitfull Praeface made by M.
I. Dee . . . London, /1570/.   It should be noted that Dee gave color to the
rumors about him by his search for the philosopher's stone and by an uncon-
scionable amount of hocus pocus both in England and on the continent.

scientist's "curiosity." The only way in which he bowed to popular belief was in insisting on the ultimate religious significance of all he did.

In the careers of the three great learned men of Elizabethan drama, Dr. Faustus, Friar Bacon, and Prospero, we find exemplified the more important aspects of this attitude. In no instance are they conceived of by the dramatists as magicians and nothing more. They are symbols of the disadvantages, even the tragedies, that may arise from this too searching inquiry after a wisdom that is no wisdom. It is particularly appropriate that Marlowe introduces the Icarus symbol in the account of Dr. Faustus in the Prologue to the play, as he presents his hero consciously choosing to go beyond the religious and other disciplines which he has mastered.

> So soone hee profites in Diuinitie,
> The fruitfull plot of Scholerisme grac't,
> That shortly he was grac't with Doctors name,
> Excelling all, whose sweete delight disputes
> In heauenly matters of *Theologie*,
> Till swolne with cunning, of a selfe conceit,
> His waxen wings did mount aboue his reach,
> And melting heauens conspirde his ouerthrow.
> For falling to a diuelish exercise,
> And glutted now with learnings golden gifts,
> He surffets vpon cursed Negromancy.
> Nothing so sweete as magicke is to him
> Which he preferres before his chiefest blisse. . .[8]

The irony of the situation is, however, that he sells his soul to the Devil only to find that he is still unable to learn all that he wishes to.

> *Faustus.* Well, I am answered, tell me who made the world?
> *Mephastophilis.* I will not.
> *Faustus.* Sweet Mephastophilis, tell me.
> *Mephastophilis.* Moue me not for I will not tell thee.
> *Faustus.* Villaine, haue I not bound thee to tel me any thing?
> *Mephastophilis.* I, that is not against our kingdome, but this is.
> Thinke thou on hell Faustus, for thou art damnd.[9]

It is only then (as his wings begin to melt) that Faustus realizes the full significance and the essential horror of the bargain he has

---

[8]Christopher Marlowe, *The tragicall Historie of Doctor Faustus*, ll. 15-27.

[9]*Ibid.*, ll. 678-685. It should not be forgotten that much of Marlowe's bad reputation in his own time resulted from his meddling with "dangerous" philosophical and religious questions. He and the other members of the Raleigh circle scandalized reputable Englishmen by their irreverent investigations of accepted beliefs. Their case was complicated by the fact that orthodoxy was a political as well as a religious issue, and many people felt that this group came perilously close to treason in their questionings. See John Bakeless, *Christopher Marlowe* (New York, 1937), pp. 200-207.

made. Like Macbeth he has been destroyed by overweening ambition, but ambition for wisdom not for power as a thing in itself.

Rather simpler are the presentations of the same theme in the two less serious plays, Greene's *Friar Bacon* and Shakespeare's *Tempest,* since in them it is apparent that no black magic is involved, no contract has been signed with the Devil. As far as Greene is concerned, Friar Bacon has not sold his soul to the Devil. True, he has the power to conjure and adjure spirits and fiends and he is learned in necromantic spells, but the chief work of his magic is to construct the brazen head which will teach him how to encircle England with a wall of brass.[10] Like Faustus, however, he finds that his most pretentious plans cannot be realized, and even the use of the "glass perspective" brings only unhappiness and disaster; so, wiser than Marlowe's hero, he abjures any further pretentions to superhuman knowledge and is content to accept a humble cell and quiet meditation as his lot in life.[11]

Even more striking an instance is that of Prospero, in whom the conflict seems at first to have been between delight in his studies and responsibility as the head of the state, a variation of the frequently discussed conflict between private pleasure and public responsibility.[12] So engrossed had he become in his books that what should have been his primary responsibility, the government of Milan, had been turned over to his brother, with the disastrous results which he recounts to Miranda early in the play. But his magic is even whiter than Bacon's, for there is no serious hint that Prospero is associated with the powers of darkness in any dangerous way at all. Furthermore, he uses his powers with good intent: to free a sprite from imprisonment in a tree, to prevent a murder or two (including his own), to bring wicked men to justice. It might seem to our minds a record to be proud of, yet Prospero in one of the best known speeches of the play casts away all his implements of magic, all the apparatus of that learning that has surpassed other men's, and turns his face to the responsibilities of rule in Milan.[13] The modern reader might feel that a ruler might well make good use of all the mysteries he could command, but the issue is clear and definite in Prospero's mind. Such studies have no place

10Robert Greene, *Friar Bacon and Friar Bungay,* ii, 49ff.

11*Ibid.,* xiii, 85ff.

12*The Tempest,* I, ii, 66ff.

13*Ibid.,* V, i, 33-57.

in the practical life of the ruler of a state. He recognizes that the
kind of power he receives from this knowledge is only a delusion
and a snare in his working world. Only in the Never-Never-Land
of his island, where he has been sole ruler, almost sole human in-
habitant, and only under the special conditions of the situation in
the play can his unnatural knowledge be a good thing.

Lest in closing I leave the impression that it is only magic as
such which is involved in this Renaissance distrust of man's too
high flights in knowledge, it is well to remember Milton's treatment of the idea in its most profound relations to human conduct.
As Adam wonders about his brave new world, he is thus counselled
by the Archangel.

> To ask or search I blame thee not, for Heav'n
> Is as the book of God before thee set,
> Wherin to read his wond'rous Works, and learn
> His Seasons, Hours, or Days, or Months, or Years:
> This to attain, whether Heav'n move or Earth,
> Imports not, if thou reck'n right; the rest
> From Man or Angel the great Architect
> Did wisely to conceal, and not divulge
> His secrets to be scann'd by them who ought
> Rather admire: . . .
> Solicit not thy thoughts with matters hid,
> Leave them to God above, him serve and fear:
> Of other Creatures, as him pleases best,
> Wherever plac't, let him dispose: joy thou
> In what he gives to thee, this Paradise
> And thy fair *Eve*: Heav'n is for thee too high
> To know what passes there; be lowly wise:
> Think only what concerns thee and thy being;
> Dream not of other Worlds, what Creatures there
> Live, in what state, condition or degree,
> Contented that thus far hath been reveal'd
> Not of Earth only but of highest Heav'n.[14]

What in base minds was essentially obscurantism, a fearful drawing back from mysteries too terrible to behold, could become that
profound humility that à Kempis had recommended to mankind
long before, a recognition that there are more things in heaven and
earth than our philosophy can account for.[15]

---

[14]*Paradise Lost,* Bk. VIII, lines 66-75 and 157-178.

[15]Thomas à Kempis, *The Imitation or Following of Christ, and the con-
temning of worldly vanities.* London, 1567. In the second chapter à Kempis
insists that there are many things, knowledge of which does not profit man's
soul, and therefore he is a fool to seek after such things. A Kempis is primarily concerned here with the distinction between worldly and godly knowledge.

SHAKESPEARE'S *RAPE OF LUCRECE*

By E. P. KUHL
University of Iowa

In all Shakespeare the *Rape of Lucrece* is the most slighted step-child. Critics disdain her, and scholars scorn her. The poem, it is urged, lacks every element of greatness; a shapeless narrative with but endless irrelevancies and tedious moralizings, and a character-ization that in its parade of learning and besprinkling of pious phrases elicits only ridicule and contempt. The truth is, however, that the very qualities for which this Cinderella is derided were highly esteemed by contemporary readers. Of all Shakespeare's printed works, dramatic or nondramatic, *Lucrece* was the most popular in its day—four editions in six years (1594-1600).

It follows then that any true estimate of the poem must consider this popular appeal; that its conspicuous success may throw light on Shakespeare's motives, perhaps even on shifting critical taste. Any discussion makes it necessary that we begin with the history of the theme sixteen centuries before the story engaged the atten-tion of Shakespeare.

Tarquin's vile deed constitutes a chapter in the early history of Rome. The story of his lust is told in full by Livy.

> Brutus, while the others were absorbed in grief, drew out the knife from Lucretia's wound, and holding it up, dripping with gore, exclaimed, "By this blood, most chaste until a prince wronged it, I swear, and I take you, gods, to witness, that I will pursue Lucius Tarquinius Superbus and his wicked wife and all his children, with sword, with fire, aye with whatsoever violence I may; and that I will suffer neither them nor any other to be king in Rome!"

Brutus accordingly raised the people against the Tarquins for the infamous offense that changed the face of Rome.

> He reminded them, besides, of the pride of the king himself and the wretched state of the commons, who were plunged into ditches and sewers and made to clear them out. . . With these and, I fancy, even fiercer reproaches, such as occur to a man in the very presence of an outrage, but are far from easy for an historian to reproduce, he inflamed the people, and brought them to abrogate the king's authority and to exile Lucius Tarquinius, together with his wife and children.

After that, "new liberty [was] enjoyed by the Roman people."

And as Livy concludes, "This liberty was the more grateful as the last king had been so great a tyrant."

Livy, it is important to remember, was no mere objective historian. "It was the ethical aspect of history then that chiefly appealed to Livy." Or, as Livy himself states:

What chiefly makes the study of history wholesome and profitable is this, that you behold the lessons of every kind of experience set forth as on a conspicuous monument; from these you may choose for yourself and for your own state what to imitate, from these mark for avoidance what is shameful in the conception and shameful in the result.[1]

It was Livy, the national historian, writing in a newly self-concious imperial Rome, who was the ultimate source for all later retellings of the Tarquin story.

In his national poem, *Fasti*, Ovid alludes to Tarquin's grievous deed and Lucrece's tragic pathos, but he too bears in mind what happened to Rome after that proud ruler's downfall. In stressing the personal tragedy he does not overlook the political consequences of Tarquin's infamous offense:

They bore her to burial, that matron of manly courage; and tears and indignation followed in her train. The gaping wound was exposed for all to see. With a cry Brutus assembled the Quirites and rehearsed the king's foul deeds. Tarquin and his brood were banished. A consul undertook the government for a year. That day was the last of kingly rule.[2]

Ovid also exerted an immense influence on later centuries.

Cicero, too, turns to political use the account of Tarquin the tyrant. In his *Republic* he reviles tyranny with fearless vigor:

For no sooner did this king alter into an unjust master than he forthwith became a tyrant, than whom no animal more foul and loathsome to gods and men or more detested can be imagined; who, though he have the figure of a man, outdoes the most monstrous of beasts in the excess of his vices.

On this "powerful defence of justice against injustice," Professor McIlwain remarks: "This, then, is the origin of tyranny among the Romans, which differs from that represented in Plato's *Republic* in this, that it was not the seizing of a new power by Tarquin, but the unjust employment of one he already had, which completely overthrew this form of regal state."[3] Cicero likewise influenced Tudor thought—and Shakespeare.[4]

---

[1]Livy (Loeb Classical Library. Translation by B. O. Foster), 1, pp. xxiff., 7, 205ff.; cf. pp. 199ff., 219.

[2]Ovid (Loeb Classical Library. Translation by Sir James G. Frazer), pp. xxf., 107ff., 119; cf. p. 394.

[3]C. H. McIlwain, *The Growth of Political Thought in the West* (New York, 1932), pp. 106f.

[4]At least indirectly.

Lydgate, "commanded" by the Duke of Gloucester to write against domestic division, began his *Serpent of Division* with the banishment of the Tarquins and the consequent change in government. Again, in the *Fall of Princes*, the misdeeds and expulsion of the Tarquins from Rome was a political lesson for English tyrants.

> Thus for luxur[y]e and ther cruelte,
> Ther tirannye and fals extorsioun,
> Thei were exilid out off Rome toun.[5]

By 1425, therefore, the Tarquin and Lucrece theme was linked with the York-Lancaster broils; Lydgate's warnings influenced succeeding generations, even the decade in which Shakespeare wrote his *Lucrece*.

Tarquin's brutal act, followed by his banishment and the change in the Roman government, exercised a hypnotic fascination upon the Tudors. With zest they seized upon his crimes-theme that offered a parallel to their own troubled times. To name the writers who moralized on the horrors and infamies of Tarquin is to list all but the entire roster.

Thus in his *Governour* Sir Thomas Elyot repeatedly turns to the story as a warning and an admonition, and ever in the background of his mind is the welfare of England. In his condemnation of the ruthless violence of Tarquin, the domestic discord and upheaval after his exile, as well as the civil wars that followed, Elyot always seeks the lesson for his own era. For example, speaking of the "insolencie and pryde" of the tyrant, he says,

Also in that citye [Rome] he maye beholde the fourme of a publike weal: whiche, if the insolencie and pryde of Tarquine had nat excluded kynges out of the citie, it had ben the most noble and perfect of all other.

Elyot elsewhere identifies England's domestic struggles with those of Rome after the exile of the Tarquins. In arguing for "one soueraigne gouernour" instead of a multitude having authority, he cites the Romans under kings: at that time, he says, they were "well gouerned, nor neuer amonge them was discorde or sedition"; but with the exile of "Tarquine and all his posteritie" power passed into the hands of the people. As a result civil wars arose and flourished, and until the time of Augustus "the cite of Rome was neuer

---

5 E.E.T.S., Vol. 121 (1924) p. 237. Lydgate, who refers repeatedly to the Tarquins, I am discussing elsewhere in connection with Chaucer.

longe quiete from factions or seditions amonge the people."[6] Elyot's oft-printed manual for future rulers, eight editions between 1531 and 1580, must have been familiar to influential Londoners of the 1590's, personages in the court circle of Shakespeare.

The internal disorders and civil wars of Rome after the exile of Tarquin were associated in Shakespeare's day with the wars of the Yorks and Lancasters. For example, in 1590, the year of the death of Walsingham, Lydgate's *Serpent of Division* was reprinted, with this warning on the title-page for tyrannical rulers: "Wherein is contened the true History or Mappe of Romes ouerthrowe, Gouerned by Auarice, Enuye, and Pride, the decaye of Empires be they neuer so sure." With Lydgate's tract was published another admonition to Tudor despots, a warning against the evils of a divided kingdom and civil wars, *Gorboduc*.[7] Holinshed, likewise, with the welfare of England at heart, equates the effect on Rome of the lust and tyranny of Tarquin with England's civil broils; "for the vice of the bodie lost the kingdome of Rome; and the name of Tarquine banished the Citie for euer: yet was not his fault so detestable as the fact of cruell Nero . . . Behold yonder Richard [III], which is both Tarquine and Nero."[8] Holinshed's account of Richard III was used by Shakespeare.

Shakespeare follows closely the plot as told by the patriot and teacher, Livy, and moralized on for more than a thousand years— down to the time of his own *Lucrece*. His Argument, presumably genuine,[9] adheres to the traditional story, not omitting the momentous political results to Rome. Speaking of the early life of Tarquin, he says,

Lucius Tarquinius, for his *excessive pride* surnamed Superbus, . . . had caused his own father-in-law Servius Tullius to be cruelly murd'red, and, *contrary to the Roman laws* and customs, *not requiring or staying for the people's suffrages, had possessed himself of the kingdom.*

And after relating the story of Lucrece, Shakespeare says:

Which done, with one consent they all vowed to root out the whole hated family of the Tarquins; and bearing the dead body to Rome, Brutus acquainted the people with the doer and manner of the vile deed, with a *bitter invective*

---

[6]*The Governour* (Everyman ed.) pp. 12f., 45; cf. p. 22.

[7]Cf. Lydgate's *Serpent of Division*, ed. H. N. MacCracken (Yale University Press, 1911), p. 47 and n.

[8]Holinshed, III (1808), p. 442.

[9]At all events the Argument reflects contemporary opinion; it must represent Shakespeare's also.

*against the tyranny of the king; wherewith the people were so moved, that
with one consent and a general acclamation the Tarquins were all exiled, and
the state government changed from kings to consuls.*[10]

Shakespeare's poem likewise ends with Brutus' appeal to the citizens to rid Rome of the monster who had disgraced the city; and in
so doing he unites the personal tragedy of ''chaste Lucrece'' with
the political story.

> Now, by the Capitol that we adore,
> And by this chaste blood so unjustly stained,
> By heaven's fair sun that breeds the fat earth's store,
> By all our country rights in Rome maintained,
> And by chaste Lucrece's soul that late complained
> Her wrongs to us, and by this bloody knife,
> We will revenge the death of this true wife.

When the citizens ''had sworn to this advised doom,'' they agreed

> To show her bleeding body thorough Rome,
> And so to publish Tarquin's foul offence.

This done ''with speedy diligence,''

> The Romans plausibly did give consent
> To Tarquin's everlasting banishment.

That Shakespeare had more than a merely decorative or dramatic
motive in *Lucrece* finds support in the dedication to *Venus and
Adonis,* in which reference is made to some future ''grave labour.''
Lucrece, the ''fulfillment of this pledge,'' contains in its dedication
a hint that Shakespeare's wish was more than to please his patron:
he calls the poem ''this pamphlet.'' Though in the sixteenth century *pamphlet* had reference to size or form, it was also a treatise
''on some subject or question of current or temporary interest, personal, social, political, ecclesiastical, or controversial, on which the
writer desires to appeal to the public.''[11] ''In *I Henry VI,* presumably by Shakespeare, ''pamphlet'' has reference to content rather
than to form.

> Com'st thou with deep premeditated lines?
> With written pamphlets studiously devis'd? (III, i, 1-2)

Contemporaries read the *Lucrece* for profit as well as for
pleasure: for example, the poem was heavily drawn upon by *England's Parnassus.* This dictionary of quotations, proclaimed on the
title-page as being both ''pleasaunt and profitable,'' is filled with
warning examples for persons in private and public life. The com-

---

[10] Italics mine.
[11] *NED.*

piler of the anthology takes it for granted that *Lucrece* contains
political maxims of conduct. I shall quote only verses appearing in
England's Parnassus, a work so popular as to call for three editions in 1600, the year that saw the third and fourth editions of
Lucrece.

Under "Justice" is this line, at a time when injustice stirred all
London,

> ——Sparing Iustice, feeds iniquitie.

"Mercy," in a period when those in authority were not inclined to
clemency, contains this verse:

> Soft pittie enters at an Iron gate.

"Opportunity" has one of Lucrece's so-called "irrelevent" stanzas,

> Opportunitie thy guilt is great,
> Tis thou that execut'st the traitors treason,
> Thou setst the wolfe where he the lambe may get,
> Who euer plots the sinne, thou points the season.
> Tis thou that spurn'st at right, at lawiers reason:
>   And in thy shady Cell where none may spie him,
>   Sits sinne, to feare each soule that wanders by him.

"Pollicie," that Machiavellian bugbear of Tudors, has this:

> A little harme done to a great good end,
> For lawfull pollicie remaines inacted,
> The poysonous simple sometime is compacted
> In a pure compound; being so applied
> His venome in effect is purified.

Under "Time" is another excerpt from one of Lucrece's "impertinent" speeches, an utterance that reflects the Elizabethan
mind of the Nineties—when an aging queen was wearing out her
welcome.

> Times glory is to calme contending kings,
> To vnmaske falshood, and bring truth to light.

Moreover, in every instance in *England's Parnassus*—thirty-nine
in all—Shakespeare appears with well-known political moralists,
writers preoccupied with problems of the hour: under "Justice"
with Spenser (Shakespeare stands between two verses from the
fifth book of the *Faerie Queene* on Justice) and Daniel (*Civil Wars,*
written with an eye on those at court, including the circle of the
Earl of Southampton); "Opportunitie" with Warner's *Albion's
England* and Harington's *Orlando Furioso*; "Pollicie" with Mark-

ham's *Devoreux*[12] and the *Mirrour for Magistrates*; and under "Time" with Spenser (two stanzas, both from the third book, in which the poet's eye glances at the English Court), and Daniel's *Civil Wars.*

Furthermore, in *England's Parnassus* ("Princes") lines from *Lucrece* stand with verses from the wars of the Yorks and Lancasters, verses moreover from Shakespeare's *Richard III*—a link recalling the equation made by Holinshed.

(1) In a time of deep political discontent intensified by uncertainty of succession and increasing tyranny from above, Shakespeare chooses a plot laden with political implications—connotations familiar to Londoners of the 1590's. And this theme of Tarquin becomes a vehicle for his own views on kingship—lust, tyranny, statecraft, justice, the laws that govern political life—precisely the problems that absorbed the contemporary Elizabethan mind. After every allowance is made for the divine spark of poetry, for a desire to please a patron or the public, for royalties on the poem, fame, advancing his social status, making connections in high places, ravishment by beauty, portrayal of delicate manhood and loyal womanhood, trafficking with the universal scheme of things, we must still believe that Shakespeare in this tragic tale was moved by patriotic impulses, that he dared protest against royal rule at a time of increasingly articulate popular opinion. In *Lucrece*, in short, Shakespeare denounces (along with other matters) crumbling outworn political theories—and he does it precisely at the time when these outworn political beliefs were uppermost in the minds of men (1592-4).[13]

(2) True, the poem suffers structurally. But grant Shakespeare's right to use a theme weighty with political import, this was inevitable. Shakespeare was risking artistic disaster the moment he subordinated form to matter. This raises a question in criticism. The *Lucrece*, as we have seen, enjoyed a wide popularity in its day; nor did this wane for a long time—not until the end of the Stuart dynasty. That is, while a monarch still believed in

---

12I have relied upon a photostat copy in the Huntington Library. The editor of *England's Parnassus*, Charles Crawford, has this note on No. 7 (p. 385): "This and other untraced passages assigned to Markham may be found in that author's *Devoreux*, printed 1595, 8vo, a work the whereabouts of which is unknown to me."

13Evidence for this statement as well as for some other remarks in the conclusion I hope to present elsewhere.

Divine Right, Shakespeare's *Lucrece* was widely read. In the next century the poem lost its national significance, and in the meantime there developed the code of dogmatic rules, what Dr. Johnson called "art reduced to principles." As a consequence, in the nineteenth century *Lucrece* was taken up by scholarly opinion and judicial criticism. In other words, while the plot had a vital relation to England's national life, the poem was valued for its meaning; when content no longer mattered, it became mummified, and arbiters of poetic theory, with different appraisals to be sure, duly labelled it.

(3) Perhaps we can glimpse a new relationship between the poet and his patron. Southampton, young in years, unmarried, eager to serve his country, in need of sage counsel, is addressed, delightfully, by an ardent patriot and poet. That Shakespeare may have been justified appears in the young man's marriage (not long before the appearance of the second quarto in 1598). One also wonders if the Earl's outstanding service to the state in the Virginia Colony is at all linked with the advice in *Lucrece*: that is, if the *Tempest* is *Lucrece* brought up to date. At all events the latter piece contains a message for those in authority; addressed as it was to a youth of impetuous blood, it is not at all impossible that in a desire to impress Southampton's mind and soul, Shakespeare gave him this example of self-control. After events proved Shakespeare right as a godlike guide.

(4) Since the Lucrece theme had been for generations associated with the wars of the Yorks and Lancasters, may not the connection also have been made in Shakespeare's mind? His contemporaries, the readers of *England's Parnassus*, made no exception in the case of Shakespeare. In that event his chronicle plays may also refer to contemporary issues.

(5) Gabriel Harvey's famous remark that Shakespeare's *Lucrece* appeals to the "wiser sort," is often airily dismissed. In the light of the above, however, his reputation as an acute critic may perhaps be in part reinstated. That Harvey in his comment on *Lucrece* voiced the sentiments of his time may be convincingly illustrated by an incident at his Alma Mater, Cambridge.

In telling the "story of Lord Brooke's attempt to found in 1627 a long-desired chair of history at Cambridge," Professor Morison writes:

As both universities had treated history somewhat lightly, no competent candidate could be found in England, and a rising young Dutchman named Dorislaus was imported from the University of Leyden. In his second lecture, the Professor made bold to touch 'upon the Excesses of Tarquinius Superbus his infringing the Liberties of the People' and to vindicate his own countrymen against Spain. In short, as Samuel Ward informed the Lord Primate, 'he was conceived of by some, to speak too much for the defence of the Liberties of the People; though he spake with great moderation and with an exception of such Monarchies as ours' . . . At Laud's instance, the professor was forbidden by a royal injunction to continue his course. Lord Brooke, in disgust, allowed the proposed endowment to lapse, and the professor returned to Holland.[14]

This was the Lord Brooke who was Sidney's intimate friend; whose life of Sir Philip reveals that to both of them history and letters were a mirror; who at the time of the popularity of Shakespeare's *Lucrece* was treasurer of the royal navy; who wrote a propaganda play on Essex "then falling"; who was a member of the literary club "Areopagus," with none other than Gabriel Harvey. Both Greville and Harvey moved in the London circle of the Earl of Southampton (to whom *Lucrece* was dedicated), himself "nursed" at Cambridge.

If in his *Lucrece* Shakespeare did not show a political awareness and a desire to enforce some warnings, then he was not in tune with his contemporaries or readers. But there is nothing in the dedication or Argument or the poem itself to suggest that Shakespeare did not consciously appeal to the hearts and minds of depressed fellow countrymen, patriots as well as patron. Shakespeare, we must conclude, stands with Daniel and Spenser and other patriotic Englishmen as a critic of contemporary issues.

---

[14]S. A. Morison, *The Founding of Harvard College* (1935), p. 49.

PERSEUS PURLOINS PEGASUS

By T. W. BALDWIN
University of Illinois

Shakespeare has given clear indication that he had information which in his day was most easily to be found in a certain contemporary form of Ovid's *Metamorphoses*. Says the braggart French Dauphin of his horse,

Ça, ha! he bounds from the earth, as if his entrails were hairs; le cheval volant, the Pegasus, chez les narines de feu! When I bestride him, I soar, I am a hawk: he trots the air; the earth sings when he touches it; the basest horn of his hoof is more musical than the pipe of Hermes.
Orl. He's of the colour of the nutmeg.
Dau. And of the heat of the ginger. It is a beast for Perseus: he is pure air and fire; and the dull elements of earth and water never appear in him, but only in patient stillness while his rider mounts him.[1]

This is the Folio version. The first quarto assigns the speech to Burbon and reads:

> I haue a steed like the
> Palfrey of the sun nothing but pure ayre and fire,
> And hath none of this dull element of earth within him.
> *Orleance.* He is of the colour of the Nutmeg.
> *Bur.* And of the heate a the Ginger.

Here clearly is the basis of the original passage, which has been revised for the Folio text. For many of the details even in the final version belong conventionally to the horses of the sun, not to Pegasus.

> nec tibi quadripedes animosos ignibus illis,
> quos in pectore habent, quos ore, et naribus efflant,
> in promptu regere est.

"Nor is it an easy thing for thee to control the steeds, hot with those strong fires which they have within their breasts, which they breathe out from mouth and nostrils."[2] Golding has it:

Againe thou neyther hast the powre nor yet the skill I knowe
My lustie coursers for too guide that from their nosetrilles throwe,
And from their mouthes the fierie breath that breedeth in their brest.[3]

---

[1]*Henry V*, III, vii, 13-25.
[2]Miller, *Metamorphoses*, I, 66-67.
[3]Rouse, *Shakespeare's Ovid*, p. 43.

A palfrey of the sun has nostrils of fire, as Pegasus also may in Shakespeare's day, and is pure air and fire as opposed to the earth and water of ordinary animals. These items, therefore, possibly including the nostrils of fire, were in the original version, but they were originally suggested, quite properly, by the horses of the sun. In the final version, Perseus and Pegasus have been substituted. Pegasus is the flying horse and brings in with him the allusions to bounding and flying. Here we have a clear indication of the nature of the quarto text. It records, no doubt imperfectly, its ancestral text, which has been revised before being recorded in the Folio text.[4]

Incidentally, while Shakespeare was touching up the mythology of this passage, he introduced still another abstruse bit in the reference to the pipe of Hermes.

Now as the 'lyre' was the invention of Hermes, and not the pipe, which was invented by Pan ('Pan taught to join with wax unequal reeds.' 'Virgil' Ecl. II. 32), the above illustration must refer to Ovid's account of the death of Argus, where Hermes approaches Argus in the guise of a shepherd playing on a 'pipe,'—

'With this (rod) he drives, in the guise of a shepherd, through the winding country lanes his flock of goats, and plays the while on his pipe.' ('Met.' I. 676.).[5]

Having made a tennis ball out of his horse, then turned him into Pegasus with Perseus-Dauphin aboard, and given him the music of Hermes' pipe, the Dauphin is now warmed up to the theme of praising his horse, but we need at this time pursue it no further.

A second allusion to Perseus on Pegasus is in the disputed *Troilus and Cressida*, so might not belong to Shakespeare personally, and besides might possibly be to the ship into which Pegasus had managed to get parabolically and allegorically (paregorically) metamorphosed.

> But let the ruffian Boreas once enrage
> The gentle Thetis, and anon behold
> The strong-ribb'd bark through liquid mountains cut,
> Bounding between the two moist elements,
> Like Perseus' horse.[6]

---

[4] There are other controllable instances which show exactly how corrupt the quarto text is in these places, but we do not enter that phase of the subject here. Since the Folio version dates itself for 1599, it follows that the quarto version was earlier. For a summary of opinion on these matters, see Chambers, E. K., *William Shakespeare*, I, 390ff.

[5] Theobald, W., *The Classical Element in the Shakespeare Plays*, p. 267.

[6] *Troilus and Cressida*, I, iii, 38-42. See the note on this passage in Professor H. N. Hillebrand's eventually forthcoming edition of the play for the Furness Variorum. It was he who set me to work on this problem.

Early critics apparently were not disturbed by the passage in *Henry V* which gave Pegasus to Perseus. At least, they neither explain nor object. But Malone thought the passage in *Troilus and Cressida* required a long note. He was of opinion that the author had followed *The Destruction of Troy*, where Pegasus the horse is given to Perseus and is allegorized and moralized into a ship.[7] Malone, therefore, thought that this ship is here alluded to, though Steevens disagreed, as have others from time to time. Douce carried the tradition back to Boccacio, who "in his *Genealogia Deorum*, lib. xii. c. 25, has quoted Lactantius as saying, that when Perseus undertook his expedition against Gorgon, at the instance of king Polydectus, he was accompanied by the winged horse Pegasus, but not that he used him in delivering Andromeda. Boccacio adds that others were of opinion that he had a *ship* called Pegasus."[8] Now in fact Boccacio merely refers to Lactantius as authority for the story that when Perseus grew up he undertook this exploit at the command of King Polydectes, not for the specific details, including the addition of Pegasus to his traditional equipment for the exploit. So Lactantius does say that Perseus "a Polydecte rege missus fuerat ad Medusam Gorgonam occidendam,"[9] but gives no details of his equipment. The same information is repeated in the commentary on Ovid attributed to Lactantius.[10] Boccacio very shortly quotes Statius, *Thebaid*, III, 460, showing that he is probably thinking of the commentary attributed to Lactantius on the *Thebaid*, but he would have got the same information from the one on Ovid. The commentary on the *Thebaid* does add one further point concerning Perseus, "qui uolatu dicitur uenisse ad interficiendum Gorgona. quod ideo fingitur, quia nauigio uenit."[11] There is no Pegasus here, merely flying is interpreted to mean that Perseus came in a ship. Even so, this note seems to be a modern insertion. Thus the works attributed to Lactantius give no authority for the horse Pegasus as belonging to Perseus, nor for a ship of that name. I do not find Pegasus either ship or horse attributed to Perseus in Servius, who is mentioned by Boccacio along with Lactantius as an authority for his article on Pegasus.

[7]Malone, *Variorum*, VIII, 254.

[8]Douce, F., *Illustrations of Shakspeare* (1807), II, 57.

[9]Jahnke, R., *Lactantii Placidi Qui Dicitur Commentarios In Statii Thebaida* (1898), III, 12.

[10]Magnus, H., *Metamorphoseon*, pp. 651, 654-5.

[11]Jahnke, *Lactantii*, III, 59.

What has happened is that by the Middle Ages Perseus has been substituted for Bellerophon as master of Pegasus, both horse and subsequent ship. For instance, Palaephatus says of Bellerophon, "Hic cum nauigium sibi praeparasset, maritima circunquaque loca depraedabatur, nomen autem nauis Pegasus erat, vt nunc quoque suum cuilibet nauigio nomen est inditum. Nomen autem id Pegasi nauigio magis, quam equo aptum, fuisse videtur."[12] Stephanus[13] gives an instance of Pegasus as the name of a ship, "Pegasus, Triarchi filius, cuius navis Pegasę monumentum accepit." Horse and ship are here connected with Bellerophon as was usual, not with Perseus. But in a mythology which survives in a manuscript of the tenth or eleventh century Bellerophon and Perseus are made identical. "Bellerophontis qui et Perseus;" "Bellerophon, qui et Perseus, Glauci filius."[14] So at one fell swoop Perseus is given even Bellerophon himself with all that he possessed. While Boccacio does not identify the two, yet in his article on Pegasus[15] he regularly brackets the two together in the use of Pegasus and in the interpretation of that use.

It was inevitable that Bellerophon and Perseus should become confused with each other in certain details as well as in the whole. For instance, the interpretation by Palaephatus of the flying Pegasus as a ship evidently led to the interpretation found in the inserted note attributed to Lactantius of the flying Perseus as having used a ship. This ship then became Bellerophon's ship Pegasus, which was also his horse Pegasus. Perseus had already purloined the horse Pegasus even in the art of classical times.[16] Since Perseus had brought Pegasus forth by a Caesarean operation, it was but natural that he should have a kind of first claim on him as a useful mode of transport in his further adventures. Thus by the Middle Ages Perseus in these various ways had acquired Pegasus, both horse and ship, from Bellerophon. So firmly did Perseus establish his claim to Pegasus that even Riley in a note to his still current translation of Ovid's *Fasti* can assert that Ovid "says that Perseus was mounted on Pegasus when he slew the sea-monster to which

[12]Hyginus, *Fabularum Liber* (Paris, 1578), p. 118a.

[13]*Dictionarium Historicum* (Paris, 1570).

[14]Maius, Angelus, *Classicorum Auctorum*, III, 27.

[15]Boccacio, *Genealogiae* (1511), Lib. X, c. XXVII.

[16]Jacobsthal, Paul, *Die Melischen Reliefs* (1931), Tables 28 and 29, Nos. 61 and 62.

Andromeda was exposed,"[17] and give a specific reference in Ovid for the fact. His reference, however, is merely to the birth of Pegasus from the blood of Medusa.

Some thought that Ovid had elsewhere placed Perseus directly upon the back of Pegasus. "In his translation of Ovid's *Elegies* [III, 11, 24] Marlowe writes: 'Victorious Perseus a wing'd steed's back takes,' and there is no doubt that by *Victor Abantiades* Ovid meant that hero, just as in *Metamorphoses*, vi. 137, he calls him *Ultor Abantiades*."[18] Ovid had written,

> nos pedibus pinnas dedimus, nos crinibus angues;
> victor Abantiades alite fertur equo—

"'tis we have placed wings on feet, and mingled snakes with hair; our song made Abas' child a victor with the wingèd horse.'"[19] It will be noticed that *fertur* of the second line is ambiguous. Showerman has translated as meaning "is said"; instead of the primary meaning "is borne." The line by itself can be translated "a victor, Abas' child is borne by the winged horse," and Marlowe has so understood it. Marlowe could not have justified his reading, as we might, by pointing out that in art Perseus might even in classical times be represented as riding the horse Pegasus.[20]

Had Marlowe examined the annotated *Amores* published in 1549, Dominicus Marius (p. 367) would have warned him against mounting Perseus upon Pegasus. He points out that some wrongly think that Perseus is meant—in which position he is himself in error—although he admits that Ovid in *Metamorphoses* refers to Perseus as *Victor Abantiades,* but it is nowhere said that Perseus was borne by Pegasus. The reference must be to Bellerophon, who was supposed to have used the horse when he conquered Chimera. So he would interpret the crucial word as it is interpreted now, "Fertur: per nos poetas, qui haec fingimus."

Thus by the sixteenth century, scholars were already attempting to evict Perseus from Bellerophon's property, but it was to take them some centuries—if they have succeeded even yet. In the second half of the sixteenth century, when Shakespeare and his contemporaries were acquiring and using their ideas, the editions of Ovid's *Metamorphoses* were no doubt the chief source of dissemina-

---

[17] Riley, H. T., *The Fasti* (1890), p. 108, n. 78.
[18] Deighton, K., *Troilus and Cressida* (Arden ed.), p. 33n.
[19] Showerman, *Heroides and Amores*, pp. 494-5
[20] Jacobsthal, *Die Melischen Reliefs*, Tables 28 and 29, Nos. 61 and 62.

tion for this bit of misinformation upon Pegasus, since I have not found it current elsewhere except in Boccacio. In 1557, was published *La Metamorphose d'Ovide figurée* at Lyons, with one-hundred and seventy-eight woodcuts by Bernard Salomon. I have used the Italian version *La Vita Et Metamorfosec D'Ovidio, Figurato & abbreuiato in forma d'Epigrammi da M. Gabriello Symeoni* (Lyons, 1559). No. 60 shows Perseus astride the winged Pegasus as with his Gorgon shield he turns Atlas into a mountain. In No. 61 Perseus on Pegasus is "bounding between the two moist elements" in most lively fashion as he kills the monster to free Andromeda. In No. 62, Pegasus has just been born as Perseus lifts the severed head of Medusa. Douce noticed the significance of these cuts. Pegasus began bounding like a tennis ball for the Dauphin, who had got tennis balls[21] on the mind from having sent a taunting gift of them to King Henry, and Pegasus continues to bound in *Troilus and Cressida,* even though he is now figuratively a ship. The action itself was suggested by the vigorous antics of Pegasus in the cut. I believe we may consider it certain that both these passages belong to Shakespeare himself and that the passage in *Troilus and Cressida* is a further evolution of the train of thought begun in *Henry V.* The passages are not likely to be far apart in time, and Shakespeare evidently had a vivid impression of that cut. In this first form of the cuts the accompanying text is nowhere specific that Perseus rides Pegasus; only the illustrations show him doing so.

These cuts of Salomon were frequently adapted and reproduced, becoming the model for practically all illustrated editions of the *Metamorphoses* in small form for the remainder of the century and beyond.[22] And the editions of this type were commonly used for school work. It is thus not surprising that Perseus rides Pegasus rough-shod through Renaissance poets, including Shakespeare and Spenser, though scholars knew better.

This set of illustrations was used also in a Latin form, my copy of which is, *Metamorphoses Ovidii, Argumentis quidem soluta oratione, Enarrationibus autem & Allegoriis Elegiaco versu accura-*

---

[21]These tennis balls came in with the reassignment of the passage to the Dauphin from Burbon in the original version. The speeches have been reassigned and refitted.

[22]See Duplessis, Georges, *Essai bibliographique sur les differentes editions des oeuvres d'Ovide ornees de planches publiees aux XV° et XVI° siecles,* Paris, 1889; and Henkel, M. D., "Illustrierte Ausgaben von Ovids Metamorphosen im XV., XVI. und XVII. Jahrhundert," *Vorträge der Bibliothek Warburg,* Vorträge 1926-1927, pp. 58ff.

*tissimè expositae, summáq; diligentia ac studio illustratae, per M.
Ioan. Sprengium Augustan,* 1583. Our illustrations are now on
the recto of the page, with a prose summary beneath, while a verse
Enarratio, ending with the *Allegoria* occupies the verso each time.
In this set the prose summary under the Medusa plate says that
Perseus, "post insidens Pegaso, quem ex Neptuno Medusa peperit,
in varias hinc inde regiones auectus est." So in plain prose
Perseus is now mounted on Pegasus.

A series of editions of the *Metamorphoses* printed by the same
printers, Hieronymus de Marnef and Gulielmus Cauellat (his
widow in 1583), at Paris embody the same cuts; and the argument
to the Medusa cut repeats exactly the words which mount Perseus
on Pegasus to go on his adventures. In this series, the cuts are
avowedly "in gratiam studiosae iuuentutis." Those who read this
form of the *Metamorphoses* would be very firmly convinced that
Perseus rode Pegasus most spectacularly. I have a much-used and
highly annotated copy of 1576 (there is one in the British Museum
also—I hope it is still in existence), which belonged eventually to
Mel(?) Barker. The story of Myrrha has been yanked out by some
firm pedagogical hand, though the illustration was spared. In an
edition of 1583 by the same printers, it was benetted Vulcan and
Venus who were thus ruthlessly expurgated, this time including the
illustration. It is not uncommon to find school editions thus muti-
lated.

I have also a copy from another series published at Frankfort by
Christopherus Corvinus for Iohannes Feyerabendius in 1582. Here
the cuts are reversed, though Perseus takes his seat on Pegasus in
the same words. In this copy,[23] the Reverend Charles J. Crawford,
D. D., has recorded on December 5, 1849, some facts concerning the
cuts from Douce's notes in his copies, then and we hope now, in the
Bodleian Library. This edition is traced to a form printed at
Frankfort in 1563 as the source. There is thus a Frankfort series
as well as a Paris series of this form. The arguments may also occur without the cuts as in an edition of 1579 at Coloniae Agrippinae.

No edition of the *Metamorphoses* in Latin is known to have been
printed in England in Shakespeare's day at grammar school. The
first edition of the *Metamorphoses* known to have been printed in

---

[23]There is an obliterated inscription of 1657 on the title page, replaced by
Henry Barnard, who gave the volume to his brother G. Barnard. There are
traces of a still earlier signature.

England was the Plantin form in 1582.[24]   This form is not illustrated, and the argument, that attributed to Lactantius,[25] does not place Perseus on Pegasus. The edition of Sabinus printed at Cambridge in 1584 has no cuts and does not directly place Perseus upon Pegasus, though one who knows the tradition might think it had done so. The moralized annotations of Sabinus, however, were sometimes attached to editions having these illustrations and arguments.

The present notes are by no means complete, and are intended merely to show that editions of the *Metamorphoses* placing Perseus on the back of Pegasus were frequent in the 'seventies and beyond, while Shakespeare was in grammar school. A great many boys of Shakespeare's age would know that Perseus rode Pegasus on his exploits. The ship Pegasus does not appear in these grammar school editions, so far as I have observed. Nor do I see anything to indicate certainly that the author of the passage in *Troilus and Cressida* knew that Pegasus might be a ship, though there is equally nothing to show that he did not. Shakespeare's information on Perseus and Pegasus is most likely to indicate that he used one of these little illustrated editions of the *Metamorphoses* in grammar school.[26]

We can now see that Shakespeare already had these pictures of Perseus in his mind's eye when he wrote

> I saw young Harry, with his beaver on,
> His cuisses on his thighs, gallantly arm'd,
> Rise from the ground like feather'd Mercury,
> And vaulted with such ease into his seat,
> As if an angel dropp'd down from the clouds,
> To turn and wind a fiery Pegasus
> And witch the world with noble horsemanship.[27]

While Perseus is not mentioned directly here, the reference is clearly to him, as Professor Root saw. For it was "feather'd Mercury" who loaned Perseus his wings, so that Perseus had dropped thus like an angel from the clouds to behead Medusa, and must have used

---

[24] Not in *S. T. C.*, but copies in the Library of the University of Illinois and the British Museum.

[25] For the arguments on the *Metamorphoses* attributed to Lactantius, see the critical edition by H. Magnus (1914). These say nothing of Perseus riding Pegasus, either horse or ship.

[26] I have materials in rough form for a volume on Shakespeare's use of Ovid, but it must wait till some thousands of pages of background can precede it into print.

[27] *1 Henry IV*, IV, i, 104-110.

these feathers to vault upon the winged Pegasus when the latter was born of Medusa's blood. In Ovid's text, Perseus did a great deal of fancy vaulting on and off the monster's back with these wings till he got the feathers wet and had to finish that job from the top of an obliging rock. The Medusa cut shows Pegasus with wings invitingly outspread as Perseus lifts the severed head. The next move was for Perseus to make his leap, and Shakespeare evidently gives here his idea of how it was done. Incidentally, Perseus is fully armed, as was King Henry. In the three cuts of Perseus and Pegasus, Perseus is not so posed as to exhibit Mercury's wings, if he is supposed to have them on, but No. 65 displays them handsomely.

Harry in *1 Henry IV* was in fact what the Dauphin in *Henry V* later was claiming to be. The picture in *Henry V* is a companion-contrast to that in *1 Henry IV*, and is clearly later. Now this is an important fact. For this companion-contrast came into the Folio version of *Henry V* when the Dauphin was being substituted for Burbon of the quarto version, displacing Burbon's palfrey of the sun with the Dauphin's Pegasus. It follows that the quarto version was almost certainly earlier than *1 Henry IV*, where a train of thought was begun which continued through *Henry V* into *Troilus and Cressida*, the latter play having also another reference. Nestor has seen Hector

As hot as Perseus, spur thy Phrygian steed.[28]

Only once more does Pegasus appear in Shakespeare, this time without Perseus. Imogen wishes ''O, for a horse with wings!''[29] that she might glide to her husband in a day instead of plodding on an ordinary horse for a week.

Perseus and Pegasus have a definite sequence in Shakespeare's plays and then disappear as suddenly as they had entered. Shakespeare exhibits his knowledge of the pair first in *1 Henry IV*. He found use only then for a pair he had likely known and greatly admired from grammar school days. But when he had thrice used them, he found for them no further use. He had not forgotten them afterward; he had not likely been ignorant of them before. He must have known a tremendous number of things from the classics and elsewhere for which he never found any literary use at

[28]*Troilus and Cressida*, IV, v, 186.
[29]*Cymbeline*, III, ii, 50.

all. Why should we constantly construe his silence as admission of his ignorance? Especially when no one ever made more brilliant use of what he chose to borrow from the classics—Perseus and Pegasus, for instance—even though he took them from the apochrypha, as it were?

TWO NOTES ON SHAKESPEARE

By GEORGE COFFIN TAYLOR
University of North Carolina

SHAKESPEARE AND THE PROGNOSTICATIONS

Sanford V. Larkey, now Welch Librarian at Johns Hopkins, in March, 1935, published an article of far-reaching importance to all scholars profoundly interested in the literature of Renaissance England. In "Astrology and Politics in the First Years of Elizabeth's Reign,"[1] Larkey calls attention to the attempt of the government to stop the "prognostications" in England as to the coming end of the world. Larkey quotes convincingly from the prognosticators and from a certain William Fulke who refutes the argument of the believers in the supernatural several decades before Reginald Scot replied to that other supernatural wave engulfing England, the writings of the believers in *witchcraft,* of which James of Scotland and England was a leader. It is difficult to overemphasize the importance of Larkey's article as bearing on the entire matter of the early skeptics of the English Renaissance. *Atheism in the English Renaissance*[2] would be even a better book if the author had known and shown what Larkey has shown. Here in William Fulke as early as 1563 is a Renaissance English skeptic talking about the supernatural in a fashion which can hardly be distinguished by a hair's breadth from a modern skeptic working in 1941.

I wish to call attention, however, to another matter. With the aid of the Larkey citations I wish to show that Shakespeare, who is classed by Hemingway as a believer in supernaturalism,[3] is thoroughly conversant with both sides of the controversy examined by Larkey, and that he synthesizes this controversy in one of his most dramatic dialogues and monologues in *King Lear* (I, ii, 111-145).

I place Larkey's quotations from the prognosticators against Gloucester's contention that all the evils falling on England are due to the stars; and I place Fulke's contention that they are not

---

[1] *Bulletin of the Institute of the History of Medicine.* III (1935), 171-86.
[2] George T. Buckley, The University of Chicago Press, 1932.
[3] See Samuel Burdett Hemingway, ed., *A New Variorum Edition of Shakespeare: Henry the Fourth Part I* (Philadelphia: J. B. Lippincott Company, 1936), p. 175.

due to the influence of the stars against the amazing statement of
Edmund, the bastard, to exactly the same effect:

The conjunction of Saturne and Mars
in this Eclipse, sygnifieth dessencions,
discordes, contencions, stryfe, great
manslaughter, murmuracions, feares,
and troubles shall happen to men, and
no pytie nor mercy almost amongst
men.

Also *Saturnus, Mars, Sol,* and *Luna,*
in *Tauro* decima domo, domus honoris,
will not leave this yere without aug-
mentinge of moche discorde, and
noughty enterprises, producinge de-
scension, betwene the higher powers,
and the lower or meaner sorte, betwene the spiritualty and the tem-
poraltie, with moche pyllage, theftes,
robberies, murmuracions, lyes, great
noyses, tumultes, comocions, a n d
suche oultrages.

The Figure of the heavens, at the
time of the Eclipse of the Moone,
1559 . . . signifieth great mischiefe,
discorde, manslaughter, hatred and
wrath, aswel betwene great princes
and ecclesyasticall persons, as the
common people: aswel private as publike, with deceite, treason, theft, bur-
nynge, adulterye, robborie, and finally
all kind of wickednes. Also betwene
secular riche and mighty princes,
warre, envy, hatred, rancour, and deceite. Also the officers of great estate
of some great prince shalbe deposed
of their offyce, and shalbe greatlye
hated of their prince.[4]

These late clipses in the sun and moon
portend no good to us. Though the
wisdom of nature can reason it thus
and thus, yet nature finds itself
scourg'd by the sequent effects. Love
cools, friendship falls off, brothers
divide: in cities, mutinies; in countries, discord; in palaces, treason; and
the bond crack'd twixt son and
father. This villain of mine comes
under the prediction; there's son
against father: the King falls from
bias of nature; there's father against
child. We have seen the best of
our time; machinations, hollowness,
treachery, and all ruinous disorders,
follow us disquietly to our graves.
Find out this villain, Edmund; it shall
lose thee nothing; do it carefully.
And the noble and true-hearted Kent
banish'd! 'Tis strange.

Sycknesse and healthe depend upon
dyvers causes, but nothyng at al upon
the course of the starres, for what
way soever the starres runne their
race, yf there be in the body abun-
dance or defect, or from outward by
corruption of the ayre infection it
must nedes be sycke: and if none of
these bee, though all the starres in
heaven with all their oppositions and
evil tokens shuld meete in the howse
of sicknesse, yet the body shoulde be
whole, and in good health. . . .[5]

This is the excellent foppery of the
world, that, when we are sick in fortune,—often the surfeits of our own
behaviour,—we make guilty of our
disasters the sun, the moon, and the
stars, as if we were villains on necessity, fools by heavenly compulsion,
knaves, thieves, and treachers by
spherical predominance, drunkards,
liars, and adulterers by an enforc'd
obedience of planetary influence, and
all that we are evil in, by a divine
thrusting on. An admirable evasion
of whoremaster man, to lay his goatish
disposition on the charge of a star!
My father compounded with my mother under the dragon's tail; and my

[4]Larkey, *op. cit.*, p. 176.
[5]*Ibid.*, p. 184.

> nativity was under *Ursa major*; so
> that it follows, I am rough and lecher-
> ous. Fut, I should have been that I am,
> had the maidenliest star in the firma-
> ment twinkled on my bastardizing.

Thus Shakespeare enters into one of the most vital of Elizabethan currents of thought. Which side did he take? No one can tell. The important matter is his awareness of up-to-date controversies and his artistic assimilation and sublimation of them. It becomes increasingly clear that Shakespeare knew pretty much all the highly controversial issues of his day, did not take any of them too seriously as we do now, and was supremely the artist in regard to his treatment of each in turn. Certainly the Shakespeare who was thoroughly familiar with Montaigne, one of the greatest of the sceptics[6], could enter with imaginative dramatic enthusiasm into the spirit of Fulke, a minor sceptic.

Incidentally, the continual reference to "eclipses" in the prognostications slightly weakens the evidence of these *late* "eclipses" as to dating Lear in 1606, because of the actual eclipses in September and October of 1605.

THE STRANGE CASE OF DU BARTAS IN *THE TAMING OF A SHREW*

Katherine's speech at the end of Shakespeare's *The Taming of The Shrew* constitutes the emotional and intellectual highpoint of the play. Her advice to wives to be obedient and submissive to their husbands, whether one likes it nowadays or not, is admirably and artistically expressed. This is all the more noticeable when one compares these lines with her lines at the same point and to the same purpose in the old play, *The Taming of A Shrew*. Notice the difference:

> Th'eternall power that with his only breath,
> Shal cause this end and this beginning frame,
> Not in time, nor before time, but with time, confusd,
> For al the course of yeares, of ages, moneths,
> Of seasons temperate, of dayes and houres,
> Are tun'd and stopt, by measure of his hand,
> The first world was, a forme, without a forme,
> A heape confusd a mixture al deformd,
> A gulfe of gulfes, a body bodiles,
> Where al the elements were orderles,
> Before the great commander of the world,
> The king of kings the glorious God of heuen,
> Who in six daies did frame his heauenly worke,
> And made al things to stand in perfit course.[1]

---

[6]George C. Taylor, *Shakespeare's Debt to Montaigne*, Harvard University Press, 1925.

[1]*The Taming of A Shrew*, by C. Praetorius, London, 1886, pp. 49ff.

Her lines in the *A Shrew* are strangely inartistic, didactic, definitely theological. I wish to call attention to the fact that the author of *A Shrew* appropriated at this point a considerable number of lines from DuBartas. I place in evidence the DuBartas passage as it appears in the original French and as it appears in Sylvester's *The Divine Weekes*:

L'immuable decret de la bouche divine,
Qui causera sa fin, causa son origine.
Non en temps, avant temps, ains mesme avec le temps,
J'entens un temps confus, car les courses des ans,
Des siecles, des saisons, des moys, et des journees,
Par le bal mesure des astres sont bornees.

Th' immutable divine Decree, which shall
Cause the Worlds End, caus'd his Originall:
Neither in Time, nor yet before the same,
But in the instant when Time first became.
I mean a Time confused: for, the course
Of yeeres, of months, of weeks, of dayes, of hours,
Of Ages, Times, and Seasons is confin'd

* * *

Ce premier monde estroit une forme sans forme,
Une pile confuse, un meslange difforme,
D'abismes un abisme, un corps mal compasse,
Un Chaos de Chaos, un tas mal entasse
Ou tous les elemens se logeoient peslemesle,
Ou le liquide avoit avec le sec querelle,
Le rond avec l'aigu, le froid avec le chaut,
Le dur avec le mol, le bas avec le haut,

* * *

That first World (yet) was a most formless Form,
A confus'd heap a Chaos most deform,
A Gulf of Gulfs, a body ill compact,
An ugly medley, where all difference lackt:
Where th'Elements lay jumbled all together,[2]

It is impossible to doubt in this case a direct borrowing from DuBartas. Whether, of course, the author of *A Shrew* saw the lost translation of DuBartas by Sir Philip Sidney, or used Sylvester's translation, or went straight to the original French is open to question. If the lines are from Sylvester, the author saw his translation before it was entered in the Stationer's Register.[3] The *First Week* of Sylvester was entered in the Stationer's Register in 1591.[4]

Three scholars of prominence have already called attention to the amazing method of composition of the author of *A Shrew*. R. W.

[2] *The Works of Guillaume de Salluste Sieur DuBartas*, by Urban Tigner Holmes, John Coriden Lyons, Robert White Linker, The University of North Carolina Press, 1938, II, 195ff, 202ff.

[3] See E. K. Chambers, the date of *A Shrew* "in or before" 1589, *The Elizabethan Stage*, IV, 48.

[4] A. H. Upham, *The French Influence in English Literature*, Columbia University Press, 1911, p. 152.

Bond,[5] F. S. Boas,[6] and H. Dugdale Sykes[7] all notice how this play is fearfully and wonderfully made. The author had a way of simply lifting lines out of Marlowe and Kyd to a greater and more peculiar extent than other writers of plays. That he should have also gone to DuBartas makes the matter all the more interesting. If he himself translated DuBartas he is the earliest translator of a part of the *First Week* on record.

Hitherto only one Elizabethan dramatist has been shown to be familiar with DuBartas.[8] Dugdale Sykes has shown that Peele was undoubtedly familiar with his works. If he had noticed this borrowing in *A Shrew*, Sykes possibly might have proposed Peele as the author of *A Shrew* rather than Samuel Rowley.[9] Of this theory E. K. Chambers says, "but Mr. Sykes has certainly made out a stylistic case which deserves consideration."[10] Familiarity of the author of *A Shrew* with DuBartas, as here made certain, helps to strengthen Sykes's contention that Rowley wrote *A Shrew*. Rowley's three lost plays bear the following titles, "Joshua," "Judas," "Samson."[11] Sidney Lee in *D.N.B.* (Vol. 17, p. 362), shows how Rowley received payments from Henslowe on all three of these plays. Anyone writing on these three subjects could get considerable help from DuBartas whose wide popularity among Elizabethans is too well known to need further comment here. He was a veritable store-house for writers of poetry.[12]

Whatever else may be true, it is evident that the author of *A Shrew* who knew how, like Pistol in *Henry IV, Part II*, to bombast out his blank verse as poor Greene says of Shakespeare in 1592, with tag ends of verse from Marlowe and Kyd, knew also how to draw on DuBartas. It follows that possibly DuBartas was pretty well known in England as early as 1589, not heretofore emphasized. It does not follow that Shakespeare in Pistol, with his much throw-

---

[5] *The Taming of The Shrew*, Arden Shakespeare, 1904, revised 1929.

[6] *The Taming of A Shrew*, Shakespeare Classics, 1908, appendix.

[7] *The Authorship of The Taming of A Shrew, The Famous Victories, and The Addition to Marlowe's Faustus*, Shakespeare Association, 1919.

[8] See Dugdale Sykes, *Sidelights on Elizabethan Drama* (1924), and "Peele's Borrowings from DuBartas," *N & Q*, CXLVII, 349-351.

[9] *The Authorship of The Taming of A Shrew*, 1920, Shakespeare Association.

[10] *Elizabethan Stage*, III, 472.

[11] See E. K. Chambers. *Elizabethan Stage*, III, 236; II, 178 and 180.

[12] My friend and former student, W. K. Abbot, Professor of English, Charleston College, Charleston, S. C., suggested to me the possible relation of Rowley's lost plays in this connection. He is one of the leading world authorities on DuBartas.

ing about of the brains of Marlowe and Kyd, was necessarily bur-
lesquing Rowley. Something like five hundred Elizabethan historical
characters have been identified as embodied by Shakespeare in his
cast of eight hundred or more dramatis personae. Let's not try to
extend the grotesque list.

SHAKESPEARE'S USE OF HIS SOURCES

By VIRGIL K. WHITAKER
Stanford University

The more probable sources of Shakespeare's plays have long been
known, and scholarly ingenuity has tracked down the remote ancestors and analogues of these sources even in primitive folklore.
But, strangely enough, very much less attention has been devoted to
considering what use Shakespeare himself made of this material.
One is tempted, in fact, to exaggerate only slightly and say that
Shakespeare's sources have been pursued everywhere but into the
mind of Shakespeare.

Scholars, it is true, have always known that Shakespeare was
often in heavy debt to his sources for his plot, his characterizations,
or even his very poetry. Recently, moreover, a few students of
single plays have proposed that Shakespeare was sometimes the vic-
tim of his sources as well: that some of the riddles of his plays
result from his failure to adapt his sources completely and consistently, and that he was sometimes careless rather than profound.
An occasional scholar has even attempted to use Shakespeare's
sources to elucidate a play, not merely to explain its difficulties and
obscurities but to enrich our interpretation of it.[1] But one looks
in vain for a general recognition of the sources as a formative element in the plays or for any systematic treatment of Shakespeare's
use of them. One is astonished, for example, that L. L. Schücking's
brilliant *Character Problems in Shakespeare's Plays*[2] contains no
chapter on the influence of sources, that there is not even a section
on them in the introductory discussion of "The Influence of Contemporary Conditions on Shakespeare's Plays."[3] This paper. therefore, is simply a brief and sketchy suggestion that any attempt to
interpret a Shakespearean play must include a detailed comparison

---

[1] Cf., in addition to the writers cited below. Harold R. Walley, "Shakespeare's
Portrayal of Shylock," *The Parrott Presentation Volume*. ed. Hardin Craig
(Princeton: Princeton University Press, 1935), pp. 229ff.

[2] London: George G. Harrap and Co. Ltd., 1922.

[3] It should be noted, however, that the section "Parts of the Original Historical Action Not Assimilated (Cleopatra: Malcolm)" (pp. 141-6) is in effect
a discussion of source influence.

of that play with its source,[4] and that such a comparison is perhaps the best single clue to Shakespeare's artistic methods. As an obvious corollary, the last part of the paper outlines some of the premises that must underlie such a study.

But, before we attempt an analysis of the use which Shakespeare made of his sources, we must recognize certain difficulties. Our generalizations obviously will be partly invalidated by the different character of the various materials which he used. Some provided almost complete dramatic plots and definite characterizations which he could take over with little change. Plutarch is an obvious example, but it has sometimes been overlooked how closely *Romeo and Juliet* is derived from Brooke's poem *Romeus and Juliet,* and how the nurse, in particular, is lifted bodily from the poem. Holinshed, on the other hand, provided a wealth of details and, for the more recent kings, enough characterization to stimulate a dramatist's imagination; but it was up to Shakespeare to select and arrange the material for his plot. A much larger group of sources provided a plot but little characterization. This was true of the old plays, if we may generalize about the many hypothetical ones from those extant.[5] But even the plot material of the source plays has been much altered and greatly complicated in *The Comedy of Errors, King Lear,* and presumably *Hamlet.* Similarly, the Italian romances or *novelle* behind so many of Shakespeare's plays could furnish little more than plot. They varied in quality from the relatively detailed sources of *The Merchant of Venice* and *As You Like It* to the fragmentary and completely inadequate tales supposedly back of *Two Gentlemen, Much Ado,* and *Twelfth Night.* In *Twelfth Night,* in fact, one feels that Shakespeare owed far more to his own earlier comedies than to Riche.

Hard as it is to generalize about the use of such diverse material, a more fundamental difficulty arises: namely, that it is almost impossible to say exactly what the sources are. In the first place, Shakespeare commonly used not one source but several, and editors confuse the matter further by listing all sources as though they were parallel in importance. *Il Pecorone* and the casket story, for example, are not equal sources for *The Merchant of Venice* at all.

---

[4]The late Professor William Dinsmore Briggs once patiently admonished the writer, then a graduate student, in almost these words. If, therefore, this paper has any point, the credit belongs to him.

[5]But note that *The Famous Victories* may have influenced Shakespeare to present Hal surrounded by his roistering companions.

Any study of the play must recognize that it is based directly on *Il Pecorone* and that the casket story, as we shall note below, is used only when *Il Pecorone* is obviously impossible. Second, we are often in doubt as to the relationship between Shakespeare and the possible source. A comparison of *Richard II* with Holinshed would be easy were it not for the vexing problem of the parallels with Daniel's *Civil Wars*. Third, a possible earlier play often intervenes between Shakespeare and the source that we have. The shadowy and hypothetical Jew play seems so doubtful as not to constitute a serious difficulty to a source study of *The Merchant of Venice*, but one hates to generalize at all about *Hamlet*, where the older play is almost a certainty. Any alteration may well have been made by the earlier playwright. Fourth, Shakespeare's use of any source was certainly influenced by contemporary dramatic practice or current theatrical fashions. It is probable that *Richard III*, *Richard II*, and Shylock owe much to Marlowe; and *Hamlet* is a revenge tragedy as well as a derivation from Belleforest. Frequently, in fact, deviations from the source are the best proof of these very influences that critics have suspected. It is at least plausible that, when Shakespeare made Shylock actually more villainous and unpitying in *The Merchant of Venice* than the usurer was in *Il Pecorone*,[6] he was following Marlowe's *Jew of Malta*. In fact, we commonly speak of the *Jew of Malta* as a "source" for Shakespeare, but the same kind of influence certainly operated in other plays where it is less obvious. Fifth and most intangible of all, we can never isolate Shakespeare's sources exactly because he was certainly affected in his use of them, and even in his own understanding of them, by contemporary prejudices and habits of mind. The plays about Henry V, *Troilus and Cressida*,[7] and *Antony ind Cleopatra* clearly reflect the popular conception of Hal, Cressida, and Cleopatra almost as much as that contained in the source; *Richard II* plays gingerly with the dangerous contemporary problem of the dethronement of a rightful sovereign; and *King Lear* becomes almost a treatise on Renaissance ethics.[8]

---

[6] E. E. Stoll notes this increase in villainy so far as the penalty is concerned, but he overlooks the essential increase in the cruelty of Shylock's actions before the trial. Cf. *Shakespeare Studies* (New York: The Macmillan Company, 1927), p. 263.

[7] Cf. W. W. Lawrence, *Shakespeare's Problem Comedies* (New York: The Macmillan Company, 1931) for a brilliant discussion of this influence.

[8] Cf. Hardin Craig, "The Ethics of King Lear," *Philological Quarterly*, IV (1925), 97-109.

All these difficulties, then, complicate any attempt to generalize upon Shakespeare's use of his sources. A statement of them is therefore a necessary preliminary to this paper. One further qualification should also be made. Shakespeare constantly fills in material only vaguely indicated in his source, as when he derives from a mere suggestion in Lodge's *Rosalynde* not merely the exiled Duke but the whole court that must surround him, including the inimitable Jaques. But this is a logical development of the source, not a deliberate variation from it, and need not concern us here. Obviously, too, a paper of this length cannot hope to treat a subject as large as Shakespeare's use of his sources with any completeness of illustrative detail. It attempts only to suggest what Shakespeare was likely to do, not to mention every occasion when he did it.

Any comparison of Shakespeare's plays with their sources shows clearly that, in general, he simply dramatized the material before him, following it as closely as its nature would permit. His earlier plays continually show this practice, but even his most mature sometimes revert to it. The loose structure of *Antony and Cleopatra* and the return to chronicle play technique in the fourth act of *Macbeth*[9] both show a mechanical dramatizing of the source narrative. Similarly, Shakespeare borrows traits of character or even entire characterizations whenever he can, not merely in following Plutarch or Holinshed, but even in using Italian *novelle*. The derivation of Iago from Cinthio's *Hecatommithi* is almost as close as that of Caesar or Brutus from Plutarch.[10] It is well known, of course, that Shakespeare frequently lifted whole passages of poetry, in substance at least, when the source provided suggestions.

But a more convincing demonstration of this method of Shakespeare's is provided by those passages in which inconsistencies or obscurities in a play can be explained only by assuming that he followed his source slavishly and unthinkingly. In *The Comedy of Errors*, although he carefully elaborated his sources, he retained from the *Menaechmi*, without working them clearly into his play,

---

[9] Cf. G. P. Baker, *The Development of Shakespeare as a Dramatist* (New York: Macmillan, 1929), p. 272.

[10] "Haveva costui nella compagnia un alfiero di bellissima presenza, ma della più scelerata natura, che mai fosse huomo del mondo. Era questi molto caro al Moro, non havendo egli delle sue cattività notitia alcuna. Perche, quantunque egli fosse di vilissimo animo, copriva nondimeno, coll' alte, e superbe parole, e colla sua presenza, di modo la viltà, ch' egli ciuidea nel cuore, che si scopriva nella sembianza un'Ettore, od un Achille." *New Variorum Shakespeare: Othello*, ed. H. H. Furness (11th ed.), p. 378.

the rôle of the courtesan, the ring episode (IV, iii; V, i), and especially the completely amoral attitude of Antipholus of Syracuse toward keeping the gold chain (bracelet in Plautus). This lack of moral scruples fits well with Plautus' comedy, but it is clearly out of place in the more realistic, humane world of law and religious houses that Shakespeare presents. In omitting from *King John* the sacking of the monasteries, Shakespeare obscured the entire action leading up to the death of John. In *Richard II* the opening triangle involving Richard, Mowbray, and Bolingbroke is almost unintelligible to one unaccustomed to English history or unacquainted with the source, and so are the allusions to Gloucester throughout the play. But most interesting of all is the way in which Shakespeare (or his predecessor) removed the entire motivation for Hamlet's assumption of madness. In the old tale it was common knowledge that Claudius had killed his brother, and Hamlet therefore feigned madness to prevent Claudius from murdering him, too, as an obvious measure of self-protection. But in Shakespeare's play Claudius had every reason to suppose Hamlet ignorant of his crime until the play within the play, or at least until the threatening remarks in the nunnery scene. The assumption of an antic disposition therefore had little value as protection and had the positive disadvantage that it must inevitably make Claudius suspicious.[11] It might perhaps be argued that Hamlet felt himself to be, and was, the rightful heir to the throne, and that he recognized that Claudius would certainly be unwilling to let the rightful claimant to the crown live, if in possession of his faculties. But this argument is clearly invalid, because Hamlet does not speak of assuming the antic disposition until after he has seen the ghost. Robertson, in his study of the relation of *Hamlet* to its sources, speculates that Shakespeare "suffered or accepted a compulsion imposed by material which, as a stage manager revising a popular play, he did not care to reject."[12]

If, then, we are right in taking it as axiomatic that whenever possible Shakespeare follows his sources, the conclusion follows in-

[11] Cf. E. E. Stoll, *Hamlet: An Historical and Comparative Study* (Research Publications of the University of Minnesota, Vol. VIII, No. 5; Sept., 1919), p. 5; Karl Young, "The Shakespeare Skeptics," *North American Review*, CCXV (March, 1922), 382-93 (especially 387); Schücking, *op. cit.*, pp. 147ff. (especially 149). Note, however, that J. Dover Wilson apparently feels no difficulty; cf. *What Happens in Hamlet* (New York: Macmillan, 1935), pp. 88ff.

[12] J. M. Robertson, *The Problem of Hamlet* (New York: Harcourt, Brace and Howe, 1920), p. 31.

evitably that any deviation from them is likely to be deliberate and to reflect Shakespeare's methods as a dramatic artist or his aims in writing the particular play. The problem immediately arises of analyzing the reasons which might lead him to depart from his sources. Such an analysis is interesting primarily because it is a clue (and let it be emphasized that it is only one clue of many) to Shakespeare's technique and aims, and because further light on these may, in turn, aid in interpreting the plays.

The first and most obvious reason for departing from the source was the need to condense the story to suit it to dramatic presentation, for, great as is the expanse of time and space in many of Shakespeare's plays, he still could not parallel the *ab ovo* technique of the biographies or *novelle* which he used.

The simplest method of compressing the action was, of course, to leave out the early stages of the story or to imply them during the dramatic exposition, and that is precisely what Shakespeare did. In *As You Like It* and *Twelfth Night*, for example, he merely omitted the preliminaries and started when the action became interesting—when, in other words, it arrived at the "love interest." Often, however, such a procedure deprived the play of motivation for the opening scenes; in such an event Shakespeare, rather than cumber the play with an elaborate exposition, was likely to proceed to heroic simplification. This extreme simplication, in fact, probably explains the opening scenes of *The Merchant of Venice* and *King Lear* that have caused so much discussion. In *Il Pecorone* a considerable narrative shows how Gianetto (Bassanio) came to be, in effect if not formally, the adopted son and heir of Bindo, the Merchant. But Shakespeare, doubtless to avoid including all this extraneous material in the play, reduced drastically what Antonio does for Bassanio and based the loan simply upon the close friendship about which the Renaissance loved to theorize. Perhaps the much-discussed melancholy is partly an attempt to explain why Antonio so much enjoyed the company of Bassanio, a gay young man, although it is also an obvious means of building suspense by foreshadowing. Similarly in *Lear* the preposterous contest of affection is part of a scheme by which Lear hopes to trick Cordella into marrying the King of Hibernia, whom he has chosen for her. The other sisters, who are quite willing to marry the men provided for them, are to promise, as proof of their love, that they will marry any man whom Lear selects. Cordella therefore has every reason to be cold and undemonstrative. Shakespeare, however, has asked us to accept Lear's whim at its face value and has relied upon the character of the participants to motivate what follows. He makes the actions of the three sisters convincing, but he deprives us of the sympathy for Lear as a man and the respect for his position as a king and father that the subsequent action of the play demands. In *Othello,* on the other hand, a similar abbreviation of the story makes the action much more probable. In Cinthio the Moor and Desdemona have been married for some time, and the harmony and peace of their life are specifically mentioned. The Moor's jealousy is therefore much more unreasonable than in the play, where he barely knows Desdemona.[13]

Shakespeare's second method of shortening the action is to telescope time sequences or to combine in one scene events actually separated by an interval of time. Any annotated text points out the frequent examples of this practice in the chronicle plays. Aside from them it is perhaps commonest in *Coriolanus.*

The third possible way of condensing the action is to hurry the conclusion by combining in one scene or sequence of scenes events that in the source occupied a much longer time. The hasty ending of *Two Gentlemen* is notorious, but the denouement of *Othello* is a much better example. In Cinthio the Ensign and the Moor make Desdemona's death seem accidental. After a subsequent quarrel the Ensign leads the Captain (Cassio) to accuse the Moor to the Signoria; being banished, he is there killed by Desdemona's kinsmen. The Ensign finally dies under torture as the result of a later intrigue. All this revelation and death Shakespeare has converted into a single scene.

The changes so far mentioned are, of course, obvious and elementary. Comparing the plays with their sources begins to bring much more interesting results when we consider devices by which Shakespeare adapted his material to the methods and conventions of his stage. Most of these take the form of developing and emphasizing characters that are unimportant in the source or introducing altogether new ones. Shakespeare had a variety of reasons for doing so. In the first place, he had to work in terms of a few actors, and he therefore could represent conflicts between large factions

---

[13]Note that this seems to refute Stoll's argument that Othello knew Desdemona well. Cf. *Othello: An Historical and Comparative Study* (University of Minnesota Studies in Language and Literature, No. 2; March, 1915), pp. 46-47.

in a state only in terms of leaders who personified them. The Tribunes in *Coriolanus* are equivalent not merely to the very minor Tribunes in Plutarch but to the whole Plebian party. They perform its actions, and they, in turn, are made by their actions to characterize the whole treacherous, inconstant mob. Similarly Menenius Agrippa is expanded from a mere hint in Plutach into a personification of the more rational Patrician point of view, as well as a character foil for Coriolanus. But Agrippa illustrates another reason for developing characters—the need for someone to serve as the dramatist's mouthpiece in the play. Enobarbus in *Antony and Cleopatra* actually lectures the audience, although part of the time he is ostensibly speaking to Cleopatra, on the technical psychology of Antony's erratic conduct (cf. III, xi, 3-11, 194-99). Horatio, however, is the best example of all. He is a tried and intimate friend of Hamlet's who remembers the former king well; yet sometimes he has to have the most obvious customs of the court explained to him. He is simply a means by which information is conveyed to the audience.[14] He has other more important functions in the play, as do all these characters, for Shakespeare is a skillful and economical dramatist; but he is obviously Shakespeare's mouthpiece.

Another major reason that led Shakespeare to add characters and episodes to his sources was the fondness for complicated and mixed dramatic action which he shared with his contemporaries. Early in his career he added to the *Menaechmi* of Plautus a twin slave to match the twin master, a sister to provide a wife for the twin brother, a father to provide a more realistic exposition than the Latin prologue and to introduce pathos and suspense into the story, and a mother to increase the pathos and make the joy complete at the end. In doing so he drew on the *Amphitruo* for one striking scene (III,i) and perhaps for the twin slave, but in general the material was his own invention. This was, moreover, only the first of such additions. They reach their most involved and effective form, perhaps, in the daring subplots in *Hamlet* and *Lear* that directly parallel the action of the main plot (granted, of course, that Shakespeare, and not his predecessor, placed Laertes in the same relationship to Hamlet that Hamlet occupies to Claudius).

---

[14]Cf. J. Dover Wilson, *Hamlet* (New Cambridge Shakespeare) (Cambridge: Cambridge University Press, 1934), pp. xlviii-xlix; *What Happens in Hamlet*, pp. 232-235. Schücking, however, proposes a different explanation; see *Character Problems in Shakespeare's Plays*, pp. 115-16.

Here Shakespeare is going far beyond his source, and the parallelism is basic to the character analysis written into the plays. Sometimes, however, a parallel episode is introduced for other reasons. The first brawl in *Romeo and Juliet* is obviously copied from the second, which alone occurs in Brooke. It furnishes the scene of tumult with which Shakespeare liked to open his plays and leads very comfortably into the exposition;[15] furthermore, it adds to the foreboding of tragedy which is so important in the play, and builds suspense.

So far we have been dealing largely with plot construction. In elaborating and complicating the stories he told, Shakespeare was undoubtedly pleasing his audience, whose main interest lay in the telling of a vivid and romantic story, however improbable and gruesome. His own attention, however, came to be centered more and more upon character rather than incident; and, as we should therefore expect, the most important variations from the sources, particularly in his later plays, are directed toward achieving a richer, more subtle personality for his characters. Such changes aim, in general, either to purify and ennoble the character or to present it more fully to the audience.

Those characters which Shakespeare drew from Plutarch or from English history were already suitable to his purpose and needed, if anything, only to be enriched. But those that came from the Italian *novelle,* in particular, belonged to an amoral, or more often immoral, world that contrasted strangely with the idealized, romantic atmosphere of the comedies or the heroic mood of the tragedies. For the "good" characters of the romantic comedies and the tragedies, though not for the clowns and villains, drastic purification was therefore necessary, and it frequently involved major alterations of the source material. *The Merchant of Venice* illustrates this better, perhaps, than any other play. In *Il Pecorone* the lady of Belmonte is a heartless gold-seeker who, after drugging her suitors, compels them to sleep with her and either possess her or forfeit all their wealth. Gianetto (Bassanio) bankrupts the Merchant (Bindo), his benefactor, by failing in two attempts; but he succeeds in the third when a maid warns him not to drink the wine offered him. He then forgets about the Merchant, whose bond becomes forfeit. After the trial, however, he generously bestows upon Bindo the maid whose

---

[15] A. C. Bradley points out Shakespeare's fondness for opening with a scene of tumult. Cf. *Shakespearean Tragedy* (2nd ed. London: Macmillan, 1937), p. 43.

warning had saved him. The substitution of the choice of caskets for the sordid bedroom scene ennobled both Bassanio and Portia, and the problem of the lapsing of the bond was solved, as we shall see, by simply forgetting it. Notice, furthermore, that Shakespeare's careful rewriting disposes effectively of that school of criticism which regards the young Venetians as "a circle of wasters," unless Shakespeare has completely failed to achieve his manifest intention.[16] When Shakespeare wished to make Shylock a villain, as we have noted, he made him worse than in the source.

But this process of purification is by no means confined to *The Merchant of Venice.* Olivia in *Twelfth Night,* bold as she is, has none of the shamelessness of Riche's corresponding Julina, who forces "Silvio" to reveal her disguise by complaining to the Duke that "Silvio" (actually the real Silvio, the brother) has made her pregnant, as indeed he has—at her earnest invitation. Nor are these changes merely a matter of morals. Shakespeare clearly ennobled Romeo and Juliet by making them younger and more impetuous than their counterparts in Brooke, and their tragedy much swifter in coming. Furthermore, he tactfully omitted the scene in Brooke in which Romeus comforts Juliet before leaving her, perhaps because it made Juliet seem weak and mawkish.

If one analyzes the methods by which Shakespeare makes clear to an audience his conception of a leading character, four stand out: other figures in the play discuss the character[17] (Shakespeare habitually prepares for the first entrance of a main character by a conversation about him) ;[18] the character explains himself in soliloquies or asides ;[19] he reveals himself by significant actions and speeches; and, most elaborate of all, he is contrasted with other individuals who point by their words or acts his weaknesses and strengths. The first two of these methods involve no departure from the source, since they are merely matters of detail such as Shakespeare would naturally supply; but the last two often cause significant alterations in the material—alterations which show Shakespeare at his best as a dramatic artist.

---

[16]Cf. Sir Arthur Quiller-Couch, *The Merchant of Venice* (New Cambridge Shakespeare) (Cambridge: Cambridge University Press, 1926), pp. xxi, xxiii, etc. Note also the remark: "With the 'sources' of *The Merchant of Venice* we have (historically) even less reason to worry ourselves" (p. vii).

[17]Cf. the discussion of this method in Schücking, *op. cit.,* pp. 53-71.

[18]See Bradley, *Shakespearean Tragedy,* p. 44.

[19]Cf. Schücking, *op. cit.,* pp. 29-35.

Perhaps no single change is so effective in developing character by significant action as the one which Shakespeare makes in portraying Coriolanus' conduct after the battle with the Volscians. Plutarch tells that Coriolanus refused all reward:

Only, this grace (sayed he) I crave, and beseeche you to graunt me. Among the Volsces there is an olde friende and hoste of mine, an honest wealthie man, and now a prisoner, who living before in great wealth in his owne countrie, liveth now a poore prisoner in the handes of his enemies: and yet notwithstanding all this his miserie and misfortune, it would doe me great pleasure if I could save him from this one daunger: to keepe him from being solde as a slave.[20]

Shakespeare reports the incident as follows:

> *Cor.* I sometime lay here in Corioli
> At a poor man's house; he us'd me kindly:
> He cried to me; I saw him prisoner;
> But then Aufidius was within my view,
> And wrath o'erwhelmed my pity: I request you
> To give my poor host freedom. . . . . .
> *Lart.* Marcius, his name!
> *Cor.*   By Jupiter! forgot.
> I am weary; yea, my memory is tir'd. (I. ix, 82-91)

Every changed detail in this passage makes Coriolanus at once more human and more clearly the man that he is throughout the play. Baker, among others, comments upon the effectiveness of "By Jupiter! forgot."[21] But surely the wrath at Aufidius which overwhelmed his pity is even more revealing of Coriolanus and gives the forgetting its point. Nor should it be overlooked that Shakespeare has made the suppliant a poor freeman. This is one of the most brilliant of Shakespeare's characterizing alterations, but he has hundreds more like it.

Many of Shakespeare's changes are, however, more fundamental. In Brooke's *Romeus and Juliet* the sequence of events leading to Tybalt's death is much simpler than in *Romeo and Juliet*. The Montagues and Capulets start brawling; Romeus tries to stop the fight and is attacked by Tybalt, whom he kills by thrusting him through the neck. The sequence of events in Shakespeare, in which Romeo refuses to fight until he sees Mercutio killed in what is essentially his quarrel, makes a much wiser, maturer individual out of him. We feel that he has become fully aware of the implications of his love for Juliet. Again, Shakespeare has immeasurably in-

---

[20]*The Lives of the Noble Grecians and Romanes* (Stratford: Shakespeare Head Press, 1928), II, 183.

[21]Baker, *op. cit.*, p. 288.

creased the power of Iago's character by substituting for the long conclusion of Iago's life in Cinthio the simple words:

> Demand me nothing: what you know, you know:
> From this time forth I never will speak word. (V, ii, 302-3)

So, in the presence of death, Iago seems to assert his superiority in mind and will to those around him.

Perhaps Shakespeare's most effective device of all in the creation of character is the balancing of one man against another, and a comparison of his plays with their sources will often show how deliberately this has been done. The best example is, of course, the way in which Shakespeare, beginning with *Richard II*,[22] makes Henry Percy twenty-four years younger than he actually was in order to use him as a contrast to Prince Hal. Often, however, much less change of the source was needed to provide a character foil. Banquo appears in Holinshed in almost exactly the same scenes as in *Macbeth*. In the first scene with the witches (I, iii) most of what he says is actually taken from Holinshed. But Shakespeare has altered our entire concept of Macbeth by adding to what Banquo says in the source the speech:

> Good sir, why do you start, and seem to fear
> Things that do sound so fair? (I, iii, 51-52)

Such touches convert Banquo from a mere companion of Macbeth into a foil who continually shows, sometimes by what he says, more often by the different way in which he reacts to the same situation, the degeneration of Macbeth's mind and character.

Much of the preceding material has dwelt upon Shakespeare's careful workmanship in transforming and elaborating his sources. But that is not the whole picture. Nothing will show so clearly as an examination of the sources that Shakespeare was willing to pass over difficulties or inconsistencies that he was sure the audience would overlook, provided by so doing he could gain a telling theatrical effect or simplify his play. Stoll has dwelt upon the way in which Shakespeare relied in *Othello* on the willingness of his audience to accept the old device of the calumniator's immediately gaining credit.[23] He perhaps overlooks the extent to which Shakespeare took pains to cover the plot weaknesses in *Othello*, as in *Romeo and Juliet*, by careful foreshadowing. Spectators who have

---

[22]So *Richard II*, II, iii, 41-4, surely implies. This may conceivably constitute evidence that Shakespeare was already looking ahead to *1 Henry IV*.

[23]*Othello*, pp. 5ff.

been told often enough that Romeo and Juliet are "star-crossed lovers" or that Desdemona "has deceived her father, and may thee" are in no mood to question the means by which the unhappy ending is brought about. Be that as it may, we have noted that *Il Pecorone* expressly states that Gianetto callously forgot the Merchant's bond in his new-found pleasure. Shakespeare obviously could not use that explanation without forfeiting our interest in both Bassanio and Portia. A new and creditable explanation would have been hard indeed to devise. So he simply ignored the difficulty. He was thereby able to gain in one scene (III, ii) an extreme shift from joy to foreboding—one of the rapid reversals of mood which he liked so much; and he made Portia even more attractive in her generous reaction to the situation. The critics notwithstanding, no playgoer has ever wished that he had done otherwise.

It will be apparent by now that the study of Shakespeare's sources is no infallible guide to an understanding of his plays; but it does afford an insight into his mind and habits. Often what it shows merely confirms what we may infer from other studies of Shakespeare, but occasionally it clears up an obscurity. It is therefore useful as one of many avenues to a better appreciation and enjoyment of the plays—the proper end of all Shakespeare studies.

SHAKESPEARE AS A CRITIC

By HEREWARD T. PRICE

University of Michigan

For generations scholars have been writing about the learning of Shakespeare and about the size and contents of his library. But for all their work we shall never know how many foreign languages he could read or how deeply he had studied philosophy. However, one thing is certain. Shakespeare's borrowings from other Elizabethans prove that he had a wide knowledge of contemporary literature. Thus it happens that scholars who recognize that Shakespeare was steeped in Elizabethan literature have a tendency to assume too lightly that he was just another Elizabethan. Their reasoning, if reduced to a syllogism, might run :—All Elizabethan writers did x: Shakespeare was an Elizabethan writer: Therefore Shakespeare did x. I propose to show that Shakespeare was keenly sensitive to the absurdities and vices of Elizabethan literature and that he often attacked what he saw going on around him. If he learned much from constant observation of other writers, he rejected as much as he accepted. It is time to stress Shakespeare's critical independence.

It would be superfluous to deal at length with all the forms Shakespeare's criticism takes. For instance, enough has been written about his attacks on excess in language. The feast of scraps in *Love's Labour's Lost,* Falstaff's ironies, the humours of Nim, the fustian of Pistol, Bardolph's little accident with the word "accommodate"—these may be left to speak for themselves. However, such criticisms of contemporary excesses show us something more than a man with a keen sense of the ridiculous making fun of certain oddities. "Wood-notes wild" may describe some of Shakespeare's song, but the man who wrote *Love's Labour's Lost* was deeply interested in literary fashions and accustomed to passing judgments on literature. He speaks as a craftsman estimating his fellows and with a certainty that yields nothing to Ben Jonson.

One of Shakespeare's most powerful weapons is parody. We are no doubt tired of hearing Shakespeare's idolators proclaim that he is the best writer of English prose or of English lyrics or supreme in whatever he undertook. Still I should like to offer Shakespeare one more crown—as the best writer of English parody. I do not know anybody who has Shakespeare's gift for hitting off sheer silliness. The stupidity of popular poetry is easy game, of course. But it is astonishing how well Shakespeare can catch its accents. There is nothing in this line so good as the clowns' play in the *Midsummer Night's Dream.* This picture of vacuity striving for utterance, doggedly determined to do its best, is the cream of silliness. It is better than the best of Wodehouse.

But Shakespeare may also employ a form of parody for something much more subtle. Occasionally when he wants to show that a character is false or not quite sound, he apes conventional forms. Naturally Shakespeare's ways are hard to trace. He is continually watching himself, learning from his mistakes, and doing better next time. He will rant or euphuize in one play and in the next make fun of rant or euphuism. The result is that one frequently does not know quite how to take him. In his early historical plays there is plenty of rant. But when he comes to write *I Henry IV* he has learned how to use it. He gives it to one particular person as a means of characterization. When he makes Hotspur say:

> Three times they breathed, and three times did they drink,
> Upon agreement, of swift Severn's flood;
> Who then, affrighted with their bloody looks,
> Ran fearfully among the trembling reeds,
> And hid his crisp head in the hollow bank
> Bloodstained with these valiant combatants (I, iii, 102-7),

he is telling us something about Hotspur—that he is a windy man who rants. It is indirect criticism of Shakespeare's early work and of his contemporaries. He had freed himself from their influence and he now sees how hollow their style was.

There is another form of parody which needs careful watching, as it has already trapped acute critics. That is Shakespeare's use of conventional poetry to stamp a man as being in some way shallow, artificial or insincere. A typical play is *Romeo and Juliet,* in which critics, from the eighteenth century onwards, have detected two styles. We have the undeniable beauty of the great scenes side by side with passages like I, i, 180-200, 224-230, III, ii, 73-88, much of III, iii, and IV, v, 32-64. Let lines I, i, 194-200 serve as an example:

> this love that thou hast shown
> Doth add more grief to too much of mine own.
> Love is a smoke raised with the fume of sighs;

> Being purged, a fire sparkling in lovers' eyes;
> Being vex'd, a sea nourish'd with lovers' tears:
> What is it else? a madness most discreet,
> A choking gall and a preserving sweet.

These lines are important. They are written in the prevailing convention of the fifteen-nineties. Being full of conceit, antithesis and paradox, they bore a modern reader, who finds them devoid both of feeling and thought and therefore quite insipid. Passages like this, which for the Elizabethans were elaborately clever and for us just as elaborately stupid, are not uncommon in Shakespeare. They occur at *Two Gentlemen,* I, i, 19-41, II, ii, 10-16; *Twelfth Night,* I, i, 1-23, and at other places. Surely Shakespeare's technique is obvious here. When he wants to suggest crudeness, triviality or insincerity, he adopts the artifices of Elizabethan convention. By indirection he reveals that he considers certain tricks of style to be cheap and flimsy. Critics often attack him for being intricate where it was so easy to be simple. These men forget that Shakespeare the dramatist sometimes imposes a duty on Shakespeare the poet, at which the latter must have groaned.

The other passages in *Romeo and Juliet* deserve more careful scrutiny. Parrott and Telfer have the following explanation.

When it came, however, to expressing the clash of contending emotions within one mind, perhaps the highest and most difficult point in tragic art, Shakespeare's hand seems to have faltered and to have turned to an extravagance of speech which, though it passed well enough in his own day, can hardly veil from us the essential emptiness of the thought behind the words.[1]

But in reality Shakespeare is making style his instrument. Juliet's speech at III, ii, 73-88 ("O serpent heart, hid with a flowering face . . .") is not the whole-hearted expression of deep indignation. Coleridge rightly describes it as "the mind's audible struggle with itself." It takes in the Nurse, but it ought not to deceive us. Shakespeare makes Juliet use the same antithetical conceits as Romeo in I, i, 181-188, and with the same purpose. She is expressing an emotion that is not completely hers.

The passage IV, v, 32-64 of *Romeo and Juliet* is to be explained from the same point of view. At first sight, it is horrible. It reminds one of Pyramus's coarse clowning in *M.N.D.* (V, i, 171-182), which in its turn is a parody of Kyd's *Spanish Tragedy* and perhaps of the Seneca translations. But surely Shakespeare's intention is perfectly clear. He is using the sight of Juliet lying dead as a

---

[1] Thomas M. Parrott and Robert S. Telfer. Shakespeare. *King Henry V, Much Ado, Romeo and Juliet, Hamlet.* Boston: Scribner's, 1931, p. 262.

touchstone to show us what sort of people Juliet's family were. He proceeds by his usual method of contrast. At first Capulet the father is deeply moved:

> Death lies on her like an untimely frost
> Upon the sweetest flower of all the field (IV, v, 28-29).

These lines anchor the scene to reality. Against them the insincerity of what follows shows up all the more clearly. The family unite around Juliet in one loud caterwauling, which in time gets hold of Capulet and causes even him to join in their banality. Kittredge says:—

Something was needed to allow for an interval of time between Act iv and Act v, and whatever was used for that purpose was required not to advance the action. A comic interlude was the conventional thing for such a purpose. Compare the Porter's speech in *Macbeth*, ii.3. High comedy would not serve, for the Elizabethan audience felt the need of utter relaxation from tragic stress and strain.[2]

I heartily detest disagreeing with the master, but I think there is more to be said for the passage than this. Surely these lines reveal character. One of the themes in the play is the contrast between the nobility of Romeo and Juliet and the vileness of the society into which they were born. The shabbiness of Juliet's family is clearly displayed. Unfeeling, coarse and vulgar, they are not touched by the sight before them. Their one thought is to put on a show. Paris's language, with its imitation of Kyd (l. 58)—i.e., he is not even original—is to be evaluated in comparison with the words that Romeo finds at Juliet's bier. With this slight touch Shakespeare hints at the kind of man Juliet's family would have forced her to marry. Thaler's explanation that "Shakespeare wrote these falsetto ejaculations with an eye and ear to the audience, which knows that real mourning, so far, is not in order, since Juliet is still very much alive,"[3] only goes half way. It shows why it was possible for Shakespeare to proclaim the shallow grief of the family just at this place. Juliet was not dead; but her family thought she was; and their behavior, based on that belief, is chiefly important as a revelation of character. When he uses Kyd's style for such characters, we can see how far removed he was from Kyd.

In a similar fashion Shakespeare can, by parodying the use of classical quotation, put a mark on a character. Of course, as his practice proves, Shakespeare knew that classical allusions may

---

[2]Edition of *Romeo and Juliet*, Ginn & Co., 1940, pp. 194-5.
[3]*PMLA*, LIII (1938), 1029.

heighten style. But the lines of Pistol and of Armado show how much amused he was by that vice of needlessly dragging in foreign scraps which disfigures so much Elizabethan dramatic verse. Occasionally the Renaissance inclination to find nothing good that is not backed up by classical authority engages his attention. He likes to expose it as pretentious intellectual snobbery. Thus in *2 Henry VI* he makes exquisite fun of Suffolk's empty self-conceit. Suffolk has been captured by "servile, abject drudges." He complains:

> this villain here
> Being captain of a pinnace, threatens more
> Than Bargulus, the strong Illyrian pirate (IV, i, 106-8).

The recondite "Bargulus" heightens the absurdity of the allusion. When he sees that death is inevitable he consoles himself:

> Great men oft die by vile bezonians:
> A Roman sworder and banditto slave
> Murder'd sweet Tully; Brutus' bastard hand
> Stabb'd Julius Caesar; savage islanders
> Pompey the Great; and Suffolk dies by pirates (IV, i, 134-8).

I do not know if it is proper to associate the term "pet aversion" with Shakespeare, but at the least one can say that the nobleman unworthy of his station was a favorite object of Shakespeare's satire. From *Henry VI* to the *Tempest* we have a long line of such people. He pours as bitter scorn on the unworthy nobleman as on the stupid and unstable mob. When one remembers the many great dying speeches in Shakespeare, it is easy to measure from Suffolk's last words how deep was Shakespeare's contempt for the man who had dishonored his class. But in thus associating classical allusion with petty snobbery Shakespeare is revealing what he thinks about a main characteristic of Renaissance style.

Another Elizabethan convention that Shakespeare fought was the delight in revenge. (I leave *Titus Andronicus* out of the discussion, as I am reserving that for special study.) Again from *Henry VI* to the *Tempest*, he returns in one play after another to the subject of revenge and forgiveness. From the political point of view Henry VI is one of that long line of rulers in Shakespeare whom some defect of character rendered incapable of rule. His weakness was a disaster to the kingdom. But with characteristic irony Henry VI is shown as the only hero of his time, the only man who is not afraid of what life may bring him. In *2,3 Henry VI* Shakespeare portrays a society demented with rage for power and revenge. If the one side scores a success, the other side immediately schemes not only to win back what it has lost but also to pay its enemies home, to inflict cruelty for cruelty, death for death. They kill out of fear; they are afraid to leave an enemy alive. Henry, however, has no fear as he has no hate. Banished from England, he returns alone, unarmed, with empty hands, to a certain death. Sheer love drives him back to the country he cannot leave. All the other exiles return with an army, breathing revenge. I am not asserting that Shakespeare was a pacifist nor am I forgetting that here as always Shakespeare shows that it is a disaster when the ruler cannot govern with a firm hand. But at the same time he insists on the ugliness of murder and revenge and on the fineness of the soul that is above revenge.

In *Romeo and Juliet* we may find the same contrast between a society mad for revenge and the lovers who are too fine for it. ''Dowered with love of love, with hate of hate, with scorn of scorn'', Romeo and Juliet are inevitably destroyed by a world which was unworthy of them. Surely Shakespeare's intention is clear: to assert that if society is to be civilized, men must love love, hate hate and scorn scorn. By showing what becomes of a world which destroys Romeo, he proves how necessary it is that the principles of Romeo should prevail. *Romeo and Juliet* is the retort gentle to the revenge-play.

The other plays of Shakespeare that deal with revenge are usually underrated or misunderstood by critics. With the *Two Gentlemen* I shall deal below. In the *Merchant of Venice* his attack is perhaps at its boldest. Marlowe's *Jew of Malta* was popular and there seems little reason to doubt that Barabbas fascinated Elizabethan audiences. Shakespeare takes this figure of hatred and revenge and strips from it all the tinsel of poetry or romance that glorifies it in Marlowe. There is nothing fine in Shylock's revenge. He is ugly and coarse of soul. Granville Barker has shown that, when foiled of his revenge, he still demands his money, he is most degraded, ''only keen to profit by his shame.'' Revenge could not be made to appear more hideous than in the figure of Shylock.

In *Measure for Measure* Shakespeare pursues the subject further and endeavors to show the necessity for forgiveness if society is to be civilized. Strangely enough, few scholars will forgive him for forgiving. I am not concerned to defend Shakespeare's art or to assert that he could not have made out a better case for himself. All that matters here is Shakespeare's intention to wean his genera-

tion from their delight in revenge. Finally, the *Tempest* is based
upon a revenge that is planned but not taken. Prospero has got
his enemies in the hollow of his hand. He can destroy them as
easily as one cracks a nut. But he opens his hands and lets his
enemies go free. It is a fair inference that Shakespeare detested
the vindictiveness characteristic of so much Elizabethan drama.
Of course he was not alone in his feelings. I need scarcely recall
the names of Dekker and Heywood. But no other dramatist treats
the revenger with such contempt and disgust; nobody else makes
forgiveness so absolute. Perhaps modern scholars would accept
Shakespeare, if he had only forgiven with some discretion.

I keep to the last a series of plays in which Shakespeare did for
his age what Bernard Shaw has done for ours. I mean such plays
as *Love's Labour's Lost*, the *Two Gentlemen*, the *Taming of the
Shrew*, and *As You Like It*. These he devotes to exploding literary
conventions, giving his age a "purge." What Bernard Shaw does
in *You never can tell* and *The Devil's Disciple*, Shakespeare did in
Love's Labour's Lost and *As You Like It*. Enough has been written
to establish Shakespeare's purpose in these two plays. For the present I only wish to dwell on one or two points with reference to the
Taming of the Shrew and the *Two Gentlemen*.

Shakespeare's independence of his age is best illustrated from
the *Taming of the Shrew*. It is well known that the Induction is
a piece of consummate parody. The jelly-like softness of Greene
and Peele at their worst is well taken off in:

> Thou hast a lady far more beautiful
> Than any woman in this waning age (Ind, ii, 64-5).

The weak imbecility of the fifteen-nineties is pilloried in:

> She was the fairest creature in the world,
> And yet she is inferior to none (*ibid.*, 68-9).

Scholars long ago recognized that parody is the life of the main
play also. Vincentio—that "boneless wonder"—is a satire on the
gilded darlings who had been the heroes of Elizabethan romances.
Hear him speak:

> O Tranio . . .
> Thou art to me as secret and as dear
> As Anna to the queen of Carthage was;
> Tranio I burn, I pine, I perish, Tranio,
> If I achieve not this young modest girl . . .
> Oh yes, I saw sweet beauty in her face,
> Such as the daughter of Agenor had,

That made great Jove to humble him to her hand,
When with his knees he kiss'd the Cretan strand . . .
Tranio, I saw her coral lips to move
And with her breath she did perfume the air:
Sacred and sweet was all I saw in her (I, i, 153-181).

The mockery of classical allusion, of love at first sight, of Elizabethan lusciousness is too obvious to need remark. The interesting thing is that this passage is answered by another one in the next scene. Petruchio is speaking of the woman he wishes to marry:

if thou know
One rich enough to be Petruchio's wife,
As wealth is burden of my wooing dance,
Be she as foul as was Florentius' love,
As old as Sibyl and as curst and shrewd
As Socrates Xanthippe, or a worse,
She moves me not, or not removes, at least,
Affection's edge in me, were she as rough
As are the swelling Adriatic seas (I, ii, 66-74).

Obviously this is set up as a counterpart to the other passage, mood against mood, classical allusion against classical allusion. The first passage must have been written with the second already in mind. Surely those scholars are wrong who say there are two styles in this play, one the work of Shakespeare, the other coming from a collaborator. Style is not the right word to apply to Lucentio's speeches. They are fine examples of parody. In Lucentio Shakespeare is criticizing not only his contemporaries but also himself. It would seem that he was like Scott in despising some of his romantic heroes. He would have understood why Scott called Waverley "a wavering piece of imbecility." However that may be, Shakespeare's delight in parody should make us cautious of speaking about two strongly personal "styles" in the *Taming of the Shrew*. His inclination for criticizing his contemporaries, shown in so many ways, ought to put the authorship of all the *Taming of the Shrew* beyond a doubt.

Another example of Shakespeare's way of turning a fashion inside out occurs in the *Two Gentlemen*. Everybody agrees that in the figure of Valentine Shakespeare is poking fun at the artificiality of the courts of love. At the same time he is gunning for the literary convention which sets friendship between men above the love of man for woman. Valentine is a man of fine and honorable character, not richly endowed with brains, who pedantically wooes according to the convention of lady, servant, and friend. In the last act Valentine not only forgives his friend for attempting—*inter alia et enormia*—to ravish Sylvia but goes on to offer him Sylvia herself. Critics cannot forgive Shakespeare for forgiving here, and of course nobody has a good word for the betrayal of Sylvia. If Shakespeare had only made Valentine and Proteus kill one another, and Sylvia and Julia commit suicide over their dead bodies, the play would have been a wow!

But surely this scene is a logical development of Shakespeare's plan. Valentine does not attempt to kill Proteus (as the audience probably expected and desired) but instead turns upon him with scorching words. This is the high-minded Valentine we have known throughout the play. Proteus repents in an abject speech and Valentine forgives him absolutely. Again he lives his creed. I do not see how any civilized—I will not say Christian—man can find fault, especially as Shakespeare has no alternative but a duel which could only end in one or both of the two gentlemen being killed. Then Valentine gives Sylvia to Proteus. It ought to be clear that by this action Shakespeare is wringing the last drop of silliness out of Valentine's conventions. With the idea of smashing a particularly ridiculous convention, Shakespeare has set out to prove Valentine a fool. Any explanation of this scene that implies that Shakespeare was serious does rather less than justice to Shakespeare's sense of humor. It is like Shakespeare to make Valentine at once noble and silly; indeed the nature of his folly is allied to his nobility and may be said to spring from it. The heroes of these romantic comedies usually have their two sides; they have their follies, of which they are cured, and their fineness which persists. When the *Two Gentlemen* is performed nowadays, the surrender of Sylvia is cut. That does not prove that Shakespeare blundered or that he did not realize what Valentine was doing. We leave it out because that special convention which Shakespeare was trying to expose no longer exists and therefore we do not understand the passage. It is not likely that the Elizabethan audience missed the point.

I have tried to show that Shakespeare followed the literature of his period with keen attention. Sometimes the absurdity of what he saw made him laugh with all the sweetness of a child. At other times he could attack with a zeal at least equal to Shaw's. Journalistic critics have described Shakespeare as a mere purveyor of fun or excitement, indifferent to the tendency of his comedy, and intent only upon the box-office. It may not be useless to put in a reminder that he criticized all sorts of folly with humor but with earnest intention, and that he could lash vicious attitudes unsparingly. He did not servilely follow where others led but he struck out his own way to such an extent that one is tempted to assert that Shakespeare was the least Elizabethan of the Elizabethans.

THE MIND'S CONSTRUCTION IN THE FACE

By CARROLL CAMDEN
The Rice Institute

Like all thinking beings, the intelligent man of the English Renaissance was anxious to know not only the secret of the universe, the macrocosm, but also of the microcosm, the little world of man; and the subject of man, his health and his fortune, has always been the subject of the pseudo-sciences. It was doubly so for the average Elizabethan because of his effervescent belief in the wonders of the new learning. Professor Hardin Craig, in his significant paper, "A Contribution to the Theory of the Renaissance," has shown that everywhere in the England of Shakespeare there was "a promise of unbelievably good things" for those who would follow the simplified directions of the learned.[1] Handbook learning came into prominence because the ordinary man could find in these manuals the practical devices which would serve as guides along the road to success. Logic had shown the Elizabethan how to confute the devil and gain salvation; ethics had told him not only how to be good, but also how to be successful. How much more important were the pseudo-sciences: alchemy would make a man wealthy and would give him the elixir of life; astrology would tell him when to marry and when to engage in business ventures, would indicate to him the deficiencies in his character so that he might correct them, and would warn him of imminent sickness and death.

Surely this was enough; but it was not! The average Elizabethan was impatient. Alchemy and astrology were long and involved studies; it took years, sometimes a lifetime to become adept in their practice. The Elizabethan wanted "short cuts to the absolute, back stairs approaches to certainty, get-rich-quick methods of acquiring the truth." For him was revived the old study of physiognomy, the claims of which were scarcely less than those of the other pseudo-sciences. It could teach a man to choose his friends and to recognize his enemies simply by observing the face and general build of the body. Thomas Hill explains in 1571 that

---

[1] Hardin Craig, "A Contribution to the Theory of the Renaissance," *PQ*, VI (1927), 321-333.

this is "a necessarie and lawdable science, seing by the same a man may so readily pronounce and foretell the naturall aptnesse vnto the affections, and conditions in men, by the outwarde notes of the bodie."[2]

According to Ptolemy's *Compost,* whizh ran through some seventeen editions from 1503 to 1631, physiognomy is defined as a science that astrologers have "for to knowe the naturall inclynacion of man and woman good or euyll, by dyuers Sygnes on them in beholdynge them onely: The whiche inclynacion we ought to folowe yf it be good. But yf it be euyll, . . . we ought to eschewe . . . it, . . . & to withstande yᵉ sayd euyll inclynacions."[3] Francis Bacon remarks that this science originated with or at least owes much to the inquiry of Aristotle, and says that although recently physiognomy has been coupled with certain superstitious and fantastic arts, yet if it be purged and returned to its true state, it has a solid ground in nature and is very profitable in use. Bacon goes on to praise Aristotle for ingeniously handling the features of the body, but insists that Aristotle and other physiognomers have neglected the gestures of the body. Bacon continues: "The Lineaments of the body do disclose the disposition and inclination of the mind in general; but the Motions of the countenance and parts do not only so, but do further disclose the present humour and state of the mind and will."[4] Perhaps Miranda, in *The Tempest,* states the fundamental thesis more succinctly as, with her naïve and simple faith in beauty, she defends Ferdinand against Prospero's allegations that he is a spy. Remember that Miranda has just seen Ferdinand for the first time, and yet she says of him: "There's nothing ill can dwell in such a temple."[5] Her beliefs are echoed by Thomas Walkington, who, writing in 1607, asserts: "When I doe gaze with a longing looke on the comelinesse of the feature without, I am more than halfe perswaded of the admirable decencie within."[6]

Many Elizabethan literary men, other than Shakespeare, have found occasion to make use of this science in their works. In

---

[2]Thomas Hill, *The Contemplation of Mankind,* London, 1571, fol. 1ᵛ.

[3]Ptolemy, *The Compost of Ptholomeus,* London, 1540?, Q4ʳ-Q4ᵛ. The *Compost* was a part of the *Shepherd's Kalinder.*

[4]Francis Bacon, *Works,* London, 1857, III, 367-368.

[5]I, ii, 457.

[6]Thomas Walkington, *The Optick Glasse of Humors,* London, 1639, p. 38.

Chapman's *Tragedy of Byron*, one of the characters refers to another in these words:

> those strange characters, writ in his face,
> Which at first sight were hard for me to read,
> The doctrine of your speech hath made so plain
> That I run through them like my natural language.[7]

Similarly, in Jonson's *Every Man in His Humor*, Edward Knowell says to Stephen:

> Come, wrong not the qualitie of your desert, with looking downeward, couz; but hold vp your head, so; and let the *Idea* of what you are, be pourtray'd i' your face, that men may reade i' your physnomie, (Here, within this place, is to be seene the true, rare, and accomplish'd monster, or miracle of nature, which is all one.)[8]

And Robert Greene has one of his characters say: "After he had sate downe a little, he looked me very earnestly in the face, as a man that had some skil in phisiognomy, to censure of the inward qualities by the outward appearāce."[9] The claims of physiognomy, then, were for the most part recognized as being quite valid. Some few, as we shall see, did cavil at what they called the pretensions of the art, but most people regarded the subject as worthy of their consideration and patronage.

In a period when arguments by authority and tradition were accepted perhaps above all others, it is no wonder that this science was thought to be on such a firm foundation. Physiognomy was a very old branch of science, which had been traced back to the fourth century B.C. It was originally connected in a somewhat vague way with anatomy, physiology, and medicine, in that the doctrine of the humors divided all men into four groups, each with its carefully described physical characteristics. Some Elizabethans, indeed, thought of this science as being over two thousand years old, as Shakespeare indicates when he writes, in *The Rape of Lucrece*:

> In Ajax and Ulysses, O, what art
> Of physiognomy might one behold!
> The face of either cipher'd either's heart;
> Their face their manners most expressly told.[10]

Not only has Aristotle had writings on physiognomy ascribed to

---

[7]I, i, 170-173.
[8]I, iii, 122-27.
[9]Robert Greene, *Greene's Neuer Too Late, Works*, London, 1881-1883, VIII, 29.
[10]1394-1397.

him, but also such well known medieval writers as Giles of Corbeil, the legendary Albert, Arnold of Villanova, Michael Scot, Guido Bonatti, Rhazes, Hippocrates, Nicolas Oresme, and innumerable others. The most important physiognomical treatise, however, at least in its influence upon later writers, was probably the pseudo-Aristotelian *Secreta Secretorum*, which Aristotle was thought to have written as a kind of *speculum regale* for Alexander the Great.[11]

The philosophical arguments which lay behind the acceptance of physiognomy as a valid science were many. Making use of the typical argument by analogy, Castiglione points out that in trees the beauty of the blossom gives token of the excellence of the fruit, and that similarly the character and thoughts of men appear in the face. Think, he reasons, how clearly we read anger, ferocity, and pride in the face of the lion, the horse, and the eagle; a pure and simple innocence in the lambs and doves; cunning malice in foxes and wolves. How much more is this true of man![12]

For those who say that of their own knowledge the laws of physiognomy do not always work, the physiognomists have a ready answer. Thomas Hill argues that the significations and judgments of this science

doe chiefely extend, and are meant rather to happen and come to passe on the brutish sort: which for the lack of grace, and being not regenerated by Gods holy Spirit, these in such manner, are moued to follow their sensuall will and appetites. . . . But to be briefe, the Creatures which are regenerated through the holy Ghost, doe not onely endeuour to mortifie their fleshly appetites, but seeke to put away and correct, all other inormities and vices resting in them.[13]

Thus free will is upheld against a mechanistic view of man. An example of one who was able to overcome the natural inclinations of a bad physiognomy is found in the following story which is often related by the physiognomists, sometimes being told of Hippocrates and sometimes of Socrates. The disciples of Hippocrates made a perfect image of him and submitted it to an excellent physiognomist, who declared it to be the likeness of a fool and of a man given

---

[11]C. H. Haskins, *Studies in the History of Mediaeval Science*, Cambridge, 1924, pp. 245, 259, 281, 286-287, 316; Hill, *op. cit.*, preface; George Sarton, *Introduction to the History of Science*, Baltimore, 1931, II, 309, 440-441, 580, 829, 941, 1083-1084; Lynn Thorndike, *A History of Magic and Experimental Science*, I, (New York, 1923), 26, 176, 667-668; II (1923), 169, 328-329, 485, 575, 910; III (1934), 13, 73, 421; IV (1934), 143, 190ff., 449, 584, 703.

[12]Baldasar Castiglione, *Book of the Courtier*, trans. Opdycke, New York, 1903, pp. 290-291.

[13]Thomas Hill, *op. cit.*, London, 1613, sigs. A3r-A3v.

to luxury, deceit, and the lusts of the body. The disciples were angered at this slur upon the character of their master, who they knew lived a sober and upright life; but Hippocrates himself told them that the physiognomist had judged aright as to his natural traits, and that it was only by the love of wisdom, philosophy, and integrity, and by a life of study and effort that he had triumphed over nature.[14]

John Evelyn, in his discourse on medals, conversely remarks that some men and women are much worse than they look, especially calling our attention to such females as Helen, Thais, and Faustina. He explains, however, that their perversions do not spring from any features which would lead one to conclude that the ladies in question were virtuous, but take their rise from some other external adventitious cause and corruption, such as neglect of early education, want, poverty, and above all from the evil examples of bad times and bad companions. It is the purest streams, he reminds us, that are most easily defiled by passing through corrupted pools.[15] The truth is, declares Thomas Hill, that "although the inner affectes of the spirite can not be judged by the outwarde notes of the body: yet may the accydences of the spirite & minde, according to those which togither alter both spirite and body, be judged. . ." It is therefore evident, he goes on, that the deductions of physiognomy based upon the natural conditions of men do cause a great probability, although they cause no necessity. The workings and passions of the spirit and mind appear to be matched and joined with the body. This fact is especially noted in the passions of the concupiscible spirit, such as anger, meekness, fear, pity, mercy, and such like, which are never found active in a person without a concurrent local motion of the heart.[16] It must be kept in mind, however, cautions John Evelyn, that many things may cause a change in the features and thus form an abatement in the outward appearance, without in the slightest altering the virtue or inclinations of the individual in question,—particularly such changes which may be attributed to age, physical pain, hard labor, religious severities, poverty, or overindulgence in food.[17]

---

[14]Walkington, *op. cit.*, p. 34; Lynn Thorndike, *op. cit.*, II, 575; John Indagine, *Book of Palmestry and Physiognomy*, 7th ed., London, 1683, sigs. A7r-A7v; Thomas Nashe, *The Terrors of the Night*, London, 1594, sig. F1v.

[15]John Evelyn, *A Discourse of Medals*, London, 1697, pp. 306-308.

[16]Hill, *op. cit.*, (1571 ed.), fols. 2v-4r.

[17]Evelyn, *op. cit.*, p. 305.

As an argument in favor of the validity of this science, Elizabethan writers call our attention to the many who have found the practice of physiognomy helpful to them. The Emperor Adrian is said to have been so proficient that he could judge the truthfulness of a witness merely by discerning his countenance. Cicero advised that kings and princes, above all others, should cultivate this study. Zacharias stated that the Arabs trusted to nothing but physiognomy in the selection of slaves and servants. Plutarch recorded that a physiognomist told Antony to avoid and beware of Octavius. Galen, Theophrastus, Pope Gregory, King James the First, Joseph Scaliger, Cardan, Philip, Earl of Pembroke, and many others attested to the usefulness of physiognomy. The story is related that Hippocrates one day passed by a brisk young maiden and saluted her by the name of 'Fair Virgin'; but meeting her again the following morning he bid her good-morrow 'Woman,' "discovering by her looks that she had play'd the Wanton . . . the Night before."[18]

We must not think, however, that physiognomy received universal acceptance. It did not. In *Macbeth*, King Duncan speaks of the traitorous Thane of Cawdor, saying,

> There's no art
> To find the mind's construction in the face.
> He was a gentleman on whom I built
> An absolute trust.[19]

At least Duncan was not adept in the science, as he was equally unable to judge Macbeth. Likewise, John Webster has a character in *The Duchess of Malfi* ask,

> Doth he study physiognomy?
> There's no more credit to be given to th' face
> Than to a sick man's urine, which some call
> The physician's whore, because she cozens him.[20]

Henry Cornelius Agrippa, Henry Howard, and others, agree with Ludovico Vives that physiognomy is one of those sciences, "inuented of the deuyll," which should be shunned because "they intreate and professe those thynges, which god hathe reserued vnto hym selfe alone, that is to saye, the knowledge of thinges to come."[21] Per-

---

[18]*Ibid.*, pp. 302-305.

[19]I, iv, 11-14.

[20]I, ii, 164-171.

[21]Ludovico Vives, *An Introduction to Wysedome*, London, 1540, sig. D3ᵛ; Henry Howard, *A Defensative against the Poyson of Supposed Prophecies*, London, 1620, fol. 25ʳ; Henry Cornelius Agrippa, *Of the Vanitie and Vncertaintie of Artes and Sciences*, London, 1569, fol. 50ᵛ.

haps the most striking description of physiognomy by an opponent
of the science is that given by Thomas Nashe in *The Terrors of the
Night*. He speaks of our faces which are often deformedly whelked
and crumpled by surfeits, grief, intemperance, and even by study;
and calling attention to some particularly bad faces, he concludes,

> there is no more to bee gathered by their sharpe embossed Ioyners anticke
> worke, or ragged ouer-hangings or pit-falls; but that they haue beene layd vp
> in slouens presse, and with miscarriage and misgouernment are so fretted and
> galled.
> My owne experience is but small, yet thus much I can say . . ., that those
> fatall brands of phisiognomie which condemne men for fooles and for idiots,
> and on the other side for trecherous circumuenters and false brothers, haue in
> a hundred men I know been verefied in the contrarie.[22]

Ben Jonson, that Elizabethan rebel, critic, and iconoclast, who had
already castigated the sciences of astrology and alchemy, also gives
the lie to physiognomy. In *Cynthias Reuells*, the character Amorphus is talking to Asotus and explaining that those who hold that
the face is the index of the mind are indulging in a paradox or a
pseudodox. Amorphus goes on to say that he can very nicely refute
any such theory simply by showing that all men of a particular
profession are likely to resemble each other. To prove his statement, he begins to describe some typical examples:

> First, for your merchant, or citie-face, 'tis thus, a dull plodding face, still
> looking in a direct line, forward: there is no great matter in this face. Then
> haue you your students, or *academique* face, which is here, an honest, simple,
> and methodicall face: but some-what more spread then the former. The
> third is your souldiers face, a menacing, and astounding face, that lookes
> broad, and bigge: The *anti-face* to this, is your lawyers face, a contracted,
> subtile, and intricate face, full of quirkes, and turnings, a labyrinthaean
> face. . . .[23]

Perhaps it would be well at this point to consider certain principles in the practice of physiognomy. Dr. Helkiah Crooke, physician
to King James and professor in anatomy and surgery, has noticed
that the hairs of the brows are particularly significant:

> if they be straight it is a signe of a soft and flexible disposition; if they be
> inflected near the nose they are a signe of a scurrulous Buffon; if they be in-
> flected near the temples they argue a scoffing Parasite; if they bend all
> downewards they are an argument of an enuious inclination.[24]

---

[22]Thomas Nashe, *The Terrors of the Night*, London, 1594, sigs. F1r-F1v.

[23]*Cynthias Reuells*, II, iii, 11-69; cf. *Philaster*, I.i (*Works*, Cambridge, 1905,
I, 82).

[24]Helkiah Crooke, *A Description of the Body of Man*, London, 1615, p. 503;
cf. Thomas Wright, *The Passions of the Minde in Generall*, London, 1621, pp.
125-141.

In *The Optick Glasse of Humors*, Thomas Walkington states that little eyes denote a flexible conscience; a great head means little wit; goggle eyes mean a fool; great ears betray the kin of Midas; a large, deep chest means long life; a brow without furrows denotes liberality; those of soft flesh are wise and quick to understand. Walkington sums up his remarks by quoting an unnamed English poet:

> Fat paunches make leane pates, and grosser bits
> Enrich the ribs but bankrupt quite the wits.[25]

The reduction of certain physiognomical generalities to mnemonic verses of a proverbial sound was quite common. John Evelyn lists the following bits:

> The Red is Witty, the Brown Trusty,
> The Pale Peevish, the Black Lusty.

> If little Men but Patient were,
> The Tall of Courage free,
> The Red Men trusty and sincere,
> The World would soon agree.
> To a Red Man read thy Read,
> At a Pale Man draw thy Knife,
> With a Brown Man break thy bread,
> From a Black Man keep thy Wife.[26]

Thomas Hill cautions us, however, that it is not sufficient to consider only the general complexion, or only certain parts of the body. "I admonish euery one," he writes, "that will rightlye pronounce and iudge in this Art, that they first consider and vew all the partes of man, and not to iudge rashly by any one member alone."[27] But of course there would be a natural tendency to concentrate on one particularly bad feature. In *Antony and Cleopatra*, a messenger has just entered with news from Rome, and Cleopatra questions him about her rival, Octavia: "Bearest thou her face in mind, Is't long or round?" Upon learning that it is "round even to faultiness," Cleopatra makes the disparaging comment, "For the most part, too, they are foolish that are so."[28] Leonato apparently looks at another feature of the face. When he learns of the supposed death of his daughter, he bursts upon the stage crying:

---

[25]Walkington, *op. cit.*, pp. 41-42; cf. Robert Burton, *The Anatomy of Melancholy*, Oxford, 1621, pp. 76-78.

[26]Evelyn, *op. cit.*, pp. 299-300; cf. pp. 295-296.

[27]Hill, *op. cit.*, preface to the reader.

[28]III, iii, 32-34.

> Which is the villain? let me see his eyes,
> That, when I note another man like him
> I may avoid him.[29]

And Othello, noticing that Desdemona's hand is hot and moist says, "This argues fruitfulness and liberal heart."[30] John Huarte, the author of *The Examination of Mens Wits*, believes in emphasizing the shape of the head, staring that Galen believed the condition of the brain to be so indicated. The shape, he tells us, should be

if taking a perfect round ball of wax, and pressing it together somewhat on the sides, there will remain (after that manner) the forehead and the nape with a little bunchinesse. Hence it followes that the man who hath his forehead very plaine, and his nodocke flat, hath not his braine so figured, as is requisit for wit and habilitie.[31]

The signs of a short life are set down thus by Philemon Holland, as he gives a free translation of Pliny's *History of the World*: "thin teeth, long fingers, a leaden hew, many lines in the palme of the hand, with crosse bars or short cuts. Contrariwise, . . . those . . . who also have in one hand two long life lines, and above two and thirtie teeth." He then makes the gratuitous remark: "Surely, these physiognomers and Chiromantines . . ., as frivolous and foolish as they be, yet now adaies are in credite, & euery man is full of them."[32]

Thomas Hill gets from Rhazes the following description of a wise man: he should be

of an vpright stature, hauing the fleshe of the bodye throughout equall: the skinne whyte, myxed with a small rednesse. The heares on the head discerned a meane, betweene the plentie and fewe, and betweene the plaine and crysped, and abourne in colour. The handes formed seemely and plaine, and the fingers . . . distaunt a sunder . . . . the eyes comely conditioned, and a meane betweene the black and variable: the fleshe soft in the feeling, gentle of countinaunce, and the looke discerned as one smyling.[33]

Physiognomy, like the other pseudo-sciences, was dependent upon astrology: as Richard Saunders puts it, "No Divination is certain,

---

[29] V, i, 268-270.

[30] *Othello*, III, iv, 36-39.

[31] John Huarte, *Examen de Ingenos. The Examination of Mens Wits*, London, 1594?, pp. 25-26.

[32] Pliny, *Historie of the World*, trans. Holland, London, 1601, I, 354.

[33] Hill, *op. cit.*, sigs. B2ᵛ-B3ʳ; Arcandam (or Aleandrin), *The Most Excellent, Profitable and Pleasant Book, . . . to finde the fatal destiny, . . . of euery man and child*, London. 1592, sigs. L4ᵛ-L8ʳ. Cf. Hill, sigs. Gg2r-Hh1r; Pliny, *op. cit.*, I, 354; Evelyn, *op. cit.*, pp. 296-299, 305, 306; Ptolemy, *op cit.*, sigs. R2ʳ-S1ᵛ.

unless it be joyned with, and assured by *Astrology*, which at present is the certainest Science for the prediction of things to come.''[34] In a like fashion physiognomy in its turn had two pseudo-sciences which were ancillary to it. These were metoposcopy and chiromancy. Metoposcopy made known the conditions and temperaments of men and judged events to come, as they affected the individual, by means of the frontal lines or the wrinkles in the forehead. This science is clearly indicated in James Shirley's *The Cardinal* when the Duchess tells Colombo, ''There's something, sir, Upon your brow I did not read before,'' and Colombo inquires, ''Does the character please you, madam?''[35] Again, it is referred to as Tamburlaine says to Theridamus,

> Art thou but Captaine of a thousand horse,
> That by Characters grauen in thy browes,
> And by thy martiall face and stout aspect,
> Deserust to have the leading of an hoste?[36]

Metoposcopy, singularly enough, was never as popular as physiognomy, chiromancy, or other pseudo-sciences. One would think that it might have been, since it was a somewhat simplified physiognomy by means of which the final prognostication could be arrived at in short order. The rapidity with which judgment could be made in metoposcopy had apparently long been recognized. The Elizabethan version of Pliny records a story told by Appion, the Grammarian, that a physiognomist once looked upon some portraits by Apelles and by means of metoposcopy foretold how long each of the originals was to live.[37] Similarly, Thomas Hill, in *The Contemplation of Mankind*, relates that a certain physiognomist was surprised by the quickness and accuracy of the physiognomical pronouncements of an acquaintance, and was further astounded to learn that this person knew nothing of the laws of physiognomy except the use of the lines in the forehead.[38] Ben Jonson, too, pays his respects to this science and the ease with which it can be practiced. In *The Alchemist*, Subtle has just read Abel Drugger's fortune, and Face

---

[34]Richard Saunders, *Physiognomie, and Chiromancie, Metoposcopie*, etc., second edition, London, 1671, p. 180.

[35]I, ii, 107-109.

[36]*Tamburlaine*, part 1, I, ii, 363-366. Cf. II, i, 1-4, and *Cynthias Reuells*, V, vi, 79-80.

[37]Pliny, *op. cit.*, II, 539.

[38]Hill, *op. cit.*, fols. 39ᵛ-40ʳ.

asks, " 'Slid, doctor, how canst thou know this so soon?" To which
Subtle replies,

> By a rule, captain,
> In metoposcopy, which I do work by;
> A certain star i' the forehead, which you see not.[39]

Although, as we have seen, Pliny speaks of a reduced physiognomy
based upon the lines of the forehead, most writers on the subject
generally consider metoposcopy to have had its origin or at least
its chief development in the Renaissance. Thomas Hill mentions
such authorities as Cardinal Morbeth, Mantuanus, Franciscus
Asculanus, Ptholomeus Parvus, Thaddaeus Hagecius, and Bartholomaeus Cocles, and we know that Jerome Cardan, Samuel Fuchs,
and Spontoni, among others, wrote on the subject. Jerome Cardan,
who in 1550 wrote his *Chiromantia* under the pseudonym of
Melampus, is apparently responsible for the pseudo-science as we
have it. Building on the basis of several hints he received, Cardan
minutely and systematically applied the science of astrology to an
explanation of the lines in the forehead.[40]

Being a somewhat new or newly revived science and not so ex-
tensively in use, metoposcopy escaped the vicious attack that the
other pseudo-sciences had to endure. Of course Henry Cornelius
Agrippa includes it among the others which he attacks, although
he merely mentions it in a brief paragraph.[41] Robert Vaughan,
however, admits that "great cunning" lies in the practice of
metoposcopy, and goes on further to say that the lines in the forehead must be there for some purpose because "God (we know) In
vaine hath nothing made in man." On the other hand, Vaughan
feels that the chief rules of this science are based on observations
and frail conjectures, and wonders how anything can be expected
of the lines in a baby's forehead.[42] Thomas Nashe, on his part,
thinks the subject fit only for "aged mumping beldams as they
[sit] warming their knees ouer a coale," and ridicules the idea of

---

[39]I, iii, 42-45.

[40]Hill, *op. cit.*, fols. 42ᵛ-44ᵛ; *Bibliotheca Osleriana*, Oxford, 1929, nos. 2242
(see quotation from Henry Morley, *Jerome Cardan*, London, 1854, II, 53),
2690, 4008. Thorndike does not list the word metoposcopy in his indexes
which thus far run through the fifteenth century.

[41]Agrippa, *op. cit.*, fol. 50ᵛ. In the *Occult philosophy*, book III, chapter 29,
Agrippa explains and defends the science.

[42]Robert Vaughan, *The Little World. Or, a lively description of all the
partes and properties of man*, London, 1612, p. 22.

trying to "show how many years a man should liue by the number
of wrinkles on his forhead." Nashe continues,

Liues there anie such slowe yce-brained beefe-witted gull, who by the riueld
barke or outward rynde of a tree will take vpon him to forespeak how long it
shall stand, what mischances of wormes, caterpillers, boughs breaking, frost
bitings, cattells rubbing against, it shall haue? As absurd is it, by the external
branched seames or furrowed wrinckles in a mans face or hand, in particular
or generall to coniecture and foredoome of his fate.[43]

According to the general theory of metoposcopy, there are seven
principal lines on the forehead, and these lines are ascribed to the
seven planets. Beginning at the hair-line and reading downward,
the first line is that of Saturn, which is followed by those of Jupiter
and Mars. Next come the lines over the eyes, that over the left eye
belonging to the Moon, that over the right eye to the Sun. Venus'
line comes next, somewhat between and below the lines of the Sun
and the Moon; it is followed by the line of Mercury which is at the
base of the nose or practically on it.[44] The lines of the planets,
according to Richard Saunders, may be fortunate or unfortunate.
The fortunate ones are those which are straight or which bend a
little toward the nose. The unfortunate ones are those that are
winding, approaching a semicircle or obelisk. Simple, straight
lines denote a simple, good, and honest soul, without any malice.
The oblique, inflexed or distorted lines denote craft, cheating, mischief, deceit. If the Sun's line be oblique, it signifies malice. If
the line of Jupiter be longer than that of Saturn, it denotes riches.
If the line of Mars be the longest, it means a warrior; but if the
line be broken, it signifies misfortunes in war. Lines at the root
of the nose and cut in the middle signify one much transported with
the vice of venery. If the Moon's line be clear, distinct, and directly above the left eye, it foretells much travel into strange nations.[45] Robert Vaughan pronounces the general principle,

> The *longer all the lines do reach, the smoother, and more plaine,*
> So much the more they luckie be, and longer life retaine,

and adds that if no lines are seen it is "a singuler most happie

---

[43]Thomas Nashe, *The Terrors of the Night*, London, 1594, sigs. E4^r-F1^r.

[44]Saunders, *op. cit.*, pp. 181, 183; Erra Pater, *The Book of Knowledge*, trans.
W. Lilly, London, 1766, p. 62. Hill (*op. cit.*, fols. 40^r-42^r) apparently has only
six lines, omitting the lines of Mars and the Sun and placing that of Saturn
over the right eye.

[45]Saunders, *op. cit.*, p 183; Vaughan, *op. cit.*, pp. 17-21; Hill, *op. cit.*, fols.
40^r-44^v; Evelyn, *op. cit.*, pp. 294-295.

lucke.''[46] Furthermore, as Thomas Hill informs us, the line of Mercury is related to childhood which runs from birth to age twenty-five; the line of Jupiter is related to youth, which runs from twenty-five to fifty; and the line of Saturn is related to old age, which runs from fifty to death.[47]

The Renaissance in England, then, had a practical side which should not be neglected. Some men may want but little here below, but not the Elizabethan. His thirst for knowledge was tremendous. And the reason lay in the element of promise—the reward which learning offered him, for he intended to have no dallying on the road to fortune. As we have seen, the sciences of physiognomy and metoposcopy definitely contributed to his needs by making him aware of the fundamental character and personality of each man who entered his life, and by preparing him for the vicissitudes of life, love, and fortune.

---

[46]Vaughan, *op. cit.*, p. 21.
[47]Hill, *op cit.*, fols. 40^r-41^v.

THAT UNDISCOVERED COUNTRY

A Problem concerning the Use of the Supernatural in *Hamlet* and *Macbeth*[1]

By MADELEINE DORAN
University of Wisconsin

The question I mean to raise in this paper· is at once historical, psychological, and aesthetic. Although I have centered it on *Hamlet* and *Macbeth,* it concerns as well any piece of literature that makes use of the supernatural to secure tragic effect.

Let me recall the distinction Coleridge made between the ends which he and Wordsworth proposed to themselves in the poems they should each write for the *Lyrical Ballads*:

> . . . it was agreed, that my endeavors should be directed to persons and characters supernatural, or at least romantic; yet so as to transfer from our inward nature a human interest and a semblance of truth sufficient to procure for these shadows of imagination that willing suspension of disbelief for the moment, which constitutes poetic faith. Mr. Wordsworth, on the other hand, was to propose to himself as his object, to give the charm of novelty to things of every day, and to excite a feeling analogous to the supernatural, by awakening the mind's attention to the lethargy of custom, and directing it to the loveliness and the wonders of the world before us; an inexhaustible treasure, but for which, in consequence of the film of familiarity and selfish solicitude, we have eyes, yet see not, ears that hear not, and hearts that neither feel nor understand.[2]

These different ends are only two faces of the same thing. They both spring from a feeling that "wonderfulness or mysteriousness" is "an essential attribute of the nature of things,"[3] and they are both concerned with stimulating an awareness of that mystery through the power of poetry. These ends, although followed in special ways by Coleridge and Wordsworth, and by them perhaps for the first time clearly recognized and stated, were not new in literature. The Coleridgean mood, which is wonder on the fringes of the known world of experience, both physical and mental, is at

---

[1] A shortened form of this paper was read before the Shakespeare group of the Modern Language Association at New Orleans, December, 1939. The paper has since been considerably revised.

[2] *Biographia Literaria*, Chap. XIV (Everyman Edition, p. 161).

[3] From William James, "The Sentiment of Rationality" in *The Will to Believe and Other Essays in Popular Philosophy* (New York, 1897), p. 75.

the heart of all fairy tale, from *Jack the Giant Killer* to *The Divine Comedy*. The Wordsworthian mood, which is wonder at the center of experience, the heart of man himself, is at the core of all tragedy. The Wordsworthian mood is present in the return of Admetus from the funeral of Alkestis to his desolate hearth:

> ὦ σχῆμα δόμων, πῶς εἰσέλθω

It is present in the reconciliation between Lear and Cordelia:

> Pray you now, forget and forgive.
> You must bear with me; I am old and foolish.

These two modes of approach to the wonder of existence, the Coleridgean and the Wordsworthian, need not be exclusive of each other, and some of the greatest tragedy, such as that of Aeschylus, of Shakespeare, and of Goethe, has used them both. Indeed, since to exhibit and emphasize the mystery of existence is apparently the business of tragedy, the quality of wonder has generally been felt to be essential to it; and to bring the supernatural into relation with the intimate feelings of man's heart may serve to deepen that wonder.

If I were merely to elaborate this point in respect to Shakespeare, I should only be saying again what has already been superlatively well said by such critics as Bradley. What I want to do is to explore rather fully the differences between the response of Elizabethan and of modern audiences to the supernatural in *Hamlet* and *Macbeth*, and hence to raise general æsthetic questions with regard to the use of the supernatural in literature.

As recent scholarship has tended to emphasize the extent of simple belief in supernatural phenomena in Elizabethan times, modern criticism has insisted on the objective character of such phenomena as they appear in the drama.[4] Not only the ghost of

---

[4]See especially E. E. Whitmore, *The Supernatural in Tragedy* (Harvard University Press, 1915), Chap. V; E. E. Stoll, *Shakespeare Studies* (New York, 1927), Chap. V, and the same author's *Hamlet: An Historical and Comparative Study*, Research Publ. of the Univ. of Minnesota, Vol. VIII, No. 5 (Sept. 1919); G. L. Kittredge, *Witchcraft in Old and New England* (Harvard University Press, 1928), and the same author's editions of *Hamlet* (Boston, 1939), Introduction and notes to ghost scenes, esp. to III, iv, 101, and of *Macbeth* (Boston, 1939), Introduction and notes; J. Dover Wilson, *What Happens in Hamlet* (Cambridge University Press, 1935), Chap. III, and the same author's edition of *Hamlet* (Cambridge University Press, 1934), pp. l-liii and notes; J. W. Draper, *The Hamlet of Shakespeare's Audience* (Duke University Press, 1938), Chap. VII; R. H. West, *The Invisible World: A Study of Pneumatology in Elizabethan Drama* (University of Georgia Press, 1939), Part II, *passim*. There is, however, dissenting opinion: see W. W. Greg, "Hamlet's Hallucination," *MLR*, XII (Oct. 1917), 393-421.

King Hamlet, but also the ghosts of Richard III's victims, of Caesar, and of Banquo are now generally considered genuine apparitions, not hallucinations, and doubtlessly "honest" ghosts into the bargain. This reaction against the tendency of romantic criticism to blur historical differences and to interpret Elizabethan ghosts subjectively is undoubtedly sound. But we should not let it blind us to the enormous complexity of the matter for Elizabethans, to the variety of opinions which were held, and to the genuine skepticism, however rare, which did exist. There is no Elizabethan state of mind; there are many Elizabethan states of mind.[5] In the same way, there is no single modern state of mind with regard to supernatural or better, supernormal, phenomena. If in Shakespeare's day King James expressed the dominant opinion, there was nevertheless a Reginald Scot; if in our day the dominant note is still the contemptuous one spoken for science in the last century by Thomas Henry Huxley, there have been, nevertheless, Sir Oliver Lodge and the highly respectable Society for Psychical Research.

Yet, allowing for all varieties of opinion in the two ages, the total complexion of each is different. This difference may be clearly realized by trying to imagine how a modern playwright retelling the Hamlet story in modern terms would have to deal with the problem of Hamlet's discovery of his father's murder. A materializing ghost would hardly do; but a message that came by way of ouija board, table-rapping, trumpet-speaking, or any of the claptrap of the séance, would be even less acceptable. For however well received these things may be in in some quarters, there would surely be too much skepticism in any theatre audience to allow the effect to be other than ridiculous. The author might make Hamlet sensitively or intuitively aware of his uncle's guilt, and so through purely psychological means arrive at a suspicion of his father's murder;[6] and a covert suggestion of telepathy would not be received as comic. But any actual disclosure would have to come, I think, through natural means.

The difference in treatment a modern playwright would have to give the supernatural elements in the Hamlet story suggests at

---

[5] For a careful distinction among all shades of Elizabethan doctrine, see Robert Hunter West, *op. cit.* He does full justice to the skepticism of Reginald Scot; see esp. pp. 10, 19-21, and index under Scot.

[6] Dr. Greg (*op. cit.*) believes indeed that that *is* the way Shakespeare made Hamlet aware of his uncle's guilt. He says that the words of the ghost are an hallucination caused by Hamlet's suspicious and overwrought state of mind.

once something important with regard to the difference in response
between Elizabethan and modern audiences. Surely the play has
lost something for us of the effect it must have had on audiences to
whom a returning spirit from the other world was an awful possibility.[7] We accept the ghost, certainly, but we accept him for the
most part, I think, simply as a convention. He does not harrow us
with fear and wonder. Those feelings are exhibited to us by the
witnesses with him on the stage, and we appreciate their response
imaginatively, at second-hand. The human tragedy, of course, remains; it is Hamlet's play, and not the ghost's. Yet by being
obliged to give the ghost a merely conventional assent, we have inevitably and irretrievably lost an important element in the play as
originally conceived. Some of its richness, some of its power, have
gone; its total quality is different.

We have raised here a psychological and an æsthetic problem that
seems to me to be worth exploring in some detail. I suggest that
there may be several levels of psychological response to the marvelous.[8] I am thinking, for the moment, of response in the real world,
not in the realm of art, which offers a more complicated problem.
And I am using "the marvelous" in the sense of any inexplicable
thing in our experience of the universe that arouses our wonder; it
is not the impossible thing, but the seemingly possible yet unaccountable thing, which gives rise to this feeling.

(1) The first level is complete acceptance of the marvelous
"fact." It is a "fact" because it happens, or seems to happen; it
is "marvelous" because it is finally inexplicable on the grounds we
accept as generally explanatory of natural phenomena. The most
credulous of the Elizabethans—and I am not here concerned with
how many or how few there were—accepted on this level such
supernatural manifestations as the apparent influence of the stars
on the lives of men, the powers of conjurors and witches, the active
agency of the Devil in the world, the presence of spirits, good and
bad, and the possible reappearance on earth of the souls of the de-
parted. Unless we happen to be spiritualists, dabblers in occult

---

[7] I am not here concerned with doctrinal differences on the character of apparitions, whether ghosts or demons; see Wilson, Kittredge, West, works already cited in note 4.

[8] What follows on the definition of the three levels (pp. 224-227) is an expanded and qualified statement of a point made in my article "On Elizabethan
Credulity," *Jour. of the Hist. of Ideas,* I (April, 1940), 151-76.

lore, or investigators as open-minded as William James,[9] we of the modern world do not regard such things as "facts" at all. But we have our own realm of marvelous fact to which we respond with wonder. It is, of course, modern science and its technical achievements. Explanation of mechanical structure or of process does not always fully satisfy us that the thing in question is not, somehow, unaccountable. Santayana says that "the wonderful and the natural are all of a piece, and that only our degree of habituation distinguishes them."[10] One still hears people exclaiming over the "wonder" of the radio. And the thought of the great interstellar spaces arouses in most people the awed wonder which is the true sign of the marvelous. But it is not the prerogative of the ignorant so to wonder; scientists themselves, who can after all only describe, not explain, have taught us how. Witness Sir James Jeans.

(2) The second level is entertainment of the possibility of an unaccountable thing without complete belief; intellectual doubt is combined with emotional willingness to believe. Many Elizabethans, if we can judge from controversies over such matters as demonic possession, the power of witches, and the return of the dead, would have responded to the supernatural on this level rather than on the first.[11] Many enlightened modern people are in this state with regard to such things as telepathy, faith healing, and the like. They are not willing to commit themselves to a belief in telepathy, for instance; on purely rational grounds they perhaps think it im-

[9]James's sympathetic and generous nature predisposed him to shut no doors on honest opinion, and to understand the "chronic belief of mankind" that life is personal and romantic: "What Psychical Research has Accomplished" in *The Will to Believe*, esp. pp. 318-27; "Final Impressions of a Psychical Researcher" in *Memories and Studies* (New York, 1911), esp. pp. 196-206; "Report on Mrs. Piper's Hodgson-Control" in *Proceedings of the American Society for Psychical Research*, III (1909), pp. 470-589; the latter is in part reprinted in *Collected Essays and Reviews* (New York, 1920), pp. 484-90.

[10]From the essay on "William James" in *Character and Opinion in the United States* (New York, 1920), p. 82.

[11]One of the liveliest controversies on demonic possession seems to have centered around William Somers, subject, and the preacher John Darrell, exorcist. Darrell had to defend himself against charges of fraud and collusion: much of the argument is on purely theoretical grounds, and his accusers argue against the possibility of possession by demons, not merely against the actuality in Somers' case. See Samuel Harsnet, *A Discovery of the Fraudulent Practises of John Darrel*, 1599; John Darrell, *A Detection of that Sinnful Shamful, Lying, and Ridiculous Discours, of Samuel Harsnet*, 1600; John Deacon and John Walker, *Dialogicall Discourses of Spirits and Divels*, 1601; Darrell, *A Survey of Certaine Dialogical Discourses*, 1602, and *The Replie of John Darrell to the Answer of John Deacon, and John Walker*, 1602. For bibliography of controversial opinion on related subjects, see West, *op. cit.*

probable. And yet they listen eagerly to stories by their friends which appear to support it, even recall strange experiences of their own which are hard to explain away as coincidences. Very likely they trust in hunches, even though they rather make fun of themselves for so doing. "Often a humorous entertainment of such ideas . . . meant to imply disbelief, really masks a willingness to believe, or at least a troubling capacity to be moved"[12] by their possible validity. The same thing is often true of a humorous indulgence in common superstitious practices like knocking on wood or throwing spilled salt over one's shoulder. Even the most skeptical of us can respond to ghosts on this level if we are sufficiently disarmed. If our primitive fears can be touched, our older emotions will overwhelm our younger heads. In the realm of art, this state of mind seems to me to be one suggested by Professor Stoll in his analysis of the effect of the supernatural in Hawthorne and Ibsen; he calls it "dubiety" and distinguishes it from direct "awe and wonder."[13]

(3) The third level applies only to art, whereas the other two, as will become apparent, may apply to both life and art. The third level is the complete rejection of the marvelous thing as possible fact; yet a willingness, for purely literary purposes, to entertain the fiction imaginatively. The question of actual belief does not enter in. The cultured Elizabethans, who would have been the only ones to read *The Faerie Queene*, would have accepted Spenser's Blatant Beast and Serpent of Error in such a spirit. So, I think, would they have accepted the purely Senecan, literary ghosts of the *Misfortunes of Arthur, Locrine,* and the *Spanish Tragedy.*[14] It is on this level, of course, that we of the twentieth century accept in contemporary literature allusions to the myths of a past age. But it is also on this level that we accept, for the most part, those appearances of the supernatural in an earlier literature which, in its own day, were responded to on a different level—a level of emotional response where belief was in question. Hence my claim that *Hamlet* is not for us, with our merely conventional, empty acceptance of the ghost, what it was for audiences who responded emotion-

---

12Doran, *op. cit.*, pp. 170-71.

13Stoll, *Shakespeare Studies*, p. 233.

14On the Senecan ghost, see Whitmore, *op. cit.*, pp. 203-20. He finds significant modifications in the plays named of the Senecan tradition. Their ghosts still seem to me, however, more conventional than "vital," if I may use the word of ghosts.

ally with greater or less degree of intellectual belief in ghosts in the real world.

Coleridge has done as much as anyone to relate the psychology of belief to this aesthetic problem, and some of his terms—like "negative faith," "poetic faith," and "willing suspension of disbelief"—are worth recalling here. When he talks of "poetic faith" as distinct from "historical faith," he clearly means merely the surrender for the time being to the apparent reality of the literary fiction.[15] In this sense, of course, the term "poetic faith" applies to our response to *Hamlet,* no matter what state of belief we are in with regard to ghosts in the real world; it simply means that, although we know the ghost we see on the stage to be no real ghost, we temporarily accept him as such. Even if we believe in ghosts we shall hardly be as naïve as the Citizen's Wife in *The Knight of the Burning Pestle,* who mistook illusion for reality. This meaning does not concern us except on the third level. My contention is that the state of our intellectual attitude towards ghosts in the real world is important in determining the character of our response to ghosts in the imaginary world of the theatre. And Coleridge's terms are still serviceable in considering this slightly more complicated problem.[16] The "willing suspension of disbelief," for instance, considered as descriptive of our state of mind with regard to the real world as we witness a play, is not applicable in this sense to the first level, since that is the level of intellectual belief. But it is, of course, applicable to the other two. Only the "willing" must be interpreted rather differently in the two cases. On the second level, it implies an emotional readiness to be convinced of the possibility in the real

---

15"That illusion, contradistinguished from delusion, that negative faith, which simply permits the images presented to work by their own force, without either denial or affirmation by the judgment," "this mere poetic *analogon* of faith," *Biographia Literaria,* p. 242. See also his discussion on dramatic probability with regard to *Bertram* and *Don Juan* (Spanish play) in Chap. XXIII, esp. p. 310: "The poet does not require us to be awake and believe; he solicits us only to yield ourselves to a dream; and this too with our eyes open, and with our judgment *perdue* behind the curtain, ready to awaken us at the first motion of our will: and meantime, only, not to *disbelieve.*" The distinction between "poetic" and "historic" faith is again made in the Ninth Lecture (*Coleridge's Essays and Lectures on Shakespeare,* Everyman Edition, p. 460).

16Professor Stoll (*Shakespeare Studies,* pp. 232-33) recognizes the problem in his distinction between poetic belief, in Coleridge's sense, and intellectual belief: "Shakespeare has only *poetic* disbelief, if we may so say, to cope with, or the state of imaginative apathy. The modern writer has not only that but positive intellectual incredulity as well. He must make his creation 'convincing,' as we say, and he must do this in a double sense."

world of a marvel similar to the theatrical marvel—ghost, supernatural power, telepathic communication, or whatever it may be.
On the third level, it implies a readiness, for the sake of enjoyment,
to surrender to the marvel merely within the limits of the fictional
world. The term "negative faith" seems to me peculiarly fitting
to describe the acceptance of marvels in this purely literary sense.
The measure of the difference between the Elizabethans and us in
our response to *Hamlet* is, I believe, that many of them would have
assented to the ghost on the first level—the level of complete belief
in the real world—that many would have assented to it on the
second level, the level of emotional willingness to believe, however
much they were in doubt rationally, and that a few would have
responded to it merely on the third level, the level of purely conventional literary acceptance; whereas we, unless we are spiritualists, respond to it entirely on this third level, or explain it away, as
Dr. Greg does.

One way to rob ghosts of their power to frighten is to psychologize
them. There was a tendency among nineteenth-century critics to
regard the second apparition of Hamlet's father, the ghost of
Banquo, and the ghost of Caesar as hallucinations on the part of
the beholder.[17] Elizabethans would have been familiar with this
explanation of apparitions and the plays do not absolutely shut the
door on such interpretations, but modern critics, especially Professor Stoll, have argued convincingly for the objectivity of most
Elizabethan ghosts. In any case, regardless of Shakespeare's intention, a large proportion of his audience would surely so have
received them.[18]

It is not that ghosts have disappeared from the world of modern
literature, either—though most of them are confined to comedies or
to frank thrillers, where at the end a naturalistic explanation is
generally supplied; they rarely occur in serious tragedy. The
ghosts of modern tragedy, such as we find in Ibsen and O'Neill, are

---

[17]Dr. Greg has made out a case (*op. cit.*) for the subjective character of
King Hamlet's ghost from the very beginning. He finds the ghost so dull as
to be unable to accept him even conventionally; he interprets his communication as an hallucination of Hamlet's, and thinks that Shakespeare so intended
it, however well he knew that "the general" would take it at its face value.

[18]Cf. Stoll, *Shakespeare Studies*, p. 241: "The poetic depends on the
imagination alone, and that . . . is not fettered to experience. In this particular case [Shakespeare's], it depends, not on the faith or superstition of
the writer, but on his cunning appeal to the faith and superstition of his
audience."

for the most part Mendelian or Freudian ghosts. The dead hand
of the past blights the lives of the young, not by appearing as
spectres with ominous messages from the nether world, but by be-
queathing them, through biological inheritance and environmental
influence, physical and mental disease. Although these ghosts demand revenge or expiation as inexorably as did their Elizabethan
ancestors, their return is controlled not by the immediate permission of God for a personal end, but by an impersonal and aimless
scientific determinism, and as they move into a naturalistic realm,
where grimness replaces wonder, they move out of our concern.

Nevertheless, if the primary springs of fear are touched, we can
still be moved by frankly supernatural beings. We can still waken
to nightmare. Witness the reception of Orson Welles's *Men from
Mars*; that was certainly response on the first level. Men could not
so have mistaken fairy-tale for fact if that particular realm of
fairy-tale (the creatures of Mars) had not already been invested by
the imagination with reality. Perhaps another of the reasons for
that immediate response of terror, so great as to overwhelm judgment, was that the play touched upon a fear constantly present to
modern consciousness, the fear of attack from the air.

In fiction that is frankly understood as such, however, a slower
approach than sufficed for the Elizabethans must be made to the
appearance of the supernatural. For example, with Shakespeare's
careful, but fairly swift preparation for the appearance of the
ghost in *Hamlet*, compare Henry James's long and elaborate preparation in *The Turn of the Screw* for the first sight of the face at the
window. By constant suggestion of something strangely, elusively
evil about the house, especially in the unaccountable behavior of
the children, our intellectual skepticism is gradually worn thin, and
when the apparition shows itself at the window the first time it
touches the spring of primitive terror which has been so carefully
laid bare, and we respond to it, if not on the first level, certainly
on the second—that is, on the level of emotional willingness to believe. Coleridge's *Ancient Mariner* is another example of this sort
of thing. The spectral ship does not appear, nor do the dead men
arise to sail the ship the mariner is on until we have been led gently
into the belief that anything is possible on this terrible voyage.
There is something more here, I think, than merely conventional
literary acceptance on the third level.

Another thing besides careful preparation is necessary to the

successful use of the supernatural in modern literature and that is
care not to explain too much.   In this respect *The Turn of the
Screw* seems to me to fail; the horror at the spectres diminishes
when we are told just who they were in life and just what they
want in returning to haunt the children.   It is a mistake to awaken
one's judging intellect when the quiescence of that faculty was the
very reason for the success of the first part of the story.   It is just
this absence of explanation which makes Maeterlinck's *L'Intruse*
so successful in arousing a fearful wonder.   A family seated in their
living-room are talking about the mother, who has recently given
birth to a child and is lying dangerously ill in the next room.   But
they have been assured she is better and will recover.   As they sit
talking, the nightingales stop singing, they hear sounds as of someone coming into the garden, and then of entering the house and the
room itself.   Yet no one actually appears.   The hypersensitive, blind
grandfather is aware of a presence, the lamp goes out, and they sit
with growing uneasiness in the dark, until just as twelve strikes
they hear a chair pushed back and the sound of someone leaving the
room.   The child cries in a neighbor room and a moment later the
Sister of Charity appears to say that the mother is dead.   The intruder has not been seen, has not been explained, has not even been
given a name.

Of course, as such a play indicates, one of the chief differences
between Elizabethan and present-day employment of the marvelous
is in the modern emphasis on symbolism.   It is here that we are
specially concerned with *Macbeth*.   But before I turn to that play,
I wish to consider the relation of symbols to our different levels of
psychological response to the marvelous.   Some symbols we clearly
respond to on the third level, the level of negative faith, of merely
conventional acceptance for purposes of the argument.   The possible
reality of the symbol hardly comes in question, since what it stands
for is what is important.   Spenser's monsters are a case in point,
as are, for the most part, references in Elizabethan lyric poems to
basilisks, mandrakes and mermaids; they would have been taken as
symbols when so indicated by Elizabethans as much as by us, the
only difference being their richer content of implication for the
Elizabethans.   From this point of view, Shakespeare's or Donne's
use of mythological creatures does not differ from the occasional
use of them in modern poets.   Shakespeare's phoenix in *The Phoenix
and the Turtle* is a symbol of perfect love; Yeats's phoenix in the

poem of that name is a symbol of peerless beauty. Shakespeare is not interested in the actual existence of such a creature, only in the associated meanings which his readers will understand; and although Yeats himself appears to believe in a kind of independent existence for certain of his smybols, to most of his readers, at any rate, his phoenix is as conventional a symbol as Shakespeare's.[19]

But there are symbols which call forth a more complicated response, which touch primitive fears or wonderings beneath our shell of sophistication, and which, therefore, evoke a willingness to believe, if not in the actual symbol, at least in the mysterious power, no less actual because not visible, for which the symbol stands. This is response on the second level. It is symbolism of this kind that makes Hawthorne's suggestion of the supernatural so moving. The state of mind which he induces in the reader Professor Stoll says is one of "dubiety" rather than one of awe and wonder.[20] I myself do not think that the dubiousness of the supernatural necessarily excludes a response of wonder, though it is clearly of a different quality than when the marvel is wholly accepted. Paul Elmer More recognizes this difference in quality when he compares the spirit of Hawthorne and Poe to that of their Puritan predecessors, Michael Wigglesworth and Jonathan Edwards:

With the passage of time the unquestioning, unflinching faith and vision of these heroic men dissolved away. Already in Freneau, himself born of a Huguenot family, a change is noticeable; that which to the earlier Fathers was a matter of infinite concern, that which to them was more real and urgent than the breath of life, becomes now chiefly an intoxicant of the imagination, and in another generation the transition is complete.

It is this precisely that we understand by the term "weird"—not the veritable vision of unearthly things, but the peculiar half vision inherited by the

---

[19] I am using *symbol* here in a wide sense, simply to mean a concrete term which stands for an abstract idea. E. M. W. Tillyard, in his *Poetry Direct and Oblique* (London, 1934; Chap. IV, pp. 54-64) distinguishes *metaphor, allegory,* and *symbol* according to the degree of permanence or permanent relevance of the comparison or substitution: "It is as the element of permanence enters that the adjectival state of metaphor shades off into the nominal state of symbol" (p. 56); allegory is sustained metaphor. The distinction I am making in the quality of a symbol (in the wide sense described) is not parallel to Professor Tillyard's: his classification is on the basis of the permanent relevance of the symbol (e.g. Herrick's *rose* is a more permanent symbol than his *daffodils*); mine is on the basis of the reader's willingness to believe in the symbol itself (Shakespeare's phoenix is substantive, or nearly so, since the phoenix, in whatever context, always suggests perfection, but we accord it only a conventional negative faith). Nevertheless, Professor Tillyard's distinction touches mine at certain points and I think illuminates it. The type of symbol, for instance, to which I refer in the next paragraph, is clearly substantive in his sense.

[20] *Shakespeare Studies,* p. 233.

soul when faith has waned and the imagination prolongs the old sensations in a shadowy involuntary life of its own; and herein too lies the field of true and effective symbolism. If Hawthorne and Poe, as we think, possess an element of force and realism such as Tieck and the German school utterly lack, it is because they write from the depths of this profound moral experience of their people.[21]

And More speaks of scenes and characters in Poe and Hawthorne which are real, yet which "are quite overlaid with some insistent shadow of the fantastic realm of symbolism."[22] Synge's *Riders to the Sea* seems to me symbolic in this sense, and deeply moving as tragedy partly for this reason. Maeterlinck's symbolism is shown by his own intention to be in this realm.[23] But in plays like *L'Intruse* and *Les Aveugles* his concern with the sensible presence of death is so great that physical fear is over-stimulated at the expense of awe. On the other hand, Eliot's *Family Reunion*, however interesting as a statement of the moral problem of sin and expiation, does not arouse either fear or awe. His symbolic Eumenides are so purely literary that they awaken, in this reader, at any rate, no troubling sense of the actuality of their power. Another play on the Aeschylean theme, O'Neill's *Mourning Becomes Electra*, is worth considering here, the more so because it is the modern tragedy most nearly comparable to *Hamlet*. Like *Hamlet* it is a play of murder, revenge, and incest. Like Shakespeare, the author is at some pains to create a pervading atmosphere of spiritual disease and moral rottenness. But the ghosts are symbolic ghosts. Some remarks of the old gardener, Seth, near the beginning of the third play, *The Haunted*, give the key:

... Between you 'n' me 'n' the lamp-post, it ain't all sech a joke as it sounds —that about the hauntin', I mean ... Oh, don't git it in your heads I take stock in spirits trespassin' round in windin' sheets or no such lunatic doin's. But there is such a thing as evil spirit. An' I've felt it, goin' in there daytimes to see to things—like somethin' rottin' in the walls ... There's been evil in that house since it was first built in hate—and it's kept growin' there ever since, as what's happened there has proved. . . .[24]

[21]*Shelburne Essays*, First Series (New York, 1904), p. 69. More's interest in this subject was pointed out to me by Professor Stuart Brown of Grinnell College, Iowa.

[22]More, *ibid.*, p. 52.

[23]In his plays, "we encounter, he says, 'a belief in immense powers, invisible and fatalistic, of which no man may know the purpose, but whose intention the spirit of the dramas assumes to be malevolent.' " From his preface to his collected plays (up to and including *Soeur Béatrice*), quoted in H. W. Church's Introduction to *L'Intruse et Les Aveugles* (New York, 1925), p. xix.

[24]*Mourning Becomes Electra* (New York, 1931), p. 197.

Orin and Lavinia, who have been traveling since the murder of their
father by their mother, the death of their mother's lover at the
hands of Orin, and her own suicide, enter at this point, Orin hag-
gard and nervous and avoiding the house with his eyes. Lavinia
makes him look at the house and admit he sees no ghosts. "She
takes his arm and leads him to the steps. He walks like an automa-
ton. When they reach the spot where his mother had sat moaning
the last time he had seen her alive . . . he stops with a shudder"
and stammers, pointing: "It was here—she—the last time I saw
her alive—" She urges him into the house, saying: "That is all
past and finished. The dead have forgotten us! We've forgotten
them! Come!"[25] The event proves that they have neither forgotten the dead, nor the dead them—for Orin, thrown off his precarious
emotional balance by returning to the house, kills himself; and
Lavinia, after a futile attempt to break free and live a normal life,
shuts herself up in the house to expiate the crimes of the family.
But the dead are not conscious spirits returning to haunt their
descendants. They are memories, inherited emotional tendencies,
youthful inhibitions, and fixations—bequeathed by the parents to
the living son and daughter in the form of Freudian psychoses.
The tragedy, perhaps because of this naturalistic conception of evil,
is more depressing than awful; the ghost symbol is so exactly
equated with psychological meaning that no sense of mystery, though
clearly tried for in the scene I have quoted from, remains.

We come to *Macbeth*. For us the witches must be taken either
as quite conventional figures or as symbols: "The weird sisters
encounter the soul in every generation."[26] If symbols, what then?
I feel unable to generalize about the response of modern audiences
to this play. Romantic criticism, generally, has found in the witches
a profoundly moving symbolism.[27] But the state of mind of a
critic in his study is not exactly the same as that of a spectator,
even if he is that very critic, in the theatre. It is a tougher, less
tractable world that he is in and his own mind will be tougher. In
the study, he may think himself into what state he chooses (the
stricture is not meant to exclude the present writer, who wrote this
paper, after all, in a study); in the theatre he has to be shown.

25*Ibid.*, pp. 200-1.

26Peter Alexander, *Shakespeare's Life and Art* (London, 1939), p. 172.

27See Coleridge, Hazlitt, Bradley. Whitmore considers *Macbeth*, because of
the treatment in it of the supernatural, to be the most sublime of Shakespeare's
tragedies and the most closely akin to the great classical tragedies.

How apt are those hard-edged grotesques, contorting themselves around a black pot, and squawking out their "boil and bubble," to lead his mind into strange realms of horror? All I can say is that I have never seen the play acted in such a way as to give the witches any more than a decorative function, certainly not so as to arouse any troubled sense of a mysterious power of evil in the world. (I do not mean that this is not suggested by other, subtler means throughout the play.) Elizabethans cannot have been so restricted in their response to the supernatural in *Macbeth*. For many of them the witches would have been representations of genuine "instruments of darkness," of something only too actual in the real world. For those few who did not believe in witchcraft, the witches taken purely as symbols would nevertheless have had an awful significance; no one denied Satan's insidious, sleepless, and powerful agency for evil in the world, and no one denied the mysterious ways of Providence. Few, if any, would have been inclined to doubt Lady Macbeth's "sightless substances that wait on nature's mischief." But I do not believe we should understand the literal and the symbolic interpretations to have been mutually exclusive. The man who believed thoroughly in witches almost certainly would still see their use in the play as symbolic of evil and of fate. And it is important to note that although the witches perform all the traditional ceremonies, in no instance are they shown exercising indubitable power by any of the familiar media—potions, the evil eye, waxen images, and the like.[28] They operate purely by suggestion, which is open either to symbolic or to literal interpretation, as one pleases— or to both. As everyone knows, the hint for their use came from Holinshed's Weird Sisters. Shakespeare chose to give them a shape less literary, more immediately familiar to his audience, and hence more emotionally exciting; but they keep at the same time the connotation of their originals—a larger evil than the personal malice of witches, a fatality in the drift of events more inexorable than the machinations of Satan. Interpretation, then, for an Elizabethan, might well have been on two planes, and his emotional response correspondingly complex. Shakespeare's superiority to his contemporaries in the field of the supernatural lay precisely in his using it, not for merely decorative or sensational purposes, but for the evocation of tragic wonder.

---

[28]See Whitmore, *op. cit.*, p. 257.

It is evident that the questions I have raised may be applied as well to the supernatural in Greek tragedy.

Tragic wonder at *Hamlet* and *Macbeth,* as at the *Oresteia,* of course remains for us. The problem of the suffering and aspiring heart in a universe of circumstance it does not understand and can only partially control is still the same. My point is simply that in so far as we accord the ghost, the witches, and the Furies merely negative faith, in so far as we take them as mere literary symbols from which the suggestion of a mysterious power actually at work in the world is gone, or in so far as we arrive at a deeper wonder through purely imaginative reconstruction of what these things must have been like for the original audiences of Aeschylus and of Shakespeare—in so far as we do these things, I say, the total complex of our response to these plays is probably of a poorer quality. It is, without doubt, essentially different.

COMEDY IN THE COURT MASQUE:
A STUDY OF BEN JONSON'S CONTRIBUTION

By T. M. PARROTT
Princeton University

The Court Masque as introduced into England by Henry VIII was rather an aristocratic form of social entertainment than a distinct dramatic genre. It was in essence little more than a dance performed by members of the court, male and female, masqued and arrayed as Moors, Russians, Shepherds, or figures from classical mythology. After completing the movement of their formal dance the masquers separated and invited members of the courtly audience to join with them in the customary dances of the day. This last was, apparently, a fashionable innovation which caused a certain amount of criticism because of the opportunity it afforded for amorous discourse and for caresses. "Sweetheart", says Shakespeare's Henry, disguised as a shepherd, to Anne Boleyn, whom he has chosen for his partner in the mixed dance,

> I were unmannerly to take you out
> And not to kiss you. (*Henry VIII*, I, iv, 94-6)

One recalls also the plea of Romeo, masked and dressed as a pilgrim, for a kiss from Juliet. After the mixed dance the masquers either removed their vizards and mingled with the audience as in the masquing scene in *Henry VIII* or, in the later and more elaborate forms of the entertainment, withdrew from the dancing floor into a pageant of some sort, a ship, a castle, or some other device, which had ushered them into the Court.

Though not a dramatic genre there was in the Masque from the very beginning a certain dramatic element, that of impersonation; like actors on the stage the masquers pretended to be other than they really were, King Henry, for example, a shepherd, Queen Anne an Ethiopian beauty. This, of course, is the very beginning of drama, the primordial germ from which all else has evolved. Furthermore, as the Masque developed it grew into an action of some kind; the dance was no longer simply a dance, it became the symbolic representation of something else, a royal or noble marriage, a profession of national loyalty, or a contest between rival divinities. This symbolic representation might take various forms; one of the most popular was the mock fight between two parties representing different ideals, as, for example, the champions of Love and Chastity. This adaptation of the medieval tournament to the spectacle of the Masque developed later into the characteristic Tudor and Stuart entertainment of the Barriers, a form which need not concern us here.

A combat is a thing easy to be understood by spectators familiar, as a courtly audience of that time would naturally be, with tilting and sword-play. On the other hand much of the symbolic representation was so elaborate and involved as quite to bewilder the audience. This difficulty was easily met by the introduction of a presenter to act as interpreter of the show. As early as 1517 we find Master Cornish, Master of the Chapel Royal, disguised as a stranger speaking a Prologue to show "the effect and intent" of the *Garden of Esperance,* a Masque or Disguising at Court. And so speech entered the Masque and also, be it noted, in this instance, the presence among the noble amateur performers of the professional entertainer, two facts of considerable significance in the evolution of the Masque.

It was a natural consequence of the growth and increasing popularity of the drama proper during the long reign of Elizabeth that the dramatic elements already present in the Masque should develop until they tended to overshadow, though never quite to obliterate, its essential feature, the masqued dance and the revels in which the masquers danced with partners chosen from the audience. In fact Sidney's *Lady of May,* performed before Elizabeth in 1578, although equipped with masquing properties of music, dance, and contest, is essentially a little pastoral play. This, however, was an entertainment presented at Leicester's country residence at Wansted, not, properly speaking, a Court Masque at all. On the other hand the splendid spectacle, *Proteus and the Adamantine Rock,* presented to the Queen in 1595 by the gentlemen of Gray's Inn, is a fully-developed Court Masque which has absorbed more than a little of genuine drama. Composed by two poets, Campion and Davison—a literary value is thus added to the spectacle— it elaborates a definite theme, the power and glory of Elizabeth, and it develops this theme by means of a contest between Proteus, symbol of inconstancy, and the Prince of Purpoole, representing the loyal devotion of Gray's Inn. The Adamantine Rock, symbol of the sovereignty of the sea, is won for England by the "virtue" of the Queen who draws to her all hearts as the Rock draws iron. In this piece, as Miss Welford (*The Court Masque*, 1927) points out, we have the norm of the masque as composed in Stuart times by Jonson and others.

One phase of drama, Tragedy, was by the very nature of things excluded from the Court Masque. The masqued dance, involving as it did the participation of members of the audience, was primarily a form of social entertainment, and tragedy, while it may thrill and startle, is not well fitted to entertain and to amuse. Comedy, on the contrary, aims just at this, and Elizabethan comedy often implied a closer rapprochement of actors to spectators than is possible on the modern stage. It is not surprising, therefore, that we find from the beginning elements of comedy in the Court Masque. At first these consisted mainly, if not entirely, in the introduction of grotesque and comic figures, devils, monsters, and such like, among the gorgeously attired dancers of the main masque. Under the influence of popular drama comic characters and comic dialogue appear as in the absurdly pedantic schoolmaster Rombus of Sidney's *Lady of May*. It is the purpose of this study to trace the specific contribution of comedy to the Court Masque made by the acknowledged master of that genre, who was at the same time the greatest living writer of comedy, the Stuart poet-laureate, Ben Jonson.

Jonson began his career as chief entertainer for the Court even before the official entry of James into London. When Queen Anne and her son stopped at Althorp on their way south, Jonson was called on to provide for them the sort of show which had greeted Elizabeth on her tours through England. This is *The Satyr*, not a Court Masque strictly speaking, but a show in which Jonson's command of graceful serio-comic verse appears in the dialogue between the Satyr and the band of Fairies led by Queen Mab, as does his readiness to employ the grotesque in the absurd figure and comic speech of Nobody, presenter of the morris-dancers. In the entertainment offered next year to the King and Queen at Highgate, the so-called *Penates*, Jonson introduces the figure of Pan, whose boorishly jocular address to the courtly company exhibits in its contrast to the graceful formal lyrics that preceded an anticipation of the Anti-masque that Jonson was later to develop so effectively.

It seems a little strange after such success that Jonson should not have been called on to compose the first formal Court Masque which Queen Anne presented at Hampton Court in 1604. Probably Lucy, Countess of Bedford, who danced in this show along with the Queen, pushed her favorite Daniel, "an honest man, but no poet," according to Jonson, into the coveted post. Certainly there is little poetry and less of comedy in Daniel's Masque, *The Vision of the Twelve Goddesses*. It was all show and spectacle, distinguished especially by the costumes of the lady masquers for whom the gorgeous wardrobe of the late Queen Elizabeth had been ransacked. Anne, who presented Pallas, must have altered an Elizabethan dress for, according to a news-writer of the time: "her clothes were not so much below the knee, but that we might see a woman had both feet and legs which," says he ironically, "I never knew before."

Jonson got his revenge next year when he was specially invited by Anne, "the most magnificent of Queens," to compose *The Masque of Blackness* for her, presented before the King and Court at Whitehall. This was the first of his formal Court Masques, the first also in which he worked hand in hand with his long ally and later enemy, Inigo Jones. It is interesting to note that in this his first Masque, Jonson retains the conventional elements of music, dance, and spectacle. All he does as a playwright is to devise a little plot to give unity to the whole performance. Acting on a suggestion of the Queen's, who had the fantastic notion that she and her fellow masquers, ladies of the Court, should first appear as 'Blackmores,' Jonson arranged to have a bevy of Ethiopian ladies, turned into negroes by the fervent kisses of the sun, come to seek relief from the milder influence of the Sun of Britain, King James. The Queen's notion was one that might easily have provoked a dash of comic satire, but Jonson prudently refrained. There is not a trace of comedy in *Blackness*.

There is little more in his marriage masque *Hymenæi* (1605), though there is plenty of learned allusion and some pleasant verse. Much the same may be said of his *Masque of Beauty* (1608), but in *The Hue and Cry after Cupid*, another marriage masque, Jonson begins to diversify the stiff formality of this genre with light comic touches. Venus in pursuit of her runaway son finds him attended by twelve boys "most antickly attired" who fall "into a subtle capricious dance"—"nodding with their antic faces, with other variety of ridiculous gesture, which gave much occasion of mirth and delight to the spectators.'' One cannot imagine spectators laughing at any earlier masque of Jonson's.

That Jonson recognized what he was doing is plain from his words in the preface to his *Masque of Queens* (1609): ''last year I had an anti-masque of boys.'' Following another suggestion of Queen Anne's that he ''think of some dance or show that might precede hers (i.e., the main masque in which she was to dance) and have the place of a foil or false masque,'' he devised a dance of witches to usher in the splendid appearance of the noble Queens from the House of Fame. Here we get Jonson's first real anti-masque, a great advance upon his hesitant use of it in *The Hue and Cry*. There the antic boys danced in silence and were promptly dismissed; here the witches not only perform ''a magical dance full of preposterous change and gesticulation,'' but they chant alternately a chorus of charms into which Jonson has packed most of the classical and contemporary traditions of witchcraft. Realism has entered into the Masque in the garb of the witches: ''some with rats on their heads—others with ointment pots at their girdles; all with spindles, timbrels, rattles, and other venefical instruments.'' It is even more apparent in their words; one might quote line after line from the anti-masque; a single specimen must suffice:

> A murderer yonder was hung in chains,
> The sun and the wind had shrunk his veins;
> I bit off a sinew; and clipp'd his hair,
> I brought off his rags that danced in the air.

This is the authentic speech of witches, and the ingredients of the charms gathered by Jonson's hags are comparable to those that enter into the caldron of Shakespeare's weird sisters. One may note also that Jonson devotes far more time and trouble to his hags than to the noble Queens. To the spectator the main masque was no doubt the most glorious part of the show; to the modern reader the only interesting part of it is this grim serio-comic anti-masque.

Pleased, no doubt, with the success of his experiment in *The Queens,* Jonson continued it in his next, *The Masque of Oberon* (1611), presented at Court by Prince Henry. In this charming work the anti-masque is composed of Satyrs whose rude gambols and wanton songs contrast with the stately declamation that ushers in and the formal odes that accompany the show of Oberon and his fairy knights. There is plenty of fun in the Satyrs, especially when they tease the sleeping Sylvans at the gate of Oberon, but the

realism that marked the songs of the hags has melted into laughing
lyric measures. There is even less of comedy in *Love Freed from
Ignorance and Folly,* also 1611. Here Jonson employs the old motif
of a contest: Love is held in chains by the Sphynx, threatened with
the fate of Orpheus by the twelve She-fools who dance the anti-
masque, and rescued by the Muses' Priests. Jonson, the writer of
comedy, has yielded here to Jonson the lyric poet.

The genius of an artist seems to advance at times by sudden
leaps. After the negligible *Love Freed* comes *Love Restored* (1612),
a mile-stone in Jonson's development as a writer of masques. Here
for the first time he opens the show with a prose induction in the
manner of his best comic scenes. Masquerade enters to warn the
expectant audience that there will probably be no masque at all
to-night. He is followed by Plutus, God of Wealth, who has assumed the disguise of Cupid, a customary Prologue to a masque,
and the tone and temper of a Puritan, protesting against courtly
extravagance: "I tell thee I will have no more masquing—no longer
endure a prodigality and riot, enough to ruin states." To him enters
"the honest plain country spirit—Robin Goodfellow, he that sweeps
the hearth and the house clean." Robin describes at some length
and with much humor the trouble he has had in obtaining admission
in various transformations. One of them was that of a fine citizen's
wife, but that disguise met with such unseemly handling by a Court
servant, because she had no "husband in sight to squeak to," that
he was fain to change his shape. The jest on the citizen's wife at
a Court Masque was good for a laugh in many a Stuart comedy.
Now that Robin is in, however, he unmasks the false Cupid, and
leads Masquerade to the presence of the true God of Love, with
which the formal masque begins. It may be noted that there is no
grotesque dance of anti-masquers; its place is supplied by the
comic chat of Robin and Plutus, which probably was spoken by
professional actors—no courtly amateur could well have been trusted with its delivery. This innovation of a comic introductory scene
in prose must have made an instant hit, for it was one which Jonson was to repeat again and again. It occurs immediately in his
slight *Challenge at Tilt* (1614), which opens with two wrangling
Cupids, distinctly recalling the quarreling boys of the Induction
to *Cynthia's Revels* many years before.

In the *Irish Masque* (1613) Jonson introduces a device new in
the Masque, but one of long standing in Elizabethan comedy, dialect

patter. Four Irish footmen come in to greet "King Yamish," quarrel among themselves in barely intelligible speech, and dance "to the bag-pipe and other rude music." Here, of course, is the comic anti-masque dance again, but a further innovation occurs when after the first movement of the main dance the comic servants break in with further patter, an anticipation of the second anti-masque which was to become an almost constant factor in later work of this kind.

By the time he wrote *Mercury Vindicated* (1615) Jonson was sure enough of his mastery of the Masque to introduce into it one of the constant elements of his comedy, satire. Mercury, who is at once the classic god and the chemical element of the alchemists, escapes from their clutches and appeals to the King for protection. He is threatened by a dancing troupe of threadbare alchemists and later by a dance of "imperfect creatures," the monstrous products of their art, which serves as the second anti-masque. Neither the alchemists nor their creatures have a word to say; the dialogue is sustained by Mercury and Vulcan, "old Smug of Lemnos," the divine patron of alchemic art. The long tirades of Mercury couched in Jonson's raciest prose are packed with satiric thrusts at the pseudo-science that he had blasted years before in the greatest of all his comedies. Like the earlier patter of Robin Goodfellow they call assuredly for delivery by a first-rate professional.

The Golden Age Restored (1616) may be dismissed with a word. In it Jonson reverts to poetry and spectacle; the comic element is noticeable only by its absence. Jonson, however, more than atoned for this in *The Masque of Christmas* (1616). Strictly speaking this little show is not really a Court Masque, since it lacks the essentials of the main masque and the mixed dance. Yet it was presented at Court in the Christmas season and the presenter, "old Christmas of London," offers the Court a masque of his own making performed by his sons "of the lanes of London, good dancing boys all." They are introduced by Cupid dressed like a prentice boy and include such appropriate figures as Carol, Minced-Pie, Wassel, and Baby-Cake. It is, in fact, Jonson's adaptation of the old-fashioned "mumming" to take the place of the formal masque. What interests us here is the lively realistic comedy of the piece. Hardly has the show begun when Venus enters, not the foam-born Aphrodite, however, but a deaf tire-woman from Pudding-lane, come to see the performance of her son, Cupid. She is a most amusing old lady, a close cousin apparently of the Citizen's wife in *The Knight of the Burning Pestle,* as proud of her son as her forbear is of her prentice, Ralph; the King's players, she says, Burbage and old Master Hemmings, have tried in vain to hire him for their company. She encourages him audibly: "speak out, hold up your head, Love," but Cupid fails to live up to his mother's boasts; after stammering a few lines he breaks down and is ignominiously hauled off, and the show ends with dance and song. Homely realistic comedy has taken the place of spectacle.

Lovers Made Men or, The Masque of Lethe (1617) was presented at Lord Hay's house "by divers of noble quality his friends." The whole was sung "after the Italian manner," Jonson tells us, "*stilo recitativo.*" As might be expected from an amateur performance, chanted rather than acted, the element of comedy sinks to a vanishing point; the main stress is laid on the music, the costumes, and the revels. Much the same is true of *The Vision of Delight,* the Christmas masque of 1617. Here, however, there are two comic anti-masques: first a "She-monster" delivered on the stage of six young ones who dance comically with six Pantaloons; then one of Phantasms introduced by Phant'sie, a comic character who rattles off a long burlesque speech much in the manner of old Iniquity in *The Devil is an Ass,* Jonson's comedy of the preceding year. Phant'sie, it may be noted, serves also to introduce the main masque, the *Glories of Spring,* and thus serves to give a certain unity to the whole.

The Masque of Pleasure reconciled to Virtue (1618) is one of the most elaborate of Jonson's compositions in this genre. It opens with the triumph of Comus greeted by a hymn in rattling doggrel rhymes:

> Room! room! make room for the Bouncing Belly,
> First father of sauce and deviser of jelly.

This is followed by the Bowlbearer's tirade in good Jonsonian prose, after which comes an anti-masque danced by men "in the shape of bottles, tuns, etc." Hercules appears to drive away the rout of Comus, but while sleeping after his victory he is attacked by the second anti-masque, a group of Pigmies. They dance about him, with jingling rhymes, but run into holes when he awakes. Then comes the very lovely main masque, the reconciliation of Pleasure and Virtue.

Strange as it may seem this show failed to please. It was the first in which the new Prince of Wales, later Charles I, had ever danced, and there was a feeling that sufficient honor had not been paid to him. Inigo Jones was blamed and Jonson too; "divers think he should return to his old trade of brick-laying again." Jonson accordingly had to revise his work; he did so by eliminating the whole Comus-Hercules part and writing a new prose Induction in which a group of Welshman patter broken English and unintelligible Welsh. It is the same sure-fire comic device that he had used earlier in *The Irish Masque.* The special tribute paid to the Prince in *The Honor of Wales,* no doubt gratified King James, but the new scenes with their dances of Goats and of Welsh peasants are a poor substitute for Comus and his crew.

Jonson yielded to pressure from above when he modified his Comus masque to suit the wish of the Court; but he came back to his own in *News from the New World* (1620). Here the prose Induction is a very lively bit of satiric comedy. In place of the monologues of earlier masques we find here a brisk dialogue between the Heralds, bringing news from the world of the moon, and three human characters, a Printer, a Chronicler, and a Factor, eager to obtain and exploit this news. It might be a scene from a Jonson comedy; as a matter of fact bits of it pass easily into his next comedy for the stage, *The Staple of News.* The dancers of the antimasque, Volatees or Moon-birds, are silent; apart from their grotesque appearance the fun of the masque is confined to the prose dialogue with its constant hits at contemporary follies. No Jonson masque up to this point has so nearly and so fully resembled a Jonson comedy.

The Gipsies Metamorphosed (1621) seems to have been Jonson's most successful masque in giving pleasure to the Court, for it was thrice repeated at three several places. Yet like other of his shows this is not properly a Court Masque. It was first presented at the home of the favorite Buckingham and was performed by members of the favorite's family. They appeared first as Gipsies, later in the "rich habits" appropriate to the main masquers. The success must have been due almost entirely to the comic patter of the supposed gipsies, to the fortunes they tell the courtly spectators, and to the tricks they play upon a group of rustics, male and female, who gather to gape upon them. The elaborate spectacle of the Court Masque has been replaced by scenes of realistic comedy, and the formal choral chants by the rowdy song of Cocklorel, the master rogue.

In the *Masque of Augurs* (1622) Jonson catches up several threads used in earlier work and weaves them into a new pattern. It opens with a prose Induction. The interlocutors are a Groom of the Court and a couple of citizens who, hearing "that neither the King's poet [Jonson himself] nor his architect [Jones] had where-withal left to entertain so much as a baboon of quality," had come in the goodness of their hearts "to fill up the vacuum with some pretty presentation," even as Old Christmas and his sons had come some years before. They are joined presently by Vangoose, Britain born but so great a traveller that he has learned to misuse his own tongue and now patters a dialect that went for Dutch-English on the Elizabethan stage. He is a "projector"—an ill-omened word at that day—of masques and presents his first offering, a dance of three bears accompanied by the Bearward, the mistress of the Three Bears Tavern, and her two barmaids. Here is a realistic anti-masque with a vengeance; Jonson has come a long way from the antic Cupids of *The Hue and Cry*. But Vangoose can do better than this; challenged to fulfill his impossible boasts, he presents the second anti-masque "a perplexed dance of straying and de-formed pilgrims." This serves as a transition to the main masque, one of peculiar splendor; it opens with the appearance of Apollo in a cloud of light, at sight of whom the pilgrims fly away, while he leads in the main masque of Augurs to greet the King.

Time Vindicated (1623) is one of the most elaborate masques that Jonson and Jones ever offered to the Court. There were three complete changes of scene and in the main masque there was a charming contest between Venus and Diana. The special note of Jonsonian comedy in this work is that of personal satire, directed here against the popular poet, George Wither, introduced in the character of Chronomastix, the scourge of time, with special ref-erences to Wither's satire, *Abuses Stript and Whipt*. He is made to boast of his reputation among the unlettered vulgar, and the first anti-masque is composed of his lovers: the printer who keeps his press in a hollow tree—a thrust, of course, at the unlicensed printers of the day,—the schoolmaster who turns his verses into Latin for boys to learn by heart, and the swaggering soldier who beats ad-miration for his poems into the heads of the incredulous with the hilt of his dagger. These are silent dancers, but a group of grotesque masquers, their vizards painted full of eyes, ears, and noses, chatter foolish talk at Fame, presenter of the whole, till they are driven out by the second anti-masque of Tumblers and Jugglers led in by the Cat and Fiddle. There is an amusing contrast between this archaic anti-masque and the pungency of Jonson's attack upon a contemporary man of letters, an innovation which does not seem to have been very well received at Court.

The pretty entertainment, *Pan's Anniversary,* apparently a masque presented to James on his birthday (1624), is remarkable rather for its lyric verse than for comedy. Yet there are comic interludes in the prose dialogue between the Shepherd, Pan's worshipper, and a Fencer who interrupts the rites with two comic anti-masques.

The so-called *Masque of Owls* (1624) is not a masque at all, but a simple country show for Prince Charles at Kenilworth. It may be disregarded here.

Jonson's magnificent masque, *Neptune's Triumph for the Return of Albion* (i.e., the return in 1623 of Prince Charles from his unlucky quest of a bride in Spain), was never performed at Court. A bitter dispute for precedence between the French and Spanish Ambassadors led first to a postponement and then to its abandonment. It was, however, published and is well worth study. It opens in the Banqueting-house at Whitehall where a Poet, "the most unprofitable of the King's servants," is challenged by the resident Master-cook. The Poet has come to present a masque, but the Cook asserts that no man can be a true poet who has not first learned to cook.

> Seduced Poet, I do say to thee
> A boiler, range, and dresser were the fountains
> Of all the knowledge in the universe,
> And that's the kitchen.

Since the Poet has neglected to devise an anti-masque, which he scorns as a mere "by-work," the Cook helps him out with an *olla-podrida* of comic characters boiled in a huge pot and poured out to dance upon the stage. After the Revels in the main masque the Cook breaks in again to offer "a dish of pickled sailors"—presumably the adjective did not carry the meaning it does in colloquial language to-day—whose noisy horn-pipe serves as a contrast to the formal dance.

When in the autumn of 1624 the betrothal of Prince Charles to

Henrietta Maria of France was announced, Jonson and Jones were ordered to celebrate the happy event with a masque at Court. *The Fortunate Isles and their Union* (January 1625), is an adaptation of the discarded *Neptune's Triumph* to the new situation. As much as possible of the old machinery and music was retained, but Jonson wrote an entirely new Induction. This, the last masque that Jonson was ever to present his royal patron—James died next June—shows Jonson's power at its zenith as a master of comedy in the masque. Instead of prose patter Jonson now writes in such verse, easy, pointed, and effective, as he had used in *Volpone* and *The Alchemist*. The presenter, Jophiel, an airy spirit from the planet Jupiter, presently encounters Merefool, "a melancholic student." This votary of the Rosy-cross is a humour character—note the labelling name—out of Jonsonian comedy, a gull who is mocked by Jophiel as the gulls in *The Alchemist* are tricked by Face and Subtle. Jophiel promises him a great reward for his devotion; he shall be "constable of the castle Rosy-cross" and "master of all learning." First of all, however, he shall be entertained by a vision, but when the gull asks for a sight of Zoroaster or Hermes Trismegistus, he is fobbed off with a show of Scogan and Skelton, who enter chanting burlesque rhymes, and with a grotesque dance led by Howleglass and performed by Elinor Rumming—Merefool would have preferred Helen of Troy—long Meg, Tom Thumb, the Queen's dwarf, and Dr. Rat, the gigantic porter of Whitehall. When the gull expresses a wish to thank the company of the Rosy-cross for the show, Jophiel replies:

> The company of the Rosy-cross, you widgeon!
> The company of the players,

a plain indication that this elaborate anti-masque had been performed by professionals. Jophiel dismisses Merefool contemptuously from the scene and turning to the King introduces the main masque which proceeds without interruption to the close.

Never again did Jonson have the chance to show his craftsmanship in the Court Masque. For five years after the accession of Charles, who cared more for spectacle and less for mirth than did his father, Jonson was excluded from participation in the Christmas shows at Court. In 1631, perhaps to console him for the sad failure of his *New Inn*, 1629, he was asked once more to collaborate with Jones. Together they devised the King's Masque, *Love's Triumph through Callipolis,* but the lion's share of the work was the architect's. Jonson wrote a few verses—one can hardly call them poetry —and suggested the figures for the anti-masque. There is not a trace of comedy in the brilliant spectacle. The wheel has come full circle with a sudden swing; after the gay comedy of *The Fortunate Isles* the Court Masque is back where it began under James with *The Masque of Blackness.* Jonson managed to secure a somewhat larger share in the Queen's Masque, *Chloridia,* a few weeks later and actually wrote some humorous prose for the Queen's dwarf who brought in the anti-masque, but his publication of the text of the two shows with his name preceding that of Jones upon the title-page roused that worthy's wrath to such a point that he definitely pushed Jonson out of the masques at Court. The best that the sick and sorry playwright could do was to devise a couple of little entertainments for his noble friend, the Duke of Newcastle, to offer King Charles during a royal progress. We need not dwell on these; they are the last poor runnings of Jonson's wit. It is enough to remark that he had enough left of his old fire to caricature his enemy as Coronel Iniquo Vitruvius, "a surveyor, a supervisor, an overseer—a busy man," he says, "and yet I must seem busier than I am, as the poet sings."

Jonson's achievement in transforming the formal Court Masque from a mere spectacle into something at least resembling drama may be briefly summarized. It is beside the purpose here to speak of the charm of the lyrics with which he lightened the stiff declamations of earlier masques or the prodigious learning that ensured a correct presentation of his witches and his augurs. Such qualities are after all not essentially dramatic. What Jonson did as a practical playwright was to devise first of all a "fable" as a thread on which to hang the show. A master of plot construction he worked consistently to give unity to what had been before a series of unrelated scenes. He stressed the value of the anti-masque as a foil to the more serious part of the entertainment, and he worked consistently to enlarge and heighten this foil until it often became the main part of the show. He introduced comic characters as speakers instead of the mute dancers of the early masques. He developed the speaking parts from the long tirades of the presenter into lively comic dialogue. His prose inductions tended more and more to resemble scenes from his own comedies including like his comedies satiric comment on the abuses and follies of his day. The Jophiel-Merefool scene in Jonson's last great masque shifts from the prose

dialogue of earlier work to the flexible verse of his own best comedies. It is not surprising that a final breach occurred between Jonson, writer of comedies, who was attempting with considerable
success to dramatize the masque, and Jones, costumer, scene-painter,
and mechanician, whose ideal of the masque was a succession of
splendid spectacles. And it was merely a logical consequence of
Jonson's expulsion from the Court Masque that this genre under
the domination of Jones became, as it rapidly did in the reign of
Charles, a heterogeneous and enormously expensive assemblage of
dances, triumphs, and transformation scenes, in which literary, to
say nothing of comedy values, vanished out of sight.

JOHN FORD AND ELIZABETHAN TRAGEDY

By G. F. Sensabaugh
Stanford University

John Ford still holds among Caroline dramatists his position of decadent high priest. From Gerard Langbaine to Stuart Sherman, except for Charles Lamb and a few modern enthusiasts,[1] Ford stands accused of nearly every dramatic and ethical crime. His comedy lacks humor or joy,[2] commentary generally agrees; his tragedy, like a fingernail scraped on cold slate, beads the brow and prickles the spine,[3] or shrieks blood and murder in stories of lust, adultery and incest.[4] Futhermore, Ford added to these decadent sins a definite prurience, titillating erotic appetites through boudoir assignations which, centering interest around affairs of the heart, effeminized the drama and hastened its final collapse.[5]

This tradition no doubt holds much truth. Fernando's rising from his lover's tomb chills the blood; Orgilus' ingenious machine-chair, catching Ithocles in bloody revenge, sends shivers along the spine; Giovanni's description of incestuous bed sports and Biancha's lascivious wooing propose simply to arouse erotic emotions. Yet such contributions to dramatic decadence may be found abundantly in other late dramatists. Webster's echo scene in *The Duchess of*

---

[1] See Charles Lamb, *Specimens of English Dramatic Poets* (London, 1887), p. 228, for enthusiastic praise; for adverse criticism, which sets the tone of most nineteenth- and twentieth-century commentary, see William Hazlitt, *Lectures on the Literature of the Age of Elizabeth*, Lecture IV (London, 1903). For a review of Ford criticism, see M. Joan Sargeaunt, *John Ford* (Oxford, 1935), pp. 167-87.

[2] *CHEL* (Cambridge, 1910), VI, 220; A. W. Ward, *A History of English Dramatic Literature* (London, 1899), III, 86.

[3] See W. A. Neilson, *The Chief Elizabethan Dramatists* (New York, 1911), p. 874; *The Bookman Illustrated History of English Literature* (eds Thomas Seccombe and W. Robertson Nicoll, London, 1906), I, 122; *Early Seventeenth-Century Plays 1600-1642* (eds. Harold R. Walley and John H. Wilson, New York, 1930), p. 26; and many others.

[4] J. J. Jusserand, *A Literary History of the English People* (New York, 1909), III, 423-4; William Francis Collier, *A History of English Literature* (London, 1869), p. 170; Emile Legouis and Louis Cazamian, *A History of English Literature* (New York, 1929), pp. 525-8; and many others.

[5] Stuart Sherman, *Shaping Men and Women* (New York, 1928), pp. 205-6; Johannes Adam Bastiaenen, *The Moral Tone of Jacobean and Caroline Drama* (Amsterdam, 1930), pp. 102-3.

Malfi, for example, equals any melodrama Ford could produce; Tourneur's tragedies run deep in blood; Fletcher could scarcely sketch an idyll of pastoral love without picturing a passionate Daphnis and Cloe, pursuing fleshy delights; and D'Avenant, shortly after Ford wrote most maturely, composed with his courtly companions a drama so full of effeminacy that in comparison Ford's most perfumed act seems strong and robust. Clearly recognizing Ford's singularity, commentary nevertheless fails to disclose that Ford's unique contribution to Elizabethan dramatic decline is not of degree but of kind.

Yet Ford's tragedy, which places upon Ford his mantle of decadent high priest, stands distinct from *Othello* and *Hamlet,* and this for reasons now clear. Fresh scientific thought made popular by Bacon began to rob man of free will; iconoclasm in politics and religion commenced to undermine old moral and ethical values; and John Ford, responding enthusiastically to these new forces, incorporated them into his plays to form a new tragic concept far different from that of his predecessors or of his companions. Deriving his science from Robert Burton's *Anatomy of Melancholy,* whose mechanistic analysis of human behavior the popular mind deemed scientific truth, Ford afflicts his characters with melancholic diseases curable or incurable according to medical formula. This formula, buttressing all Ford's plays to lesser or greater extent, may be put thus:

1. Melancholy is a disease arising from specific causes.
2. Dread physical and mental symptoms mark the course of this disease.
3. Persons afflicted run a headlong course to destruction.
4. Cure may be effected by application of proper treatment.
5. Custom and law often forbid treatment and thus prevent cure.[6]

Finding his revolt from conventional ethics in Queen Henrietta Maria's platonic love cult in court, Ford created heroes and heroines speaking courtly love jargon, worshipping beauty in woman, and

---

[6]See especially S. Blaine Ewing's *Burtonian Melancholy in the Plays of John Ford* (Princeton, 1940); see also G. F. Sensabaugh, ''Burton's Influence on Ford's *The Lover's Melancholy,*'' *SP*, XXXIII (1936), 545-71; *idem,* ''Ford's Tragedy of Love-Melancholy,'' *Englische Studien,* Band 73, Heft 2, 212-9; Lawrence Babb, ''Abnormal Psychology in John Ford's 'Perkin Warbeck,' '' *MLN,* LI, (1936) 234-7; Mary E. Cochnower, in *Seventeenth Century Studies* (ed. Robert Shafer, Princeton, 1933), pp. 147-74.

arguing individual rights even to the defense of adultery and incest. Concisely, the cult's main tenets and ethics may be put thus:
1. Beauty and goodness are one and the same.
2. Beautiful women are saints to be worshipped.
3. Love is all-important and all-powerful.
4. Marriage and convention are secondary to true love.
5. True love condones any liberty of action and thought.[7]

These two particular forces Ford organically fused, backing up his moral revolt with accepted scientific law, a combination which creates conflicts peculiarly modern and not Elizabethan at all. An analysis of Ford's three tragedies will show clearly these conflicts and the new tragic concept which grows from them.

The Broken Heart, dramatically Ford's most powerful play, presents clear-cut dilemmas born of the clash of medical demands and conventional law. Ithocles has forced his sister Penthea into loveless marriage with Bassanes subsequent to her pledging vows of true love to Orgilus, a situation in which Burtonian formula decrees that she will die unless she can satisfy her passion of love. Unable to satisfy her passion because of the iron laws of custom she dies, a fairly common event which Ford portrays in a new light.

The dilemma in which Penthea finds herself placed becomes pregnant with meaning only because Ford sees an ethical question through medical eyes: he not only observes her physical suffering but also believes that society has committed a crime. Ithocles addresses her as "Wrong'd soule," expressing concern over his injuring so excellent a maid;[8] Calantha, possibly thinking of her own thwarted love, deems her a "wrong'd Lady!" (l. 1633); and Orgilus, after Penthea's extended sad commentary upon reasons for her childless life, again pledges true love to such a "wrong'd creature" (l. 1916). As the play further progresses Ford subtly suggests that convention rather than Ithocles committed this wrong so freely expressed. Fully agreeing with custom that conventional marriage may bring lasting comforts and joys unknown to promiscuous lovers (ll. 1493-1504), Ford nevertheless makes it clear that Penthea's case is exceptional because she swore vows of true love and that she lies deathly ill merely because her heart lies where her

---

[7]See G. F. Sensabaugh, "Love Ethics in Platonic Court Drama, 1625-1642," *The Huntington Library Quarterly*, I (1938), 277-304; *idem*, "John Ford and Platonic Love in the Court" *SP*, XXXVI (1939), 206-26.

[8]*The Broken Heart*, l. 1245. All references to *The Broken Heart* are taken from *John Ford's Dramatic Works* (ed. Henry De Vocht), Louvain, 1927.

body cannot (ll. 1593-4). Is she not in her heart wife to Orgilus (ll. 1200-02) ? At any rate, Orgilus considers Penthea his wife (ll. 947, 972) and Crotolan observes that his son has been "vnwiu'd." In fine, Penthea and Orgilus are married in soul and only convention, which they observe in letter but hardly in spirit (ll. 1295-9, 1573-6), keeps them apart, a situation violating their pledge of true love. Literally turning upside-down the ethical order, Penthea considers chaste and pure her longing for Orgilus' embrace and deems her married life with Bassanes an existence of whoredome and faith-breaking (ll. 1195-7), a state in which her "leprous soule" (l. 1976) records foul dishonor to true love for all time:

> Oh my wrack'd honour ruin'd by those Tyrants,
> A cruell brother, and a desperate dotage!
> There is no peace left for a rauish'd wife
> Widdow'd by lawlesse marriage; to all memory,
> Penthea's, poore Penthea's name is strumpeted (ll. 1951-5).

Ford sounds here a new tragic note. Penthea's health depends upon her cooling love's hot desires aroused before her unfortunate marriage, yet custom demands that she be "whore" to her husband; science decrees and court ethics approve her throwing aside scruples so as to give her ills proper treatment, yet society commands that she observe marriage vows and so die. Such a dilemma, tolerant of evil and lacking in logic of cause and effect, smacks of the impasse born of modern skeptical thought and shows little kin to the tragic concept of Shakespeare.

Love's Sacrifice presents similar problems. Marrying Biancha because of her beauty, the Duke of Caraffa raises her from low estate to high; and apparently she dutifully returns his love until Fernando, the Duke's handsome friend, wins her heart with true love. Immediately a triangle situation arises, an old plot which Ford views with new, scientific eyes. For though the true lovers embrace clad only in night-clothes, since their passions demand satisfaction and since the love code sanctions all their actions and thoughts, right lies on their side and wrong on the side of the Duke, who is made to seem unjust in his revenge.

This is the dilemma as Ford sees it. The marriage bond, solemnized between the Duke and Biancha, tyrannically keeps true lovers apart and by so doing afflicts them with melancholic diseases which eventually bring about their death and destruction. Hence it logically follows that any bar to the desires of true lovers is of itself evil. But Ford hardly dared to encircle all iconoclasm with a

halo of pure light. Ferentes, for example, ranging through subplots of incredible dullness lusts after three women, all of whom
appear later with child; and for him and for his victims Ford's
disapproval at times becomes almost audible. Opening Act III,
Nibrassa enters cursing his daughter Julia, one of Ferentes' victims with child; "strumpet, infamous whore," he cries, aiming at
Julia choice epithets as he accuses her of leading a lewd and lascivious life.[9] Petruchio next leads in his daughter, Colona, bitterly up-
braiding her for stooping to whoredom (ll. 1418ff.); and finally
Ferentes himself enters, guiding Morona, a stale widow of forty-
six, whose virtue, if she had any, he also has taken with fecund results. Viewing his three partners in sin, Ferentes dismisses them
with a wave of the hand: thirty-odd years ago Morona might have
given him pleasure, but not now; Julia, young enough, looks scurvy
of face; Colona dallied prettily but was too easily won. He then
advises them to rip up a shirt or two with which to ease themselves
of their burdens, an injunction fully justifying Morona's earlier
scathing remark that he is a "periur'd-damnable-vngracious-defiler
of women" (ll. 1502-3). Later, when Ferentes falls pierced with
daggers, the Abbot pronounces sage judgment:

> Here's fatall sad presages, but 'tis iust,
> He dyes by murther, that hath liu'd in lust (ll. 1903-4).

Ferentes' adultery merited Ford's clear disapproval, yet Fernando's
adulterous affection, less open and much less productive, receives
his clear benediction.

For Ford sees tragic issues involved only in heroes and heroines
loving by the court code. In the first few lines of the play, before
he intimates a serious analysis of dilemmas arising from the clash
of custom and physical law, Ford suggests that "forme" should
never prevail over affection, even in the observance of funeral rites
(ll. 245ff.). Consider, he continues through the mouth of the Duke,
the "gray-headed Senate," which would tie the limits of "free
effects" through the "lawes/ Of strickt opinion and seuere dispute"
(ll. 269ff.). Should princes do this? He is sure they should not.
Now such admonitions, dropped conveniently at the very time
Biancha and Fernando exchange glances of true love, must suggest
to Fernando that mere custom should not tie down his already un-
ruly, adulterous desires; and shortly after this scene his passion

---

[9] *Love's Sacrifice*, ll. 1388ff. All references to *Love's Sacrifice* are taken
from *John Fordes Dramatische Werke* (ed. W. Bang), Louvain, 1908.

rises so high that he reasons reasonably against reason that he should quench his flames in the sweet waters of clandestine love (ll. 857ff.).

His love runs on apace. Biancha, having coldly rejected his first pleas but secretly burning herself, in full tide of passion steals, dressed in her night mantle alone, from her own boudoir to Fernando's bed, pausing at its edge to awaken him with sweet words of love. The night is short, she begins, and she has much to say. Could it be that she comes to make him master of his best desires? Fernando responds, seemingly at once wide awake. Well, listen, she replies: with shame and passion she must now confess that since she first saw Fernando love became tyrant over her heart; every word he spoke sounded like music, and should he now, in her weakness, tempt her, she would compassionately yield to his pleasure. Fernando breaks in with "Perpetuall happinesse!" but she cuts him off short. The Duke, she admits, took her to bed without dower, for which she vowed to live constant and so far has done so; nor exists a man in the whole world who could snatch from her that vow save Fernando. Then in ecstasy she offers her body to him, threatening to take her life ere morn shall christen new day; but Fernando, discarding her offers of death, asks only for kisses, readily granted since she now is all his. Kneeling before his bed in agonized love she repeats pledges and vows, swearing by her very "Bridall vowes" to hold him dearer than all earthly joys. As they part they again pledge eternal love, sealing their souls with a kiss bound by ties stronger than marriage; truly, as Biancha murmurs, never had woman loved so unfainedly or true (ll. 1285ff.).

The last act heightens the problem the foregoing scene raises. Below a drawn curtain Biancha and Fernando appear, she in a night dress, holding his hand. Why shouldn't Fernando be hers, she argues; should the "Iron lawes of Ceremony, barre/ Mutuall embraces?" (ll. 2353ff.). What's in a vow? Can there be any "sinne in vnity?" Could she dispense with conscience, which apparently still faintly speaks, as easily as she could throw aside the title of Duchess, she would rather sleep one night with Fernando than be for a thousand years the Duke's wife. The small hurt in her conscience she quickly salves with kisses of true love, at which point the Duke of Caraffa enters, catching them deep in their passion. "[S]hamelesse harlot," he justly accuses; "Shamelesse intolerable whoore" (ll. 2424ff.). But Biancha quickly retorts: Could

the Duke imagine she could continue to love him with Fernando
nearby? True, the Duke raised her from a simple gentlewoman's
position in court to the high honor of his bed, a commendable action
which nevertheless only meant that she possessed more beauty than
any woman of his former acquaintance. Furthermore, the "selfe
same appetite" which led him to marry her led her to love Fernando. Could the Duke's "crooked leg," "scambling foot,"
"bloodlesse lip," hope to compete with Fernando's miracle of flesh
and blood? Nor is it her fault that the Duke's sheets have never
been soiled, for had she had her will she and Fernando would have
long ago coupled. Shamelessly she continues to whitewash her love;
yes, she lost no time in winning Fernando's affection, but he kept
"So holily, with such Religion" the laws of friendship, that even
had she procured his complete surrender of body she would not
blush to speak it (ll. 2484ff.), whereupon the Duke breaks in, scorn-
ing her apparent adultery. Drawing his poinard he stabs her and
Biancha dies with Fernando's name on her lips.

Hot in blood the Duke turns next to Fernando, resolved to complete his revenge. A duel appears in the offing, but upon hearing
that "*chaste Biancha* /Be murther'd," Fernando lets fall his
weapon, asking death for himself. She was "Innocent," "free
from lust," he further explains to the Duke, who pauses to hear out
Fernando's peans of praise; possibly he exceeded in "lawlesse
Courtship" but from any actual folly he is free. Such a "spotlesse
wife" the wealth of all worlds could scarcely redeem (ll. 2623ff.).
When Fernando swears these truths on his sword, the Duke mumbles
"Chast, chast, and kild by me" (l. 2651), offering to stab himself
for his foul deed; but reserving self-destruction for some later date
he rushes off to worship at Biancha's tomb, before which he
prostrates himself in awed adoration:

> Peace and sweet rest sleep here; let not the touch
> Of this my impious hand, prophane the shrine
> Of fairest purity, which houers yet
> About those blessed bones inhearst within: . . .
> To thee, offended spirit, I confesse
> I am *Caraffa*, hee, that wretched man,
> That Butcher, who in my enraged spleene
> Slaughtered the *life of Innocence and Beauty*: . . .
> So chast, so deare a wife was neuer man,
> But I, enioyed (ll. 2742-59).

As Caraffa chants these solemn orisons, Fernando, hidden within
Biancha's tomb, arises to drink off a vial of poison thereby cutting

off his unhappy life; then forgiving Fernando the Duke stabs himself, predicting that future ages will weep whole nights contemplating their wretched story of love.

Love's Sacrifice thus ends according to Burtonian formula. Thwarted by custom, Fernando's passion burns so hot that he risks all to satisfy it, an action which in turn arouses jealousy in the Duke so gripping that he inflicts death upon himself and upon others. Again Ford implies that the laws of society conflict with the cure of disease, in Fernando's case a therapy of adulterous passion fully approved by the love code in court. But custom is strong and an impasse is reached, stretching man on the rack of confusion.

'Tis Pity She's A Whore, however, strikes the most decisive blow against the established moral order. Giovanni loves his sister Annabella, an affection which Ford paints so white that incest becomes a problem of ethics. Why, he argues with Friar Bonaventura, customary form should not bar love between brother and sister; belief in retributive justice marks a mind superstitious and old-fashioned. Disregarding the Friar's admonitions, he fortifies his beliefs with casuistic reasoning before he dares put his thoughts into action, consulting "wit or Art" for good counsel only to find them mere dreams and old men's tales to fright unsteady youth.[10] Now feeling sure of his ground, he plunges into incestuous relations, but almost immediately he comes again to the Friar to argue about love, and about heaven and hell. By all rights Annabella should be his, he contends; she is beautiful and therefore her love must be pure; and since her love is pure, so is his love for her, "Since in like Causes are effects alike" (ll. 906ff.)—an argument based upon the tenets of the Queen's cult of love which elicits warm rebukes from the Friar. But despite the Friar's admonitions Giovanni stands firm in his rebellion through the entire play, deeming the hell which Bonaventura threatened "naught else/ But Slauish and fond superstitious feare" (ll. 2145-65) and asking the gods to relieve him from the "Curse / Of old prescription" (ll. 2223-31).

But Giovanni is not only rebellious; he suffers from a combination of heroical love and religious melancholy, the first of which calls for satisfaction of incestuous desires. The dilemma which immediately arises is this: Should Giovanni cure himself of heroical

---

[10] *'Tis Pity She's A Whore,* ll. 306-7. All references to *'Tis Pity* are taken from Henry De Vocht, *op. cit.*

love at the expense of society, or should he follow custom and die of disease? Though both horns are sharp, the dilemma is made even more real in that again Ford carefully distinguishes between true love and mere lust. Take Hippolita, for example. Married to Richardetto, she clandestinely loves Soranzo, for whose sake she sends her husband abroad in search of a niece. Richardetto, suspecting his wife, releases rumors of his death, leaving Hippolita free to pursue her adulterous desires, which she prosecutes with such vigor that Richardetto, upon returning in disguise, comments openly upon her "lasciuious riotts" and "loose adultery" (ll. 783-91). Such love as this Ford heartily condemns; and he clarifies his position by making the oaths which passed between them "wicked and vnlawfull," which to keep were more sin than to break (ll. 700-05); and at her death resulting from passion and crime no Fernandos praise her spotless purity and chaste love, no repentent Caraffas step up to absolve her from sin. Instead, with poison of Soranzo's scheming coursing her veins, she dies damning her clandestine lover and all agree that she has met "Wonderful Iustice" (l. 1708).

But Giovanni's love is celestial and pure, a passion which not only demands satisfaction but which because of its purity merits sympathetic attention. Recalling Annabella's "matchlesse beauty" just before he rips out her heart, he bids her go white in her soul "to fill a Throne / Of Innocence and Sanctity in Heauen" (ll. 2300ff.). Then admitting that "The Lawes of *Conscience* and of *Ciuill vse*" may justly blame them, he clears their incest from sin because their love, springing from beauty, could not be other than pure (ll. 2379ff.). Even the couplet closing the play rings with sympathetic approval:

> *Of one* so young, so rich in Natures store,
> Who could not say, *'Tis pitty shee's a Whoore?* (ll. 2600-01).

'Tis pity indeed and a problem as well. For the play ends tolerant of incest, suggesting that because of Giovanni's disease and because of his celestial love he should stand as an heroic exception, more exalted than the wisdom of ages.

Scientific necessity and revolt from authority thus make Ford forever a stranger to Shakespeare: Romeo and Orgilus speak in different languages of star-crossed and unfortunate love; Fernando and Antony in their adultery stand as far apart as the poles; Giovanni and Hamlet, both mightily questioning, claim no kinship in word or in deed. Yet it would be presumptuous to say that Ford's three serious plays are not tragic; it would be still more presumptuous to generalize on the spirit of tragedy, except to say that it deals with problems of human suffering and evil. To determine, however, Ford's unique contribution to dramatic decline, some general notion of Elizabethan tragedy, with particular reference to its nature and function, need be established.

Generally, according to Aristotle's *Poetics*, tragedy is the story of human blindness and error leading to effects opposite from those intended, the truth of which is ironically revealed.[11] The errors may or may not be moral, the universe need not necessarily proceed by justice; but the laws of cause and effect must objectively function, man's errors finding him out in unvarying patterns. No drowned man must revive because his motives were pure, no grain must spring from tares; and the excellence of this sort of tragedy is that its logic convinces, its form is concise, its irony evident and sharp. Though it is not the only kind of tragedy, it is one of the best.

Now this same essential concept, though owing little to the Greeks, emerged again with a Christian difference in Tudor England after a long medieval development.[12] In the *Mirror for Magistrates*,[13] a veritable storehouse of tragic material, medieval mutability began to be but another name for man's responsible action; tragedy again became a dramatic progress from cause to effect. Shakespeare, taking over this concept and stamping it with indelible life and unforgettable character, again made tragedy excellent for its logic, conciseness, and irony, comparable to any drama the Greek age produced. Neither he nor the Greeks make tragic justice an open book, but both make life magnificently heroic in intolerance of evil, villainy never remaining victorious and prosperous in the end. In truth, Greek tragedy and Shakespeare differ in form rather than in idea, Tudor drama following the *De Casibus* rise-and-fall structure which it inherited from the Middle Ages.[14] Furthermore, the Renaissance, child of both Christianity

---

[11] *Aristotle on the Art of Poetry* (trans. by Ingram Bywater, Oxford, 1920), *passim*. See also F. L. Lucas, *Tragedy in Relation to Aristotle's "Poetics"* (New York, 1928), for an excellent analysis of the nature and function of tragedy.

[12] See Willard Farnham, *The Medieval Heritage of Elizabethan Tragedy* (Berkeley, 1936), for a detailed treatment of this idea.

[13] See Lily B. Campbell, *Tudor Conceptions of History and Tragedy in "A Mirror for Magistrates"* (Berkeley, 1936).

[14] Farnham, *op. cit.*, Chap. XI.

and the ancient world, developed more than one concept of tragedy, though the Christian idea that evil results from wrongdoing received the most widespread treatment.[15] In both Renaissance and Greek concepts man's free will in a world of human values stands out clear, questions of right and wrong separating as easily as black and white; and deepest tragedy came when free will not necessity struck man down, when tragic heroes of their own unwitting hands worked their own doom, or killed the thing they loved most.

Macbeth exhibits excellently the main nature and function of this sort of tragedy. Struggling in a world both hostile and fearful, goaded by ambition and by Lady Macbeth, Macbeth kills Duncan to forward his own plans, by his own hands thereby bringing grief to himself and to others. What is remarkable is that his resulting fears and conscience-stricken dreams seem wholly natural and logical; and what is even more remarkable is that events, moving inexorably to tragic ends, allay tragic qualms: fear of man's dreadful struggle in a world of blind forces, pity for man's weakness. For contemplation of logical cause and effect purges pity and fear, making somehow the struggle endurable in intolerance of evil and leaving a sense of relief in the demonstration that cold winds pierce shorn lambs and villains alike.

Ford's tragic sense, however, is quite different. All Ford's heroes and heroines struggle in a world of physical forces crossing swords with the laws of society. Orgilus and Penthea declare their plighted love more sacred than her nuptial vows to Bassanes, a legal bond which in its very insistence on keeping the two lovers physically apart leads to their dying of definite diseases; Fernando and Biancha actually exalt their mental adultery, making it clear that the iron laws of ceremony which kept them from satisfying their physical desires promoted their untimely deaths. But perhaps Giovanni best illustrates Ford's tragic concept. Driven by passion, he seeks to allay his disease first by counsel and second by incest, the latter of which, though breaking society's laws, for a time solves his physical problem. Then as retributive justice for smashing the moral order sets in Giovanni argues on courtly love grounds that since Annabella is beautiful and their mutual love pure the logical chain of cause and effect should be broken, that events once set in motion should not move inexorably but should exempt their

---

15Hardin Craig, "The Shackling of Accidents: A Study of Elizabethan Tragedy," *PQ*, xix (1940), 1-19.

particular incest which, as Giovanni admits, in others would be abhorred; and the tragic qualm aroused by his early struggle grows with confusion in a world where no law prevails, where figuratively wheat grows from tares. Contemplation of such events fails to purge pity and fear; and life becomes in its tolerance of evil unheroic, an existence to be merely endured.

This is the change Ford effected in the nature and function of tragedy. Absorbing from science an idea of material necessity and from Henrietta Maria's love cult an oblique code of ethics, Ford created a tragic concept void of dignity or idealistic purpose, a tragedy which neither elevates nor enlightens but which bludgeons man's spirit numb with despair. In thus failing to leave a sense of relief, Ford's plays hardly square with *Macbeth* or *Othello*, whose portrayal of man's tragic course in the world purges fear and gives rise to grim joy; in both meaning and purpose they differ from Shakespeare's in kind. Perhaps in this difference, so sharp and distinct, lies Ford's unique contribution to Elizabethan dramatic decline.

RICHARD HOOKER AMONG THE CONTROVERSIALISTS

By ELBERT N. S. THOMPSON
University of Iowa

When the first four books of the *Ecclesiastical Polity* appeared
in 1593 and the fifth in 1597, the Puritan controversy was already
far advanced. It had begun on matters of ceremony, things indifferent as the Puritans regarded them; but even then graver issues
were apprehended. As the authors of the *First Admonition to
Parliament* declared in 1572, "Neither is the controversy between
them and us . . . for a cap, a tippet or a surplice, but for great matters concerning a true ministry and regiment of the church according to the word." Before Hooker wrote, the reformers had denounced the fundamental organization of the English Church as
indefensible, and the bitter campaign waged by the Marprelates
had been crushed. Then a compromise seemed possible. Lord
Burghley favored a reconciliation, Francis Bacon turned his influence toward appeasement, and only the insistence of Elizabeth
on uniformity and obedience to the crown blocked the way. Not
unreasonably Hooker could hope that the strife would be neither
"earnest nor long."

Hooker was certainly one of those "wary and respective men"
who "had rather seek quietly their own, and wish that the world
may go well, . . . than with pain and hazard make themselves advisers for the common good." Conscious, though, that in his day
"zeal hath drowned charity, and skill meekness," he felt forced to
undertake "the plain and impartial defence of a common cause."[1]
The *Ecclesiastical Polity* was first inspired by the Presbyterian
sermons of Travers; it rebuts more often than any others the arguments of Thomas Cartwright; but Hooker was not by nature a con-
troversialist, and his book rises far higher than the strife of his
time.

In this regard the *Ecclesiastical Polity* may well be compared to
another work of very similar title, Milton's *Reason of Church Government*, which was written almost fifty years later. Milton, also,
professed himself to be averse to controversy. "Surely to every

---

[1] *E.P.*, 5.1.1; 4.1.1.

good and peaceable man," he wrote, "it must in nature needs be a hateful thing to be the displeaser and molester of thousands." But duty called him from the work for which "the genial power of nature" better fitted him. By that year, 1642, all hope of appeasement was gone and moderation had vanished. Nevertheless, Milton began in the spirit of philosophical inquiry, not of controversy. His little essay on discipline is not unlike Hooker's praise of the ordered universe, and his description of it as "not only the removal of disorder; but if any visible shape can be given to divine things, the very visible shape and image of virtue," could easily be attributed to Hooker. Milton also recognized the educative force of law, a force promoting "love of that which is really good," and again like Hooker he grounded law on what he called reason. But soon Milton descended from this higher plane of thought to deal with law simply as a restraining force and to recognize for Christian living only one guide, the Bible. Not till the last chapter but one did he rise again to higher matters and give his mind free play.

Take first what Milton wrote of the Bible's authority:

> Let them chant while they will of prerogatives, we shall tell them of scripture; of custom, we of scripture; of acts and statutes, still of scripture; till the quick and piercing word enter to the dividing of their souls, and the mighty weakness of the gospel throw down the weak mightiness of man's reasoning.

Then for contrast read Hooker's judgment:

> As her [wisdom's] ways are of sundry kinds, so her manner of teaching is not merely one and the same. Some things she openeth by the sacred books of Scripture; some things by the glorious works of nature: with some things she inspireth them from above by spiritual influence; in some things she leadeth and traineth them only by worldly experience and practice. We may not so in any one special kind admire her, that we disgrace her in any other; but let all her ways be according unto their place and degree adored.[2]

In the marked disparity between these two passages one sees how the range of Hooker's thought transcended the level of contemporary controversy. On large issues, such as the relation between church and state, Milton wrote nobly; but here his thought is sadly restricted. Hooker, on the other hand, at the start set controversy aside to offer his fine analysis of law, from the immutable law that God has prescribed for his own acts to the temporary statutes that man frames for his own governance. He was at his best in his discussions of natural law, which breathe the spirit of the finest human-

---

[2]*Church Government*, 2.2, p. 485; *E.P.*, 2.1.4.

ism, and of supernatural law, in which he established a life higher than the natural, where alone man's full satisfaction can be gained. But all, as he saw it, work harmoniously together. Divine law, or ultimate truth, is revealed to man not through any one channel,— through Scripture, to be sure, but through the human reason also and human experience as expressed in the opinions of man through the ages. In this way, against the less reasoned arguments of Travers and Cartwright, Hooker defended the regimen of the English Church.

To find another such cordial acceptance of both the natural and the supernatural laws one must look forward fifty years to Nathanael Culverwel's *Discourse of the Light of Nature*. He too, but with less calm poise and more lyric fervor, accepted both as harmonious, though variant, expressions of the eternal will. Hooker was a rational churchman of the old school, in which matters of ceremonial and organization were uppermost. Furthermore, the demands of English law carried great weight with him. Culverwel approached more nearly the rationalism of a later age. Like other Cambridge Platonists, he looked on religion as chiefly a matter of the spirit, and gave little attention to ceremonies or the regiment of the Church or Parliamentary legislation. But he was at one with Hooker in tracing natural law back to its eternal source and in regarding reason as the link uniting human and divine.

In praise of reason Culverwel was less restrained than Hooker. "So that to blaspheme Reason, 'tis to reproach Heaven it self, and to dishonour the God of Reason," he finely argued. It may be only a candle compared to the brighter light of revelation, but "would they put out this Candle of the Lord, intellectuals of his own lighting?" Again he asked pertinently: "If Reason be content with its own Sphere, why should it not have the liberty of its proper motion?" Less ecstatic than some of the repetitions of this idea is the statement: "God hath breathed into all the sons of men reasonable souls, which may serve as so many candles to enlighten and direct them in the searching out their Creator."[3] This has something of the calm dignity of Hooker's comment on St. Paul: "His meaning is, that by force of the light of Reason, wherewith God illuminateth every one which cometh into the world, men being enabled to know truth from falsehood, and good from evil, do

---

[3] Chapter 1.

thereby learn in many things what the will of God is.''[4]   Strange it
may seem that the fundamental position of the *Ecclesiastical Polity*
should become within fifty years the staple argument of one of the
Cambridge Platonists with at least some Puritan leanings and connections.

One may suspect, though, that the term reason had no one well
defined meaning.   Hooker designated by it all that man learns by
exercise of his proper faculties and through intuition; it was not
the product of mind alone but of his whole being, and is attested
even by common usage and the consent of nations.   It was, therefore, a composite of the individual and the communal.   Less in-
clusively, Milton interpreted it as man's private judgment, and
identified it, just as Hooker was apt to do, with what he thought
to be right.   Culverwel's view resembled Hooker's more nearly but
was colored by the rationalism then emergent.   He recognized with
Hooker ''those first bublings up of common Principles that are
own'd and acknowledg'd by all.''   He also saw in *sensus communis*
an evidencing of nature's law.   But he inclined more to metaphysical speculation.   He cited not simply Plato, Aristotle, the
Church Fathers, and the Schoolmen, but also later thinkers like
John Selden, Grotius, and Salmasius.   He spoke admiringly of the
''great and noble Verulam'' and showed especial interest in Lord
Brooke's *De Veritate*.   Platonist though he was, he pitted against
Plato's doctrine of innate ideas and pre-existence Lord Herbert's
explanation of the natural instincts as simply capacities of the soul
stimulated by contact with external objects, and he discarded
Lord Brooke's retention of the Platonic doctrine of remembrance
for John Wallis's more observational theory in *Truth Tried*.   Culverwel stood closer to rationalism than Hooker.

Naturally Culverwel thought of reason more exclusively as an
intellectual power, and, although he recognized that the capacity
for knowledge is spiritual, he still believed that its content comes
from without through the senses; ''all knowledg comes flourishing
in at these Lattices.''[5]   Hooker, writing before the new philosophy
had come, fell back on old conceptions of the supernatural law, and
succeeded better in uniting it and other forms of law in one
harmonious system.   Faith, Culverwel admitted, is the brighter of
the ''two great Luminaries in every Heavenly soul''; for ''the most

---

[4] *E.P.*, 1.8.3.
[5] Chapter 11.

that Man's Reason can do, is to fill the Understanding to the brim; but Faith, that throws the Soul into the Ocean, and lets it roll, and bath it self in the vastnesse and fulnesse of a Deity.'' Hooker, though, shows more convincingly that the object of ultimate desire and complete happiness lies beyond this world. In a passage that reminds one of Tamburlaine's lyric outburst on ideal beauty Hooker wrote: ''although the beauties, riches, honours, sciences, virtues, and perfections of all men living, were in the present possession of one; yet somewhat beyond and above all this there would still be sought and earnestly thirsted for.'' Or again he wrote: ''For man doth not seem to rest satisfied, either with fruition of that wherewith his life is preserved, or with performance of such actions as advance him most deservedly in estimation; but doth further covet, yea oftentimes manifestly pursue with great sedulity and earnestness, that which cannot stand him in any stead for vital use.''[6] No writer since Hooker, save only Newman, has been able to make so absolutely real this world that lies beyond human reach.

This union of natural and supernatural determined Hooker's attitude toward Scripture. All parties agreed that the doctrines necessary for salvation are plainly revealed. Cultured men, however, saw that Biblical texts, like all other documents, need interpretation, or in Hooker's words: ''The Scripture could not teach us the things that are of God, unless we did credit men who have taught us that the words of Scripture do signify those things.''[7] The Catholic gave the sole right of interpretation to the Church. Hooker allowed more to human reason, although *men* as used above hardly means men in general. To this view Chillingworth, the godson of Laud, advanced more nearly. In the *Religion of the Protestants* he accepted as the sure source of truth the Bible and a human mind illumined by God's spirit. Still, he insisted that the individual judgment must be based on solid evidence. This caution was disregarded by Milton in *Christian Doctrine* as he insisted that there are really two scriptures, one external on the printed page and the other internal in the human heart. This extreme view was altogether too unstable for Hooker. He was curious to know how the testimony of the spirit could be discerned and what sort of check could serve. ''When they and their Bibles were alone together, what strange fantastical opinion soever at any time entered into

6Chapter 16; *E.P.*, 1.11.4.
7*E.P.*, 2.7.3.

their heads, their use was to think the Spirit taught it them.'' He refused to trust his own judgment against the settled opinion of the Church or established usage, for these to Hooker were plain evidence of natural law. With that understanding he flatly declared: ''inasmuch as law doth stand upon reason, to allege reason serveth as well as to cite Scripture.''[8] Thus reason is opposed both to the dogmatism of the Presbyterians and the unchecked individualism of later Puritans. Hooker did not foresee how this same argument was to be used soon by Lilburne, Parker, Overton, and the Republican party in general.

Hooker's immediate opponents, the ''old Nonconformists'' as they were later called, seemed conservative to radicals of the next generation. Milton dubbed tradition a ''perpetual cankerworm to eat out God's commandments,'' and to the hypothetical question, ''is the government of episcopacy . . . so weaved into the common law?'' answered: ''In God's name let it weave out again.''[9] As Professor Woodhouse has suggested, the Puritan concern for Christian liberty promoted a revolutionary attitude.[10] Here again Hooker's conception of natural law brought him into direct opposition to the Puritans. His work is filled with ingots of conservative philosophy like: ''the Law of the Church, whereby for so many ages together we have been guided,'' or: ''allowed as fit in the judgment of antiquity, and by the long continued practice of the whole Church.'' When he declared that ''the general and perpetual voice of men is as the sentence of God himself'' and drew from that the deduction that ''infinite duties there are, the goodness whereof is by this rule sufficiently manifested, although we had no other warrant besides to approve them,'' he revealed how essential this conservatism is to his whole system of thought.[11]

Hooker's application of these soundly established principles to the specific issues of the day is not always persuasive. He saw, for example, that the externals of the Christian religion could not be the same in all nations, and he insisted that it suffices if all accept the same fundamental doctrines. ''How should we think it agreeable and consonant unto reason,'' he asked, to demand uniformity in ceremonials, especially since such a policy would create only

---

[8]*E.P.*, 3.8.15; *Pref.*, 1.8.7; *E.P.*, 2.5.7.
[9]*Church Government*, p. 459; *Of Reformation*, p. 412.
[10]*Univ. of Toronto Q.*, IV (1935), 483-513.
[11]*E.P.*, 1.1.3; 5.7.1; 5.20.5; 1.8.3.

dissension? Hooker here combated the Presbyterians' effort to force continental usage upon the English Church. But one might well ask why it was not counter to reason to demand strict uniformity in England. Lord Brooke, in fact, in his Discourse on episcopacy in 1642 argued just that. Hooker can rest his case only on statute law. The Act of Uniformity, though, might have been repealed or modified. Our conservative philosopher, however, shrank from that with the warning that "the change of laws, especially concerning matter of religion, must be warily proceeded in," and indeed that "alteration though it be from worse to better hath in it inconveniences." Here, of course, he should have faced such reminders as a Catholic could offer of alterations made at the time of the Reformation; but this is barely mentioned, for the argument is leveled against Presbyterian claims. So Hooker seems to lose his footing in substituting "the law which belongeth unto each nation" for that more fundamental law "whereunto by the light of reason men find themselves bound in that they are men." Apparently forgetting that enforced conformity is repugnant to reason, he closed with the words: "No doubt if men had been willing to learn how many laws their actions in this life are subject unto, and what the true force of each law is, all these controversies might have died the very day they were first brought forth."[12]

Engrossed in universal truths Hooker thus failed to meet some actual issues squarely. Just as Burke, the heir to much of his habits of thought, closed his eyes to abuses in England's electoral system and to inequalities in taxation in France, so Hooker disregarded evils that seemed obvious to other, even moderate, men. The silencing of nonconforming clergymen certainly fell within Hooker's purview. The Puritans who suffered deprivation faced actual facts and found theory of little consolation. One of them, Dudley Fenner, in a manly protest entitled *A Defence of the Godlie Ministers* (1587) answered an opponent's assertion that the churches were "aboundantlie replenished with Preachers" by alleging "the great complaint of all the shires."[13] He knew that men had to go from five to twenty miles to hear a sermon, only to be fined "twelve pence a Saboth for being absent from their parishe Church." Francis Bacon, whose judgment may carry greater weight than Fenner's, called the deprivations ill advised "in such great scarcity

12*E.P.*, 4.13.8; 4.14.1; 1.16.1; 1.16.5.
13P. 49.

of preachers,'' and suggested that the bishops might better consider the good that those preachers were doing than fix all attention on the hurt supposedly owing to them.[14] Hooker himself admitted that not enough learned clergymen were to be found. Nevertheless, he dismissed the question with the remark: ''it being better that the Church should want altogether the benefit of such
men's labours than endure the mischief of their inconformity to
good laws.''[15]   To this summary verdict a silenced preacher or a
practical statesman would hardly acquiesce.

Much more effectively Hooker met the bitter attack on the episcopal organization of the Church. His opponents argued their case
along two general lines: that since there is no Biblical authoriza-
tion for the office of bishop it therefore is unwarranted, and that
the bishops then in office abused their power. Already everything
in either sacred or profane history that could by any possibility
serve the purpose of either side had been unearthed. In the weari-
some dispute Hooker, at least, showed a sense of true historical
perspective in his insistence that the bishop could still be in essentials what he always had been even if in some ''accidental
properties'' his status had been altered. But again Hooker seemed
not quite to meet the bitterest assault, that on the wealth, pomp,
and worldly power of the prelates. Martin Marprelate had stressed
most these abuses. Even a conservative, constitutional reformer
like Lord Falkland, who approved of episcopacy as an institution,
spoke plainly in Parliament against the conduct of the bishops.
Francis Bacon mildly admitted part of the Puritan indictment, and
Lord Brooke in 1642 argued that the social background and training of the churchmen poorly fitted them for high secular office.
But Hooker in his second book had disclaimed all intention of considering ''the dealings of men who administer government, and
unto whom the execution of that law belongeth.'' His concern was
only with ''those things which in the very whole entire form of our
church polity have been . . . injuriously blamed.'' He regarded the
honors bestowed on prelates as deserved recognition of merit, and
called it fortunate that the honors were often of so trivial a nature
that no man would be too eager to claim them and no one quick to
withhold them. As to the bishops' wealth, it was theirs and cer-

[14]*Advertisement Touching the Controversies of the Church of England.
Works*, ed. B. Montague, VII, 52.
[15]*E.P.*, 5.81.11.

tainly not the reformers' to seize.[16] So he did not waive altogether
the social and political objections that had been raised. But his
defence of episcopacy rests really on broader foundations. The
institution had existed in England from earliest times; it was
sanctioned by long usage and law; it had contributed to the culture
of the clergy and the dignity and efficacy of the Church. All this
is a direct outgrowth of his reasoned theory of natural and supernatural law. It is the position not of a combatant but of a philosopher.

As time went on royal authority was to be attacked just as bitterly as the prelacy had been. But when Hooker wrote the assault
had not yet begun and he could indulge more at ease his inclination
for broad, philosophic analysis. Like earlier political theorists,
Hooker derived royal authority from the will of the people. In
the fine tenth chapter of the first book he so traced the growth of
societies and states. Strangely enough, Milton's exposition in *The
Tenure of Kings and Magistrates* is so much the same that Michaelis
has suspected the direct influence of Hooker.[17] There are differences,
however, between them. Hooker does not accept the theory of contract between king and people squarely, and he surely holds back
from the extreme deductions often made from it. Milton certainly
would not have said with Hooker: "Unto kings by human right,
honour by divine right is due; Man's ordinances are many times
presupposed as grounds in the statutes of God."[18] Hooker also
denied the right to depose a monarch. He really seems to be contracting his first broad view out of respect for law and common
English feeling. Yet the authorities objected to the eighth book,
where this problem holds the center of interest, and it was not
published until 1648. Taking this uncertain position, the *Ecclesiastical Polity* stands apart from the controversy and is best in that
finely written chapter of the first book and in the "character" of
the true king in the fifth.

An issue with such far reaching import was needed to rouse
Hooker to his best. In his justification of tithes he resorted to the
same sort of argument that Milton used against tithes in 1649; as
in a joint debate Biblical example is pitted against example, the
sole difference being that Hooker made more of custom and that

16 *E.P.*, 7.24.1.

17 *Richard Hooker als politischer Denker.* Berlin, 1933.

18 *E.P.*, 8.2.

Milton was more aware of social abuses. If to either, the decision would be in Milton's favor. But on the question of the Livings of Ministers Hooker's sound judgment was operative.[19] He could advance three propositions, that clergymen should be learned men, resident in their parishes, and limited to one parish, and still see that actual needs may force the Church in certain instances to disregard them. He argued, then, cogently that such an exemption or special privilege does not imply opposition to the general principle. Hence he justified the Church for ordaining some poorly trained men when fit men were not available, and he approved of clergymen's leaving parish duties to continue their studies in the university, laboring "to grow in knowledge that so they may afterwards the more edify and the better instruct their congregations." Bacon, whose respect for universities was slight, disagreed with this; for he felt that a clergyman would progress faster who combined parish work with study at home. His position is not surprising, but Milton's is.[20] He saw no reason for a preacher's remaining long under tutelage since the Bible and solid books on divinity were easily available in English, and since the truths of the Christian religion are so plain and simple that one can quickly master them and become a teacher. Even a simple artizan could easily be trained for such service, whereas the university man usually acquires only expensive tastes and great expectations for himself from his calling. Such arguments sound little like Milton, the poet and scholar. It was Hooker, who, disregarding possibly some temporary abuses, would provide for the culture and intellectual growth of the Church.

In general, therefore, although Hooker shared in the controversy of his day, he rose well above it, feeling with Bacon that "the disease requireth rather rest than cure." He was really himself when he handled the questions under debate from solidly grounded general principles. As a psychologist he drew a clear distinction between appetite and will; as a political philosopher he traced the growth of civic life; in the field of ethics he handled the problem of good and evil; and as an active churchman he reflected on the nature of the ministry. All these topics were surveyed from two points of view. He faced them as an Englishman concerned over

---

[19]*E.P.*, 5. 79; 5.81.

[20]*Certain Considerations Touching the Better Pacification and Edification of the Church of England. Works*, VII, 91 *et seq.; Hirelings from the Church.*

the needs of his own country. He was conscious, also, of the larger, universal significance that they bore. His spirit is never bitter; his style in its calm dignity and rhythmic flow is never beneath his subject. He may lack the force and the range of some others in the fray, but even when he is most serious an apt phrase or a pointed epigram lightens his expression. "To see life steadily and see it whole" has become a much abused phrase, but it sums up Hooker's purpose and describes his achievement.

THE MYTH OF JOHN DONNE THE RAKE

By Allen R. Benham
University of Washington

If you had been a frequenter of the book stalls in Paul's Walk in the spring of 1633 you might have been surprised on seeing a small book on sale there. This volume had on its title-page the following: *Poems, by J. D. with Elegies on the Author's Death. London. Printed by M. F. for John Marriot.* The identity of the author, J. D., was perhaps disclosed when you read the first poem, *The Progress of the Soul,* for that work had been published with the author's name in 1612. But possibly you had not read the *Progress of the Soul* in the earlier edition and then you would be dependent for the identification of J. D. on the elegies toward the close of the 1633 volume, whence you would discover that J. D. was John Donne, D. D., late Dean of St. Paul's, who had died in an odor of sanctity in 1631.

The 1633 volume is prefaced by a statement *The Printer to the Understanders*[1] and the title of that statement is a very suggestive one. The printer comments on his use of the term "understanders" rather than "readers." He obviously does not want to interfere with the sale of the book and hopes "that very few will have a minde to confesse themselves ignorant." He does not suggest that there are esoteric references in the poems[2] printed in the volume and explains that on account of their excellence he has transferred from the early pages of his venture to the end thereof the customary eulogies of the author.

There were two groups of readers who would have examined the poems with very different feelings. There were *understanders,* like Ben Jonson and George Chapman, who would reread these poems as the works of their old friend and fellow poet, John Donne, long

---

[1]This is reprinted in the now standard edition of Donne's poems by H. J. C. Grierson, 2 vols., Oxford University Press, 1912; in the Muses Library Edition edited by E. K. Chambers, 2 vols., George Bell & Sons, 1896; and in the Oxford University Press volume of 1929 edited by H. J. C. Grierson.

[2]But Drummond reports that Donne told Jonson that Donne wrote his Epitaph on Prince Henry to match Sir Edward Herbert (i.e., Lord Cherbury) in "obscurenesse" (*Jonson's Conversations with Drummond of Hawthornden,* Ed. Patterson, p. 12). And on a later page Drummond reports Jonson as saying "that Donne himself, for not being understood, would perish."

lost to the craft of poets and regretted perhaps as a preacher; though they would admit that from 1620 to 1631 he had been the best as well as the most spectacular preacher in England. Other purchasers of the 1633 volume would be somewhat mystified by the term *understanders* as applied to them; for their main immediate reaction to the contents of the volume would be that they couldn't make head or tail of them. Perhaps the bookseller was making fun of them or perhaps he was challenging them to become understanders. The poems in the book are printed in no systematic sequence and this disorder suggests that Marriot had got his copy from one or more of the numerous manuscripts that were circulating in London, to the author's expressed distress. The volume at any rate sold, it found a market and was reprinted with additions and changes in 1635 and 1639.

In 1640, the eldest son of J. D., also John Donne, D. C. L., decided to publish a volume of his father's sermons and when this volume appeared it was provided with a life of the preacher by Izaak Walton. The latter had furnished one of the elegies in the 1633 volume and was later to become well-known as the author of *The Complete Angler*: but his *Life of Donne* is his earliest extended piece of prose and the earliest synoptic view of Donne.

Walton as a biographer of Donne suffers from the fact that he did not become acquainted with his subject till Donne was already a fairly well-known clergyman, and did not have access to Donne's extensive correspondence, which was not, in fact, published until the late Edmund Gosse brought out in 1899 his two volume *Life and Letters of John Donne*.[3] Walton's *Life of Donne*, therefore, is but sketchy for the early years and must have been supplemented by reference to the letters and other materials. There is this difficulty, however, about using Donne's letters as a basis for an account of his life—the letters are for the most part dated in only the most casual way. Donne apparently did not when he wrote to his friends have a future biographer in mind. He too frequently dates a letter merely *Tuesday* and, as in the course of his 59 years there were several Tuesdays, it at times becomes difficult to determine which Tuesday is meant. Sometimes, of course, well-known and datable events are referred to and then we can with some certainty locate a letter in its proper chronology. But this happy

---

[3]London, William Heinemann.

possibility is all too infrequent. I might say here at once that this difficulty of dating is true of Donne's poems also.

Now, how about his poems and the confusion into which they threw his readers who were not already *understanders*. They would probably have no trouble with many of Donne's poems such as his pious *To God the Father* and perhaps his *Valediction Forbidding Mourning*. But with many other poems they were bound to have trouble. The latter would arise not so much from the sheer obscurity of the poems as from the difficulty some readers would find in fitting given poems into the picture of Donne formed in the public mind from 1620 to 1631.

It is no wonder that, according to report[4] the Reverend Dr. John Donne was rather worried about the interpretation which would be put on his poems and endeavored to call in his MSS: but they were too numerous and scattered for him to do this.[5] Since none of these MSS was reprinted in Donne's life time he was spared some of the embarrassment he might have experienced, had they been published. But how about the non-"understanding readers" of the 1633 volume? Since this appeared only two years after Donne's death, they might very properly assume that the poems were of recent composition. And, if they did make that assumption, would it not give rise to such a question as, "Did the good Dr. Donne give such moments as he could spare from his work on his edifying and moving sermons to the 'enditing' of such sceptical and fleshly poems?"[6]

Of course such old friends of Donne's as Ben Jonson and George Chapman, when they examined the 1633 volume greeted again poems that they had read thirty years before in manuscript.[7] Jonson, in fact, told Drummond of Hawthornden that Donne wrote all his best pieces before he was 25, i.e., *ante* 1598.[8]

Of Donne's importance for the history of English poetry *circa*

---

[4]See the comments in the Muses Library Donne, I, xxxvi-xxxviii.

[5]See the comments on Donne MSS still extant in Gosse, *Life and Letters of John Donne* and in Grierson's edition of the *Poems*.

[6]See Sir Thomas Browne's elegiac lines on Donne, Grierson's *Donne*, I, 372.

[7]See Drayton's letter to Reynolds on contemporary poets in which he comments on the difficulty of assessing the total poetic production of the time because of the probable mass of MS material to which he did not have access. The editor of the Muses Library Donne hints that probably Drayton had seen no MS versions of Donne's poems, and would have difficulty in dating the poems.

[8]See *The Conversations*, ed. R. F. Patterson, Blackie and Son Ltd., 1924, p. 11.

1600 there can be no question, even if the poems were in MS only. Thus. Francis Davison "apparently when collecting material for his *Poetical Rhapsody* in 1600, includes in a memorandum of 'MSS. to get.' certain poems of Donne.'"⁹ Jonson, who was very chary of bestowing praises on his contemporaries, and whose critical attitude toward Shakespeare is well-known, wrote three poems to or about Donne in which the latter is highly praised. Drummond also reports that Jonson regarded Donne as "the first poet in the world for some things,"¹⁰ though Donne "deserved hanging, for not keeping of accent";¹¹ and that in Jonson's preface to his *Art of Poesie*, Donne has the rôle of Criticus.¹²

"Few lyrical poets," remarks Professor Schelling,

have ever rivalled Donne in contemporary popularity. Mr. Edmund Gosse has recently given a reason for this, which seems worthy of attention, while by no means explaining everything. 'Donne was, I should venture to suggest, by far the most modern and contemporaneous of the writers of his time . . . . . He arrived at an excess of actuality of style, and it was because he struck them as so novel, and so completely in touch with his age, that his immediate coevals were so . . . fascinated with him.'¹³

Donne's influence on English poets was very great up to about the middle of the seventeenth century.¹⁴ It then declined¹⁵ and

---

⁹F. E. Schelling, *Elizabethan Lyrics*, Athenaeum Press Series, Ginn & Co., 1895, p. xxi.

¹⁰The *Conversations, ed. cit., ibid.*

¹¹ *Ibid.*, p. 5.

¹²*Ibid.*, pp. 8, 36.

¹³Schelling, *op. cit.*, p. xxii.

¹⁴For the critical opinion of a Jacobean and Caroline poet on Donne see the elegy by Thomas Carew 1594-1639 in the Everyman Library volume *Minor Poets of the 17th Century*, p. 122; in Grierson's Donne and Muses Library edition of Carew. For Donne's influence in action see the poems of George Herbert, John Cleveland, Abraham Cowley, Richard Crashaw, Henry Vaughan and Dryden's poem on the death of Lord Hastings.

¹⁵See the following articles by Professor A. H. Nethercot: "The Reputation of John Donne as Metrist," *Sewanee Review*, xxx (1922), 463-474; "The Reputation of the 'Metaphysical Poets' during the Seventeenth Century," *JEGP*, xxiii (1924), 173-198; "The Reputation of the Metaphysical Poets during the Age of Pope," *PQ*, iv (1925), 161-179; *The Reputation of the Metaphysical Poets* during the Age of Johnson and the Romantic Revival, *SP*, xxii (1925), 81-132. See also George Williamson, *The Donne Tradition*, Harvard University Press, 1930 and Mary E. Fowler, *The Metaphysical Tradition in English Poetry*, 1937, MS in University of Washington Library. Robert L. Sharp in his *From Donne to Dryden*, University of North Carolina Press, 1940, regards Donne and his influence as the thing which the seventeenth century in English literature has been trying to live down. But Leah Jonas in her *Divine Science*, Columbia University Press, 1940, considers Donne as a minor matter in the seventeenth century.

Donne almost disappeared from view[16] until interest in his work was revived in the romantic generation 1790-1830.[17] The interest then aroused continued through the nineteenth century and was the impulse that led Gosse to start his studies that resulted in the publication of *The Life and Letters of John Donne,* 2 volumes, 1898. Gosse was much troubled by the contrast between Donne's poems and his sermons and is responsible for the orthodox explanation of the contrast, as follows: Donne lived a wild life as a young man as we can see from his poems. He was converted along about 1612-15, went into the church and his life for his last sixteen years was one long repentance. Gosse's diagnosis may be correct, but I think that the evidence presented for it is not demonstrative.

In the first place, consider the following passage from Sir Richard Baker's *Chronicles of the Kings of England* (1641) :[18]

And here I desire the Readers leave to remember two of my own old acquaintance, the one was Mr. John Donne, who leaving Oxford, lived at the Innes of Courts, not dissolute, but very neat; a great Visiter of Ladies, a great frequenter of Playes, a great Writer of conceited Verses; until such time as King James taking notice of the pregnancy of his wit, was a means that he betook him to the study of Divinity, and thereupon proceeding Doctor, was made Dean of Pauls; and became so ĩ..re a Preacher, that he was not only commended, but even admired by all that heard him.

This is one of the few pieces of evidence we have about Donne's early life.

In the second place, consider some Elizabethan and Jacobean theories of poetry, e.g., Sidney in his *Apologie,* arguing versus the charge on poets that they were liars, holds that since poets make no claims for the truth of their verses they are not guilty of being falsifiers. Touchstone's well-known statements in *As You Like It*[19] are in point, though we need not hold Shakespeare responsible for them. Michael Drayton in the introductory sonnet to his sequence *Idea* makes the following remarks:

To the Reader of These Sonnets

Into these Loves, who but for Passion looks;
   At this first sight, here let him lay them by,
   And seek elsewhere in turning other books,
   Which better may his labour satisfy.

16But see T. Cibber's *Lives of the Poets,* 2nd ed., 1753, I. 202-211. There is no life of Donne in Johnson's *Lives of the Poets*; but see his *Life of Cowley.*

17See the remarks on Donne in A. Burnett, *Specimens of English Prose Writers* (1807), I. 402-414.

18Ed. 1679, p. 426.

19III, iii, 19, 20, "The truest poetry is the most feigning." Cf. Sidney, *Apologie for Poesie,* ed. Cook, pp. 35, 36.

> No far-fetched sigh shall ever wound my breast;
> Love from mine eye a tear shall never wring;
> Nor in "Ah me's!" my whining sonnets drest
> A libertine! fantasticly I sing!
>   My verse is the true image of my mind,
> Ever in motion, still desiring change;
> And as thus, to variety inclined,
> So in all humours sportively I range!
>   My Muse is rightly of the English strain,
>   That cannot long one fashion entertain.[20]

Francis Bacon in his essay *Of Truth* and in *The Advancement of Learning*[21] comes out flatly with the statement that all poets are liars; because they never represent things as they are but as either better or worse than they are. Donne himself, writing to Sir Robert Ker (or Carr) remarks, ". . . you know my uttermost when it was best, and even then I did best where I had least truth as it defeats all Poetry."[22]

My argument versus the traditional view that Donne translated a vicious life into bawdy poetry has so far brought forward two sorts of evidence—a passage from Sir Richard Baker on Donne's early life and character and passages from several writers, including Donne himself, on the relation between fact and poetry. In view of these facts and considerations it seems to me rather naive in a critic to assume that he can argue from the kind of poems a man writes to the kind of life he lives. Browning's *How It Strikes a Contemporary* presents some rather telling comments on the situation. In fact, the psychology of literary composition and indeed of creative art in general[23] is a subject that still, I think, could stand a good deal of research on it. If Gosse had been writing of Donne a little later, he might have interpreted his poems as wishful living rather than as transcripts of accomplished facts. I am inclined to think, moreover, that the traditional view of the relation between Donne's life and his poetry is further belied by Donne's

---

[20]See *Daniel's Delia and Drayton's Idea*, ed. Arundell Esdaile, King's Classics Series, London Constable & Co., 1908, p. 67.

[21]See the passages quoted in Spingarn, *Critical Essays of the Seventeenth Century*, I, 5-7, and Spingarn's notes.

[22]Quoted by G. R. Potter in *John Donne's Discovery of Himself* in *U. of Cal. Essays in Criticism*, Second Series, U. of Cal. Press, Berkeley, 1934, p. 9.

[23]Consider the controversies regarding autobiographical phases of Byron's *Manfred*; the opium scenes in Charlotte Bronte's *Villette* (see Mrs. Gaskell, *Life of Charlotte Bronte*, Everyman ed., p. 386); the uproar in France over Zola's naturalistic novels. And see F. C. Prescott, *The Poetic Mind*, (The Macmillan Co., 1922), *passim*; and Agnes M. Mackenzie, *The Process of Literature* (George Allen and Unwin, 1929), *passim*. See also E. M. W. Tillyard and C. S. Lewis, *The Personal Heresy*, Oxford University Press, 1939, *passim*.

own theory of poetry. He apparently was nauseated by the conventional current poetry.[24]

A comparison of Donne's poetry with that of his contemporaries will disclose the differentiae of his verse. The most obvious of these are: no euphuism; very sparing use of conventional figures of speech; little use of classical mythology; a resolute refusal to adopt the conventional poetic virtues; e.g., whereas most of his fellow poets glorified constancy in love, he sings the praises of inconstancy. He throws overboard the whole Petrarchan technique and apparently resolved as a poet to be himself, as he advised his friend Woodward to do in morals and as he advises all men to do in religion. So far as his verse technique is concerned he went so far that Ben Jonson, who thought highly of Donne as a critic and sent his poems to Donne for criticism, told Drummond of Hawthornden, that Donne was the first poet in the world for some things, but that Donne himself deserved hanging for not keeping accent (i.e., for refusing to follow the conventional standards for polished verse) and that Donne would perish for not being understood.

In the place of the conventional sources of poetic ornament (i.e., classical mythology, Petrarchan or pastoral nature images, euphuistic biology and similes drawn from or modeled on the Greek and Latin classics, inversions of the sentence order and other forms of "poetic license") Donne used materials drawn from contemporary geography and astronomy, from scholastic disputation and renaissance philosophy (Paracelsus and Bruno),[25] and from the useful arts. He wrote a direct and sometimes rough style and his obscurity is due to the multiplicity and the novel and subtle character of his references. His contemporary Drummond of Hawthornden wrote probably of him as follows:

It is more praiseworthy in noble and excellent things to know something, though little, than in mean and ignoble matters to have a perfect knowledge. Amongst all those rare ornaments of the mind of Man *Poesie* hath had a most eminent place and been in high esteem, not only at one time, and in one climate, but during all times and through those parts of the world where any ray of humanity and civility hath shined. So that she hath not unworthily deserved the name of the Mistress of human life, the height of eloquence, the quintessence of knowledge, the loud trumpet of Fame, the language of the Gods. There is not anything endureth longer: Homer's Troy hath outlived many Republics, and both the Roman and Grecian Monarchies; she subsisteth by herself, and after one demeanor and continuance her beauty appeareth to all ages. In vain have some men of late (transformers of everything) consulted

---

[24]See Satire II, Everyman *Donne*, p. 111, and the verse letter to Rowland Woodward, *ibid.*, p. 139.

[25]Cf. the passage from *An Anatomy of the World*, Everyman *Donne*, p. 182.

upon her reformation, and endeavoured to abstract her to metaphysical ideas and scholastic quiddities, denuding her of her own habits, and those ornaments with which she hath amused the world some thousand years. *Poesie* is not a thing that is in the finding and search, or which may be otherwise found out, being already condescended upon by all nations, and as it were established *iure gentium* amongst Greeks, Romans, Italians, French, Spaniards. Neither do I think that a good piece of *Poesie* which Homer, Virgil, Ovid, Petrarch, Bartas, Ronsard, Boscan, Garcilasso (if they were alive and had that language) could not understand, and reach the sense of the writer.[26]

Donne, then, apparently had resolved to be different[27] from his coevals in his poetic theory and practice. If, now, Donne wished to write a narrative poem involving a love story, what lines would he follow? Isn't it likely that, as his contemporaries were prevailingly romantic, he would be what we call realistic? That where they idealized the chivalric and courtly virtues in love (e.g., constancy, reserve, etc.), he would do the opposite? I think the answer to these questions is "Yes." Consider his lyrics that imply a love story and his elegies that embody one or more and I think you will find confirmation of the above answer. Gosse bases his theory on his interpretation of these poems and has overlooked the fact that the poems fit perfectly into Donne's poetic canon as contrasts to the conventional love poems of the day. Gosse gives away his hand where he admits that the strongest argument he can find for his diagnosis of Donne is that the oftener he runs over the poems the more vivid and sincere (i.e., transcriptual of facts) they seem—a purely subjective sort of evidence. As a final argument, however, he asks, "Why, if these poems are not autobiographic, was Donne so anxious, after he became Dean of St. Paul's, to recall and destroy them?"[28]

[26]Quoted in *Oxford Lectures on Literature*, 1908-1922, p. 4. So far as I know Donne indulged only once in parody of a contemporary; but this one effort is very telling. Compare his poem *The Bait* with Marlowe, *The Passionate Shepherd to His Love* and Raleigh, *The Nymph's Reply*.

[27]That Donne was different, and designedly so, from his contemporaries, is clearly brought out in Carew's *An Elegy upon the Death of Dr. Donne, Dean of Paul's* in The Muses' Library Carew, p. 100.

[28]Walton in his *Life of Donne* (Saintsbury's ed. in the Oxford World Classics, p. 34) apparently suggests in the "irregularities" mentioned there some basis for Gosse's theory. But these "irregularities" might have to do with Donne's relations with Sir Robert Drury. Jonson thought Donne's *Progress of the Soul* was "prophane and full of blasphemies," see *Drummond's Conversations with Jonson*, ed. Patterson, p. 5. Gosse's article on Donne in the *Encyclopaedia Britannica*, 11th ed. (1889), has no suggestion of the theory expressed in *The Life and Letters of John Donne* (1898). Sir Herbert J. C. Grierson in his 1912 ed. of Donne's poetry seems to accept Gosse's theory but in his 1929 ed. Grierson is not so sure of it. Hugh I. Anson Fausset bases his *John Donne: a Study in Discord* (Harcourt, Brace and Co., 1924) on Gosse's theory. R. Balfour Daniels in his *Some Seventeenth Century Worthies* (The University of North Carolina Press, 1940) says, p. 64, "Perhaps Izaac Walton's *Life of Donne* touches too lightly upon the great Dean's dissolute

The reason is obvious. Take the parallel case of Zola. When it was learned that Zola after all was a rather puritanical sort of person and not the person who lived the sort of life described in his novels, some critics maintained that these very facts showed that Zola was an even worse kind of man; for a man who would deliberately, in cold blood so to speak, write the kind of thing Zola wrote, must be a lower grade person than the one who was merely writing of his actual adventures. Donne was nothing if not critical and I think he saw that he was in for censure whether his surviving poems were interpreted as autobiographical or otherwise. Donne of course, since the time of Samuel Johnson's *Lives of the Poets* (1779-81), has been known as the leader of a group of 17th century poets called the metaphysical poets.[29] These poets were so called, not because their poems set forth a philosophical system or expounded a synoptic view of life and the world in its deepest aspects, but because apparently they set out to make men think, to shake them free of conventional practice in literary art, and because in pursuit of these ends, they were willing even to shock them.

Gosse's theory, as I said earlier in this paper, may be true but, in view of the facts and considerations herein set forth, unless more and better evidence for it is forthcoming, is properly denominated *The Myth of John Donne the Rake*.

---

youth.'' On p. 71 Mr. Daniels inquires regarding Carew and Donne, ''Was it not the writing of verses that started them on their wild careers?'' These remarks imply the acceptance of the Gosse theory.

[29]See Johnson's *Life of Cowley*, the background of the term *metaphysical* in Dryden and Walton's *Elegy on Donne* and the references to the articles of Professor A. H. Nethercot, note 15, *supra*.

A PROTEST AGAINST THE TERM *CONCEIT*

By George Reuben Potter
University of California

Literary criticism is not an exact science; and most of its terms have meanings which are vague about the edges. Some terms, however, are vaguer than others. The meanings of *didactic* and *simile* are pretty clearly defined. Those of *tragic* and *lyric* are not clearly defined at all. The only thing of which a reader can be sure when he sees one of the latter two terms used in print is that the writer is trying to convey a certain emotional attitude that the reader has also felt.

The noun *conceit*, however, as applied to a poetic figure—a term used frequently enough in critical writing to be called common—is in a worse state still. When a writer uses it today, his readers can tell neither the precise concept he has in mind nor his emotional attitude toward the poetic figure he is naming; not, that is, unless he defines his term at the time he uses it.

Conceit in the sense of "a conception, an idea" was commonly used in English as early as the fourteenth century; and in the sense of "the power of conceiving or of understanding" as early as the fifteenth.[1] The word became applied to poetry as Englishmen began to be critically conscious of the art, in the latter sixteenth century. By the end of that century, a newer, more specialized meaning of the word came into existence, taken from the Italian *concetto*. Mario Praz, in his recently published *Studies in Seventeenth-Century Imagery*,[2] has clarified greatly our understanding of this term, as it was used in Italy and Spain during that period, by showing its close relations to the "emblems" and "devices" that were tremendously popular at the time, and by quoting many times from writers of those years who themselves discussed the subject. He quotes, for example, Gracián's definition of the term in *Agudeza y*

---

[1] See *NED*.

[2] Originally published in Italian, Milan, 1934, under the title *Studi sul Concettismo*. English version published in London by The Warburg Institute, 1939.

Arte de Ingenio (1649) :[3] "It is an act of the understanding which expresses the correspondence which is found between objects." And again, "Understanding without wit or conceits is a sun without light or rays. . . . What beauty is to the eyes and harmony is to the ears, the conceit is to the understanding."[4]

A *concetto* was, in short, a symbolic or imaginative comparison, especially one used in poetry. The enthusiasm which Italian and Spanish writers showed for *concetti,* as well as for emblems, is, it seems fairly evident, a sign that they were discovering the value—a twentieth-century critic would say, the necessity—of poetry's expressing ideas and feelings through images and symbols.

Englishmen attracted to things Italian naturally came across the word, and used it in referring to their own countrymen's poetic comparisons. The Italian meaning was, however, close enough to the older English sense of the term so that English writers were when using it not at first clearly conscious of a distinction. When Sidney wrote[5] of "This purifying of wit, this enriching of memory, enabling of judgment, and enlarging of conceit, which commonly we call learning," he obviously meant by *conceit* "the power of understanding." When later in the same famous essay he referred to the Puritans as saying that "the comedies rather teach than reprehend amorous conceits," the meaning of the word is a little less certain; but without much question he still was thinking of "ideas" or "notions." When Ben Jonson[6] wrote of literary grace as yielding "a pleasure to the conceit of the reader," he meant obviously "understanding," "mind." When, however, he urges young writers to "seek the best, and be not glad of the forward conceits, or first words, that offer themselves to us," and when he says, "The conceits of the mind are pictures of things, and the tongue is the interpreter of those pictures," we cannot be quite so sure. Probably Jonson even in these latter sentences did not have poetic imagery specifically in mind. Henry Peacham, however, while his meaning is still a little doubtful, seems to have used the word in a sense closer to the Italian when he wrote[7] of Chaucer's verse that "As under a bitter and rough rind there lieth a delicate

---

[3]Baltazar Gracián y Morales, 1601-165∂. See Mario Praz: *Studies in Seventeenth-Century Imagery* (London, 1939), I, 24.

[4]Praz, *op. cit.,* p. 18.

[5]In his *Defence of Poesie.*

[6]In *Timber: or Discoveries.*

[7]In his *Compleat Gentleman,* 1622, 1634; Chapt. X, "Of Poetry."

kernel of conceit and sweet invention." And Sir William Alexander, in 1634,[8] is clearly thinking of the term in its restricted sense:

> I compare a poem to a garden, the disposing of the parts of the one to the several walks of the other; the decorum kept in descriptions and representing of persons, to the proportions and distances to be observed in such things as are planted therein; and the variety of invention to the diversity of flowers thereof; whereof three sorts do chiefly please me: a grave sentence, by which the judgment may be bettered; a witty conceit, which doth harmoniously delight the spirits; and a generous rapture expressing magnanimity, whereby the mind may be inflamed for great things.

The English writers of the earlier seventeenth century who most often used the term in its restricted sense were, naturally enough, those in the group headed by Donne, who were attracted to the striking poetic comparisons in the verse of southern Europe. Most members of the group tended also—as did their Italian and Spanish predecessors—to fix their attention upon the beauty or the cleverness of a poetic comparison, or upon the unusual and witty connection which the comparison might have with its object, rather than upon the usefulness of that comparison to the main course of thought in the poem. Hence *conceit* came to bear the connotation of "a strikingly beautiful, clever, or ingenious poetic comparison," sometimes simply *any* striking or clever idea whether a comparison or not.

The connotation of the term in these latter two senses, among the writers who liked and worked with such comparisons, was entirely favorable. But the danger of thus emphasizing striking poetic comparisons is clear enough: the process leads to an over-emphasis on the details at the expense of the whole; and, when carried on by weaker heads, it leads to the search after clever comparisons for their own sake, to artificial, conscious writing in which the comparisons are present only because they are—or are thought to be—pretty, clever, or unusual, not because they illuminate any central thought or feeling in the poem. Plenty of critics during the seventeenth century, especially during the latter part of it, saw this danger, and believed that not only Donne's weaker imitators but even Donne himself had fallen into this sort of artificiality. *Conceit* came then to have in the minds of Dryden and his contemporaries a depreciatory connotation. A conceit was not *any* idea, or any poetic comparison, or even any striking poetic com-

---

[8] In his *Anacrisis*. Printed in J. E. Spingarn's *Critical Essays of the Seventeenth Century*.

parison, but a poetic comparison that was artificial, conscious, strained, or far-fetched. Donne's images were still called conceits, but the word became a term of reproach.

"The vulgar judges," said Dryden, "which are nine parts in ten of all nations, who call conceits and jingles, wit, who see Ovid full of them, and Chaucer altogether without them, will think me little less than mad for preferring the Englishman to the Roman. Yet, with their leave, I must presume to say, that the things they admire are only glittering trifles, and so far from being witty, that in a serious poem they are nauseous, because they are unnatural."[9]

Pope wrote,

> Some to Conceit alone their taste confine,
> And glitt'ring thoughts struck out at ev'ry line;
> Pleased with a work where nothing's just or fit;
> One glaring chaos and wild heap of wit.[10]

Dr. Johnson defined the word in his dictionary as "Opinion, generally in a sense of contempt; fancy; imagination; fantastical notion."

Gradually, down through the eighteenth and nineteenth centuries, this use of *conceit* to brand a poetic comparison as obtrusive, artificial, far-fetched, or not completely fused with the main idea of the poem in which it appeared, became more firmly established; until by the first decades of our own century it had become a decidedly useful word for criticism, a term universally understood to be one of reproach. If a poet referred to the sun rising over a mountainous horizon as an egg breaking on the edge of a bowl, critics might disagree as to whether the metaphor was a conceit, but if any critic called it that, he knew he was damning it, and his readers understood that he was. The fact that this depreciatory sense of the term was firmly established in the earlier years of our century, and has by no means lost all its force even now, appears clearly from the various standard dictionaries. The original definition in the *N.E.D.* dates from 1891; but it appears in the 1933 edition, and no new sense is given to the word in the *Supplement* of that edition: "A fanciful, ingenious, or witty notion or expression; now applied disparagingly to a strained or far-fetched turn of thought, figure, etc., an affectation of thought or style; = concetto."[11]

---

[9]*Preface to The Fables.*

[10]*Essay on Criticism.*

[11]*The Shorter Oxford English Dictionary* of 1933 makes no change in this definition, simply abridges it slightly.

The Century Dictionary (1891-1913) is similarly clear: "A witty, happy, or ingenious thought or expression; a quaint or humorous fancy; wit; humor; ingenuity; especially, in modern usage, a quaint or odd thought; a thought or expression intended to be striking or poetical, but rather far-fetched, insipid, or pedantic."[12]

Later dictionaries are somewhat vaguer, but still emphasize the depreciatory connotation. *The Universal Dictionary* (1932) has: "Fanciful and rather trivial idea or notion; a quaint, humorous, or witty fancy." Funk and Wagnalls' *New Standard Dictionary* of 1940 is very vague as to the application of the term to literature: "A fantastic notion or fanciful idea. . . . A quaint or humorous fancy; clever thought or expression." Webster's Unabridged of 1940 is a little more definite, but less so than the *N.E.D.* and the *Century Dictionary*: "A fanciful, odd, or extravagant notion; variously; a quaint, artificial, or affected conception, or a witty thought or turn of expression; a whim, quip, or trick."

The conventional connotation of the term during the first two decades of the century was, then, decidedly derogatory. Even during those years, however, there was some uncertainty about the word; and in 1917 Raymond M. Alden, feeling this uncertainty, tried to re-define it. His two thought-provoking articles on the subject (the second published in 1920)[13] are significant for two reasons: first, fortunately, because they were a pioneer effort to defend Donne's highly intellectualized poetic comparisons as serious and genuine art, and this renewed recognition of Donne's importance has now become so nearly universal that it will probably be permanent; second, less fortunately, because they began a series of re-definitions of *conceit* which have reduced its former clear connotations to confusion.

Alden started by saying, "I have often used the term 'conceit' with the secret wish that I knew what I really meant by it." He objected to definitions such as that in the *N.E.D.* because in his opinion "the statements amount practically to the doctrine that a conceit is a poor metaphor, and to use the term in this way leads to no useful end." The present writer does not agree with Alden

---

[12] *The New Century Dictionary* of 1927 abridges the definition but makes no essential change: "A fanciful thought, idea, or turn of words, esp. of strained or far-fetched nature."

[13] "The Lyrical Conceit of the Elizabethans," *SP*, XIV (1917), 129ff; "The Lyrical Conceits of the 'Metaphysical Poets,'" *SP*, XVII (1920), 183ff.

here—surely if a term could be generally understood as denoting the sort of poetic comparison which is poor because it is obtrusive or artificial, the use of that term *would* lead to a useful end; no terms are more useful than clear terms of condemnation. But to return to Alden—after rejecting the *N.E.D.*'s definition, he evolved his own working definition for the word by attempting "to inquire what the process of composition may be which we find producing certain characteristic effects in the verse of given types or periods, and thus to arrive inductively at *something* which deserves a characteristic name." The definition which Alden evolved by following the above process reads as follows: "A conceit is the elaboration of a verbal or an imaginative figure, or the substitution of a logical for an imaginative figure, with so considerable a use of an intellectual process as to take precedence, at least for the moment, of the normal poetic process."

The definition, considered as an attempt to put in critical terms the distinguishing characteristics of certain sorts of Elizabethan imagery, especially the comparisons in Donne's verse, marks a decided step forward in our understanding of poetry in that period. It has, however, at least two marked weaknesses, into which Alden fell because he deliberately tied himself and his analysis to the term *conceit*. He failed to make clear—though he tried to do so—the precise nature of "the normal poetic process"; and, more important, he slipped into the very doubtful position of thinking that this "something" which he termed the "conceit" is true poetry but at the same time abnormal. He still, that is, held more or less consciously to the feeling that if he called a poetic image a conceit he was thereby marking it off from the images of normal poetry. During the decades since Alden wrote his articles it has become increasingly evident that the sort of poetic process he tried to describe is not abnormal at all, but entirely normal—that the various sorts of poetic imagery which he classified as "verbal conceits," "imaginative conceits," and "logical conceits" are, when successfully made part of a genuine poem, simply different varieties of the "normal poetic process."

The fortunate effect of Alden's articles was that they stimulated other scholars to work more intensively toward an understanding of the sort of imagery that he classed as "logical conceits"—the intellectualized imagery, that is, of Chapman, Donne, and the seventeenth-century writers who have come to be called the "metaphysical poets.'' But the unfortunate effect of the articles was that they led most of these later writers to continue calling such intellectualized images, even when wholly successful in poetry, ''conceits,''and thus led to successive attempts at re-defining *the term* which have obliterated its former clear depreciatory connotations, have twisted its meaning into something far more specialized than that in which any Elizabethan or seventeenth-century critic would have used it, and have thus led to confusion.

The writers who have used the word ''conceit'' most frequently in the past two decades have been the critics of Donne. They have concerned themselves almost exclusively with the particular sort of poetic comparison which appeared in Donne's poems and those of his followers; and they usually qualify their use of the term by an adjective—writing of ''the metaphysical conceit'' or ''the Donne conceit.'' They sometimes tend, however, to identify *conceit* with ''metaphysical conceit,'' thus leading many less careful readers to think of the term *conceit* itself as applying only to the sort of comparison found in Donne. Four such writers are George Williamson, Cleanth Brooks, Robert L. Sharp, and F. O. Matthiessen.[14] Williamson gives an excellently clear exposition of Donne's poetic imagery. Others are not so clear. Sharp, for example, seems frequently to use *conceit* in the sense of any ingenious or witty simile or metaphor, sometimes qualifies his use by connecting the term with a ''far-fetched'' idea (proceeding to defend as sometimes good poetry ideas that are far-fetched, and leaving a reader helpless to understand what then is the connotation of ''far-fetched'' itself!), and sometimes restricting the term as Williamson does.[15] Incidentally, T. S. Eliot, the most famous of these newer critics of Donne, uses *conceit* seldom, and then in a much less restricted sense. ''Distended metaphors and similes'' is as near as he comes to defining himself in his best-known essay on the ''metaphysical'' poets;[16] and his statement in a later essay[17] is but little more restricted, and

---

14Williamson, *The Donne Tradition*, Cambridge (Mass.), 1930; Brooks, ''A Note on Symbol and Conceit,'' *American Review*, III (1934), 201ff; Sharp, ''Observations on Metaphysical Imagery,'' *Sewanee Review*, XLIII (1935), 464ff., and *From Donne to Dryden*, Chapel Hill, 1940; Matthiessen, *The Achievement of T. S. Eliot*, London, 1935, 1939.

15Sharp's uncertainty in the use of *conceit* is observable in both his article and his book.

16''The Metaphysical Poets,'' *Homage to John Dryden*, London, 1924.

17''Donne in Our Time,'' *A Garland for John Donne*, ed. Theodore Spencer, Cambridge (Mass.), 1931.

implies something very close to the formerly conventional depreciatory use of the term: "The conceit itself is primarily an eccentricity of imagery, the far-fetched association of the dissimilar, or the overelaboration of one metaphor or simile."

Other writers, too, have continued to use the term with more or less derogatory implications; for example, Herbert Read, Kathleen Lea, Elisha Kane, and W. P. Ker.[18] Such writers seem, however, a good deal less certain of their ground than earlier writers have been. Kathleen Lea, for example, admits that the Elizabethan conceit "failed,"[19] but nevertheless defends it as a natural product of an excited imagination, and as frequently created in earnest. Ker makes various distinctions, which are far from clear, between "false" and "true" conceits in poetry.[20]

Other critics have consciously tried to define the term as the Elizabethans used it. Louis Untermeyer does this cautiously in his book *The Forms of Poetry*:[21] "Conceit. In the literary sense, a conceit is a witty conception or ingenious thought; a diverting or highly fanciful idea. A brief piece of imaginative writing which is neither too flippant nor too profound is often referred to as 'a happy conceit.' The Elizabethans were particularly fond of these playfully conceived inventions."

Esther C. Dunn, in her book *The Literature of Shakespeare's England*,[22] insists that *conceit* meant to the Elizabethans simply *any* of "the qualities in the realm of non-action which may be named *imagination* or *fancy*." This definition is, it may be noted, in contrast to attempts such as those by Ker and Sharp to limit *conceit* to something fanciful and *not* imaginative—though both of these last writers emphasize the difficulty in drawing a sharp line between those two Coleridgean qualities.

Still other critics use the term with no definition either stated or implied.[23] And, finally, an increasing number, including some of

---

[18]Read, "The Nature of Metaphysical Poetry," *Criterion*, I (1923), 246ff; Lea, "Conceits," in *MLR.* xx (1925), 389ff; Kane, *Gongorism and the Golden Age*, Chapel Hill, 1928; Ker, *Form and Style in Poetry*, London, 1928.

[19]Lea, *op. cit.*, p. 389.

[20]Ker, *op. cit.*, pp. 145, 259-263.

[21]New York, 1933, p. 8.

[22]New York, 1936, pp. 161-162.

[23]A recent example of such an undefined use is that of H. F. Fletcher in the new Cambridge *Milton*, (1941) p. 71, referring to Milton's verses on Hobson: "Both poems are a succession of quips, puns, and 'metaphysical' conceits."

our best critics. when writing of poetry avoid the term entirely.   J.
L. Lowes, J. M. Murry, John Sparrow, and E. M. W. Tillyard[24]
have all found it possible, and evidently advisable, to write about
the style of poetry without using *conceit* at all.

From this badly confused state of affairs, several reasonable conclusions can be drawn.   First, it seems clear that the various attempts to clarify criticism by re-defining more accurately the term
conceit are not succeeding in their purpose.   Writers agree less than
they did twenty years ago as to what they mean when they use the
word.   Second, it seems equally clear that the more serious attempts by critics of the school of Donne to define *conceit* or *metaphysical conceit* are valuable not because they define *the term* more
satisfactorily, but because they increase our understanding and appreciation of Donne's poetry itself.   Third, it is extremely unlikely
that an Elizabethan who used the word had in mind any of the
more subtle distinctions which these recent critics are trying to
make between a poetic comparison which is a conceit and one which
is not.

As a matter of fact, while English poetry itself flourished greatly
in the late sixteenth and early seventeenth centuries, the analysis
and criticism of that poetry was only in its beginnings.   Nobody then
thought it worth while to analyse poetic imagery in order to determine the precise relation of a simile or metaphor to its object, or
the exact artistic effect of one sort of poetic comparison as distinguished from another.   It is only in the past twenty years that
we have made serious attempts at this sort of analysis; and we have
not progressed very far yet towards any complete and universally
satisfactory results.

What is really needed at present is more balanced work on *all*
the varieties of poetic imagery, not more attempts to separate one
sort from the rest.   Henry W. Wells some twenty years ago,[25] by
his description of what he called "the radical image" and his distinctions between that and other sorts of imagery common among
Elizabethan writers, shed more light on the precise nature of
Donne's comparisons than has any one of the re-definers of *conceit*;

---

[24]Lowes, *Convention and Revolt in Poetry*, Boston and New York, 1919;
Murry, *The Problem of Style*, London and New York, 1922; Sparrow, *Sense
and Poetry*, New Haven, 1934; Tillyard, *Poetry Direct and Oblique*, London,
1934.

[25]Wells, *Poetic Imagery Illustrated from Elizabethan Literature*, New York,
1924. Wells states in his Preface that he wrote the book in 1918.

and he did so because instead of bothering about older terms and their definitions, he tried to analyse and classify poetic images as such, and worked out new terms for newly perceived relationships. Some just fault has been found with his term "the radical image" and his explanation of it;[26] but it was brilliantly conceived, nevertheless; and so were one or two of his other terms, such as "the sunken image." His treatise was only a start at the clear, comprehensive classification of poetic imagery which we badly need and do not yet have; but it was a start in the right direction.

Doubtless historians of literature will have to continue making reference to *conceit* as a word which was used by the Elizabethans to refer to a striking poetic comparison. But to go on using the word as a part of *our own* critical terminology, re-defining as we go, will lead us nowhere except into more confusion. Several of our best reasoners about style are avoiding the term. In the name of our beloved mistress Poetry, why cannot we all stop using it? Why cannot we also stop treating poetic imagery like Donne's as if it were pathological? It has been abundantly proved not to be so. Finally, why cannot we try more clear-headedly than we have thus far to understand how many varieties of imagery poets need and employ, in making us see the strange lands which they discover beyond those well-travelled highways that are paved with our conventional diction?

---

[26]See, for example, J. B. Douds, "Donne's Technique of Dissonance," *PMLA*, LII (1937), 1051ff.

THE THEME OF PRE-EXISTENCE AND INFANCY IN
THE RETREATE

By MERRITT Y. HUGHES
University of Wisconsin

For some years interest in Vaughan's poetry has been divided
between the attraction of his treatment of childhood for modern
readers and the curiosity of scholars about the origins of "the doctrine hinted at in *The Retreate,* of a sinless pre-existent state, which
the child in some sort remembers and in some degree inherits."[1]
Those who, like Professor Martin in his essay on "Henry Vaughan
and the Theme of Infancy," are concerned with the background
of the poem, have admired its 'Wordsworthian' feeling for childish
innocence in part because they have found its tap-root in Hermetic
and Rabbinic literature.[2] So keen has been the search for Cabbalistic influence upon Vaughan's imagination, and so uncritical the
sympathy with his treatment of childhood that we have not stopped
to ponder the evidence for its esoteric origin. Most readers accept
the value put upon his treatment of infancy in Mr. Edmund Blunden's book *On the Poems of Henry Vaughan,* and most scholars
accept the position of Miss Elizabeth Holmes in her study of *Henry
Vaughan and the Hermetic Philosophy*[3] and of Mr. R. M. Wardle[4]
in his investigation of the influence of Thomas Vaughan, "the most
interesting figure in the Hermetic literature of the seventeenth
century in England."[5] upon his brother. Miss Holmes's critics may
not acknowledge that she has contributed to our appreciation of
Vaughan's poetry, but they almost all recognize that she has made

---

[1] L. C. Martin. "Henry Vaughan and the Theme of Infancy." *Seventeenth
Century Studies Presented to Sir Herbert Grierson.* Oxford, 1938, p. 246.

[2] Professor Martin is familiar with the doubt raised by Miss Helen N. Mc-
Master ("Vaughan and Wordsworth," *RES,* July, 1935.) and others about the
evidence for the influence of *The Retreate* on *Intimations of Immortality.* The
main interest in his essay is his proof that other channels than Vaughan's
poetry brought the surmise that "We lived, ere yet this robe of flesh we
wore" to Coleridge (in his sonnet on Hartley's birth) and to Wordsworth.

[3] Oxford, 1932.

[4] "Thomas Vaughan's Influence upon Henry Vaughan". *PMLA,* LI (1936),
936-952.

[5] Arthur E. Waite in his Introduction to *The Works of Thomas Vaughan:
Eugenius Philalethes.* London, 1919, p. xxv.

"a knowledge of the elements of Hermetic philosophy . . . necessary for the appreciation of Vaughan."[6]

The exact relation of Henry Vaughan and even of as tiny a fragment of his mind as we have in *The Retreate* to Hermetic and Cabbalistic thought cannot be determined, but we can at least chart his position at the confluence of many streams of speculation about the origin of the soul—oriental, Greek and Roman, medieval, and contemporary—in the Renaissance. At the outset we can discount the fanatical Cabbalism of the harshest of Miss Holmes's reviewers, Mr. Edouard Roditi.[7] Condescending to her "fundamental ignorance of occultism," he deplores the incompleteness of her analysis of the "so-called Hermeticism which was vulgarized by Pico, Sebonde, Weigel and Drexelius," and which "transmuted the dull lead of theoretic scholasticism into living gold of Cartesian, Spinozist or Leibnitzian idealism." Without an equipment of oriental languages Mr. Roditi implies that Vaughan's debt to Thrice-great Hermes and the Cabbala cannot be studied; but we may recall that Vaughan himself was no orientalist, that his Oxford training seems to have given him only "sufficient Latinity to find his chief reading, outside his professional studies and contemporary poetry, in the fathers of the church,"[8] and that—as Mr. Wilson Clough points out in the most judicious of all studies of Vaughan's 'Hermeticism'[9] —he derived much of it from Cornelius Agrippa and Paracelsus. Mr. Clough concludes that "Vaughan was . . . poet first, and Hermeticist, if at all, only by a temperamental attraction to the mystic view of man and of nature."[10]

The opening reference in *The Retreate* to this world as

this place
Appointed for my second race,

seems to say plainly that—at least by an act of poetic faith— Vaughan accepted the idea that he had left a conscious antenatal life for this one. Throughout the first twenty lines runs an implication of the perfect moral beauty of that former life, memories

---

[6] *The Times Literary Supplement* review, October 12, 1932, p. 724.

[7] In *The Spectator*, CXLIX, 211.

[8] Rev. F. E. Hutchinson in "The Sacred Poets," *Cambridge History of English Literature*, Cambridge, 1933, VII, 43.

[9] "Henry Vaughan and the Hermetic Philosophy," *PMLA*, XLVIII, 1108-1130. In this study Mr. Clough acknowledges indebtedness to Professor A. C. Judson's "Cornelius Agrippa and Henry Vaughan", *MLN*, XLI, 178-181.

[10] *Ibid.*, p. 1129.

of which still haunted his "Angell-infancy." "Shadows of eternity" give the poem its glory, but pre-existence is so treated that the imaginative rather than the philosophical value of the idea is uppermost. The key image in the poem is the lines:

> But felt through all this fleshly dresse
> Bright *shootes* of everlastingnesse.

Upon our interpretation of these two lines and upon the undertones of reminiscence that we find there our appreciation of the poem depends. For their background Professor Martin sends us[11] to Owen Feltham's Resolve *Of the Soul,* where we find the image of *"a shoot of everlastingness."*[12] The language is not precisely Vaughan's, nor may the thought be quite the same as his. Most readers of *The Retreate* who are familiar with Thomas Vaughan's work will associate the lines with his Hermetic image in *Anthroposophia Theomagica:* "Man in his original was a branch planted in God."[13] Or they may associate Henry's image with Thomas' notion that "the Land of the Living . . . buds and sprouts, hath her fiery spiritual flowers, which we call souls."[14] Feltham's context, however, indicates that the origin of "Bright *shootes* of everlastingnesse" is classical, not Hermetic:

> Cicero is there *divine* where he says, *Credo Deum immortalem sparsisse animos in humana corpora*: and where he says again, *Mihi quidem nunquam persuaderi potuit, Animos, dum in corporibus essent mortalibus, vivere: cum exissent ex iis, emori: I could never think souls to live in mortal bodies, to die when they depart them. Seneca does raise it higher, and asks, Quid aliud voces hunc, quam Deum, in corpore humano hospitantem? What other canst thou term it, but a God, Inning in the flesh of man?*[15]

In sending us to the classics Feltham surely indicates the main literary tradition behind Vaughan's image. If now we take leave of the more esoteric influences upon *The Retreate,* we need not share Mr. T. S. Eliot's contempt for those who "have professed to discover in Vaughan the traces of an Hermetic philosophy of profound depths", or agree with him that, if it is there, "it belongs

---

[11]*The Works of Henry Vaughan,* edited by L. C. Martin, Oxford, 1914. I, 283.

[12]*Resolves: Divine, Moral, Political.* By Owen Feltham. 11th ed., London, 1696, p. 89.

[13]*The Works of Thomas Vaughan,* edited by A. E. Waite, p. 10.

[14]*Ibid.,* p. 297.

[15]The first allusion is to Cicero's *De senectute,* xxi, where he pleads for the Pythagorean and Platonic doctrine of the soul's reminiscence of truth that it has known in a life before birth, and the second allusion is also to that context. Seneca's passage occurs both in *Epistles* 31 and *De Vita beata,* 23.

not to literature but to cryptography."[16] Neither need we accept
his verdict that "The mystical element in Vaughan . . . is 'mysticism' only by a not uncommon extension of the term." The fact
will prove to be that by examining Vaughan's classical and medieval
backgrounds we can relate *The Retreate* to Christian theology definitely enough to set our fears of his mystical unorthodoxy at rest.
Finally it may prove possible to correct a common prejudice against
Vaughan's treatment of the theme of infancy which is put very
sternly in Mr. Eliot's review of Mr. Blunden's book:

> Wordsworth's Ode is a supreme piece of verbiage, and Vaughan's poem is
> a sincere statement of feeling. But Mr. Blunden's praise of this poem, and
> praise of this sort of poetry which is reminiscent of childhood and its imagined
> radiance, is significant of the weakness of both Vaughan and Blunden.

Most readers of *The Retreate* take Vaughan's belief in pre-
existence for granted, and perhaps there are few who would
question Mr. Kenneth Winterbottom's dogmatic assertion that
"Vaughan . . . clearly explains the intuitions of childhood by assuming them to be intuitions of a former life."[17] Yet nowhere else
is Vaughan more definite in suggesting a doctrine of pre-existence
than he is in this poem. Elsewhere he is less definite about it than
he is about his faith in the resurrection of the body—a belief which
is not easily reconcilable with that in a pre-incarnate life, but which
is the core of such poems as *Resurrection and Immortality, The
Evening Watch,* and *Burial.* One of his most characteristic utterances about a former life occurs significantly invol.ed with his
most definite assertion about the body's resurrection:

> Nor are those births which we
> Thus suffering see
> Destroy'd at all; But when times restles wave
> Their substance doth deprave
> And the more noble *Essence* finds his house
> Sickly, and loose,
> He, ever young, doth wing
> Unto that spring,
> And *source* of spirits, where he takes his lot
> Till time no more shall rot
> His passive Cottage: which (though laid aside)
> Like some spruce Bride,
> Shall one day rise, and cloath'd with shining light
> All pure, and bright

---

[16] T. S. Eliot's review of Edmund Blunden's *On the Poems of Henry
Vaughan: Characteristics and Imitations* (London, 1927.) in *The Dial,* LXXXIII,
260.

[17] Kenneth M. Winterbottom. *Certain Affinities to Wordsworth in the Poetry
of Vaughan and Traherne.* Unpublished M. A. thesis of the University of
Pittsburg, 1933, p. 49.

Remarry to the soule, for 'tis most plaine
Thou only fal'st to be refin'd againe.[18]

While declaring the resurrection in *Eastern Hymn* and *The Sap*
Vaughan turns aside to assert the doctrine of original sin, and in
the latter poem he flatly addresses the soul as thou "who in the
first mans loyns didst fal."[19] The soul's first birth is "not from
dust" because, says Vaughan, of its "growth and stretch for
heav'n"—not because of any nostalgia for a "shady city of palm
trees" remembered from its ante-natal life. The yearning of the
soul for God, "who is its home," is easy to mistake for evidence
of that pre-existence which Wordsworth said that his *Intimations
of Immortality* did not assume.[20] That yearning is everywhere in
Vaughan's work,[21] as Lionel Johnson remembered when he ended
his essay on "Henry Vaughan, Silurist" with the lines:

O Father of eternal life, and all
Created glories under thee!
Resume thy spirit from this world of thrall
Into true liberty.[22]

Nostalgic though Vaughan's longing for the life to come was, however, it never crystallized into a statement of Platonic belief in pre-
existence any more definite than that which is traditionally read
into *The Retreate*.

In his moments of conscious orthodoxy—and Vaughan's nostalgic
longing for reunion with God is the root of Christian orthodoxy—
he is likely to have thought of all souls as created at the moment
of the birth of the body. That "men have their souls by creation"
was a view which Richard Hooker thought might be considered
"probable and not unlikely to be true," although he put the question among those "matters divine" about which "we may lawfully

---

[18]*The Works of Henry Vaughan*, II, 401-402. *Resurrection and Immortality*.
[19]*Ibid.*, p. 475.

[20]Wordsworth, says Professor Arthur Beatty, was "interested in establishing
this . . . visionary quality of the experience of childhood, and not in establishing the doctrine of pre-existence." *Wordsworth. Representative Poems*, New
York, 1937, p. 661.

[21]As it is much more explicitly in the faith of the more definitely Platonic
Drummond of Hawthornden that "pure and virgin souls" may look backward
as well as forward to "the place of their rest, for this world is their inn, and
not their home." *A Cyprus Grove. The Poems of William Drummond of
Hawthornden*, edited by William C. Ward, London, 1894. II, 257.

[22]In *Post Liminium: Essays and Critical Papers* by Lionel Johnson, London,
1912, p. 276. The essay was first published in *The Daily Chronicle* in December,
1896. The passage occurs in Vaughan's *Ascension-Hymn, Works*, II, 484.

doubt and suspend our judgment.''[23] To the Dissenter, Richard Baxter, the idea of the soul's pre-existence seemed to be familiar, but he thought of it as an opinion of the minority and stigmatized it as ''an unproved imagination of men's own brains.''[24] In his *Dying Thoughts* he found comfort in a bleak denial that the soul is ''a *radius* of the *anima mundi vel systematis*,'' and that before birth ''it did intellectually animate *hunc mundum, vel mundi partem*.'' We think of Calvin, who, though he did not entirely repudiate the doctrine of the soul's moral reminiscence of God, yet warned against the conception that it is ''un surgeon de Dieu.''[25] Baxter was sympathetic enough with those who thought that ''the soul, as vegetative, is an igneous body, such as we call ether, or solar fire, or rather of a higher, purer kind; and that sensation and intellection are those formal qualities which specifically difference it from inferior fire or ether''[26] to provoke the Bishop of Dromore, George Rust, to attack him as no less of a 'psychopyrist'—and therefore a materialist in his conception of the soul—than Dr. Henry More himself.[27] In spite of all that More could do philosophically and poetically too, in *The Praeexistence of the Soul*, to convince men of his belief, the majority clung stubbornly to the orthodox view of the Church as St. Thomas delivered it in the *Summa Theologica*:

Cum Deus primas res instituerit in perfecto statu suae naturae; anima autem, quae est pars humanae naturae, non habeat naturalem perfectionem nisi secundum quod est corpori unita; dicendum est animam humanam non esse productam ante corpus.[28]

[23]Richard Hooker. *Of the Laws of Ecclesiastical Polity*, Books I to IV. Everyman, London, 1903 and 1925, p. 269.

[24]*Select Practical Writings of Richard Baxter*, edited by Leonard Bacon. New Haven, 1844, p. 106.

[25]Calvin's conviction of original sin, although he admitted (*Institutes*, I, iii, p. 24) that the most hardened sinners had a trace of God's ''divinité imprimée aux coeurs,'' was hostile to imagery resembling Vaughan's ''*shootes of everlastingnesse*.'' ''Or la creation n'est point une transfusion, comme si on tiroit le vin d'un vaisseau en une bouteille, mais c'est donner origine à quelque essence qui n'estoit point; et combien que Dieu donne l'esprit, et puis le retire à soy, ce n'est pas à dire pourtant qu'il le coupe de sa substance comme une branche d'arbre.'' *Institutes*, I, xv. *Institution de la Religion Chretienne* par Jean Calvin, edited by Frank Baumgartner. Geneva, 1888, p. 87.

[26]*Writings of Richard Baxter*, p. 64.

[27]Joseph Glanvill. *Two Choice and Useful Treatises: The One Lux Orientalis, or An Enquiry into the Opinion of the Eastern Sages Concerning the Praeexistence of Souls. The other, A Discourse of Truth*, By the late Reverend Dr. Rust, Lord Bishop of Dromore in Ireland. London, 1682. (Rust's) *Annotations upon the Foregoing Treatises*, pp. 192-194.

[28]*Summa Theologica S. Thomae Aquinatis*, edited by De Rubeis, Belluart and others, Turin, 1927, I, 595. Pars prima, Quaestio XC, Article iv. Marsilio

The glory of God, it was felt, demanded that the act of creation out of nothing or out of the dust of the earth should be performed fresh every day at the birth of every human being. As John Donne phrased it, repeating a formula of St. Augustine, *Creando infundit, infundendo creat.*[29]

Typically humanistic Protestant theology defined the soul as Melancthon did in the *De anima*, quoting Aristotle, as something divine infused from without the body. Melancthon reviewed the Stoic conception of the soul as an essence of celestial fire and the Platonic view of it as a charioteer in a vehicle of flesh, but he warned against such speculations and was content with the formula: "quod vita, sensus, racionatio et electio ostendunt, esse in nobis animas, et esse eis insitas noticias . . quae testantur, et esse Deum, et animas ab ipso conditas esse."[30] He liked the biblical image of the soul as something breathed into man by the breath of God; he called it *spiraculum*; and, confusing his images in a way that suggests Vaughan's "*shootes* of everlastingnesse," he described God as transfusing his "light, wisdom, and even mathematical and ethical knowledge" into the newly inbreathed soul.[31]

No one can fully understand the hold of the doctrine that souls are individually created at birth in the seventeenth century unless he follows it into the natural philosophy of that time. As in.the nineteenth and twentieth centuries, theology found support in 'science.' The great danger was, of course, the disturbing denials of the possibility of the soul's existence apart from the body by men like Epicurus and Lucretius and, in more modern times, the great Italian, Pietro Pomponazzi. The Lucretian position had been challengingly reviewed by Montaigne in the *Apology for Raimond Sebond*. Against the Platonic doctrine of pre-existence he brought Lucretius' question about the soul:

Ficino reconciled this dogma with Platonic pre-existence by declaring that God conceives all souls from all eternity, but gives them being (parit) at the various times of the births of their respective bodies. "Creat igitur assidue animas hominum." Marsilii Ficini *Opera*, Paris, 1641, I, 394, 1. *Theologia Platonica*, Liber XVIII, iii.

[29]Quoted by Itrat Husain. *The Dogmatic and Mystical Theology of John Donne*, London, 1938, p. 81. Compare Charles M. Coffin. *John Donne and the New Philosophy*, New York, 1937, pp. 47-48.

[30]Philippi Melancthonis *Opera quae supersunt omnia*, edited by Charles Gottlieb Bretschneider. Halle, 1846. *Corpus Reformatorum*, XIII, 18.

[31]Adflatur hominibus anima foris, et tale spiraculum est, in quod Deus transfudit suae lucis, ut ita dicam, radios, videlicet suam sapientiam, noticias numerorum, discrimen honestorum, et alias noticias." *Ibid.*, pp. 15-16.

si in corpus nascentibus insinuatur,
Cur super anteactam aetatem meminisse nequimus,
Nec vestigia gestarum rerum ulla tenemus?[32]

And he went on to suggest that, because the soul is impotent at
birth and often lapses into impotence in old age, its life is bound
up with the body's. More confidently Pomponazzi, with his un-
matched command of Arabian Aristotelianism and his critical mastery of the thought of St. Thomas, although he was no crude materialist, questioned whether the soul could "exist in a disembodied
state,"[33] either before birth or after death.

In reply to men like Pomponazzi and his disciples[34] orthodox
theology consolidated its defence by reaffirming the miracle of the
soul's birth with the body. The great position to maintain—and
by far the more tenable one—was that of the soul's survival of the
body's death. On that problem men worked with a perhaps unconscious desire to compensate for the fading of the old Platonic
myth of the descent of the soul from a region where it saw the
blessed gods in the heavens[35] by asserting an even more certain
future for it beyond the grave. This is the position of Sir Kenelm
Digby in *Of Bodies, and of Mans Soul. To Discover the Immortality
of Reasonable Souls.* Beginning with the stubborn facts of em-
bryology, he states what is essentially the orthodox theological
doctrine that "of necessity, the Soul must be begun, lay'd, hatch'd,
and perfected in the Body."[36] Yet he no less confidently affirmed
the soul's immortality and final self-fulfilment beyond the confines
of the body. The antipathy between his position and the traditional
Platonic one comes out clearly in his challenge to "the Platonick
Philosophers (who are persuaded that a humane Soul doth not
profit in this life, nor acquire any knowledge here, as being of herself compleatly perfect; and that all our discoursings are but her

---

[32]Michel de Montaigne. *Essais,* edited by Jean Plattard, Paris, 1931. Livre
second, Premier volume, p. 318. The Lucretian reference is Book III, lines 671-
673.

[33]Andrew H. Douglas. *The Philosophy and Psychology of Pietro Pomponazzi,* Cambridge, 1910, p. 56.

[34]Francesco Vicomercato, as Mr. George T. Buckley points out (*Atheism
in the English Renaissance,* Chicago, 1932, p. 27), disseminated the influence
of the *Tractatus de Immortalitate Animae* in Paris from 1542 to 1567, and
was followed by men like Des Perriers, Rabelais and Jerome Cardan.

[35]*Phaedrus,* 246-247.

[36]*Of Bodies, of Mans Soul. To Discover the Immortality of Reasonable
Souls. With Two Discourses Of the Power of Sympathy, and Of the Vegetation
of Plants.* By Sir Kenelm Digby, Knight. London, 1669. Chapter XI, p. 114.
Digby's death occurred in 1665.

rememberings of what she had forgotten).''[37] They would, he believed,

find themselves ill bestead, to render a Philosophical and sufficient cause of her being lock'd into a Body. For, to put forgetfulness in a pure Spirit (so manifest an effect of corporeity,—so great a corruption, in respect of a creature whose nature it is to know it self) is an unsufferable error.[38]

Digby may not have been representative of his medically trained contemporaries, but he was not an eccentric. Sir Thomas Browne similarly balanced his belief that ''the souls of men . . subsist beyond the body, and outlive death by the priviledge of their proper natures, and without a Miracle''[39] against the solution of the thorny question of pre-existence by ''that *Antimetathesis* of *Augustine*, *Creando infunditur, infundendo* creatur.''[40] Much as he was attracted by the possibility of the soul's pre-existence, Browne was confident only of '' a piece of Divinity in us, something that was before the Elements, and owes no homage unto the Sun.''[41] But his vision has no Platonic clarity, and when he says that Nature tells him that he is ''the Image of God, as well as Scripture,'' we hear the naturalist's voice as clearly as the theologian's. Browne was incapable of such faith in the ''sensible communion'' of the soul ''with God and his holy Angels, . . before it falls into this Terrestrial Region'' as Henry More expressed in the *Defence of the Philosophick Cabbala*, II, 19, which openly invokes Plato's winged soul and vision of preincarnate life in the *Phaedrus*.[42]

Nearly forty years ago, when Professor Harrison wrote his study of *Platonism in English Poetry*,[43] it was possible to accept without qualification the over-simplified statement that ''the idea which Vaughan carries over into his own poetry is found in Plato's account in the *Phaedrus* of the pre-existence of the soul in a world

---

[37]*Ibid.*, p. 85.

[38]*Ibid.*, p. 102.

[39]*Religio Medici*, I, xxxvii. *The Works of Sir Thomas Browne*, edited by Charles Sayle, Edinburgh, 1927; I, 55.

[40]*Ibid.*, chapter xxxvi, p. 53.

[41]*Ibid.*, Book II, chapter xi, p. 105.

[42]In general the Cambridge Platonists accepted the pre-existence of the soul, but Culverwell (as Ferris Greenslet indicates, *Joseph Glanvill*, New York, 1900, p. 29.) ''rejects absolutely the doctrine of innate ideas through reminiscence,'' and ''criticizes Lord Brook's presentation of that doctrine very acutely.''

[43]John Smith Harrison. *Platonism in English Poetry of the Sixteenth and Seventeenth Centuries.* New York, 1903.

of pure ideas before its descent into the body.''[44] In Vaughan's poetry however—in his exaltation of the body's resurrection and his faith in original sin—and in the theological and philosophical opposition of his contemporaries to the doctrine of pre-existence we have found reason to qualify Professor Harrison's view. By deliberately Platonizing poets like Spenser that doctrine had been vaguely reconciled with Christian dogma as we find it in the *Hymne of Beautie*—

> the soule, the which deriued was
> At first, out of that great immortall Spright,
> By whom all liue to loue, whilom did pas
> Downe from the top of purest heauens hight,
> To be embodied here.[45]

But Vaughan shows no trace of the conscious syncretism which Spenser inherited from the Florentine Neo-Platonists. Unlike Spenser's, Vaughan's poem was not written to affirm the soul's pre-existence or direct derivation from God. *The Retreate* is less outspokenly Platonic than the *Hymne*. Is it possible that one key to that difference is to be found in the development of Plato's doctrine of pre-existence which we have now to notice?

If Vaughan was interested in pre-existence from theological points of view, he may have been led by his attachment to the church fathers to think about it in terms of the theory which Origen developed early in the second century, and which Bishop Rust was to try to popularize again in his *Letter Concerning Origen* eleven years after the publication of *Silex Scintillans*. The several Platonic arguments for the soul's transcendence of generation which Origen adduced in support of his view that all spirits are ''an Essence capable of eternal existence''[46] and that ''the souls of men do prae-exist''[47] need not detain us here. The point in Origen's thought which may arrest us because it challenged Vaughan's conception of the soul as a child coming celestially innocent into life is his transfer of original sin from earth to heaven. Justice, as Rust explains, requires that men must have sinned in heaven, or how else explain their descent to earth? ''We all become . . . *terrestrial*

---

[44]Harrison, *Platonism*, p. 203.

[45]Lines 106-110. *Daphnaida and Other Poems by Edmund Spenser*, edited by R. W. Renwick. London, 1929, p. 131.

[46]*A Letter of Resolution Concerning Origen and the chief of his Opinions*, by George Rust. Reproduced from the edition of 1661 with a bibliographical note by Marjorie Nicolson. New York, 1933, p. 24.

[47]*Ibid.*, p. 21.

men by sin," he wrote, "but since we are such from our first coming into this world, and the fault must needs be before the conse-
quents of it, that sin and transgression by which we became such
must be look'd for higher or in some former state."[48]

In Rust's eyes and in those of Joseph Glanvill, who wrote more
ambitiously than Rust did in defence of *The Praeexistence of
Souls*,[49] the transfer of man's first sin to higher worlds was a welcome solution of the problem of the justice of God's ways to man
in this world. A retributive extension of the Platonic myth of the
soul which loses its wings and falls into a mortal body and a retributive emphasis upon the Platonic metaphor of the body as the
prison of the soul, might explain the abandonment of whole nations
to ignorance and superstition by Providence. In this way incarnation came to be regarded—as Cyril of Alexandria is said to have
regarded it—as a punishment for the pre-existent and sinful soul.[50]
The purity of the child at birth, which is assumed in Vaughan's
Retreate, was unthinkable in the theory of pre-existence which Glanvill and Rust inherited from Origen.

At every point Origen's conception of pre-existence conflicts with
Vaughan's. When Glanvill writes that "the Soul in its *first* and
pure nature hath no *idiosyncrasies*, that is, no *proper* natural inclinations which are not competent to others of the same kind and
condition,"[51] he seems to be on the verge of an idea like that in
the first lines of *The Retreate*—the coming of the new-born soul
into a world which it cannot understand. At once, however, he
reverses the thought by asking how it happens that we come into
the world with such strong propensities to evil as we bring with us:

And therefore since we find this determination to one or other falsehood in
many, . . and since 'tis very unlikely 'tis derived *only* from the *body, custom,*
or *education,* what can we conceave on't, but that our Souls were tainted with
these *peculiar* and *wrong corruptions* before we were *extant* upon this *stage
of Earth!*[52]

Unlike Vaughan, Glanvill felt the shadow of heresy upon his
conception of the soul's pre-existence. The last words in *Lux
Orientalis* are an act of submission to the authority of his church

---

[48]*Ibid.,* p. 52.

[49]*Lux Orientalis,* the first of *Two Choice and Useful Treatises* mentioned in
note 27 *supra.*

[50]Cited without reference by Robert Sencourt, *Outflying Philosophy.* London, 1925, p. 230.

[51]*Lux Orientalis,* p. 78.

[52]*Ibid.,* pp. 78-79.

and "to the maturer judgments of graver and wiser men." Perhaps he feared the ridicule of shrewd readers hardly less than he did the bigotry of the orthodox. Although he liked to think that his argument would stand by its own intrinsic strength, he regretted its lack of Scriptural support. In his fourth chapter he denied the need of such authority, violently forced the argument from Scriptural silence on the matter, wrenched a few insignificant passages to support his theory, and finally fell back upon 'the Rabbins.' His most striking quotation from them is important because, although it might have been used like the three Talmudic passages which Professor Martin cites as representative of that influence in *The Retreate,* and as illustrative of the principle that "The Rabbins emphasize untiringly the spotless purity of the new-born babe,"[53] Glanvill applied his quotation in reverse as evidence for the capacity of the pre-incarnate soul to sin. He quoted the "*Author* of the Book of *Wisdom,* who certainly was a *Jew,* probably *Philo,*" and who "plainly supposeth the same Doctrine in that Speech, *For I was a witty Child, and had a good Spirit, wherefore the rather being good, I came into a body undefiled.*"[54]

Glanvill's only impressive Scriptural proof of pre-existence is an interesting interpretation of Job 38, 7. In his fourth chapter he first mentions it as having been used in the *Conjectura Cabbalistica* by that "great *Restorer* of the *antient Cabbala,* the Learned Dr. H. More,"[55] to prove the creation of all souls and spirits at the foundation of the world. In his eleventh chapter he returns to the passage, surmising that in Job "God himself . . seems to intimate somewhat of his purpose, viz. that all *spirits* were in being when the *Foundations* of the *earth* were laid; when saith he, *the morning stars sang together, and all the Sons of God shouted for joy.*"[56] The words recall the flight in Sir Thomas Browne's *Christian Morals :*

Where we were when the foundations of the earth were lay'd, when the morning Stars sang together, and all the Sons of God shouted for Joy, He must answer who asked it; who understands Entities of preordination, and beings yet unbeing; who hath in his Intellect the Ideal Existences of things, and Entities before their Extances. Though it looks but like an imaginary kind of existency to be before we are; yet since we are under the decree or pre-

---

[53]Quoted from Abelson's *The Immanence of God in Rabbinical Literature,* p. 281, by L. C. Martin in *Seventeenth Century Studies,* p. 248.

[54]*Lux Orientalis,* p. 41.

[55]*Ibid.,* p. 38.

[56]*Ibid.,* pp. 84-85.

science of a sure and Omnipotent Power, it may be somewhat more than a non-entity to be in that mind, unto which all things are present.[57]

Browne concludes by noting the possibility of interpreting the verse from Job in Glanvill's way, but his retreat into God's fore-knowledge attenuates the interpretation so as to destroy its force as evidence for Glanvill's belief in the chequered pre-existence of all souls. Vaughan's recollection of the same Scripture in *The Day-spring* to crown his mood of worship on a walk at dawn takes us into an emotional experience very different from the speculative temper in which Browne and Glanvill leave us:

> But *mornings* new Creations are,
> When men all night sav'd by his Care,
> Are still reviv'd; and well he may
> Expect them grateful with the day.
> So for the first *drawght* of his hand,
> Which finish'd heav'n and sea and land,
> The *Sons* of God their thanks did bring,
> And all the *Morning-stars* did sing.[58]

If Vaughan thought of himself as having sung with all created spirits on the first cosmic morning, we can at least be sure that he regarded himself as untainted at birth by any original sin except Adam's, and as having come to earth trailing clouds of glory.

In Vaughan's translation of the Jesuit Johannes Eusebius Nieremburgeus' *Of Life and Death* there is one fugitive passage, insignificant in itself, which proves that he was not ignorant of the twist given by Origen to the Platonic myth of the descent of the soul. Johannes explains the banishment of souls from the 'Empyreal light' on what he regards as Platonic grounds, and in consequence betrays a dread of "the suspension of Reason in Infants, and the *hallucinations* of Childhood."[59] In its main channels of transmission, however, the myth of the descent of the soul to earth represented it as bringing its heavenly splendor to the threshold of incarnation and losing it on contact with the body. So Petrarch imagines St. Augustine as revealing his own origin to him. "Listen!" he imagines the saint as saying to him in their dialogue:[60] "Listen! It was from Heaven your soul came forth; never will I assert a lower origin than that. But in its contact with the flesh,

---

[57]Part II, xxv. *Works*, edited by Sayle, III, 505-506.

[58]*Works of Henry Vaughan*, II, 643-644.

[59]*Ibid.*, I, 10.

[60]*Petrarch's Secret*: or, the soul's conflict with passion. Three dialogues between himself and S. Augustine, translated by William H. Draper. London, 1911, p. 41.

wherein it is imprisoned, it has lost much of its first splendor. Have no doubt of this in your mind.'' In Ficino's *Platonic Theology* the third essence, the home of the rational souls which, when incarnated, endow their bodies with life, is a refulgent realm of splendor and fertility.[61] Elsewhere, describing the descent of souls, Ficino refused[62] to speculate like some of his disciples about the excursions of descending spirits among the planets, but—in language which suggests both Vaughan's *"shootes* of everlastingnesse''* and the opening of *The World*—he gave his voice for the instantaneous descent of the soul like the rays of the sun, which take color from the clouds on their way to earth:

Descensus huiusmodi ita fermè subito potest fieri, ut radii descensus a Sole, qui quamvis subito demittatur in terram, variis tamen in ipso casu nubium vestitur coloribus.[63]

In metaphors like these of Ficino and in the Neo-Platonic and Stoic conceptions of the soul as sprung from a super-celestial fire which was closely bound up, if not identical with God himself, we may look for the remoter origins of Vaughan's

Bright *shootes* of everlastingnesse.

Popular theology liked to go back to the classics for such conceptions of the soul, and it liked to confirm them out of Scripture, the Talmud, and even the great medieval Arabian philosophers, as did Pierre Charron, that barometer of all that was theologically correct in France in the late sixteenth century, at least among lay readers. His conclusion from the gamut of polyglot authorities was that the soul may be ''a substance still more subtil and purify'd than even the Ætherial and Cœlestial itself.''[64] To Guez de Balzac, writing not far from the time when Vaughan was at work on *Silex Scintillans,* it seemed that ''l'Ame de l'homme est un feu inextinguible & Perpetuel; qu'elle est originaire du Ciel; que c'est une

---

[61]Prior enim in divinis vita est quam splendor, quoniam splendor eorum est tum reflexio, tum effusio vitae. Quapropter inde prius manat in animam vitae immortalis ubertas, quam divinarum splendor imaginum. *Theologia Platonica,* Liber v, xv. Ficini *Opera,* I, 148, 2.

[62]Nonnulli vero putant animas in qualibet sphaera ad certum tempus vitam agere sphaerae illi convenientem. . . Nos autem in omnibus quae scribimus, eatenus affirmari a nobis aliisque volumus, quatenus Christianorum Theologorum concilio videatur. *Ibid.,* Liber xviii, v. P. 396, 1.

[63]Liber xviii, v. P. 396, 1.

[64]*Of Wisdom.* Three Books. Written originally in French by the Sieur de Charron. Made English by George Stanhope. Third Edition. London, 1739. I, 55.

partie de Dieu mesme."[65] What charm such speculations had even
for Dissenting clergymen we have seen in Baxter's case. Their hold
upon thinkers of poetic temper is best indicated by Henry More's
diatribe on the fiery home and nature of the soul in the opening
stanzas of *The Praexistency.* Vaughan may never have listened to
More or to any of the other voices whose echoes we have just heard,
but he was of their society. Even if he was not familiar with
More's most concrete expression of his vision of the fiery soul of
man—

> This is that nimble, quick, vivacious Orb
> All ear, all eye, with rayes round shining bright,
> Sphear of pure sense which no perpessions curb,
> Nor uncouth shapen Spectres ever can disturb.[66]

it would have been characteristic of him to condense that conception
of the soul's vivacity and serenity into the single metaphor,

> Bright *shootes* of everlastingnesse.

Behind that figure is the entire tradition of Christianized Platonism
and Stoicism which Henry More reinterpreted, but which had previously been directly shaped toward Vaughan's embodiment of it
in that image by the Biblical tradition which Melancthon fused
with the classical in the *De anima.*

Whatever the provenience of Vaughan's thought in *The Retreate,*
we may be confident that the nostalgia for a lost beauty which
inspired the poem is not puerile. Some modern criticism has in-
jected puerility into it, but that fact does not justify Mr. T. S.
Eliot in the inference that Vaughan shared the sentimental attachment of certain twentieth century poets for childhood. The psychic
infirmity with which Mr. Eliot charges him is, from the historical
point of view, almost as recent a phenomenon on the spiritual scene
as is its diagnosis by Freud. There is no more of it in *The Retreate*
and *Childe-hood* than there is in the words of Jesus to which those
poems finally go back: "Verily I say unto you, Except ye be converted and become as little children, ye shall not enter into the
kingdom of heaven."[67] If, like Renan, we choose to do so, we may

---

[65] *Socrate Chretien,* par le Sr de Balzac, et Autres Oeuvres du mesme Auteur.
Rouen, 1661, p. 9.

[66] *The Praeexistency of the Soul,* stanzas 14, 6-9.

[67] Matthew 18, 3.

regard Christ's teaching as fundamentally an appeal to men's craving for escape from a complex world, but that is hardly Mr. Eliot's view of it, nor should it be our view of its reflection in *The Retreate*.

Vaughan's treatment of the theme of childhood should be judged in comparison with its treatment by his contemporaries. It is no less adult than Traherne's.[68] Both men valued their "pure and virgin apprehensions . . . from the womb," and "that divine light wherewith" they were "born" because, as Traherne put it, they had found them "the best unto this day, wherein" they could "see the universe."[69] It was not a desire to return to childhood which sent Henry More back to the "Pure and Ætherial sort of Touch and Sensibility he was then under,"[70] or made George Fox say, with characteristic consciousness of his own precocity in realizing how 'happy those early days': "When I came to the age of eleven, I knew pureness and righteousness."[71] Mr. Leishman puts the right interpretation on *The Retreate* when he says that it is a vision of "the Creation as God intended all men to look upon it, as a glorious thing, the garment of God."[72] This does not mean that the poem should be read as a classic of 'nature mysticism' or 'natural religion.' It should be read as the work of a poet who, though he may have been as deficient as one of his most sympathetic interpreters says that he was in experience of "the central core of . . . developed mysticism,"[73] was no less mature in his outlook upon childhood than the best of his contemporaries. *The Retreate* is a supremely poetic statement about childhood in relation to the soul's possible pre-existence and certain divine origin. It fully corresponded to the best intellectual as well as poetical position of its time upon a matter which then naturally seemed more theological than psychological. "Nous ressemblons," wrote

[68]Miss Gladys I. Wade ("Thomas Traherne as 'Divine Philosopher,'" in *Hibbert Journal*, XXXII, 400-408) makes a good case for Traherne's mastery of the best formal philosophy of the seventeenth century.

[69]Quoted by E. N. S. Thompson in "The Philosophy of Thomas Traherne," *PQ*, VIII, p. 98.

[70]Quoted by Geoffrey Bullock in his Introduction to *Philosophical Poems of Henry More*. Manchester, 1931, p. xiii.

[71]*George Fox; An Autobiography*, edited by Rufus Jones. Philadelphia, 1919, p. 26.

[72]J. B. Leishman. *The Metaphysical Poets, Donne, Herbert, Vaughan, Traherne*. Oxford, 1934, p. 166.

[73]Helen C. White. *The Metaphysical Poets. A Study in Religious Experience*. New York, 1936, p. 305.

Guillaume du Vair, first president of the Parlement of Provence and one time French ambassador to the court of Queen Elizabeth, at the head of his treatise on *La Saincte Philosophie,* in language which clearly strikes Vaughan's note: "Nous ressemblons à ceux qui en leur plus tendre jeunesse estans menez captifs en quelque lointaine contrée, perdent auec le temps la memoire de leur pays, l'usage de leur langue, & l'amitié de leurs parens."[74] Du Vair and many practical men of the Renaissance had set the example for Vaughan's century of regarding philosophy as simply the study of the art of making the kind of retreat from evil which Vaughan had in mind when he chose his title for his poem.

---

[74]*La Saincte Philosophie avec plusieurs traictez de pieté.* Par G. Du Vair. Paris, 1618. p. 1, recto.

A NOTE ON TWO WORDS IN MILTON'S *HISTORY OF MOSCOVIA*

By HARRIS FLETCHER

University of Illinois

Milton's *History of Moscovia,* turned over to the printer 'sometime before his death,' has been prepared for print and published eleven different times;[1] but has never been annotated except for Milton's reference notes appearing in the margins of the first and all subsequent editions. It is a very brief work, occupying only [vi] + 109 small pages set in large type in the first edition, and but 55 of the generous Columbia pages in the latest printing of it; but a few words in it really need explaining. Two of these will baffle most readers completely, and no reference work will help very much to explain them. The first is the word *Cursemay,* in the following passage:

. . . in every good Town there is a drunken Tavern, call'd a *Cursemay,* which the Emperour either lets out to farm, or bestows on some Duke, or Gentleman in reward of his Service;[2] . . .

The entire passage in which this statement occurs is taken, as Milton's marginal note points out, from Hakluyt (margin reads, *Hac.* 314.) and reads therein as follows:

In every good towne there is a drunken Taverne called a Cursemay, which the Emperour sometime letteth out to farme, & sometimes bestoweth for a yeare or two on some duke or gentleman, in recompense of his service:[3] . . .

---

[1] Separately printed in the first edition of 1682, in London, by M. Flesher for Brabazon Aylmer; 1694 (1697) in John Toland's edition of the prose; 1738, in Thomas Birch's edition of the prose; 1753 in the second edition of Birch's editing; 1806, in the edition of the prose edited by Charles Symmons; 1833, in the edition of the prose edited by Robert Fletcher; 1845, in the two volume edition of most of the prose, edited by Rufus W. Griswold, published at Philadelphia; 1848, the prose in 5 vols. edited by J. A. St. John (Bohn); 1851, John Mitford's edition of prose and poetry; 1929, D. S. Mirsky, London: The Blackamore Press, the only separate printing since the first edition; 1932, in vol. 10 of the Columbia edition, edited by G. P. Krapp. This volume in the Columbia is exceedingly ill-starred; not even the pasted leather label is correct on any of the three copies available to me.

[2] *Columbia* ed., x, 338. Lines 3-6.

[3] *The Principal Navigations, Voyages, Traffiques, & Discoveries of the English Nation.* 1598. I quote fom the edition of Glasgow, 1903. 12 vols. II, 424. The account Milton was using is the 'first voyage made by Master Anthonie Jenkinson, . . . 1557.'

The word 'Cursemay' is unknown, apparently, to English lexicographers. It occurs in no English dictionary so far as I have been able to determine. There is no particular reason why it should so occur, although Hakluyt and Milton together would seem to be important enough writers to have all their words included in some, if not all English dictionaries. The word is either a highly corrupt and inaccurate transliteration of the Russian word for a 'drunken tavern'; or it is an accurate transliteration of a Russian form that has changed since the sixteenth century. It is at least akin in the Hakluyt-Milton form to a Russian word that means a hovel-like building, frequented by low persons, or by ordinary persons for low purposes. It was apparently applied originally to a peasant's hut containing an oven with no chimney, and constantly therefore filled with smoke. The Russian stem transliterated *kyr-* in certain compounds has such a meaning.[4] But no Russian word seems to have been the exact original of the form 'Cursemay' in Hakluyt, and how the word originated in Hakluyt's passage is not clear. It was almost certainly transliterated from a collateral word **korqmā,** the Russian word used as long ago as the 16th century and still in use today for exactly the kind of inn, tavern, or pot-house mentioned in Hakluyt-Purchas.[5]

Another word in the *History of Moscovia* is, in a way, equally easy to explain, on the one hand, and difficult to account for as Milton used it on the other. He used it and then explained the word at greater length than he did the word 'Cursemay.' It occurs in the following passage:

Riphaean   Touching the *Riphaean* Mountains whence *Tanais* was anciently
Mountains.   thought to spring, our men could hear nothing; but rather that
           the whole Country is Champain, and in the northernmost part huge
           and desert Woods of Firre, abounding with Black Wolves, Bears,
           Buffs,[6] and another Beast call'd Rossomakka, whose Female

---

[4]*Cf.* A. Alexandrow, *Complete Russian-English Dictionary.* 5th edition, Revised and Enlarged. Berlin, n.d. 2 vols.

[5]*Ibid., loc. cit.* I wish to thank [Prince] Zlatoff-Mirsky for confirming the form and meaning of this word.

[6]Buffs: this word offers no difficulties, occurs only here in all Milton's works ('buffe' in *Of Prelatical Episcopacy, Columbia* 3:1:102:24, means 'buffet, cuffing, blow' as in *Samson Agonistes,* 1239), and means a definite kind of animals. It is the same word as 'buffalo,' and is so treated by Edward Phillips, the elder of the two nephews, in his *New World of Words, or A Universal English Dictionary;* 1658, "*Buffe,* a wilde Oxe"; *idem,* 1662; 1678, "*Buffe* or *Buffalo, (Bubalus)* a sort of Beast very frequent in the *East-Indies,* and other parts of *Asia.* It resembles an Ox, most of any other Beast among us, and is by some called a Wild Ox"; 1700, *idem.;* 1706, "*Buff, Buffle,* or *Buffalo,*" [otherwise] *idem.*

> bringeth forth by passing through some narrow place, as between
> two Stakes; and so presseth her Womb to a disburthening.[7]

What did Milton mean by the 'Rossomakka' and whence came the
word? There can be no doubt of his immediate source for it. He
took it, along with the entire passage in which it occurs, as he
pointed out in the margin, from Purchas.[8] It occurs both in
Purchas and in the earlier Hakluyt,[9] the passage in Purchas to
which Milton referred reading as follows:

Riphean hils,   Touching the Riphean Mountaines, whereupon the Snow lyeth
a tale of   continually, and where hence in times past it was thought that
Antiquitie.   Tanais the river did spring, and that the rest of the wonders of
nature, which the Grecians fained and invented of old, were
there to bee seene: our men which lately came from thence,
neither saw them, nor yet have brought home any perfect relation of them, although they remayned there for the space of
three moneths, and had gotten in that time some intelligence of
the language of Moscovie. The whole Countrey is plaine and
champion, and few hils in it: and towards the North, it hath
very large and spacious Woods, wherein is great store of Firre
trees, a wood very necessarie, and fit for the building of houses:
there are also wilde beasts bred in those woods, as Buffes,
Rossomakka, a   Beares, and blacke Wolves, and another kinde unknowen to us,
strange beast.   but called by them Rossomakka: and the nature of the same is
very rare and wonderfull: for when it is great with young, and
ready to bring foorth, it seeketh out some narrow place betweene two stakes, and so going through them, presseth it selfe,
and by that meanes is eased of her burthen, which otherwise
could not bee done.[10]

Milton's use of this passage is noteworthy. Except for the phrase,
meaningless in Milton, 'our men,' his account is bettei written and
clearer, because more compressed, as he stated in his Preface it
would be, than Adams's rambling letter.[11]

But what is the meaning of 'Rossomakka,' this strange beast
with such outlandish parturient habits? It seems obvious that Milton either did not recognize it, or that he trusted entirely to his

---

[7]*Columbia* ed., **x**, 333. Lines 13-21.

[8]Samuel Purchas, *Hakluytus Posthumous, or Purchas His Pilgrimes*. London,
1625-27. 3 vols.

[9]Richard Hakluyt, *The Principal Navigations, etc. op. cit.*, II, 253. There
is almost no difference between Hakluyt and Purchas, Purchas taking his text
from Hakluyt with a few differences in spelling.

[10]Purchas, *op. cit.*, III: 200 [220, as page is misnumbered]. The account
occurs in 'Some additions for better knowledge of this Voyage, [i.e., the Wil-
loughby-Chancellor to the north and northeast, 1553] taken by Clement Adams,
Schoolemaster to the Queene Henshmen, from the mouth of Captaine
Chancelor.' See also *Guloines* in Chancellor's account, p. 213, line 34.

[11]On the treatment of his authorities in the *Hist.*, *cf.* D. S. Mirsky's edition,
London: Blackamore Press, 1929, p. 20.

authority, Purchas. At least there is no indication whatever in the
passage that he was in any way familiar with the Rossomakka. And
it is a difficult beast to identify, with this single occurrence in Milton. No dictionaries in English list the word, and no lexicons in
any language of Milton's day or earlier are acquainted with it. But
it was not entirely unknown to scholars of his time and of even a
century earlier.[12] The earliest appearance of the word 'Rossomakka' in a word-list that I can discover is in the index to Bochart's
Heirozoicon.[15] Bochart lists the beast in his *Index Rerum* as '*Roso-
maccha* hyænæ species Sclavis' and his discussion of the animal occurs under the general heading *De Hyæna*, a very general heading,
indeed, in view of the many strange animals included therein. He
discussed one type of hyena that led him to our beast, the Rossomakka, as follows:

[After dealing with the Hebrew word for a beast named in Jeremiah 12:9 and
elsewhere, and deciding that it was a hyena; then describing its coloration,
Bochart continues] Neque aliter ab *Olao* describuntur eæ hyænarum species in
Septentrione frequentes, quas Sclavi *rosomachas*, Sueci, *Jerf*, Germani *Wilfras*
nominant.[14] [He then continues with a discussion of the various colors of the
animal's coat.]

---

[12]The stakes or trees which the beast was said to use started me on the false
trail of the *alce* (elk), a fascinating animal as described in the ancient
bestiaries and lexicons, which, like the elephant and, in some accounts, the
tragelaphus, cannot bend its knees, and consequently sleeps leaning against
stakes or trees. In some accounts, the female employs stakes or trees during
the process of parturition; but only for support. The *alce* or *macclis* (frequently *machlis*) was well known to the ancients, and hence to the bestiaries
of the Middle Ages and the zoologists of the Renaissance. The forms, *macclis,
machlis, macclia, machia,* suggest the second syllable (*-makka*) of Rossomakka.
But there is no real connection between the two beasts.

[13]Samuel Bochart, *Hierozoicon . . . de Animalibus Scripturæ.* London, 1663.
2 vols. This learned Frenchman (1599-1667) produced this work some time
after he had been at Oxford, and Thomas Roycroft printed it in England. It
was re-edited by Johannis Leusden and printed as the first two vols. of the
three volume *Opera*, Lugduni Batavorum, 1692, very little changed from the first
edition.

[14]Bochart, *op. cit.,* either 1st or 2nd edition, vol. I, col. 837, lines 49ff.
Bochart correctly cites the Russian, Swedish, and German forms of the name
of the beast. Rossomakka, or Rosomakka, or Rossomacha, or Rosomacha, any
or all these forms are direct transliterations of the Russian word that is the
name of the animal known today as the *gulo borealis, gulo luscus,* or, in English, *wolverine, glutton,* or *caracajou.* (Cf. A. Alexandrow, *Complete Russian-
English and English-Russian Dictionary.* St. Petersburg, 1897-99, 2 vols.
Variously reprinted. Both spellings, Rossomakka and Rosomakka, appear
in various printings of this dictionary.) The word *Jerf,* more properly *Järf,*
in Swedish means this animal, and is defined in Swedish-English dictionaries as
gulo borealis, or zool. glutton, wolverine. Bochart erred on the German form;
but not much. The true form is, of course, *Vielfras,* not *Wilfras;* but that is
a very minor error, and in 1663 would not have been regarded as an error at
all. The German word, of course, is the name of the beast we in English call
a *glutton*.

The word 'Rossomakka,' or, to preserve Bochart's form, 'roso-machas,' was, as already stated, duly recorded in the *Index Rerum*. But there is nothing in Bochart to suggest the extraordinary parturient habits of the female. However, the entire passage, properly accredited to Bochart, was included in the second edition (not in the first) of John Jacob Hofmann's *Lexicon Universalis*, printed in two volumes at Basle in 1683 (first edition, Basle, 1677; and a third at Lugduni Batavorum, 1698). This is the first inclusion of the word in an actual lexicon that I know of.

The special nature of this animal, as noted by Milton, came from another source, not from Bochart. Bochart cited his own source for the beast as *Olao*, who is, of course, Olaus Magnus (1490-1558). This writer on the northern countries of Europe, described the beast as follows:

Of the Gulos. Amongst all creatures that are thought to be insatiable in the Northern parts of *Sweden*, the *Gulo* hath his name to be the principall; and in the vulgar tongue they call him *Jerf*, but in the *German* Language *Vielfras*, in the Sclavonish speech Rossamaka, from his much eating; and the made Latin name is *Gulo*; for he is so called from his gluttony. He is as great as a great dog, and his ears and face are like a Cats: his feet and nails are very sharp: his body is hairy with long brown hair, his tail is like the Foxes, but somewhat shorter, but his hair is thicker, and of this they make brave Winter Caps. Wherefore this creature is the most voracious: For when he finds a carcasse, he devours so much, that his body by over-much meat is stretched like a Drum, and finding a streight passage between trees, he presseth between them, that he may discharge his body by violence; and being thus emptied, he returns to the carcasse, and fills himself top full: and then he presseth again through the same narrow passage, and goes back to the carcasse, till he hath devoured it all; and then he hunts eagerly for another. It is supposed that he was created by nature to make men blush, who eat and drink till they spew, and then feed again, eating night and day, as *Mechovita* thinks in his *Sarmatia*, The flesh of this Creature is altogether uselesse for man's food: but his skin is very commodious and pretious. For it is of a white brown black colour, like a damask cloth wrought with many figures; and it shews the more beautiful, as by the Industry of the Artists it is joyn'd with other garments in the likenesse or colour. Princes and great men use this habit in Winter made like Coats; because it quickly breeds heat, and holds it long; and that not onely in *Sweth-land*, and *Gothland*, but in *Germany*, where the rarity of these skins makes them to be more esteemed, when it is prised in Ships among other Merchandise. [There follows a short section *Of honouring strangers with the coverings of these Skins*. And another *Of the way of hunting of Gulo's.*][15]

---

[15]Quoted from the English translation, Olaus Magnus, *A Compendious History of the Goths, Swedes, & Vandals, and Other Northern Nations.* London: J. Streater (to be sold by Humphrey Moseley *et al.*), 1658, pp. 180-181. The dedication, signed J.S.. may indicate that it was translated by Streater. It was originally written in Latin and published as *Historia de gentibus septentrionalibus.* Rome, 1555. The Latin of the passage just quoted in English reads as follows (edition published at Antwerp, 1558, p. 137):
De Gulonibus, Inter omnia animalia, quæ immani voracitate creduntur insatiabilia, Gulo in partibus Suetiæ Setentrionalis præcipuum suscepit nomen, ubi patrio sermon Ierff dicitur, & lingua Germanica Vielfras, Sclauo nice

Here is the original of Milton's creature, the Rossomakka; but the strange habit of pressing between two stakes or trees was originally connected with gluttony in the beast, not with parturition.

Olaus speaks of the didactic remark of Mechovita in the latter's *Sarmatia* concerning the purpose of the beast in creation. The reference is to a work that appeared nearly forty years before that of Olaus, and the account just cited was drawn almost *verbatim* from Mechovita, as Olaus' notice admits. Maciej z Miechowa (d. 1523), Maciej Miechowita, or Mathis von Michaw, or Mechovita, as Olaus styled him, was a Pole or Russian who wrote of Sarmatia, the ancient name of Poland and Russia.[16] Olaus drew heavily on

---

Rossomaka a multa comestione: Latino vero non nisi fictitio, Gulo, videlicet a gulositate appellatur Grossities eius, ut magni canis: aures & facies, velut catti: pedes & ungulae asperrimæ: corpus villosum, & prolixorum pilotum subfuscorum: cauda ut vulpis, licut brevior. sed crinium densiorum: unde optima conficiuntur hyemalia capitum tegumenta. Hoc igitur animal voracissimum est. Reperto nanque cadaure, tantum vorat, ut violento cibo corpus instar tympani exendatur; inuentaque angustia inter arbores, se stringit, ut violentius egerat; sicque extenuatum, reuertitur ad cadauer, & ad summum usque repletur: iterumque se stringit angustia priore, repetitque cadauer, donec eo consumpto, aliud solicita venatione inquirat. Creditur a natura creatum ad ruborem hominum, qui vorando, bibendoque vomunt, redeuntque ad mensam, noctes & dies continuaturi, prout Mechouita in sua Sarmatia opinatur. Caro huius animalis omnino inutilis est ad humanam eacam: sed pellis multum commoda, atque pretiosa. Candet enim fuscata nigredine, instar panni Damasceni, diuersis ornata figuris, atque puchrior in aspectum redditur, quo artificum diligentia & industria, colorum conformitate, in quocunque vestium genere fuerit coadunata: soli Principes & magnates eo indumento tunicarum more confecto, hyemis tempore utuntur: quia calorem adducit citius, & eum diutius seruat inductum: idque non solum in Suetia & Gothia, sed in Germania, ubi raritas harum pellium maiorem sortitur æstimationem, quando nauigijs una cum cæteris mercibus fuerit appretiata.

[16]Maciej z Miechowa, or Miechowita, *Tractatus de duabus Sarmatiis Asiana et Europiana et de contentis in eis.* Auguste Vindelecorum, 1518. Also, translated into German by J. Meyer von Eck, Augspurg, 1518. It was included in *Novus orbis regionum ac insularum veteribus incognitarum, etc.* [Edited by S.G. (i.e., Simon Grynæus) from materials collected by J. Huttichius.] Basle, 1532. I have only the German of this, *Die New Welt, der landschaftén unnd Insulen, etc.,* Strassburg, 1534. On folio 153r, begins "Mathis von Michaw von den Sarmatien in Asia/ und Europa gelegen." The work is in two books. Book 2, chapter 3, "Von der grösse des grossen Hertzogthumbs der Lithaw/ unnd was darinnen begryffen wurdt." Folio 163r, C reads, "Inn Lithaw und Moscouiten ist ein unnutz thier/ das findt man sunst nicht/ das nennen sie Rosomacka/ inn grösse als ein hundt/ am angesicht wie ein katz von leib und schwantz wie eyn fuchs/ von farben gantz schwartz. Dat frisset schelmen und keyben. Und so es ein ass findt/ so frisset es so viel/ das es sich blehet wie ein baucken. Darnach sücht es eyn enge zwyschen zweyen beumen/ do tringt es sich mit gewalt inn/ das es dazu gefressen mit gewalt wider von im geb. Wann es dann lehr wurdt/ so laufft es wider zu der ass/ und fullt sich widerumb/ das treibt es noch einander mit fressen und scheissen/ bis es den keyben odder schelmen gar gefressen hatt: Und ist villeicht das fressig thier inn dem landt darumb geschaffen/ das es die fressigen menschen straffe. Dann so die gewaltigen an heben zu prassen/ so sitzen sie von mittag an/ bis zu

Mechovita for his account of the beast.   Here is the earlist occurrence in print that I can find of the word 'Rossomakka.'   Note how
Olaus has added to Mechovita's Russian beast, the Rossomakka, the
Swedish and German names for the creature.   From this account,
it is now clear as to what the beast actually was, and is.   It is the
glutton, or wolverine (*gulo borealis,* or *gulo luscus*), known to both
northern Europe and America.   Under the Russian, Swedish, and
German names, the beast was apparently first brought to the notice
of western Europe by the work of Mechovita and Olaus.   Both
writers accurately describe the gluttonous nature, the size, and color
of the animal, although perhaps the two trees and their function
are a slight exaggeration.   This animal, the glutton, as Olaus states,
was unknown to the ancients, and knowledge of it was acquired
late and only slowly disseminated in western Europe, as the following brief history of the knowledge of the animal and its name,
glutton, will indicate.

Pliny, the natural fountain-head for animal names and descriptions after Aristotle, knew no more of the beast than did the Greeks.
No beast Pliny describes fits the glutton, and the word 'gulo' in
Pliny only means 'gullet' when used technically, although some
uses of it, but never as the name of an animal, apparently mean
'glutton.'[17]   But for our purposes, the classics may be dismissed as
ignorant of a beast actually worthy, as is the wolverine, of the name
'glutton.'

Gula (*est inordinatus appetitus delectabilium*) or unreined appetite, gluttony, was a sin,[18] and was properly so treated in theological works of the Middle Ages and later.

Probably the earliest description of the animal as a glutton or
gulo, and the one that was most influential in the dissemination of
the knowledge of the animal, as Mechovita and Olaus certainly were
not although they were probably the first to describe it in print,

mitternacht/ und thundt nichts dann fressen und sauffen/ und stohnd so offt
innen von nöthen ist von dem tisch auff/ und scheissen und kotzen/ auff das
sie dester mehr fassen mögen/ das treibend sie/ bis sie alle irer sinnen beraubet
werden/ dann so wissen sie kein underscheyd zwyschen dem ars und dem
kopff.''

[17]*Cf. Hist. Mundi,* Book 19, chapter 4. 'in voluptatem gulæ' *et passim* for
other uses of the word.   Philemon Holland (London, 1601) translated this
'wanton gluttons.'   But the reference is to men, not animals.

[18]An excellent example of its exposition as a sin may be found in *Polyanthea
Opus suassimis floribus exornatum compositum per Dominicum Nannum Mira-
bellium.*   Venice, 1507, folio 95v-97ra.

was Conrad Gesner's account of it. His description of the animal
was as follows:

DE GULONE. Gulonis nomen de Septentrionali quadam voracissima fera etsi
nouum est, & ab Olao Magno, vt puto, ad imitationem Germanicæ vocis primum
confictum, placuit t tamen retinere, & ad hoc in loco collocare, cum vereribus
ignota hæc fera indictaque videatur. Plurima tamen concurrunt vt aut ipsam
hyænam, seu crocutam quam aliqui eandem hyænæ putant, alij ex hyæna &
cane, alij ex hyæna & leena (*sic*) natam: omnia dentibus frangit, protinusque
deuotata conficit ventre, Plin. aut omnino congenerem bestiam existimem, vt
facile iudicabunt qui vtriusque historiam conferent: & commode quidem accidit,
vt hyænæ historia proximi subijicienda literam ordine sic poscente sequator.
In Lithuania & Moscouia (verba sunt Matthiae a Michou ex libro 2. descrip-
tionis Sarmatiæ Europæ, cap 3) animal voracissimum & inutile, quod alibi non
comparet, rossomaka nominatum, magnitudine canis, facie catti, corpore &
cauda vulpinis (myæna videtur quasi ex lupo & vulpe composita) colore nigro:
(pedes & vngues asperrimi, corpus villosum, prolixis pilis subfuscis, cauda
vulpis, sed brevior & pilis densior, Olaus Magnus:) cadaueribus vescitur.
Inuento caduere tantum vorat, vt extendatur & infletur tympani instar: itaque
angustiam aliquam inter arbores ingreditur, & per vim se ipsum intrudit, ac
ventrum premens stringensque exonerat, vt violenter ingesta violentibus egerat:
sic extenuatum rursus ad caduer properat & rursus impletur, ita vt vicissim de
caduere quantum potest deuoret & excernat, donec totum absumpseret. [Next,
a section, such as that found in Mechovita and in Olaus on the similarity of
the voracity of this beast to that of the men of the region, aid on the iniquities
of gluttony[ ] Sed redeo ad rossomacam: de qua esdem Lithuanus quidam
nobilis sic narrabat: Rossomaka minor lupus, breuiroibus cruribus, adeo
repletur vt venter propendens terram fere contingat. Rictum fere suis habet,
dentes lupinos, longos. Genera sunt duo, vnum nigrum, & aliud lupino fete
colore . . . Scribit Olaus Magnus . . . Animalia, inquit, quæ Germani *vilfras*, id
est multiuora, Suedi ieff appellant, immodicæ voracitatis: nimium repleta
ventrum inter duas arbores stringunt vt exrementa protrudent. [Continues
with complete description and discussion from Olaus.][19]

This came into English as follows:

OF THE GULON. This beast was not known by the ancients, but hath bin
since discovered in the Northern parts of the world, and because of the great
voracity thereof, it is called (*Gulo*) that is, a deuouer in imitation of the
Germans, who call such deuouring creatures *Vilfruss*, printed, *Vilsruss* and
the Swedians, *Cerff*, in *Lituania* and *Muscouia*, it is called *Rossomokal*. It is
thought to be engendered by a *Hyæna* & a *Lionesse*, for in quality it resem-
bleth a *Hyæna*, & it is the same which is called (*Crocuta*:) it is a deuouring
and vnprofitable creature, having sharper teeth then other creatures. Some
thinke it is deriued of a wolfe and a dog, for it is about the bignesse of a
dog: it hath the face of a Cat, the body and taile of a Foxe; being black of
colour: his feet and nailes be most sharp, his skin rusty, the hair very sharp,
and it feedeth vpon dead carcases.
    When it hath found a dead carkas he eateth thereof so violently, that his
belly standeth out like a bell; then seeketh he some narrow passage betwixt
two trees, and there draweth through his body, by pressing whereof, he driueth
out the meat which he had eaten: and being so emptied returneth and
deuoureth as much as he did before, and goeth again & emptyeth himselfe as
in former manner; and so continueth eating and emptying til al be eaten. It

[19]Conrad Gesner, *Historiæ Animalium. Liber Primus. De Quadrupedibus
viuiparis. (1st ed., Tiguri, 1551.) Frankfort, 1603, p. 554. Gesner's account
is a blending of Mechovita and Olaus, with almost nothing added; but with a
more systematic summary of the physical characteristics of the beast.

may bee that God hath ordained such a creature in those countries, to expresse the abhominable gluttony, of the men of that countrie, that they may know their true deformed nature, and liuely vgly figure, represented in this monster-eating-beast: for it is the fashion of the Noble men in those parts, to sit from noon till midnight, eating and drinking, and neuer rise from the table, but to disgorge their stomacks, or ease their bellies: and then return with refreshed appetites to ingurgitate and consume more of Gods creatures: wherin they grow to such a highth of beastlinesse, that they loose both sence and reason, and know no difference betweene head and taile. Such they are in *Muscouia*, in *Lituania*, and most shamefull of al in *Tartaria*.
These things are reported by *Olaus Magnus*, and *Mathias Michou*; . . .[20]

Topsell follows Gesner, and both depend upon Olaus Magnus and Mechovita. It is especially noteworthy that Gesner-Topsell insist that "this beast was not known to the ancients, but hath bin since discovered in the Northern parts of the world." It is also worth noting that Topsell did not use the name 'glutton' as the English name of the animal, calling it rather a *gulo* or *gulon*, a quasi-scientific name.

The word 'glutton' as the name of an animal does not seem to have been used in English much before 1674. The *OED* cites the translation in that year of Ioannes Scheffer's *Lapponia*,[21] under the title of *The History of Lapland*, and printed at Oxford. Scheffer therein describes the 'gulo' after the manner of Olaus and Mechovita, and the English translator used the word 'glutton' as the name of the beast.[22] Such a use of the word would have been perfectly understood and very easy to effect, as the dictionaries of both the 16th and 17th centuries known or printed in England list 'gulo' as meaning 'glutton' or 'gluttonie' but in connection only with human beings.[23] But so far as I can determine in a careful if limited search, no actual occurrence of the word as the name of an animal appeared much earlier than that date.[24] So far as I can

[20]Edward Topsell, *The Historie of Fovre-Footed Beastes . . . Collected out of all the Volumes of CONRADUS GESNER, and all other Writers to this present day.* London, 1607, p. 261.

[21]Frankfort, 1673.

[22]P. 134.

[23]*Cf.* John Baret, *An Alvearie or Quadruple Dictionary.* London, 1580, *sub* 'glutton' and 'gluttonie'; William Morell and Richard Hutton, *Verborum Latinorum cum Græcis Anglicisque Coniunctorum.* London, 1583; various printings of Rider, Holyoke, Littleton, Blount, and the many Continental editions of vernacular and Latin lexicons and dictionaries, *sub* 'glutton, gourmand, gula, gulo, Vielfras, etc.' But for the slow dissemination of knowledge of the creature to which these names were finally applied, cf. J. J. Hofmann, *Lexicon Universalis.* Basle, 1683. 2 vols. The first edition (1677) lists none of the forms, and the second edition lists *Rosomacha* only as Bochart described it.

[24]John Swan, *Speculum Mundi, or a Glasse representing the Face of the World.* Cambridge, 1635, p. 484, makes a passing reference to Sir Richard

determine, the first English dictionary to apply the word 'glutton' to the animal, *gulo borealis* or the wolverine, was the seventh edition or printing of Edward Phillips, the elder nephew, *New World of Words* in 1706, some years after his death.[25] In that edition, but in none of the earlier editions, the word 'glutton' is definitely applied to the beast that Milton called a Rossomakka, and is made identical with the name 'gulo,' with the main entry under 'glutton.' The next printing of this dictionary, in 1720, repeated this definition, as have English dictionaries since in one form or another.

Milton, therefore, drawing heavily on Purchas and Hakluyt, used the word 'Rossomakka' in his *History of Moscovia* as the name of a strange beast to be found in Russia and other parts of northern Europe. He took the word into his text exactly as he found it in Purchas and gave his reference for it. Because of this exact citation and usage, it is impossible to tell whether or not Milton knew what the beast actually was. It is equally impossible to determine whether or not he had ever encountered the same animal in Olaus Magnus or Mechovita, to both of which writers he would have had

Barckley's citation of the beast called a 'gulo' from Olaus, as a horrible example of gluttony to mankind. Barckley (*A Discourse of the Felicitie of Man or his Summum Bonum.* London, 1598, 1603, 1631) says [I quote from the edition of 1603] p. 26: "*Olaus Magnus* maketh report on a beast in the North-part of Suetia called a Ierffe, whose propertie is, vvhen hee hath killed his pray, or found some carkasse, hee deuoureth so much, and neuer leaueth feeding, untill his belly be puffed vp, and stroweth like a bag-pipe; then not beeing able to hold any more, hee goeth presently between two narrow trees, and straineth out backward that which he hath eaten, and so beeing made emptie, returneth againe to the carkasse, and filleth himselfe as before, and then straineth it out between the two trees and returneth to the carkasse to eate againe; and thus he continueth to doe vntill hee hath deuoured all: which being consumed, he hunteth after more, in this sort continually passing his life. This beast it seemeth God hath created to the shame of gluttonous men, that passe whole dayes and nights in eating and drinking, & when they haue filled," etc.

25The first edition, 1658, contains only, "Gulosity, (lat.) gluttony" as do succeeding editions until that of 1696 which has "Glutton, a Gourmandized, a Greedy Eater," (see the English parts of Rider, Holyoke, Littleton, etc., for many fearfully and wonderfully made definitions of 'glutton,' all applied, however, to human beings) and "Gulosity, (Lat.) Gluttony," and the next printing, 1700, repeats these. In 1706, John Kersey edited and published this dictionary, Phillips, so far as we know having died perhaps ten years before this. This edition, 1706, contains "Glutton, one that devours much Meat, a greedy Eater: Also the Name of a strange greedy Beast, that stuffs it selfe with Carrion till its Paunch sticks out like a Drum; afterwards getting between two Trees and Rocks, it presses out the Ordure upwards and downwards, and then returns to the Carcas to gorge it selfe again. This Beast is found in *Lithuania, Muscovy,* and other Northern Countries." Also, "Gulo, (Lat.) a strange greedy Beast that stuffs it self with Carrion. See Glutton."

fairly easy access. Gesner-Topsell cannot be connected with Milton's use of the word.

It is equally impossible with the meager evidence before us to determine why Milton, or indeed why Clement Adams described the parturient habits in connection with the stakes or trees rather than the more disgusting digestive habits. About all that could be actually accomplished here, therefore, was to 'gloss' the word 'Rossomakka' for readers of Milton's *History of Moscovia*. As in the case of 'Cursemay,' we have another transliterated Russian word. 'Cursemay' was most corruptly transliterated, whereas 'Rossomakka' was very correctly transliterated; but Milton was responsible for neither transliteration, taking both from practically the same source, Purchas-Hakluyt.

GRUNDTVIG ON *PARADISE LOST*

By Kemp Malone
Johns Hopkins University

The great nineteenth-century Danish reformer and man of letters, Bishop N. F. S. Grundtvig, is best known to the English world as a *Beowulf* scholar, and in fact his critical discussion of *Paradise Lost* appears in a paper devoted primarily to the OE poem.[1] If this discussion has eluded any Milton specialists, it will prove of some interest to them, I think, for more reasons than one. Grundtvig reaches the Miltonic epic indirectly enough. He first considers whether *Beowulf* is an epic or not, and concludes (p. 273) that

we have in this poem an epic outlook (or vision) but no epic before us; we have all the letters but they are not properly put together into a great picture-word. It will be seen that by *epos* I mean what the name indicates [i.e. "word"], and without raising the question at this time how far any poem actually exists that can be so called, it is enough for me that such a poem *can* exist, and that the present poem [i.e. *Beowulf*] apparently tries to express what I mean by the epic name. The Word, as Holy Writ teaches, and as we now can grasp, is the highest and deepest expression for Life's revelation, and all history must be regarded as the Word's fight for victory. Now we see well enough that only the whole of history, seen in the light of truth, constitutes and expresses the true epic and heroic poem, but even as each individual man (however weakly and darkly) expresses and represents the race, even so every event with battle and victory undoubtedly expresses and represents (more or less plainly) the one great achievement in the stream of time which is accomplished among men [i.e. the victory of the Word]. If such a [particular] event is viewed spiritually, in the light of truth, it is quickened to a visible, concentrated picture of all history, and a poem which expresses such a view we can call an epic as justly as we call an offshoot of mankind a man. . . .

Grundtvig now proceeds to a brief consideration of certain poems to which the epic name is usually given. He maintains (pp. 274f.) that

all epic poems either try to include or at least play upon an event which, in the view of the poet and many others, best stood for (or represented) what was thought to be the greatest world-event, just as the famous poems in that [i.e. the epic] kind all have a recognizable relationship to the event which at bottom is the one and only event, be the relationship what it may: friendly or hostile, right or wrong. Thus, we may be certain that the cycle of poems dealing with the Trojan War represents or stands for history as a whole when it includes a fight in which truth wins and brings ravished beauty back in triumph, for that is precisely what happens when history is taken as a whole. But it by no means follows that the *Iliad* deserves the epic name, for the event [celebrated]

---

[1] "Om Bjovulfs Drape," *Danne-Virke*, II (Copenhagen, 1817), 207-289.

may be viewed awry or only in part, as in fact it is, I think. Again, Jerusalem's deliverance by the crusaders is undoubtedly a very epic event, which represents the same thing that the expedition to Troy represents, but with the difference that the picture is far clearer and more spiritual, since it is not a bodily but a spiritual beauty that is being fought over, inasmuch as the army strives to win, not for itself, but for the invisible, living, eternal truth.   Yet I have not the slightest hesitation in setting the Homeric poem high over Tasso's, for it [Tasso's poem] does no more than play upon and play with the great event, as it plays upon and plays with history as a whole. Finally, who dares deny that Christ's life upon earth, the Word become flesh, is an event that not only represents but contains the fight and the victory of truth, and it would seem that this event, spiritually viewed, would of necessity produce the only true epic that can be made in history. But I am far from thinking that Klopstock's *Messias* is such an epic.

Grundtvig next takes up the *Æneid*, to which he refuses the epic name, not because Vergil made too little of his theme, but because the theme itself was an unworthy one. He says (pp. 275f.),

that the *Æneid* is in every way a false and lying epic hardly calls for proof. It will be enough for me to point out that it is based upon the view that the history of Rome (that is, slavery, dishonor and the rape of beauty) is the great world-event.

Having thus disposed of the Latin poem, he continues as follows (pp. 276f.) :

Next I turn to the island of the English. Here we meet three great attempts to produce epic poems, two of which have tied themselves to the Bible, the third [*Beowulf*] . . . to the history of the North. Let us first have a look at the former. The only one that is well known is, of course, Milton's *Paradise Lost*. Certainly the fall of man is, in itself, the worst event that any poet could possibly choose as the central point of an epic poem, but its centrality in Milton's poem [was needless and] comes only of the poet's bad taste. Milton saw that existence as a whole, seen with the Bible's eye, made a great epic, which begins with the devil's rebellion against God, and continues with the fight between truth and falsehood over mankind, and [he saw] that here the fall is the turning-point, but instead of letting the rebellion and fall stand in the background and making the redemption the central point, he made the rebellion and fall a fight in which it was falsehood that really won, and he frustrated the victory of truth, a victory which in the poem comes to nothing more than empty threats. Instead of contemplating spiritual battle in history, he has turned the relationship about and has tried to contemplate history in spiritual battle, and thereby has given us airy shadows instead of clear pictures. But we see well enough that the true subject-matter of the epic of history [i.e. of history taken as an epic] hovered darkly before him in a huge incomprehensible shape, and we might well be able to show what the shadows would say if they could speak.

Here Grundtvig ends his discussion of *Paradise Lost*. He makes no mention of *Paradise Regained,* and evidently considers that *Paradise Lost* was meant to be taken as a whole, not as a part of a larger whole. Or perhaps he considers merely that the poem is commonly taken (or must be taken) as a whole, whatever the intention of the poet. But even if he had taken *Paradise Regained* into account, he would presumably have condemned it as a mere tailpiece, and his objections to Milton's procedure would hardly have been affected. These objections are rooted in Grundtvig's understanding of the term *epic* and in his interpretation of the historical process. The latter I have discussed elsewhere;[2] here it will be enough to say that Grundtvig thought of history as the course or career of mankind, and defined this career as "the gradual development of human nature to clarity about itself," a progress which in time would bring about fulness of understanding and "an everlasting blessed life,"[3] presumably in accordance with the millenial perfection described by St John in his "Revelation." But since the historical process is a struggle which ends in the victory of good over evil (or of truth over falsehood, as Grundtvig prefers to put it), an epic, therefore, which (according to Grundtvig) by definition is a representation or illustration of history as a whole, must tell the story of some particular fight between good and evil (or truth and falsehood) which ends with the victory of goodness (or truth). Milton in choosing the story of the fall of man and his redemption chose the greatest of all subjects, namely, the fight between God and the devil for the soul of man, but in dwelling on the fall rather than on the redemption he put the emphasis on the wrong thing and thereby distorted his theme. Moreover, his elaborate account of the events that preceded the fall made the distortion even more marked.

So far, all is plain sailing. But when Grundtvig reproached Milton for turning the relationship about between spiritual battle (*aandekamp*) and history, what did he mean? Possibly the word *aandekamp* (which I have not found elsewhere) is to be taken in a double sense; it may refer both to the warfare between good and evil generally, and to the warfare which had been brought about by the rebellion of Lucifer against God. In either case, Milton obviously thought of history (i.e., the story of mankind) as only a small part of a very great whole, a whole which Gruntvig calls existence in one place and spiritual battle in another. Now the proper procedure of the epic poet, according to Grundtvig, is to celebrate some particular struggle between right and wrong as representative of all history. Milton, however, celebrated all history (summed up,

---

[2]"Grundtvig's Philosophy of History," *Journal of the History of Ideas*, I (1940), 281-298.

[3]*Haandbog i Middel-Alderens Historie* (Copenhagen, 1836), pp. 1f.

not merely represented, in the fall and redemption) as representative of the struggle between right and wrong. In so doing (we are
told) Milton gave us airy shadows instead of clear pictures. Apparently Gruntvig felt that Milton's "picture-word" was too vast
to admit of the particularity needful if an epic effect was to be
achieved; Adam was too much man in general to be a living, clean-
cut man in particular, and most of the characters, in virtue of their
superhuman nature, could not be made to come alive, except by
sacrifice of their essential quality. In sum, Milton gave us shadows
because he was dealing with spirits, or (in Adam and Eve) with
generalized figures, instead of with fellow-mortals, individuals of
flesh and blood. Without discussing the justice or injustice of this
criticism, let me say that particularity and vitality loom large in
Grundtvig's thought (and in his practice). The *logos* or Word of
God became known to man only through the incarnation, and the
epos or picture-word likewise becomes real to us only through living
men and women, in action on the stage of history, or so Grundtvig
believed.

Our critic's conclusion is that Milton had the right idea but saw
it darkly instead of seeing it clearly. As he puts it, *det virkelige
indhold af historiens epos dunkelt svævede for ham i en uhyre,
ufattelig skikkelse,* "the true content of history's utterance darkly
swayed before him in a prodigious, incomprehensible figure." To
this darkness of vision, at bottom, is to be attributed the poet's faulty
execution of his great design. Here as everywhere down the centuries the Englishman exhibits his characteristic muddleheaded-
ness. And with this judgment we may take leave of Grundtvig, as
he takes leave of Milton.

THE ENGLISH RELIGIOUS RESTORATION, 1660-1665

By HARRY G. PLUM
University of Iowa

It has been the habit of historians of seventeenth-century England to assume that the fall of the Commonwealth closed the period of puritan influence, and that after 1660 the unfortunate remnant of puritan legislation served only to check free expression of the English nature and to plague England as the blue laws of colonial New England did the later development of American life.[1] For some time it has been the writer's opinion that this view of Puritanism is erroneous and that the real puritan influence, the constructive work of Puritanism, has been largely lost sight of while the extraneous and largely irrelevant excrescences have so claimed attention that the whole movement has been misunderstood. This brief study of the Restoration period was undertaken to try to find out what happened when England so gladly welcomed home the wandering Stuart King, Charles II; whether what was worth saving, and there was much worth saving, was discarded and the earlier revolution was proved wholly mistaken.

Puritanism in its religious thought was very largely responsible for asserting the Englishman's right to individual liberty, which quickly widened into civil, economic and constitutional liberties. It was during too brief a period a united party. In the main it was represented within the Anglican organization under James and Charles, not without it. The fear that the Laudian regime was a preparation for the return of Catholicism effected a unity of those within and without the organized Church that secured the body of legislation under the Long Parliament, which in turn served as the bulwark against all the efforts of Charles II and James II to establish an absolutist system of government. Lucius Carey, who died in the King's service, and Chillingworth, Hales, Usher and other Anglican churchmen, as well as Pym, Hampden, Prynne and Eliot, were essentially Puritan, opposed to the Laudian system and to the theory of a divine clerical hierarchy.

---

[1] See Green's description which has been so largely followed. It will be found in his *History of England*, Vol. I, Ch. 2.

It must not be forgotten in the period of military power and in the efforts of the time toward political control by a minority of the nation that Puritanism had lost much of its lustre and had had its skirts sullied in the political arena. As in all periods many so-called supporters gave it only lip service and by their lives tended to weaken its character. Nor must it be forgotten that the small group of Independents, far in advance of the nation in its acceptance of the principle of toleration, was yet quite unable to realize its great principle in political control. So it was in 1660 that Puritanism, divided against itself, was again put into its place as a minority group, hated for its period of power, feared, and in large part misunderstood. So the whole of the Restoration period was necessary for Puritanism to regain the position it had held in 1640.

There has been a rather general tendency to minimize the part taken by the Presbyterians in the Restoration or to suggest that they were out-manouvered and inefficient in the part they played. It is worth while to call attention to the fact that they had ever been monarchial in their attitude, had faithfully backed the Long Parliament in its efforts to tie the King's hands by legislative effort, and, while supporting the civil war against the King, had strongly advocated agreement with the King until the radical army drove them from Parliament. In general they had not sympathized with the Scotch alliance and, when in 1646 the Scottish Covenant was accepted in England, the Presbyterians were half-hearted in effecting the organization of the Presbyterian church. The English Presbyterians were distinctly English and Puritan in their make-up, and to them comprehension meant only the Anglican acceptance of certain changes in organization and ritual which should give a freedom of individual action beyond that which Charles I and Laud had contemplated. They had no objection to the state church, but the basis of a divinely ordained state church was to their way of thinking impossible to accept. Their great antipathy was to the Catholic church because of its foreign and arbitrary control over men's lives. They asked only for Bishop Usher's plan, which would have combined the two systems and have given a modified democratic control, leaving room for individual initiative; but they opposed toleration because toleration would have admitted the Catholic group which they feared beyond the devil himself. Hence they declined to accept the program of the Independents for a general toleration, and, if they had ever had it, lost the support of Charles II, who favored toleration in order to give a legal status to Catholics. From this position they never wavered through the long period of persecution which followed,[2] though they came to embrace toleration as an alternative when it excluded the Catholics.

On coming to London, Charles at once appointed a group of ten Presbyterians as Chaplains and designated this group with a group of Bishops to consider the proposed settlement. The latter, however, refused to meet the Presbyterians, and Charles then proposed the conference at Savoy; it was undoubtedly this announcement that influenced the Convention Parliament to put over the religious settlement[3] to a new Parliament. Before the dissolution of the Convention Parliament the attitude of the Anglican Bishops and the council had become clear. Speaking to the Lords at the dissolution after the King had retired, Clarendon had thanked God that so many of the displaced Bishops had been able to return that the sacrament of the consecration of priests might be passed on to the new generation of churchmen unimpaired.[4]

The issues were clearly brought out in many pamphlets. Altogether the Presbyterians seem to have had the better of the argument in the presentation of the respective positions. Their pamphlets are characterized by more sober thought and reasoned argument[5] and by a broader grasp of the problems at stake; they were able to point to Anglican writers who supported their views, to Jeremy Taylor, Edward Stillingfleet,[6] Bishop Usher and others. The Anglican pamphlets, on the other hand, were naturally filled with the bitterness of long-suppressed desires and hopes and with long-sustained enmity of a group driven from office and often from the country. How much influence either group may have had it is difficult to say, but they at least make clear to the present-day reader the great significance of the issue at stake—a free conscience, individual self-respect, and liberty of thought.

Charles II generally lost patience with the slowness of his parliaments, and his message to the Convention Parliament that he was

---

[2]Clark, H. W., *History of English Non-conformity*, I, 10ff.

[3]*Ibid.*, I, 14; and Calamy, *The Non-Conformist's Memorial*, I, 20-22.

[4]*Lords Journals*, 1660-65, p. 239.

[5]See Baxter, R., *A Petition for Peace with Reformation of the Liturgy as it was presented to the Bishops and Divines.* Also *An Exact Collection of Farewell Sermons Preached by the Late London Ministers*, London, 1662.

[6]Stillingfleet's *Irenicum, A Weapon's Salve for the Churches Wounds*, was published first in 1659 and gave great offense to the Anglican church by its liberalism.

about to appoint a commission for revision of the prayer book may have decided the final vote on the bill to settle religion. It certainly influenced the general feeling that Charles was still prepared to stand by his Declaration. Soon after the dissolution Charles appointed a group of Presbyterian divines to represent the non-conformist element and a group of Anglican churchmen headed by Archbishop Juxon, and presented to them the task of the settlement of the government of the church and a revision of the prayer book within a period of four months.

There was much uncertainty as to the procedure of the Commission. Satisfied with things as they were, the Anglicans insisted that the Presbyterian group present a complete statement of the changes demanded, leaving the Anglicans to review such a list and to accept or reject it in part or in whole. When the Presbyterians found that they were to have no chance to debate the matter, they lost heart, and only at the last moment did Baxter draw up a rather complete list which was accepted by the group, and five members were chosen to present the request to the Bishops.[7]

At this session the Presbyterians found themselves overwhelmed and embarrassed and only Baxter and Calamy attempted to defend their position. The conference was soon over and the Bishops agreed to prepare and send their answer to the Presbyterian group in due time. When the answer was finally sent it was found to be a complete denial of the changes asked for. The Presbyterian group then drew up a general defense of their position,[8] which was later supplemented by ''The Humble and Earnest Petition of Others in the Same Commission.'' This procedure, which had dragged over the period allotted for the revision, ended the work of the conference. It was clear that few among the Anglicans were prepared to make any compromise that would admit the Presbyterian clergy to a place within the Anglican fold. It was in fact stated by Archbishop Juxon that, had it been thought that the position taken by the Anglican group would have won over any Presbyterian, the conditions would have been made more uncompromising.

With the efforts of the Commission out of the way, the Convocation appointed a committee of twenty members with eighty-five

---

[7] *The Grand Debate between the most Reverend Bishops and the Presbyterian Divines appointed by the Sacred Majesty as a Commission for Review & Alteration of the Book of Common Prayer.* London, 1661.

[8] Baxter, R., *A Petition for Peace with Reformation of the Liturgy as it was Presented to the Right Reverend Bishops by the Divines.* London, 1661.

clerks to review and revise the Liturgy and Prayer Book. Some few of the Presbyterian suggestions were introduced, a very cursory and superficial group of revisions was made and the report was accepted by the Convocation and presented to Parliament for its sanction. But even the Cavalier Parliament put little faith in the sincerity of the revision and, after some delay and debate, finally accepted it by a vote of ninety-six to ninety votes. The debate raised the question of the right of the Convocation to proceed independently of Parliament and as well indicated dissatisfaction with the work done.[9]

The failure of the Savoy Conference had a far-reaching effect. A considerable number of the non-conformists remained in office even though they disliked the new liturgy. They felt it wise to remain in order to try for further reform and reopen the way for the inclusion of their brethren. The general body of Presbyterian pastors refused to accept a prayer book published only on the day on which their decision was to be made, and they left the Anglican church.[10] There was thus established a strong body of dissent which was to make a final settlement of the religious problem most difficult and which was to trouble the church through the rest of the Stuart period. For the great problem of the seventeenth century, the problem of individual liberty, the exclusion was of great significance. It made it clear to the largest and strongest body of non-conformists that since the church would have none of them, their only course must be to throw in their lot with the other sects, and gradually in the twenty years following, the Presbyterian group came out on the side of and in full support of toleration. So again under the later Stuarts the leadership of the opposition to absolute government in church or state is found in the religious group which from the Tudor period had stood for individual liberty as against the absolutist idea of authority.[11]

Charles's first regular parliament, the Cavalier Parliament, met in May 1661. The King in his address to Parliament emphasized the need of religious peace: ''The peace of State is concerned in peace of Religion. There is no order in civil affairs when there is

---

[9]Sykes, Norman, *Church and State in England in the 18th Century*, Cambridge, 1934, pp. 11ff.

[10]*Ibid.*, pp. 12ff. It was probably off the press some two weeks but had not yet become available.

[11]Sykes contends that the organization of the party opposition to Charles II in 1672 was due to this group.

none in ecclesiastical affairs.'' The address commended the Presbyterians for their moderation, their attachment to the Episcopal form of government, their learning and piety. The King declared against the use of the prayer book until the ecclesiastical problem should be settled. Clarendon, who addressed Parliament after the King had retired, gave quite a different color to the problem and made quite clear what the Anglicans desired from Parliament.[12] The House began to work without delay. A general Committee was at once appointed for religion. By the time the Convocation's Book of Common Prayer was disposed of, the bill for the Government of Corporations was ready for introduction. While this was going through its regular course the Act of Uniformity was introduced and had some discussion in the House before the prorogation, at which time the King gave his sanction to the Corporation Act in December 1661. Early in 1662 the Act of Uniformity was agreed to by both houses and Charles gave it his assent. This was followed in 1663 by the Conventicle Act. Later, after the cessation of the plague in 1665, the Five Mile Act was passed.

These four acts constituted the famous Clarendon Code and set definitely the policy of the Restoration toward religion. They provided for the exclusion of all non-conformists in borough and local government, made obligatory the repudiation of the Covenant, exacted an oath to support the King and to abhor all opposition to his authority, and to accept and use the Book of Common Prayer as the one church service. All services outside the parish church were made illegal and a fine and imprisonment fixed as punishment for such illegal preaching. Finally the Five Mile Act forbade any non-conformist pastor to reside within five miles of any borough where he had formerly preached to a congregation.

The first act was intended to destroy the political influence of the Presbyterians and other sects, while the second was intended to drive the Presbyterians into dissent. The Act of Uniformity made impossible the exercise of any religious or educational work within the established church unless the minister was prepared to abjure the Covenant, use the Book of Common Prayer, and take an oath to support the King whatever he might choose to do. The Presbyterian and other sects gave up their pulpits. As nearly as it is possible to estimate the numbers, about two thousand Presbyterians and five hundred Independents were forced out of the church at this

---

[12]*Lords Journals*, 1661, p. 179.

time.[13] Most of them did not wait for the act to come into legal effect. A considerable number, when they read the act, decided to remain within the Anglican church, but it is impossible to say how many.[14] The London ministers addressed a protest to Charles and received Charles's assurance that the law would be modified by an indulgence, but, by this time, few put much trust in Charles's word. In 1662 a volume of farewell sermons preached in the city of London was issued.[15] In it very generally the advice is given to attend the Anglican services, to be constant in Godly service, and to take punishment meekly; and the hope is expressed of a return at some future time. This readiness to accept and act according to law should perhaps have been taken by the Anglican church as evidence of the character and Godliness of the displaced ministry, but there is nothing in any of the writings to suggest that it was. The church was jubilant at its easy success, and determined to destroy nonconformity.

To supply twenty-five hundred new places within the church was no easy matter and all too many unfit ministers were set over the churches. The discontent which this soon caused and the pleas of the congregations to their old ministers led to a changed non-conformist policy before the end of the year. By that time both Presbyterian and Congregationalist had decided that since the Act of Uniformity did not forbid preaching outside the church, the work might go on as supplementing the inefficient work of the Anglican ministry. This new policy was met in 1663 by the Conventicle Act,[16] which refused the right of the dissenters to preach or teach anywhere to more than five persons in addition to the family. The new act was not received in the spirit of resignation that yielded to

---

[13]Calamy, E. *The Non-Conformist Memorial Religion;* See Turner, *Original Records of Early Non-conformity,* III, 35-65.

[14]Halley, R., in his *Lancashire, Its Pulpits and Non-conformity* finds three out of one hundred remaining. Reynolds and one or two more accepted Bishoprics. No attempt to establish the number has been found by the author. Lancashire had been a stronghold of Presbyterians who were so confident of Breda that almost a solid delegation of Cavaliers were sent to the first Parliament of the Restoration. In 1689 the city of Lancashire was emphatically Jacobean. See Halley, p. 344.

[15]*An Exact Collection of Farewell Sermons Preached by the Late London Ministers,* Calamy, Watson, Jacomb, Case, Sclater, Baxter, Jenkin, Manton, Lye and Collons. Later, too, there were added the sermons of Bates, Brook, Mede, Caryl, Seeman, Vennin, Newcomen, Cradicot, Bull, Pledger and Bierman. (Baxter had left his congregation in Kidder-minister earlier and had come up to London).

[16]Car. II. C, 4., *Pickering Statutes,* VIII, 209.

the earlier act. By this legislation the government had made itself as responsible as the Anglican group to enforce the law. There followed a period of earnest and passionate persecution. Officials were everywhere brought to hand, the churchmen were in accord and the informers busy. Persecution had, however, all too little effect. The Anglican church had assumed that, driven into dissent, the ministers would soon lose their influence and Anglicanism would stand supreme. This, however, did not follow. Too many churchmen were averse to active persecution, too many borough officials refused to enforce the law. The informers were soon repudiated by local officials, and the King, uneasy perhaps at the inclusion of Catholics and at the complaints boldly asserting his forgotten promises, issued in 1662 a declaration of indulgence to alleviate persecution. Parliament at its early meeting objected to this and it was withdrawn, but its effect was to emphasize lenity in some quarters and to strengthen resistance in others.

The early period—1662-1665—definitely established the non-conformist opposition to the efforts of government and church. The Government as well as the church early assumed that every small and large movement of dissatisfaction with government policy was directed by the religious opposition. The jails were filled with all sects but especially with Friends and Anabaptists. The church, too, over-emphasizing the non-conformist sympathy with political discontent, ere long had crystalized religious opposition. In 1662 the Presbyterian ministers had advised their congregations to conform to the laws, attend the services, and, if dissatisfied, supplement the service with reading sermons and the scripture. The complaints of ignorance and the evil lives of some of the conformist clergy soon changed the character of the advice. Non-conformist congregations were formed. Secret services continued. Ministers and congregations went to prison or paid fines and those in prison were cared for by the faithful. When in 1664 the Code was strengthened by the Conventicle Act, which was intended to separate pastor and people, it was disobeyed or some newly ordained minister took up the work. Many of the churchmen revolted against the persecutions, the borough officials were lax or refused to take the testimony of informers. The church was well aware of the unfitness of many churchmen. The Convention Parliament had legalized the return of deprived churchmen but had emphasized the limitation to but one benefice. The ink was hardly dry upon the statute before the church had sanctioned the breaking of it. It was notorious that some Bishops had no religious interest in their diocese. The need of supplying twenty-five hundred places in the church in 1662 had brought in many time-servers. The court of Charles proceeded to set a very poor example in discipline of character. The rabble followed the court practice with enthusiasm and many churchmen found the moral laxness to their taste.

In 1662-1663, the Archbishop of Canterbury issued a set of "Articles of Visitation" for the use of the dioceses, and his example was followed by most of the Bishops. These efforts, however, were ineffectual in the face of opposite example. The careful churchmen were busy hunting out those who neglected to come to church or, coming, refused communion. Many, of course, who were spiritually inclined and who loved the church service, yet had sympathy for those who remained outside but kept their Christian character and were honest and industrious.[17]

When the plague began in 1665 and grew worse day by day, many of the conformist ministers fled their posts, partly because they were time-servers only and partly because services were largely discontinued and the Anglicans had not yet developed the habit of visiting the homes and carrying on the pastoral work. Many, of course, fled through fear. The non-conformist clergy very readily stepped into the breach, took up the pastoral work, ministered to the sick, buried the dead, and preached in the vacant pulpits unless the authorities forbade. It was the period when any wavering of the non-conformist flock had been brought back to steadfastness and when generally the tide was turned against persecution. So also the unrest among the soldiers of the Commonwealth, the fifth-monarchy men and republicans, was largely passing. The fears of the re-established monarchy were allayed and the government had less reason for persecution of religion for political purposes.

Complaints were also rife by 1665 of the economic consequences of the government's religious policy. In one pamphlet it was complained that thirty or forty thousand men, active in trade and commerce, had been driven from the country or despoiled, and that England was suffering in consequence. With less, yet with some, reason, perhaps, the author complained that funds needed for commerce were being taken in large amounts to turn into plate for the churches or were lying idle in the hands of the clergy. The author

[17]Overton, J. H., *Life in the English Church, 1660-1714*, pp. 7-15.

maintained that four hundred and fifty thousand pounds were being drawn from use each year by the clergy where two hundred thousand pounds could easily maintain them.[18] It was seen very early that the middle classes were the main supporters either openly or covertly of the non-conformist groups, and from 1664 to 1672 the pamphlets discussing the economic results of the persecutions increased in numbers and in definiteness.[19]

There seems little doubt that the church suffered greatly from its activity as police officers for both church and state.[20] The churchmen assumed the attitude of coercion, and gave more attention relatively to this aspect of their work than to the regular offices of the church. This, with the loosening of morals at the court, tended to spread the contagion of immorality throughout England and thus strengthened the non-conformist activity. There was much attention given to the work of education by the non-conformist clergy. Many well-to-do families employed them as tutors and chaplains. Schools were organized by the non-conformist ministers, sometimes with the support of individual conformist ministers, sometimes independently of any support other than themselves, and in spite of efforts to destroy them, they continued to thrive.[21]

By late 1665, three years had passed in the effort to destroy non-conformity. Persecutions had been bitter and all the arguments possible had been used to further the cause of persecution. In spite of its severity, it had failed to accomplish its purpose, and many Anglicans had come to doubt its effectiveness. The Government, too, felt more secure; the small rebellions or riots had been mostly dispersed. The local officials were less interested in the success of the Anglican church; some were disgusted with the severity of its methods and many were sympathetic with the persecuted. Many well-to-do members of the local community gave them support, thus

---

[18]*Et à Dracone, or Some Reflections upon a Letter out of the West called Omnia, à Bello Comesta.* These two argued the economic effects of persecution over a period of several years. See also, Fortney, *England's Interest and Improvement, etc.,* Cambridge, 1663; and Audley, Hugh, *The Way to be Rich,* London, 1662.

[19]The Seligman collection of economic documents in Columbia University contain the most important of these.

[20]*Dissenters Magazine,* I, 142.

[21]See Turner, *op. cit.,* II, for list of well-to-do supporters, also Baxter, R., *The Poor Husbandman's Advocate,* London, 1926, pp. 1-25. In Baxter's memorial to Thomas Goudge, p. 23, he states that he alone was responsible for many schools in Wales. The Act of Uniformity was the first legislation to demand subscription to the Liturgy by teachers and physicians and this section was not followed so closely possibly. See Turner, *op. cit.,* III, 65.

intimidating the Anglican effort and offering an excuse for the Justices. It seemed a time to take stock, to see how effective the efforts had been.

In 1665 Archbishop Sheldon asked of his Bishops a survey of each Diocese to discover the numbers of non-conformist ministers, their places of residence and the numbers of the laity.[22] The reports came in slowly; twenty out of the twenty-six Bishops seem to have ignored the request, or their reports have been completely lost. One, St. Asaph in Wales, simply reported that there were no non-conformists in the diocese![23] The reports were certainly discouraging to the Archbishop, in so far as they came. Whether non-conformity had grown or diminished—and both contentions were made —the strength of non-conformity had not been broken. The non-conformist ministers had not conformed in any numbers; the non-conformist laity were still strong and where they had conformed there was left the doubt of their sincerity. The Conventicle Act, which had been in force only about a year, had undoubtedly strengthened the morale and stiffened resistance and, what was still more serious, had developed a more sympathetic attitude on the part of the low-churchmen and many magistrates. When the plague struck London and spread over England, the zealousness of the non-conformist clergy as compared with the Anglican ministry made them many supporters and friends.

The effort to force conformity was a complete failure. The three years had purged the dross from the Puritan and non-conformist character, had deepened its spiritual nature and emphasized its unselfishness. Moreover, the brief period had made it clear to the Presbyterian element that there was little chance for comprehension and thus had emphasized for them the need of toleration. The sects within the non-conformist group were unified in spirit and strengthened. From this time there is a rapidly growing number of pamphlets urging the need of toleration—pamphlets from the pens of Presbyterians and Low-Churchmen as well as from those who had long espoused the cause of liberty in religion.

---

[22]He sent his request to Bishop Henchman of London who was asked to send out the orders. See Turner, *op. cit.*, III, 758.

[23]The Diocesan returns included St. Asaph and St. David in Wales, Donset, Bristol, Devon and Cornwall in England. The records remarkably substantiate Calamy's account. See Turner, *op. cit.*, III, 66. Calamy reported twenty ministers ejected in St. Asaph.

BIBLIOGRAPHY OF THE WRITINGS OF HARDIN CRAIG FROM 1901 TO 1940[1]

By FRANCIS R. JOHNSON
Stanford University

1901   "An Edition of the Weavers' Play of Coventry." *The Princeton University Bulletin*, XIII, 8-12.

1902   *Two Coventry Corpus Christi Plays. 1. The Shearmen and Taylors' Pageant. 2. The Weavers' Pageant. With a Plan of Coventry, and Appendixes containing the Chief Records of the Coventry Plays.* Early English Text Society, Extra Series, No. 87. London. Pp. xxxviii, 133.

1903   "The Manuscripts of the Weavers' Pageant at Coventry." *The Princeton University Bulletin*, XIV, 199-207.

1905   *Little Masterpieces of English Poetry by British and American Authors.* Ed. by Henry Van Dyke, assisted by Hardin Craig. New York: Doubleday, Page & Company. 6 vols. (Reprinted in 1922 as vols. x-xv in "The Pocket University.")

1912   *The Tragedy of Richard the Second.* Ed. by Hardin Craig. The Tudor Shakespeare. New York: The Macmillan Company. Pp. xvii, 158.

1913   *Byron's Childe Harold, Cantos III and IV, The Prisoner of Chillon, and other Poems.* Ed. by Hardin Craig. New York: Henry Holt and Company. Pp. xxix, 232.

"The Coventry Cycle of Plays." *The Athenaeum.* No. 4477 (Aug. 13, 1913), p. 166.

"Effectual Culture." *Minnesota Public Library Commission: Notes and News*, IV, 57-61.

"Lincoln as the possible Home of the so-called Coventry Plays." *The Nation*, XCVII, 308-9.

"The Origin of the Old Testament Plays." *Modern Philology*, X, 473-87.

1914   "The Corpus Christi Procession and the Corpus Christi Play." *Journal of English and Germanic Philology*, XIII, 589-602.

"An Elementary Account of Miracle Plays in Lincoln." *The Lincoln Diocesan Magazine*, XXX, 135-39.

---

[1]This bibliography does not attempt to list all of Professor Craig's reviews. From 1926 to 1940 he regularly included several short reviews of Renaissance studies in his annual bibliography, "Recent Literature of the English Renaissance," published in the April number of *Studies in Philology*. These have not been separately noted; the present list merely records a selection from the more important reviews appearing in other journals.

"Note on the Home of Ludus Coventriae." *University of Minnesota Studies in Language and Literature*, No. 1, pp. 72-83.

1915   "A Conversation on Emerson." *The Minnesota Magazine*, XXII, 53-58.

"The Mantle of Browning." *Mid-West Quarterly*, II, 162-68.

1916   *The Works of John Metham, including the Romance of Amoryus and Cleopes.* Ed. from the unique MS. in the Garrett Collection in the Library of Princeton University by Hardin Craig. Early English Text Society, Original Ser., No. 132. London. Pp. xlii, 184.

1917   "The Doomsday Play in England." *Publications of the Modern Language Association*, XXXII, lv-lvi.

"The Pater Noster Play." *The Nation*, CIV, 563-64.

"Thoreau and Concord." *The Bellman* (1917), pp. 272-73.

"The Lincoln Cordwainers' Pageant." *Publications of the Modern Language Association*, XXXII, 605-15.

1921   "Dryden's Lucian." *Classical Philology*, XVI, 141-63.

Review of: *The Stonyhurst Pageants*, ed. by Carleton Brown (1920). *American Journal of Philology*, XLII, 280-83.

1922   "Some Problems of Scholarship in the Literature of the Renaissance, particularly in the English Field." *Philological Quarterly*, I, 81-99.

"The University of Padua (Il VII Centenario)." *The Iowa Alumnus*, XX, 57-60.

Review of: F. M. Padelford, *The Poems of Henry Howard, Earl of Surrey* (1920). *Philological Quarterly*, I, 74-76.

Review of: J. M. Berdan, *Early Tudor Poetry* (1920). *Philological Quarterly*, I, 79-80.

1923   "*Hudibras*, Part I, and the Politics of 1647." In *The Manly Anniversary Studies* (Chicago, 1923), pp. 145-55.

"Terentius Christianus and the Stonyhurst Pageants." *Philological Quarterly*, II, 56-62.

1924   *Jonathan Swift: Selections.* Ed. with an introduction by Hardin Craig. The Modern Student's Library. New York: Charles Scribner's Sons. Pp. xxviii, 448.

"Shakespeare Today." *The English Journal*, XIII, 539-49.

1925   "The Ethics of *King Lear*." *Philological Quarterly*, IV, 97-109.

"Shakespeare's Depiction of Passions." *Philological Quarterly*, IV, 289-301.

Review of: B. A. P. Van Dam, *The Text of Shakespeare's Hamlet* (1924). *Philological Quarterly*, IV, 187-88.

Review of: Lane Cooper, *An Aristotelian Theory of Comedy with an Adaptation of the Poetics and a Translation of the "Tractatus Coislinianus"* (1922). *Philological Quarterly*, IV, 186-87.

Review of: A. M. Witherspoon, *The Influence of Robert Garnier on Elizabethan Tragedy* (1924). *Philological Quarterly*, IV, 188.

1926 "Recent Literature of the English Renaissance." *Studies in Philology*, XXIII, 200-325.

Review of: G. C. Taylor, *Shakespeare's Debt to Montaigne* (1925). *Philological Quarterly*, V, 91-92.

1927 "The Relation of the First Quarto Version to the First Folio Version of Shakespeare's *Henry V.*" *Philological Quarterly*, VI, 225-34.

"Recent Literature of the English Renaissance." *Studies in Philology*, XXIV, 290-382.

1928 "A Contribution to the Theory of the English Renaissance." *Philological Quarterly*, VII, 321-33.

"Recent Literature of the English Renaissance." *Studies in Philology*, XXV, 178-293.

Review of: Frances Theresa Russell, *One More Word on Browning* (1927). *Philological Quarterly*, VII, 412-13.

1929 *Great English Prose Writers.* Ed. by Hardin Craig and J. M. Thomas. New York: F. S. Crofts & Co. Pp. xii, 841.

English Prose of the Nineteenth Century. Ed. by Hardin Craig and J. M. Thomas. New York: F. S. Crofts & Co. Pp. xi, 831.

"Shakespeare and Formal Logic." In *Studies in English Philology: A Miscellany in Honor of Frederick Klaeber* (Minneapolis, 1929), pp. 380-96.

"Recent Literature of the English Renaissance." *Studies in Philology*, XXVI, 192-303.

1930 "Recent Shakespeare Scholarship." *Shakespeare Association Bulletin*, V, 39-54.

"Scholarship, Old and New." In *University of Southern California: The Semi-Centennial Celebration of the Founding of the University, 1880-1930* (Los Angeles, 1930), pp. 131-49.

"Recent Literature of the English Renaissance." *Studies in Philology*, XXVII, 293-409.

1931 *Shakespeare: A Historical and Critical Study with Annotated Texts of Twenty-one Plays.* Chicago: Scott, Foresman and Company. Pp. vi, 1194.

"Shakespeare and Wilson's *Arte of Rhetorique,* an Inquiry into the Criteria for Determining Sources." *Studies in Philology*, XXVIII, 618-30.

"Shakespeare's Revisions." *The Johns Hopkins Alumni Magazine*, XIX, 331-48.

"Recent Literature of the English Renaissance." *Studies in Philology*, XXVIII, 273-398.

1932 "The University and the College." *Journal of Higher Education*, III, 487-92.

"Recent Literature of the English Renaissance." *Studies in Philology*, XXIX, 252-365.

Review of: *Twelfth Night*, ed. by A. Quiller-Couch and J. Dover Wilson (Cambridge, 1930), and *The Merchant of Venice*, ed. by R. Adelaide Witham (Boston, 1929). *Modern Language Notes*, XLVII, 204-6.

Review of: S. A. Tannenbaum, *The Handwriting of the Renaissance* (1930). *Modern Language Notes*, XLVII, 192-93.

1933   "Recent Literature of the English Renaissance." *Studies in Philology*, XXX, 243-363.

"Unity in Shakespeare." *New Republic*, LXXV, 131-32.

1934   "Hamlet's Book." *Huntington Library Bulletin*, No. 6, pp. 17-37.

"Recent Literature of the English Renaissance." *Studies in Philology*, XXXI, 236-350.

1935   *Essays in Dramatic Literature: The Parrott Presentation Volume.* By Pupils of Professor Thomas Marc Parrott of Princeton University, published in his Honor. Ed. by Hardin Craig. Princeton University Press. Pp. 470.

Edgar Allen Poe: Representative Selections, With Introduction, Bibliography, and Notes. Begun by Margaret Alterton . . . and Completed by Hardin Craig. New York: American Book Company. Pp. cxxxvi, 563.

"Ethics in the Jacobean Drama: The Case of Chapman." In *The Parrott Presentation Volume*, pp. 25-46.

"Recent Literature of the English Renaissance." (With David Patrick.) *Studies in Philology*, XXXII, 259-375.

1936   *The Enchanted Glass: The Elizabethan Mind in Literature.* New York: Oxford University Press. Pp. ix, 293.

"Recent Literature of the English Renaissance." (With David Patrick and William Wells.) *Studies in Philology*, XXXIII, 283-396.

1937   "Recent Literature of the English Renaissance." (With David Patrick and William Wells.) *Studies in Philology*, XXXIV, 260-382.

1938   *Great English Writers.* Ed. by Hardin Craig, Oscar James Campbell, J. F. A. Pyre, and J. M. Thomas. New York: F. S. Crofts & Co. 2 vols.; pp. xii, 1039; x, 1049.

The Tragedy of Hamlet: A Critical Edition of the Second Quarto, 1604, with introduction and textual notes. Ed. by Thomas Marc Parrott and Hardin Craig. Princeton University Press. Pp. ix, 247.

"The Profile of a Philologist (Dr. Thomas A. Knott)." *Word Study*, XIII, No. 6 (May, 1938), 2-4.

"Recent Literature of the English Renaissance." (With David Patrick and William Wells.) *Studies in Philology*, XXXV, 279-403.

Review of: W. C. Curry, *Shakespeare's Philosophical Patterns* (1937). *Philological Quarterly*, XVII, 319-20.

Review of: W. W. Greg (ed.), *The Play of Antichrist, from the Chester Cycle* (1935), and F. M. Salter, *The Trial and Flagellation, with other Studies in the Chester Cycle* (1936). *Journal of English and Germanic Philology*, XXXVII, 97-99.

1939 "Recent Literature of the Renaissance" (general editor). *Studies in Philology*, XXXVI, 253-432.

Review of: M. M. Knappen, *Tudor Puritanism: A Chapter in the History of Idealism* (1939). *Modern Language Notes*, LIV, 600-03.

1940 "The Shackling of Accidents: A Study of Elizabethan Tragedy." *Philological Quarterly*, XIX, 1-19.

"Recent Literature of the Renaissance" (general editor). *Studies in Philology*, XXXVII, 283-460.

Types of English Fiction. Ed. by Hardin Craig and John Wendell Dodds. New York: The Macmillan Company. Pp. ix, 745.